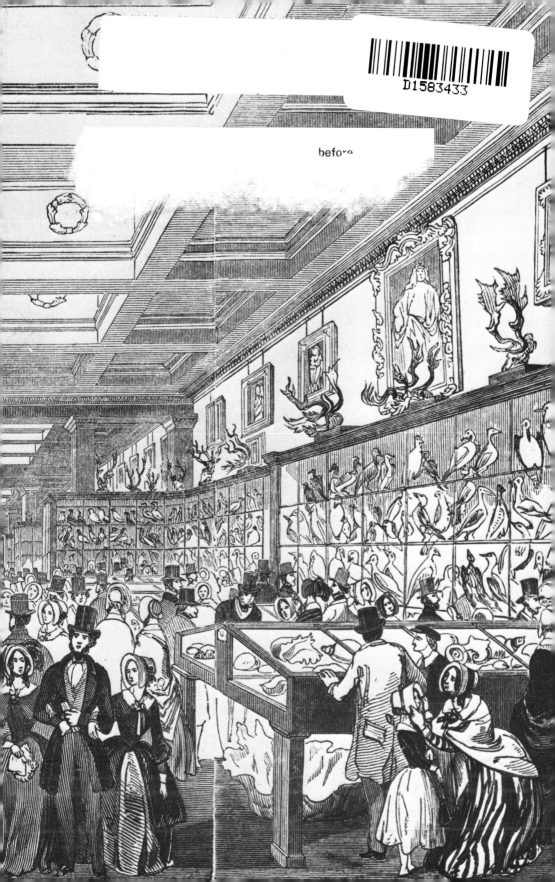

before

The Natural History Museum
at South Kensington

The Natural History Museum at South Kensington

A History of the British Museum (Natural History) 1753 - 1980

WILLIAM T. STEARN

HEINEMANN : LONDON

Published in association with the British Museum
(Natural History), London

William Heinemann Ltd
10 Upper Grosvenor Street
London W1X 9PA
LONDON MELBOURNE TORONTO
JOHANNESBURG AUCKLAND

Published in association with the
British Museum (Natural History) London

First published 1981

434 73600 7

Printed in Great Britain by
The Fakenham Press Ltd, Norfolk

To
the memory of
Edward John Miller
1914-1980

Scholar and bibliophile, devoted servant and historian
of the British Museum at Bloomsbury, in gratitude for
his *Prince of Librarians, The Life and Times of
Antonio Panizzi* and *That Noble Cabinet, A History
of the British Museum*

'It is indeed wonderful to consider, that there should be a sort of learned men who are wholly employed in gathering together the refuse of nature, if I may call it so, and hoarding up in their chests and cabinets such creatures as others industriously avoid the sight of.'

Joseph Addison, 26 August 1710

Contents

List of Plates

Acknowledgements

The author and publishers wish to thank the following for their permission to use the following illustrations:

Aerofilms (plate 75), Associated Newspapers Group Ltd. (figure 21), Bassano Studios Ltd. (plate 80), Trustees of the British Museum (plates 1, 5, 6, 8), Daily Herald (figure 22), A.E. Gunther (plate 19), The Geological Society of London (plate 54), *Illustrated London News* (plates 7, 13 and Endpapers), Linnean Society of London (plate 71), London Transport (figure 20), *Punch* (figures 11, 17, 23, 24, 27).

Preface

Aᴅɪᴠᴇʀsɪғɪᴇᴅ ᴀɴᴅ ᴠᴇɴᴇʀᴀʙʟᴇ institution, such as the British
Museum (Natural History) has become during its hundred years
of growth at South Kensington, confronts its historian with difficult
problems of selection and presentation. The Museum's collective
existence derives more from the proximity of different branches of
natural history in the one building than from resemblances in their
subject matter and techniques. Diamonds and meteorites have seemingly little in common with diatoms, molluscs, dinosaurs, mammoths,
dolphins, moths, doves and man, yet all come within the Museum's
scope. The gathering and study of such varied natural objects are now
divided between the Departments of Botany, Entomology, Mineralogy, Palaeontology and Zoology, with the support of the Departments
of Administrative Services, Central Services, Library Services, and
Public Services. All these have proliferated from the Department of
Artificial and Natural Productions, formed in 1756. This was a section
of the organisation created at Montagu House, Bloomsbury, London,
after Sir Hans Sloane's extraordinary private museum at Chelsea had
been moved there to become the major part of a national one — the
British Museum.

The early history of the Natural History Museum, as it is popularly
known, relates to the growth of individual departments in the British
Museum, until their intolerable congestion and competition, under
such dominant and often hostile officials as Panizzi, Gray and Owen,
led to the splitting in two of the Bloomsbury collections. The antiquities
and the main library stayed at Bloomsbury. The natural history
collections, unfortunately without the Banksian library hitherto closely

associated with them, moved in 1880 to the grand new South Kensington building designed by Alfred Waterhouse.

The concept linking the assemblage of the Museum's material is that of the unity and progressive development of the natural world from inanimate rocks to the manifold kinds of life now dominated, and often being irrevocably destroyed, by modern man. Their study rests upon belief in the validity of scientific method as a means of revealing and recording in an orderly manner this diversity of nature, both as a worthy exercise of the intellect and as a contribution to its understanding, utilisation and preservation. These considerations underlie the whole work of the Museum which, despite its extraordinarily mixed character, deals predominantly with description and classification based on the first-hand study of specimens. A common aim of elucidating the intricate natural world, in which the activities of every organism somewhat affect those of others, makes the Museum much more than a tenement of independent departments. It may be that in the following history of the Museum, its function of service to the general public and the world of learning through research, publications, exhibits, lectures and furnishing of information, becomes obscured amid details of collections acquired, of decisions made, of personalities in conflict or in co-operation, but nevertheless the concept of service implicitly pervades the Museum's activities.

Since the individual departments of the Museum have often been completely independent of one another, though developing in parallel through a common purpose and constrained by the same conditions, a continuous story involving them must necessarily record together events and matters which happened at about the same time, but lack any obvious causal link. Regretfully unable to impose a pattern upon these accidents of chronology, I have simply chronicled them as they have come. Added to this problem of presentation, there has been the allied one of selecting what appears to be significant, necessary or interesting out of the enormous amount of information, most of it tedious, dull or irrelevant, to be dug from official reports, Minutes of Trustees' Meetings, etc. Wilfrid Blunt described his *In for a Penny: a Prospect of Kew Gardens* as being 'personal, capricious, irreverent and perhaps even prejudiced' in approach and the treatment here probably merits the same adjectives. Indeed, it would seem almost inevitable.

The first three sections of this book try to outline in chronological order the development of the Museum as a whole but necessarily contain some material taken from the histories of individual departments, forming the fourth section, which has seemed relevant to the general history or simply of general interest. To aid the continuity of the book, the chapters on the individual departments have been arranged so that those whose history is most intimately linked with the more general aspects of Museum history come first.

The abiding impression from the Minutes of the Trustees' Meetings is how fortunate the Museum has been in having been controlled by the public-spirited, conscientious, well-informed, deeply interested, and highly intelligent men who have served the Museum as its active Trustees. Among these must certainly be included King Edward VII when Prince of Wales. The Museum owes to his initiative one of its most conspicuous exhibits, the gigantic dinosaur, *Diplodocus carnegii*. The Trustees and their servants over the years, the often poorly-paid Museum scientific workers and attendants, together with the amateur naturalists who have enriched the Museum by the gift or bequest of their collections, have constituted an assemblage of talent such as probably no other museum in the world has possessed. They have included some extraordinary characters: the gentlemanly big-game hunter Frederick Selous, killed in action at the age of sixty-four; the distinguished and cunning soldier Richard Meinertzhagen, who studied bird-lice as well as birds; the entomologist James John Joicey, three times bankrupt, who caused Mr Justice Darling to describe the collecting of butterflies and moths as 'this infantile taste'; the Marlborough classics master Edward Meyrick, who became a world authority on microlepidoptera; the Port of London Police chief Edward Charles Stuart Baker, who thrust his left arm down the throat of a man-eating panther to the disaster of both arm and panther; the banker Charles Rothschild, who assembled the world's largest collection of fleas; Thomas de Grey, Baron Walsingham, another authority on microlepidoptera, who boasted of having shot 1,070 grouse in one day and of owning 19,200 acres (7,776 hectares); and the solicitor, novelist, circus rider, Persian scholar, palmistry expert and bibliographer of violins Edward Heron-Allen, whose work on Foraminifera nevertheless gained him fellowship of the Royal Society. These are but a few of the Museum's notable benefactors who come into the following pages. The Museum's staff has also included, as might indeed be expected, some remarkable characters whose idiosyncrasies can sometimes only be hinted at.

My association with the Natural History Museum began about 1931 with a visit to the old Department of Botany and was continued by frequent visits when in the employment of the Royal Horticultural Society, until in 1952 I became a member of the Department's staff. The opportunity of working in such a dynamic institution as the Museum is, with its rich collections and its comprehensive libraries, its cordial staff relations and its talented and scholarly individuals, among whom I especially esteemed the late Alexander Cockburn Townsend,

the late Sir Gavin de Beer and the late Edgar Dandy, is one for which I
have always been grateful. Thus, having retired from the Museum's
service, I have been happy, despite pressing claims from too many
other commitments, to try to give the historical background to the
Museum's numerous activities. Presumably aware of my
shortcomings and inexperience as an author, and presumably
acquainted with my *Botanical Latin*, the Secretary to the Board of
Trustees stated that the book was to be 'written in a style which is
neither colloquial nor aridly academic' and must provide a readable
and definitive record. The plain unadorned story of varied endeavour
by a multitude of zealous, capable and devoted workers presented in
the following pages conforms, I hope, at least to some of those
specifications.

As already indicated, in compiling this history I have drawn upon
many official and unofficial sources, both published and unpublished.
The usually laconic and discreet Minutes of the Trustees' Meetings
have provided the skeleton onto which the flesh from newspaper
reports, articles and correspondence, obituaries and biographies,
scientific works, memoranda and, as regards recent times, personal
recollections by long-serving staff members has been added. General
sources of information are indicated throughout the text. Those who
are acquainted with *The History of the Collections contained in the Natural
History Departments of the British Museum* (3 vols, 1904-1912), Edward
Edwards' *Lives of the Founders of the British Museum . . . 1570-1870* (1870),
Edward Miller's *That Noble Cabinet, a History of the British Museum*
(1973), and Albert E. Gunther's *A Century of Zoology at the British Museum
through the Lives of two Keepers* [J.E. Gray and Albert Günther],
1815-1914 (1975), will quickly recognise my great debt to these
excellent, detailed and well-documented works, which I gratefully
acknowledge. Ray Desmond's *Dictionary of British and Irish Botanists and
Horticulturists* (1977) and Pamela Gilbert's *A Compendium of the
Biographical Literature on Deceased Entomologists* (1977) have greatly
lightened the task of finding biographical information. *The Natural
History Magazine*, published by the Museum from 1927 to 1936, is a
mine of interesting information for that period. If there should chance
to be included here any revelations of times long past which some might
consider indiscreet, I plead the example of such reputable historical
books as Miller's *That Noble Cabinet* and Peter Sutcliffe's *The Oxford
University Press, an informal History* (1978); the frankness with which they
have dealt with the events, intrigues and personalities of their
respective institutions provides acceptable precedent, I think, for
matter included here. Possibly there are too many quotations, but it
seemed better to quote some documents and contemporary accounts

direct, rather than to paraphrase them. I have been impressed by the widespread and accurate reporting of Museum affairs by newspapers and popular magazines, by the space they gave in their closely printed pages to long letters relating to Museum controversies and by the crucial influence exerted in the past by correspondence printed in *The Times, The Morning Post* and others. One must be grateful for so much freedom of comment on a great national institution. If in making some quotations I have unwittingly infringed copyright, I trust that this will be taken as a compliment to the goodwill and perspicacity of those concerned.

Since the designations of academic people and others tend to change with the years, e.g. from Mr to Captain, Major, Colonel, Dr, Professor, or even to Sir, I have omitted them almost entirely, Quaker fashion, to avoid inconsistency in the text, which can give no offence to the dead and will, I hope, be pardoned, if need be, by the living.

It is a pleasure to record the ungrudging help received from the Museum staff in all departments, above all from the librarians who have called attention to sources of information that I would probably have overlooked. Of these many kind and co-operative individuals, I must thank in particular Mr Maldwyn J. Rowlands, Head of the Department of Library Services, for encouragement and facilities without which this history could never have been written, and Mr Ron Driver, Mrs Doris Bromley and Mrs E.D. Johnson of the Photocopying Services for much time-saving help, always cheerfully given. I am indebted to Miss D. Norman for her invaluable assistance in locating many of the illustrations for this book and providing information for the captions. Mr Peter J. Green, Mr Colin B. Keates, Mr P. Lund and Mr Harold Taylor of the Photographic Unit have likewise been most helpful by providing copies of illustrations with remarkable promptness. Most of the typing of the manuscript, in places almost a palimpsest, has been skilfully undertaken by Mrs Theresa Dartnall and Miss Patricia Hill. I am grateful to the Keepers of the Museum Departments, Dr H.W. Ball (Palaeontology), Dr A.C. Bishop (Mineralogy), Mr J.F.M. Cannon (Botany), Dr P. Freeman (Entomology) and Dr J.G. Sheals (Zoology), who read the original text and who from their special knowledge and experience have made helpful contributions.

In particular, thanks are due to Mr Anthony P. Harvey who, in addition to making valuable contributions, undertook the onerous, time-consuming and hazardous task of steering the text patiently and conscientiously along the pitfall-scattered editorial road from typescript to finished copy, together with Miss Rosalind D.S. Edwards and Mr John St. John of William Heinemann Ltd.

A history such as this must inevitably leave out much more than it includes. If all the material collected during the preparation of this book had been used it would, so far as the publishers are concerned, have made it unacceptably lengthy. However, all of these preliminary scripts have been deposited in the Manuscript Collections in the General Library of the British Museum (Natural History). My regrets go to all who fail to find here what they had expected. I trust, however, the book will leave its readers with the impression of a vigorous many-sided British institution created through the zeal and efforts of numerous talented individuals dedicated to the advancement of science and to the education and entertainment of the public, with the potential to emulate in the future the achievements of its remarkable past. The Venetian printer of R.G. Boscovich's *Theoria Philosophiae Naturalis* (1763) ended his prefacing words to the reader with the wish, likewise appropriate here, *Tu laboribus nostris fruere et vive felix*: may you enjoy the fruits of our labours and live in happiness.

William T. Stearn

March 1980

Foreword

SIR HANS SLOANE'S interest in the 'knick-knackeries' of Nature exemplifies a curiosity that is widely represented in his fellow countrymen, although in his generation it was largely dormant. His contemporary, the writer Joseph Addison, expressed amazement that 'there should be a sort of learned men who are wholly employed in gathering together the refuse of nature'. Now, nearly three centuries later, over 27,000 people may visit the Natural History Museum at South Kensington (as it is popularly called) in a single day to wonder at, enjoy and learn from what are termed 'exhibits': a less colourful, but less perjorative description than either 'knick-knacks' or 'refuse'.

The British Museum (Natural History) — its formal title — has played an important role in awakening the curiosity of such a large proportion of the population. Its riches have been gathered by many: by the wealthy, such as Sloane, the founder, and Rothschild, the founder of the satellite organisation at Tring; by the professional naturalist and by the amateur. The source of the specimens is not important; what is important is that through such gifts one has only to travel to South Kensington to see a whale, a piece of meteorite, a section of an ancient Redwood tree, all the British butterflies or a dinosaur's skeleton. No longer the preserve of the 'cabinets of the curious', everyone can now see them; knowledge can be gained, even by the illiterate.

It might have been supposed that the development of photography, which would convey the appearance of animals, plants and natural objects through books, films and television without the effort of a visit to South Kensington, would lessen the Museum's attraction.

Paradoxically the reverse has occurred and for those who can reach London a visit to the 'Natural History Museum' has become part of virtually everyone's experience.

Although the Museum's role has remained unchanged throughout this growth in the public's knowledge, the way that it has discharged this role has changed. The exhibition policy has evolved from one involving the display of the maximum number of objects, through an arrangement that portrayed the great diversity of nature, to the present one that seeks to illustrate major biological ideas in, for example, ecology and the origin of man. An institute like the Natural History Museum must not age; like those potentially immortal organisms, a coral colony or a clump of bracken, it must replace the old units by new. However, the Museum's visitors do age and their requirements and perception of an exhibit when an eight-year-old are different from those when a teenager or when, as a grandparent, they accompany a second generation of eight-year-olds. The challenge to the Museum staff is to meet these varying needs, whilst at the same time evolving so as to play a positive role in the development of public understanding of and attitude to natural history: to be the leader, not the follower.

If to the world at large the Museum's exhibition galleries are its shop window, the goods displayed there are but the minutest fraction of what is stored behind the counter. Even in Sir Hans Sloane's day, his 'Cabinet of Curiosities' was the envy of natural historians throughout Europe and was valued at what would now be the equivalent of about three million pounds. Sloane was always delighted to make his collections and libraries freely available to visiting scholars, and his philosophy of serving international science has been a cardinal principle of the institution that derived from his foresight and his philanthropy. It seems more than coincidental that the Museum's inception exactly coincided with the publication of the First Edition of Linnaeus's *Species Plantarum* in 1753 and broadly with the Tenth Edition of his *Systema Naturae* in 1758, which are respectively the foundation of modern botanical and zoological nomenclature, and thus of taxonomy. Taxonomy is the science of determining, describing and naming of organisms, and classifying them in a way that attempts to reflect their inter-relationships. This has been the main commitment of the Museum throughout its history. Moreover, it is essentially a science of comparison and as such is dependent on large collections and libraries.

The origin and early years of the Museum coincided with the so-called heroic age of the biological and geological sciences in which the Museum played a major role. At the same time, the first half of the nineteenth century, new technologies enabled the exploration of the world to an hitherto unprecedented degree; and as the newly-discovered wonders of natural history poured into the Museum, then housed in Bloomsbury, an ever-increasing pressure was put on the already over-crowded accommodation there. This was resolved by the erection of a new building in South Kensington, whose opening in 1881 is commemorated by this volume. At this time the structure and relationships of living organisms were in the forefront of scientific advance, and the Museum was prominently in the vanguard, not only as a repository for the enormous wealth of materials, but as a centre for research. In particular, the battles for the establishment of the Theory of Evolution were much fought on discoveries made within its walls. The Museum was the source of national pride and interest, and its activities and internal wrangles made headline news. Yet, in addition to the latter less laudable aspects, the history of the Museum is remarkable for how much has been achieved despite the slender resources that have been made available to it. Such achievements have been largely due to the ability and devotion of the staff and the many scientists who have worked in association with the Museum.

By the early part of the present century, the natural sciences had begun to diversify and the major new frontiers in biology had moved to other levels, to physiology, cytology, behaviour, and ecology, which were undertaken in the newly burgeoning universities and subsequently by other research institutes. For a while the Museum languished in the wake of these newer and more overtly exciting fields of biology, but as they have matured, it has become more and more evident that they need to be based on a firm foundation of taxonomy, of which the Museum is guardian and dispenser. Above all, true to the ideals of Sloane, the Museum is devoted to the cause and service of international science, non-applied and applied. The researches of the Museum staff have been of direct aid to the underdeveloped countries in the prevention of disease and the control of agricultural pests, as well as in the preparation of geological maps and the search for oil and mineral resources. The Museum's scientific staff comprises one of the world's largest concentrations of specialists, whose expertise is ever at the service of the man-in-the-street, no less than to their professional colleagues both in Britain and overseas.

Yet it is the collections and libraries, built up with dedication and conserved with devotion, that form the heart of the Museum. Their importance lies in their breadth, enabling the many distinguished scientists and students who visit them each year to obtain an unrivalled conspectus of the materials of natural history. This accessibility of the collections is augmented by its loans of specimens to other research institutions and universities throughout the world.

For many people and in particular many naturalists, biologists and geologists, the Museum evokes strong memories. Although only the beginning of a long association with the Museum for me, early memories remain vivid. The stunning wonder, especially when a mere three feet in stature, of seeing a dinosaur for the first time is overlaid by the excitement when as a youth, with specimens and letter of introduction in nervous hand, one is ushered 'behind the scenes' to meet the leading authority on this or that. Thus for the individual the Museum may have a place akin to a natural shrine: it is somewhere from which inspiration has been drawn and pleasure sought. It is vitally important to provide the young of today and tomorrow with the same opportunities for similar experiences. Therein lies, however, the seeds of the conflict and controversy that surround, and as this account shows, have always surrounded the changes in the Museum's arrangements. The Museum must change so that it may serve future generations in the way that it has served past ones.

Professor Stearn and his colleagues have captured the dynamic spirit of the Museum. Neither the exhibits nor the personalities, who devote their lives to its objectives, are as 'dry as dust'. It is easy, if unworthy, to be gripped by the controversies that are revealed in this History; to read on, anxious to discover the victor! But the important message that is implicit throughout the account is that in many research fields the Museum has long been, and remains, in the vanguard. In some other areas the very success of its activities has led to the eventual development of an independent activity. Thus the conservation movement owes much to the continued but little-publicized endeavours of the Trustees collectively and members of the scientific staff individually. These have included support as early as 1874 for the preservation of the then threatened giant tortoises of Aldabra as well as vigorous opposition to the slaughter of birds for the feather trade, to the unregulated killing of whales and seals and the introduction of animals into countries where they are not native; they have taken an active part in promoting legislation for the protection of wildlife, often 'behind the scenes'. Non-native birds and mammals may not only become directly noxious pests when introduced in foreign countries; they may cause, as is all too evident, the extinction or diminution of native species through competition, destruction or change of habitats and the introduction of virus and other diseases to which native species have no immunity. The Museum Trustees and their staff have long been aware of these dangers and have continually though not always successfully warned governments against them; in 1952 they even had to protest against the proposed introduction of polar bears into the Antarctic! Another example is the guidance and advice on insect pests, now largely the responsibility of the Ministry of Agriculture and others, where the Museum's *Economic Series* and specialist staff played a leading role in the dissemination of information.

On behalf of my fellow Trustees, I should like to thank all those unnamed staff who have been involved in the production of this history, without their dedicated effort the account would have been impossible to compile. They include all the various staff members in the Museum's departments and in particular the Department of Library Services which has researched not only information, but also provided editorial skills. We are grateful to the representatives of William Heinemann Ltd who have been so helpful throughout the preparation of the book for publication. Today's Trustees share with their predecessors a great pride in their trust. They are most grateful to Professor Stearn and his colleagues, Mr A.P. Coleman and Dr H.W. Ball, for this excellent account of 'how it got to where it is'. The Museum is a provider of a sound foundation and pivot for modern biology and geology and a powerful contributor to the public's awareness and appreciation of the world in which we live.

T.R.E. Southwood
Chairman of the Board of Trustees

October 1980

Part I

The Bloomsbury Years
1753 - 1880

1

Sir Hans Sloane
and the origin of the
British Museum

Without formality on Easter Monday, 18 April 1881, the British Museum (Natural History) at South Kensington, London, opened its doors to the general public for the first time. Some 16,000 visitors thronged in, 'people of a most orderly and respectable class', dutifully depositing their umbrellas and walking sticks before gazing at the vast cathedral-like main hall, the arcaded galleries, stained-glass windows and ornamental pillars. They had little else to see. Mineral, fossil and plant specimens were on display but, although the Superintendent of the Natural History Departments, Professor Richard Owen, was believed to have asked for room sufficient to accommodate sixty whales, not one had come from Bloomsbury. The stuffed elephants and giraffes, the stuffed bears which a crazy well-meaning and kind-hearted old gentleman had tried to feed with buns, in fact all the zoological specimens so popular with the public, were still at Bloomsbury. Visitors had to wait until 1883 for the opening of the zoological galleries.

Neither the Trustees nor the staff of the British Museum regarded either occasion as the birth of a new institution. To them the new museum was simply a distantly-located part of the British Museum at Bloomsbury containing its Natural History Departments and legally, though not in fact, it thus remained until sundered by an Act of Parliament in 1963.

The British Museum owes its origin to the collecting zeal of Sir Hans Sloane (1660-1753), President of the Royal College of Physicians from 1719 to 1735 and President of the Royal Society from 1727 to 1741. At his death, in 1753, his enormous and extremely varied collection, his 'knick knackatory' as Thomas Hearne called it, must have been the largest ever assembled by any private individual in Europe and was certainly the most famous, most extensive, most visited and most admired one in Britain. John Evelyn saw 'Dr Sloane's curiosities' in 1691. Pehr Kalm, on his way from Sweden to North America, made a special visit to see them in 1748 and wrote a detailed and enthusiastic account. Over fifty years Sloane's collection, first at Bloomsbury and later at Chelsea, was one of the sights of the London area, attracting a succession of distinguished visitors, both British and foreign. Sloane told his curator, James Empson, not long before his death, that assembling his collection had cost him £100,000, but the question of the true cost is more fully discussed in G. de Beer's *Sir Hans Sloane and the British Museum* (1953). The money for it, as also for his other property, had come from his practice as a fashionable London physician, charging heavily the rich and well-to-do for his professional services, but treating without payment the poor who attended his consulting room before 10 o'clock in the morning. He was a shrewd Protestant Ulster Irishman of Scottish descent, born at Killyleagh by Strangford Lough in County Down on 16 April 1660. His father, a receiver of taxes for the Earl of Clanbrasil, evidently could well afford to send Hans, the youngest of his seven sons, to London for medical instruction. It is significant, in view of his later collections, that recalling his boyhood in Ireland, Sloane remarked how he had 'from my Youth been very much pleas'd with the study of Plants, and other Parts of Nature, and had seen most of those Kinds of Curiosities, which were to be found either in the Fields, or in the Gardens or Cabinets of the curious in these Parts'. He noted how Irish peasants gathered edible seaweed and chewed it to cure scurvy.

Hans Sloane arrived in London in 1679 and lodged next door to the Apothecaries' Hall. He studied chemistry, pharmacy, anatomy and medicine, and became a friend of Robert Boyle (1627-1691), the celebrated chemist, and John Ray (1627-1705), the celebrated botanist. Then, after his four years of study in London, he went in 1683 to Paris, where he attended the botanical lectures of Joseph Pitton de Tournefort (1656-1708), and the anatomical lectures of Joseph Guichard Duverney (1648-1731), both celebrated men. Thus qualified, Sloane went to the little principality of Orange, in Vaucluse, southern France, from which the Dutch House of Orange took its name. Here was a Protestant university where, like Harderwijk in the Netherlands, a doctor's degree could be quickly obtained. Sloane took advantage of this Orange facility, as Tournefort had done. Both universities were examining bodies for those who came to them well-qualified by learning and experience. Thus on 27 July 1683 Mr Hans Sloane supplicated for the degree of the Faculty of Medicine, was examined and found competent, and then next day at 7 o'clock in the morning was again examined. He then argued and maintained a disputation before the whole university academic staff, was awarded high honours, and became Dr Hans Sloane. He then went to Montpellier for further medical studies. Leaving Montpellier in May 1684, he began a homeward journey, visiting Toulouse, Bordeaux and Paris, before returning to London.

Back in London Sloane quickly made the acquaintance of the celebrated and unconventional physician Thomas Sydenham (1624-1689), who told him at once that in practical medicine his knowledge of anatomy and botany was nonsense: 'young man, all this is stuff: you must go to the bedside, it is there alone you can learn disease'. Nevertheless, Sydenham was impressed enough to take Sloane on his rounds and to recommend him to his own patients when unable to attend them himself. Above all, he taught him the importance of diagnosis by a systematic observation and evaluation of symptoms, the same approach that a taxonomic naturalist employs in the study of organisms. Sloane's own reputation evidently grew, for in 1685 he was elected to the Royal Society, and in 1687 to the Royal College of Physicians.

The years 1687 to 1689 gave Sloane the greatest adventure and natural history opportunity of his life, his visit to Jamaica as physician to the new Governor, the Duke of Albemarle. The observations which he made and the specimens which he collected during his stay in that biologically rich and beautiful island provided him with the material for his *Catalogus Plantarum quae in Insula Jamaica sponte proveniunt vel vulgo coluntur* (1696) and his ample *A Voyage to the Islands Madera, Barbados, Nieves, S. Christophers and Jamaica with the Natural History of the Herbs and Trees, four-footed Beasts, Fishes, Birds, Insects, Reptiles, etc. of the Last of those Islands* (2 vols, folio, 1707-1725). This stay in Jamaica also acquainted him with chocolate, which as taken in Jamaica he found 'nauseous, and hard of digestion, which I suppose came from the great oiliness'. He found it much better when mixed with milk and imparted his recipe to Nicholas Sanders, Soho, who manufactured and sold it, as did his successor, William White: the last-named advertised it as 'Sir Hans Sloane's Milk Chocolate . . . Greatly recommended by several eminent Physicians, especially those of Sir Hans Sloane's Acquaintance, for its Lightness on the stomach & its great Use in all Consumptive Cases'. During the nineteenth century Messrs Cadbury took over its manufacture, using Sloane's recipe.

Sloane's subsequent career as a physician, as Secretary and President of the Royal Society, as a public benefactor, notably in connexion with the Chelsea Physic Garden, and as a great collector, has been adequately covered in Gavin de Beer's *Sir Hans Sloane and the British Museum* (1953), and E.St. John Brooks, *Sir Hans Sloane, the great Collector and his Circle* (1954), together with J.E. Dandy's *The Sloane Herbarium* (1958), and numerous smaller publications cited in these. His hobby, indeed his dominant interest, became the increase of his collection. There are several accounts of what it had become, in addition to the synopsis made by his executors in 1753 after his death, when towards the end of his life he moved it from Bloomsbury to Chelsea. One of the most detailed accounts is that written in Swedish in 1748 by Pehr Kalm and translated into English in 1892 as *Kalm's Account of a Visit to England* (pp. 97-106) from which the following extract is abbreviated:

'In the morning I went . . . up to Chelsea where we spent some time in looking at Chelsea Garden, but afterwards went to see Sir Hans Sloane's collections, in all three Natural Kingdoms, Antiquities, Anatomy, and many Curiosities. We saw here a great collection of all kinds of stones, partly polished, partly such as still lay in their matrix as they are found in nature. We saw all sorts of vessels, Tea-cups, saucers, snuff-boxes, caskets, spoons, ladles, and other small instruments, all manufactured out of agates and Jaspis, etc.; a number of different kinds of pearls, several learned men's Contrefaits, among which we particularly devoted ourselves to the study and admiration of the great botanist and student of natural history, John Ray . . . A very large collection of insects from all parts of the world, all of which were now preserved in four-sided boxes, with clear glass glued on both over and under, so that one could see them quite well, but these boxes or cases were also so well stuck together and so tight that no worms or other injurious insects could get at them, and spoil them . . . Some of the East and West Indian *Butterflies* were far more showy than a peacock with its matchless variety of colours. A very large number of all kinds of corals, and other harder sea plants, a multitude of various sorts of crystals, several head-dresses of different races of men, musical instruments, etc. Various stuffed birds and fish, where the birds often stood fast on small bits of board as naturally as if they still lived. Skeletons of various four-footed beasts, among which were particularly noticed that of a young elephant, the stuffed skin of a camel, and an African many-striped ass [i.e. a zebra]. Several human skeletons larger and smaller, the head and other parts of a frightfully large whale. This whale was said to have been 90 feet long. The length of its head bone was nearly 18 feet. Humming birds from the West Indies, which there made a show with their many colours, and set in their nests under glass as though they had been living; the bird's nest which they eat in Asia as any other food which they eat in the East Indies. It was white and looked almost as if it had been made of white wax. A great collection of snakes, lizards, fishes, birds, caterpillars, insects, small four-footed animals, etc. all put *in spiritu vini* in bottles, and well preserved; dried skins of snakes from the East and West Indies, of many ells length and proportionately broad; very many *tomes* of a *herbarium*, among which we particularly examined those which Sir Hans Sloane himself had collected in Jamaica; 336 volumes of dried plants in Royal folio; on each leaf there were as many plants stuck on as there was room for. Sir Hans Sloane's *Library*, which probably has few like it among private collections gathered together by one single man, and consists of somewhat more than 48,000 volumes, all bound in superb bindings. To describe all this great collection in detail, would fill several *Folios*: for any who has not himself seen this collection would probably have very great difficulty in picturing to himself that it is so large. In another room were several of such books as consisted of coloured pictures of all sorts of Natural objects. Such were Meriana's, Catesby's, Seba's, Madame Blackwell's etc., costly works, Egyptian Mummies, Roman and other Antiquities, etc. In the garden we saw Sir Hans Sloane's Chair with three wheels under it, and a little one behind, in which he was drawn about in the garden . . . Afterwards the most costly stones were shown us, which were arranged in a box made in a particular manner. The box was quadrilateral, a little more than 6 inches long and not quite 6 inches broad, and nearly 6 inches high. On the top it sloped from all sides together, so that it resembled a monument on a grave, or a house with an Italian roof. It consisted of a great many boxes, which are not drawn out as usual, but the upper box was always a lid to the under, so that the lowest box had for a lid all the boxes above it. The gems were small and lay in small round holes turned or cut in the boxes. It was said that in this box there were 1,300 different kinds of gems . . .'

As Sloane's collection grew, so did his anxiety for its future preservation. It was a unique assemblage, his life's work, and he wished it not to be dispersed but, if possible, to remain a national treasure. No existing institution in Britain could then provide it with a suitable home. As long ago as 1739, he had made a will desiring very much that his curiosities of all kinds 'may remain together, and not be separated, and that chiefly in and about the city of London, where I have acquired most of my estates and where they may by the great confluence of people be most used.' The 'use and improvement of physic, and other arts, and sciences, and benefit of mankind', which such a collection as his could promote, stayed always in his mind. A copy of his will is printed in Thomas Faulkner's *Historical and Topographical Description of Chelsea* (1810). In it he offered the collection to the King for the nation, provided that his two daughters were paid £20,000 between them, a sum much below the value of his material. Sloane died on 11 January 1753. He had appointed executors, whose first task was to summon the numerous trustees he had nominated to decide the fate of his museum. The result of his far-seeing disposition of his property was the creation of the British Museum at Bloomsbury, where Sloane had lived most of his life, and in due course its sister institution — the British Museum (Natural History).

Admittedly Sloane had been a very miscellaneous collector. Nevertheless, he more than any other man of his time had contributed to the realization of the desire expressed by his older contemporary Robert Hooke (1635-1703), the most versatile scientist of the seventeenth century: 'It were therefore much to be wisht for and indeavoured that there might be made and kept in some Repository as full and compleat a collection of all varieties of Natural bodies as could be obtained, where an inquirer might be able to have recourse, where he might peruse, and turn over, and spell, and read the book of Nature, and observe the orthography, etymologia, syntaxis and prosodia of nature's grammer'. Such a repository 'for the most serious and diligent study of the most able proficient in natural philosophy' as envisaged by Hooke, but also 'for divertisement, and wondering, and gazing', the Natural History Museum has become. Its initiation goes back to Hans Sloane. In Chelsea several places, such as Sloane Square, Sloane Street, and Hans Place, commemorate him, as do his statue in the Chelsea Physic Garden and his monument in Chelsea churchyard, but the best memorial to his achievements and interest in natural history is the Museum facing Cromwell Road in nearby South Kensington.

1. Sir Hans Sloane (1660-1753), physician, naturalist and collector, the virtual founder of the British Museum.

2. Sir Joseph Banks (1743-1820), traveller, naturalist and patron of science, founder of the Banksian Herbarium and Library.

Robert Brown

3. Robert Brown (1773-1858), botanist librarian to Sir Joseph Banks 1810-1820, Keeper of Botanical Department 1827-1858.

4. John Edward Gray (1800-1875), naturalist, Keeper of Zoological Department 1840-1875.

5. South front of Montagu House, Bloomsbury, 1714, opened to the public in 1759 as the British Museum.

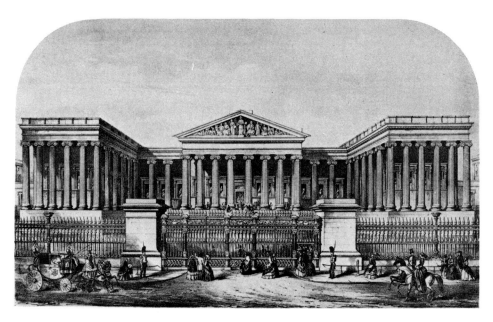

6. South front of the British Museum, Bloomsbury, 1853, designed by Robert Smirke, which replaced Montagu House.

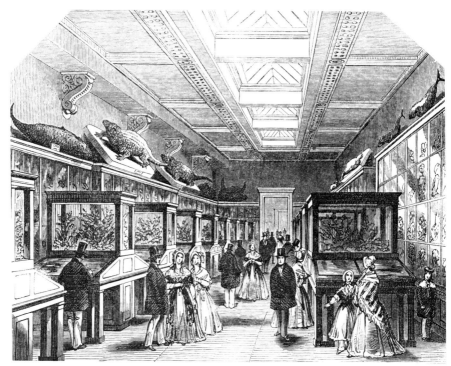

7. The new Coral Room in the British Museum, 1845 (from *Illustrated London News*, 11 October 1845).

8. The great staircase of Montagu House in 1845 (drawing by G. Scharf).

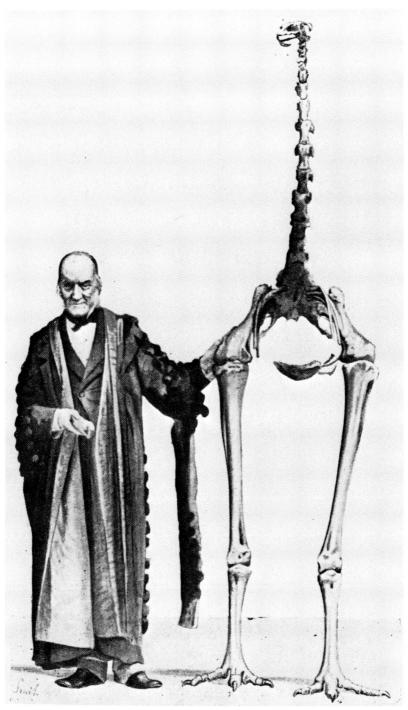

9. Sir Richard Owen (1804-1892) and skeleton of the Giant Moa
(Dinornis maximus) about 1877.

2

The Trustees of the British Museum 1753-1963

T HE FIRST HALF of the eighteenth century was one of much religious indifference and cynicism in high places and of widespread jobbery and corruption, which were the dark sides of patronage, and which, together with embezzlement of funds, sometimes weakened or ruined projects begun with high intent. Of such dangers, the worldly-wise eighteenth-century founders of the British Museum, like Sir Hans Sloane himself, needed no warning. Sloane stipulated in his will that his collections were to be placed at his death in the care of Trustees, who were to offer them to the King for the nation. Obviously believing that among a large body of gentlemen, honesty and good sense would prevail, Sloane nominated fifty-one of his relations and friends as Trustees and thirty-four of them came to a meeting on 27 January 1753 summoned by his four executors. They appointed a committee to draw up a memorial for presentation to the King. Horace Walpole, a member of this group, wrote to Sir Horace Mann on 14 February 1753: 'we are a charming wise set, all philosophers, botanists, antiquarians and mathematicians'. Despite earlier opposition from the Premier and First Lord of the Treasury, but highly influenced by the Speaker of the House of Commons, Arthur Onslow (1691-1768), the House after a long debate on 19 March 1753 accepted the conditions made in Sloane's will for the preservation of his collections. 'An Act for the Purchase of the Museum, or Collection of Sir Hans Sloane, and of the Harleian Collection of Manuscripts; and for providing One General Repository for the better Reception and more convenient Use of the said Collections; and of the Cottonian Library, and of the Additions thereto' (26 George II.c 22) was then drawn up. It eventually received the Royal Assent on 7 June 1753.

9

The delay was due to a lack of money with which to purchase the collections. Indeed a memorial from Sloane's Trustees to George II met with the rebuke 'I don't think there are twenty thousand pounds in the Treasury'. Onslow therefore suggested a public lottery to provide the necessary funds. Such lotteries were frequently corrupt and the management of the one to provide funds to establish the British Museum, shocked even the eighteenth-century Houses of Parliament. However, sufficient funds were raised not only to purchase the collection, but to house it in Montagu House, Bloomsbury, and provide substantial investment.

The Act authorized the appointment of Trustees for putting its provisions into action and gave the 'One General Depository' the name of 'British Museum' in the following terms: 'And be it further enacted by the authority aforesaid, That for the better Execution of the Purposes of this Act, the said Trustees hereby appointed shall be a Body Politick and Corporate, in Deed and in Name, and have the succession for ever, by the Name of *The Trustees of the* British Museum; and by that Name shall sue and be sued, implead and be impleaded, in all Courts and Places within this Realm; and shall have Power to have and use a Common Seal to be appointed by themselves; and to make Bye-laws and Ordinances for the Purposes of this Act.' It also stated that the Trustees, or 'the major part of them, at any general Meeting assembled, shall, from Time to Time, and as often as they shall think fit, make, constitute, and establish, such Statutes, Rules, and Ordinances, for the Custody, Preservation, and Inspection, of every Part of the several Collections hereby intended to remain in the said General Repository, as to them shall seem meet; and shall and may in like Manner assign such Salaries and Allowances as they shall think fit, to the Officers and Servants, who in Manner herein-after mentioned shall be appointed to attend and assist in the Care and Preservation of the several Collections contained in the said General Repository; and shall and may, at their Pleasure, in like Manner, suspend or remove any such Officer or Servant, for Misbehaviour or Neglect of Duty.'

In a paper on 'The Royal Society and the foundation of the British Museum, 1753-1781' in *Notes and Records of the Royal Society of London* 33: 207-216 (1979), A.E. Gunther has pointed out that no less than forty of Sloane's Trustees in his will were Fellows of the Royal Society; of these only nine could be classified as active scientists. The prestige of the Royal Society, an assembly of well-educated and reputable gentlemen interested in the arts and sciences, was obviously important for the implementation of Sloane's plans, since the institution he intended had to secure the support of learned and influential people, with a broad range of interests. The 1753 Act gave this justification for maintenance of the Museum: 'all Arts and Sciences have a Connection with each other, and Discoveries in Natural Philosophy, and other Branches of speculative knowledge, for the Advancement of Improvement whereof the said *Museum* or Collection was intended, do and may, in many Instances, give Help and success to the most useful Experiments and Inventions.' Though the specialization of branches of knowledge necessarily tends now to hide from consideration this view of the continuity of knowledge, two directors of the Natural History Museum, Sir William Flower and Sir Gavin de Beer, were ever conscious of this, as also that the institution embodying it was, in the words of the Act, to be 'preserved and maintained not only for the Inspection and Entertainment of the learned and the curious, but for the General Use and Benefit of the Publick'.

Those drafting the Act took no chances over the respectability and standing of the Trustees to put it in execution. They were the Archbishop of Canterbury, the Lord Chancellor, the Lord President of the Council, the Lord Treasurer, the Lord Privy Seal, the Lord High Admiral, the Lord Steward of his Majesty's Household, the Lord Chamberlain, the Bishop of London, each of the three Principal Secretaries of State, the Speaker of the House of Commons, the Chancellor of the Exchequer, the Lord Chief Justice of the King's Bench, the Lord Chief Justice of the Court of Common Pleas at Westminster, the Master of the Rolls, the Attorney General, the Solicitor General, the President of the Royal Society and the President of the Royal College of Physicians for the time being, all *ex officio,* and thus *Official Trustees.* Then there were Lord Cadogan, Hans Stanley, Thomas Burroughs, Thomas Hart, the Duke of Portland and the Earl of Oxford, these being *Family Trustees* representing the Cavendish, Cotton and Sloane families. These Trustees or the major part of them, always including the Archbishop of Canterbury, the Lord Chancellor and the Speaker of the House of Commons, the three *Principal Trustees,* had to elect and nominate fifteen other persons to be associated to them in the execution of their Trust, 'which Fifteen Persons, so elected and nominated, shall be and continue for the Term of their Natural Lives, Trustees for putting this Act in Execution, with the like Power, in all Respects, as hereby is given to the Trustees herein before first appointed'. These were the *Elected Trustees,* the real governing body of the British Museum. They in their turn formed a smaller *Standing Committee,* an executive body meeting regularly, initially weekly, later monthly, with the officers of the Museum for the conduct of its affairs.

The origin of the *Standing Committee* goes back to a general meeting of the Board of Trustees of the British Museum on 17 May 1755. The relevant minute of this meeting is as follows:

Ordered:—
That the Committee appointed by the Order of the 12th April, together with the Duke of Argyle, Duke of Portland, the Earl of Northumberland, Mr West, the President of the College of Physicians, and Dr Ward, be a Standing Committee of this Corporation: And that they do meet on Thursday in every Week at Eleven o'clock in the forenoon, and on any other days, which they shall think fit: And that all such of the Trustees who shall come, shall have Voices: And that the said Committee have power to take into their Consideration any Matters relating to the Business and affairs of this Corporation, and from time to time to make their Report thereupon, or any proposition, which they shall think fit to a General Meeting: And that they have also powers to give directions to the Surveyors or Workmen touching the Repairs of Montagu House with the Appurtenances, and the putting the Gardens thereof in Order, or any other Matter which shall be necessary to be carried into immediate Execution: and likewise to direct Summons to be Issued for General Meetings.

Ordered:—
That it be referred to the said Committee to consider what Officers and Servants may be necessary, and what Salaries may be reasonable to be allowed to each of them: and for that purpose they do form a Scheme consisting of the following heads, viz.

1st . . . The Fund which will remain as the Estate of the Corporation, after the Repairs of Montagu House with the Appurtenances & Gardens and the preparing and fitting up the Repository, shall be completed.

2ndly . . . What may be the Annual Income of such Fund.

3rdly . . . What Salaries they shall think proper to propose to be allowed to such Officers and Servants.

And that they do State the same with their Opinion thereupon to a General Meeting.

A further clause dealt with the appointment of the Principal Librarian, as the Director was first designated: 'And be it enacted by the Authority afore-said, That the Principal Librarian, to whom the

Care and Custody of the said General Repository shall be chiefly committed, shall, from Time to Time, be nominated and appointed in Manner following; that is to say, The said Archbishop of *Canterbury*, Lord Chancellor, or Lord Keeper, and the Speaker of the House of Commons, or any Two of them, shall recommend to His Majesty, His Heirs and Successors, Two Persons, each of whom they shall judge fit to execute the said Office; and such of the said Two Persons so recommended, as His Majesty, His Heirs and Successors, by Writing under His, or Their Sign Manual, shall appoint, after he shall become bound to the said Trustees by this Act appointed, for the due and faithful Discharge of his Office, in such penal Sum not being less than One Thousand Pounds, as the said Trustees, at any General Meeting assembled, or the major Part of them, shall think proper, shall have and hold the said Office, during such Time as he shall behave well within.'

It very much reflected the state of public morality of this period, that a person appointed as Principal Librarian by the three Principal Trustees should nevertheless deposit a guarantee of £1,000, then a very large sum of money indeed, for his good behaviour. No age limit was set for his retirement from office. He could remain so long as he duly and faithfully discharged his duties. This became a very important matter of argument in the twentieth century when Ray Lankester, as Director of the Natural History Departments of the British Museum at South Kensington, contended that his status was that of the Principal Librarian of the British Museum at Bloomsbury and that he was in no way bound to retire at sixty, or indeed at any definite age, so long as he could discharge his duties (p.88).

When 'the Trustees' are mentioned, as they frequently are, in the following chapters of this book, they are the Elected Trustees, together with the Principal Trustees from time to time and an occasional Official Trustee, who attended the Standing Committee meetings and whose decisions are recorded in the Minutes. Nevertheless, appointments of Museum officers remained the exclusive prerogative of the Principal Trustees, who could exercise their right against the wishes of the Elected Trustees if they thought fit or were subjected to pressure. Although on paper these Trustees as a whole would appear to be an excessively large body, as mentioned, their number was essentially a safeguard considered necessary in the corrupt eighteenth century and never impeded the efficient management of the Museum by the Elected Trustees. According to Gunther (1979), of the thirty-one Elected Trustees in the first thirty years of the Museum's existence, at least twenty-three were Fellows of the Royal Society. This is not surprising in view of the Society's interest in science and the fact that the Museum contained so much scientific material.

The contents of Sloane's museum, as listed at his death, included, besides a library of about 50,000 volumes, about 32,000 coins and medals, 1,125 antiquities, 268 seals and about 700 cameos and intaglios, also the following essentially natural history material: 'Pretious Stones, Agates, Jaspers, etc., 2,256; Vessels, etc., of Agates, Jasper, etc., 542; Chrystals, Sparrs, etc., 1,864; Fossils, Flints, Stone, etc., 1,275; Metals, Mineral-Ores, etc., 2,725; Earths, Sands, Salts, etc., 1,035; Bitumens, Sulphurs, Ambers, Ambergreese, etc., 399; Talcs, Micae, etc., 388; Testacea, or Shells, 5,843; Corals, Sponges, etc., 1,421; Echini, Echinites, etc., 659; Asteriae, Trochi, Entrochi, etc., 241; Crustacea, or Crabs, etc., 363; Stellae Marinae, etc., 173; Fishes, and their Parts, 1,555, Birds, and their Parts, Eggs and Nests of different species 1,172; Vipers, Serpents, etc., 521; Quadrupedes etc., 52; Insects, 1886; Humana, as Calculi, Anatomical Preparations, etc., 756; Vegetables, as Seeds, Gums, Wood, Routs, etc., 12,506; Hortus Siccus, or Volumes of dried Plants, 334; Miscellaneous Things, Natural, etc., 2,098; Picture and Drawings, etc., Fram'd 310; Mathematical Instruments, 55.'

The British Museum at its founding was thus as much a natural history museum as one of artefacts and books and was so regarded. A distinguished doctor, Gowin Knight (1713-1772), offering himself for the post of Principal Librarian in 1754, claimed that a regular physician, whose training included medical botany, deserved preference over others not of that profession. An anonymous writer of the time, quoted by Edward Miller in *That Noble Cabinet*: 59 (1973), said: 'Here the young Physician, Chemist and Apothecary may become well acquainted with every Substance, Animal, Vegetable or Mineral that is ever employ'd in Medicine . . . In short the Naturalist will find in this Museum almost everything which he can wish and will be greatly assisted in his Inquiries and Observations.' Gowin Knight was appointed Principal Librarian and remained in office until 1772. His two successors, Matthew Maty, first appointed to Keeper of Manuscripts, and Charles Morton, first appointed as Keeper of Printed Books, were likewise medical men. James Empson (d. 1765) who had charge of Sloane's collection at Chelsea and was an executor of his will, became Keeper of Natural and Artificial Productions, his department being the ancestor of the Department of Natural History and thus ultimately of the Natural History Museum at South Kensington. These four men were the first servants of the Trustees.

The business of the Museum was from its beginning in the hands of able, public-spirited men and so it has remained. At the meetings of the Standing Committee, the Principal Librarian brought to their attention the need for improvements, purchases and the like, as well as much business of a trivial character which presumably they thought should be placed on record in their minutes; these provide for the most part tedious, soporific reading. Various senior members of the staff had direct access to the Trustees. In later years, when the Keeper (i.e. the Head) of a department had submitted a report on the working and needs of his department, the Trustees usually called him or his deputy to discuss and explain it to them more fully. As the British Museum grew, the Trustees became responsible for a much wider range of material than individually they could have any first-hand knowledge or indeed interest. The Standing Committee there-fore appointed four sub-committees on Buildings, on Finance, on Printed Books and Manuscripts, and on Natural History in the middle of the nineteenth century; to them were subsequently added sub-committees on Antiquities, Prints and Drawings, on Coins and Medals, and on the Greek Inscriptions. These brought their con-clusions before the Standing Committee for consideration and usually approval. After the transfer of the natural history collections to South Kensington, the Sub-Committee on Natural History was divided into the Sub-Committee on Zoology (later Zoology and Entomology) and the Sub-Committee on Geology (Palaeontology), Mineralogy and Botany.

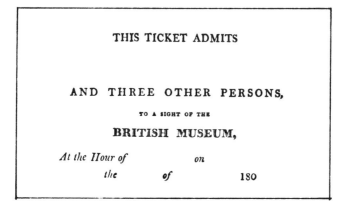

THIS TICKET ADMITS

AND THREE OTHER PERSONS,

TO A SIGHT OF THE

BRITISH MUSEUM,

At the Hour of   *on*

the   *of*   180

Fig. 1.   Ticket of admission to the British Museum in the first decade of the nineteenth century when entry was still restricted.

The Trustees have been subject to much criticism from time to time, some of it justified, much of it ill-informed and occasionally malicious. During the nineteenth century, scientific men resented their lack of representation on the governing body of an institution housing so much scientific material. The Principal Librarian, Henry Ellis, as he made clear in 1835 certainly did not want them as Trustees: the Secretary, the Rev. Josiah Forshall, and Panizzi were of the same opinion: 'The scientific men would spoil the men of rank and drive them from the board.' Nevertheless, men of science were admitted to the Trustees with no evils ensuing.

The British Museum, including the Natural History Museum, continued to be governed under the provisions of this 1753 statute, with Trustees appointed accordingly, until 1963, when a new Act of Parliament legally separated the two museums of Bloomsbury and South Kensington and placed them under independent bodies of Trustees differently constituted. Thus, the Archbishop of Canterbury no longer had any responsibility for the upkeep of the world's largest collection of fleas.

3

The Natural History Collections at Bloomsbury 1756-1856

FOR TWELVE YEARS before the death of Sir Hans Sloane on 11 January 1753 at the age of ninety-two the care of the vast collection of books, antiques, medals, coins, minerals, fossils and botanical and zoological specimens in his Manor House at Chelsea had rested upon James Empson (d.1765) his curator. He appointed Empson as one of his executors and, when the Trustees assembled in accordance with his will, they appointed him as their Secretary and requested him to continue with the care of the Sloane museum. Removal of the collections from Chelsea to the renovated Montagu House at Bloomsbury, which thereupon became the British Museum, took place in 1756. Sloane's material was allocated to three departments, each in the care of the Under-Librarian responsible to the Principal Librarian, in modern terminology a Keeper responsible to the Director. Empson was given charge of everything not a printed book or manuscript. His division of the Museum received the designation 'Department of Natural and Artificial Productions'. It included not only Sloane's extremely valuable 'Hortus siccus' or herbarium in 334 volumes, the subject of J.E. Dandy's, *The Sloane Herbarium* (1958), which is well preserved, but numerous minerals and fossils which were almost all sold or discarded later, and numerous zoological specimens, notably insects and stuffed mammals and birds, which could not be effectively preserved and were later destroyed. Charles Konig stated in 1835 that when his predecessor George Shaw became Keeper of the Natural History Department in 1806, 'most objects of the Sloane collection were in an advanced state of decomposition and they were buried or committed to the flames one after another. Dr Shaw had a burning every year; he called them his cremations.' Konig's assistant

17

William Elford Leach (1790-1836) is also said to have been another incendiarist. 'He despised the taxidermy of Sir Hans Sloane's age and made periodical bonfires of Sloanian specimens . . . the attraction of the terraces and the fragrance of the shrubberies were sadly lessened when a pungent odour of burning snakes was their accompaniment.' Nevertheless, these vanished Sloane collections established natural history as an important part of the British Museum and provided the occasion for acquiring more material, and led ultimately to the foundation of the Natural History Museum.

In 1765 Empson became seriously ill and Matthew Maty (1718-1776), a Dutchman who had come in England in 1741 and had been Under-Librarian in charge of the Department of Printed Books, was transferred to the Department of Natural and Artificial Productions. Maty's appointment in 1772 as Principal Librarian made a vacancy which was filled in 1773 by the appointment of a Swedish naturalist and medical man Daniel Carlsson Solander (1736-1782), who had already worked in the Museum. He had helped Linnaeus to classify three important zoological collections enumerated in Linnaeus's *Museum Tessinianum* (1753), *Museum Adolphi Friderici* (1754) and *Museum Ludovicae Ulricae* (1764), as well as the herbarium of Patrick Browne (?1720-1790) acquired in 1758. However, he came to England in 1760 and never again set foot in Sweden.

In England, where the works of Linnaeus were becoming widely known, Solander was immediately welcomed as an authority on Linnaean method, classification and nomenclature. Richard Pulteney, referring in his *Historical and Biographical Sketches of the Progress of Botany in England* 2: 350(1790) to 'the much-lamented Dr Solander' stated:

> 'His name, and the connexion he was known to bear as the favourite pupil of his great master, had of themselves some share in exciting a curiosity which led to information; whilst his perfect acquaintance with the whole scheme enabled him to explain its minutest parts, and elucidate all those obscurities with which on a superficial view it was thought to be enveloped. I add to this, that the urbanity of his manners, and his readiness to afford every assistance in his power, joined to that clearness and energy with which he effected it, not only brought conviction of its excellence in those who were inclined to receive it, but conciliated the minds, and dispelled the prejudices, of many who had been adverse to it.'

Solander's usefulness as a naturalist made his friends in England anxious to keep him here and the naturalist and antiquary, Peter

Collinson (1694-1768), and John Ellis (?1710-1776) whom Linnaeus termed 'the main support of natural history in England', helped to get him a post in the British Museum in 1763.

Unlike his predecessors, Solander possessed a remarkable knowledge of all branches of natural history, except perhaps mineralogy, though nowadays he is most admired for his botanical work on Captain Cook's global voyage in the *Endeavour*. He was thus a very important acquisition for the Museum staff, because Linnaeus's works supplied what natural history collectors most needed, orderly comprehensive enumerations covering both the animal and vegetable kingdoms by which specimens could be arranged and retrieved when required. He set to work with enthusiasm on the classification and cataloguing of the Museum's natural history collections and produced in 1766 *Fossilia Hantoniensia collecta et in Musaeo Britannica deposita* (see p.226). His election to the Royal Society in 1764 acquainted him with young Joseph Banks (1743-1820). Later, when advising Banks on natural history preparations for voyaging to the South Seas with Cook, he became so excited about the prospect of so much investigation in unknown lands that he volunteered to come himself, an offer which Banks gladly accepted. Then he temporarily left the full-time service of the British Museum.

The voyage of the *Endeavour* lasted from 25 August 1768 to 12 July 1771. Banks and Solander made botanical collections in Madeira, Brazil (but obtained few specimens here owing to the hostility of the Portuguese governor at Rio de Janeiro), Tierra del Fuego, Tahiti, New Zealand, eastern Australia and Java. The artist Sydney Parkinson (1745-1771) made an immense number of coloured drawings of the plants and also some fishes and birds. The sad fate of the zoological material collected on Cook's voyages has been described by P.J.P. Whitehead in the *Journal of the Society for the Bibliography of Natural History* 5: 161-201 (1969) and *Pacific Studies* 2: 52-93 (1978). The botanical specimens and drawings were carefully preserved by Banks and are now in the Natural History Museum, but they did not come to the British Museum until 1827, which was long after Solander's sudden death on 13 May 1782 aged only forty-six.

Solander was a very competent and hard-working naturalist, whose reputation formerly suffered much because so little of his work was published under his own name; nevertheless, Th.O.B.N. Krok, *Bibliotheca botanica Suecana*: 655-660 (1925), listed sixty-six publications in which work by Solander is included and to these should be added W. Blunt and W.T. Stearn, *Captain Cook's Florilegium* (1973).

Solander was a genial easy-going man of high ability and solid worth, respected and liked by such good judges of character as Sir

Joseph Banks and Captain Cook — a man to be trusted. Thus it may be due to the presence of Solander, the Museum's only qualified scientist, that the Royal Society decided to transfer its natural history collections to the Museum in 1781. The most valuable part of these would appear to be the collection of dried specimens of plants, in all 3,750, grown in the Chelsea Physic Garden between 1722 and 1796 (p.279). They provide a first-hand record of plants cultivated during the curatorship of Philip Miller from 1720 to 1772 and have proved very useful for ascertaining the correct application of names published in Miller's important *Gardeners Dictionary* (8th ed., 1768).

On Solander's premature death, Paul Henry Maty (1745-1787), the son of Matthew Maty, who had been in charge of the Department of Printed Books, moved to the Department of Natural and Artificial Productions. Not much seems to have happened during his short period of keepership, and not much more, apart from some valuable accessions, during the nineteen years spent in the Department by his successor, Edward Whitaker Gray (1748-1806), the dimness of whose undistinguished career in the Museum contrasts strongly with the brilliance and eager activity of his great-nephew John Edward Gray (1800-1875) (see p.164). E.W. Gray was Keeper from 1787 to 1806. After a medical training and admission to the Royal College of Physicians, he went out to Portugal and spent between 1773 and 1778 as surgeon to the English merchants' Factory House at Oporto. From here he wrote to Joseph Banks offering to collect material for him and in 1777 he sent Banks some botanical specimens. This may have stood him in good stead when in 1778 he entered the service of the British Museum, apparently on the recommendation of the anatomist William Hunter (1718-1783). There he set about arranging the ornithological collection. Two very remarkable acquisitions came to the Museum in 1799, the Charles Hatchett collection of minerals by purchase and the Mordaunt Cracherode collection of minerals and shells by bequest (see p.258), which by their excellence led to the sale or discarding of Sloane's minerals. The big natural history collections of the eighteenth and early nineteenth centuries were made by wealthy amateurs, like Greville (see p.260) and Joseph Banks. The British Museum, which became ultimately the repository for their material, had neither the means nor the will to compete with them. It refused some collections, such as Sir Ashton Lever's private Leverian Museum, from lack of space to house them. Neither Maty nor E.W. Gray were worthy successors of Solander, whose standing, had he lived longer, would have promoted the flow of collections into the Museum from private collections esteeming him.

The lethargic attitude of such custodians as E.W.Gray became more and more a matter for condemnation. The Trustees in petitioning Parliament in 1805 for extra space thus brought down upon the Museum an enquiry into the state of the collections. Gray obviously found this embarrassing. His health had been declining for some years and he died in the Keeper's Apartments of the Museum on 28 December 1806. In his paper on 'Edward Whitaker Gray (1748-1806), Keeper of Natural Curiosities at the British Museum' in *Bulletin of the British Museum (Natural History),* Historical Series 5: 191-210 (1976), A.E. Gunther sees him as 'a man of general ability, acceptable to those to whom he owed his advancement, lacking incentive and concentration, who evidently regarded natural history as an occupation suited to a gentleman of his inclinations', and concludes that 'he devoted his life and means to the cause of science and, whether as medical man, museum curator or as secretary of a scientific society, he lent his presence to a background of considerable events. He lived and worked on the fringe of the activities of the great scientists of the period, but he lacked the capacity to contribute to the progress they inspired'. The creative intellect, so evident in many generations of the Gray family, does indeed seem to have passed him by.

After his death the Trustees appointed the more ebullient George Shaw (1751-1813) as Keeper of the newly-created Department of Natural History and Modern Curiosities. Shaw, who had become Gray's assistant in 1791, was a physician who studied theology, medicine, botany and zoology and whose enterprising ways, such as admitting a surgeon into the museum to investigate the internal structure of animals and a draughtsman to portray them, must have been very disconcerting for Gray and also for the Trustees; they refused him permission to lecture in the Museum in 1795 and they reprimanded him in 1799 and 1800 for his 'irregularities'. He was one of the founders of the Linnean Society of London. His publications include *Speculum Linnaeanum* (1790), *Museum Leverianum* (1792) and *Zoology of New Holland* (1794).

Shaw's appointment marked the end of an era for the natural history collections as that of Joseph Planta (1744-1827), Principal Librarian from 1799 to 1827, did for the Museum as a whole. Shaw had as his assistant a German naturalist of like versatility, Charles König, originally Carl König (1774-1851) (p.260), appointed in 1806. The Hatchett and Cracherode mineral collections occupied much of König's attention, but Shaw and he were obliged in 1808 to tackle the accumulation of natural history specimens in the basement. Undoubtedly many of the stuffed mammals and birds had sadly deteriorated and Shaw probably enjoyed burning them in the

Museum gardens. Medical and anatomical material was sent to the Hunterian Museum of the Royal College of Surgeons. The specimens remaining were sorted into those suitable for exhibition in the rooms on the upper floors of Montagu House and those to remain below as duplicates. Sir Joseph Banks, as a leading Trustee, supervised the operation. Shaw died in July 1813 and in September that year Konig became Keeper.

The death of Sir Joseph Banks in 1820 deprived the Museum of a sagacious and devoted Trustee and a generous benefactor and Konig of a helpful adviser. Banks had first entered the Museum in 1765 and attended his first Trustees Meeting on 18 December 1778; on one occasion he and his retainers had come to the Museum armed to defend it against a rioting London mob. At an earlier period, Banks under-standably had not considered the Museum a suitable repository for natural history specimens and on his advice some zoological material went elsewhere. Under Planta and Konig the Museum was on its way to rival the prestigious Muséum d'Histoire Naturelle in Paris, but it had still far to go. Banks manifested his confidence in its future by bequeathing his library and herbarium, one of the richest in the world, to the Trustees through the intermediary of his curator and librarian, Robert Brown (1773-1858), on whose death they were to pass to the Museum unless Brown preferred to transfer them earlier, which he did in 1827. In fact the Trustees began negotiations in July 1823 for what was called the Sir Joseph Banks' Botanical Collection, although Brown referred to it as the Banksian Botanical Collections. Brown was appointed Keeper under very favourable terms, with long holidays and a weekly attendance of only two days. The Museum's already existing botanical collections, consisting of the Sloane herbarium, the Chelsea Physic Garden plants from the Royal Society and the herbarium which came with the minerals of Carl Ehrenbert von Moll (1760-1838) remained for the time being under Konig, who was himself a botanist of standing. These original collections and the Banksian botanical material were eventually joined, in 1835, to create a Botanical Branch which foreshadowed the division of the Department of Natural History into several independent departments.

This took place in 1837 and was carried further in 1857. It resulted from the report of a House of Commons Select Committee appointed to enquire into the condition, management and affairs of the British Museum in 1835. 'The real purpose of this Committee', as stated by Edward Miller, 'was to reveal the nepotism, corruption, inefficiency and maladministration said to be rife within the Museum'. In fact it revealed how understaffed the Museum was for scientific research, indeed for the proper curation and cataloguing of its material, and how galling that was for its over-worked scientists with no trained understaff and only cleaners and warders to support them and how handicapped they were by inadequate funds.

Konig, Brown, Children and J.E. Gray gave evidence. John Edward Gray (p.164) had now risen to an influential position within the Museum, even though only a temporary member of its staff, and he gave the most forthright and well informed evidence of them all. He revealed an intimate knowledge of the Museum's deficiencies and he proposed remedies based on comparison, in particular with the Muséum d'Histoire Naturelle which he knew well. He recommended that zoology and mineralogy should no longer be kept together as one department, that more funds should be made available and that more trained staff should be employed. He contrasted the state and size of the Museum collections with those on the Continent which he had visited on several occasions. It must have been evident to all that here was a man of both knowledge and drive.

Another man of knowledge and drive also gave evidence, Antonio Panizzi (1797-1879), when the Select Committee met again in 1836. 'This tough, brawny man, with the face and sometimes the manners of a bandit', was a lawyer and a scholar, exiled from Italy with a price on his head, ambitious to make the main library of his adopted country, the Department of Printed Books at the Museum, the finest in the world. In many, many matters he and Gray were bound to conflict violently. On this occasion, with his own attitude radically democratic, Gray must have agreed completely with Panizzi's bold challenging declaration of aim: 'I want a poor student to have the same means of indulging his learned curiosity, of following his rational pursuits, of consulting the same authorities, of fathoming the most intricate enquiry, as the richest man in the country, as far as books go, and I contend that the Government is bound to give him the most liberal and unlimited assistance in this respect.' That was what Panizzi strained all his redoubtable powers to achieve. Replace, however, 'as far as books go' in that statement by 'as far as natural history specimens go' and it could have come from Gray. He himself said that the Museum's function was 'to encourage a taste for science among the people generally and to advance it . . . by opening the collection to all who are desirous of studying it and capable of profiting by it'. Such worthy aims should not have been incompatible. They were made to appear so by the failure in 1799 to buy land to the north of Montagu House, offered by the Duke of Bedford for the Museum's expansion, together with the continuing financial stringency. Enough money and space to achieve both were not then available and their conflicting needs aroused a bitter animosity between these two, great strong-minded men. Moreover,

Panizzi made it clear even then, in 1836, that he would like the Museum to be rid of its natural history collections and the men associated with them: 'The department *Natural History* ought to have better assistance and be transferred somewhere else, in which case I wish to impress upon the Committee the absolute necessity of this separation.' In later years he fought for such a separation against Gray in particular. For him 'Scientific men are jealous of their authority, themselves infallible' and he preferred their room and indeed their rooms to their company in the institution of which he later became the Principal Librarian.

The Select Committee accepted Gray's recommendations, including the one that the Natural History Department should be divided and in 1837 it became three branches: the Botanical (already formed in 1835 when all Museum botanical specimens were put in Brown's charge), the Zoological under Children and the Mineralogical and Geological under Konig, who much resented this lessening, as he saw it, of his status. On 27 March 1837 the Trustees formally appointed Gray as assistant to the ageing Children.

The meetings of the Select Committee had brought Gray into public notice, but he was already very well known and esteemed among fellow naturalists, both at home and abroad. With Children's resignation impending, he sought their support in applying for the Keepership of Zoology. Among those who supplied letters of recommendation was Children himself, who had an appreciative paternal attitude towards his brilliant and energetic assistant, Thomas Bell, William Yarrell, Thomas Horsfield, Richard Owen, Peter Mark Roget, the compiler of the invaluable *Thesaurus of English Words and Phrases,* Charles Darwin, Lorenz Oken, C.G.C. Reinwardt, Eduard Rüppel, C.J. Temminck, Charles Lyell, C.G. Ehrenberg and Prince Charles Lucien Bonoparte. These were great names then as now. No one else in Britain could have mustered so many recommendations from men of such eminence. Accordingly, on 11 April 1840 J.E. Gray became Keeper of Zoology. A new era in the Museum's history began.

Once Keeper of the Zoological Branch in 1840, Gray immediately set about getting more specimens for the new extension to the British Museum and planning a more logical arrangement. The writer of an obituary of Gray in *The Athenaeum* no. 2472: 363 (13 March 1875) remarked that 'those who are old enough to remember the confusion that reigned in the dark rooms of Montagu House, where camelopards [giraffes], crustacea, and corals were crowded together, can appreciate the changes effected under the superintendence of Dr Gray. In this he was ably seconded by his assistants'. He knew the increasing prestige of the zoological collections of Berlin, Leyden, Paris and other continental cities and he resolved that the one under his care should equal or surpass them. He soon found the grant of £1,000 allocated for his yearly purchases too small; for 1841 he wanted £1,600. Throughout his keepership he never had enough money for all the purchases and publications his ambitious mind conceived.

The collections having been placed in the new building, Gray tackled their cataloguing. The catalogues he had in mind were not to be simply lists of specimens, but reviews of groups with synonyms and descriptions, which became more elaborate and detailed with the passing of time until, particularly with Albert Günther, they became monographic.

Thanks to Gray's enterprise and enthusiasm, specimens continuously came into the Museum and from time to time catalogues and synopses came out, despite the working conditions of the staff. They toiled in the basement. P.L. Sclater, writing as late as 1877, stated that 'No lights are allowed, and when the fogs of winter set in, the obscurity is such that it is difficult to see any object requiring minute examination'. According to Albert E. Gunther, his father Robert Günther 'never forgot being taken, as a small boy, to the spirit room in the basement by the faithful attendants, old John Saunders and Edward Gerrard, through endless dark passages, stuffy with the heat of boilers, into the gloomy vaults. There, packed tight on shelves, stood the dust-covered bottles with their thousands of specimens. Those friends whose privilege it was to be admitted to those cellars often referred to Albert's sunless life surrounded by his fishes'. The cellars were, moreover, often damp and had no ventilation.

Appreciation of the Museum's zoological collections received formal recognition in 1854 when the University of Munich, which had earlier honoured a great English botanist John Lindley with the honorary degree of Doctor Philosophiae, now conferred the same degree on Gray for having formed the largest zoological collection in Europe. Another testimony to the esteem which the zoological branch had now attained came from the Zoological Society of London. In 1841 the Society was anxious to find alternative accommodation for its important museum to the unsafe building which then housed it but did not consider the British Museum a properly-managed repository for such valuable materials. During the next ten years Gray's administration gained the Society's confidence. Its Council decided in 1855 that the remarkable development within the Museum made superfluous the need to maintain a second zoological museum in London and it sold to the Museum for £500 such of its collections as the Museum required. Thereafter government departments, as well as private individuals, accepted the Museum as the proper repository for zoological material.

Meanwhile, the Botanical and the Mineralogical and Geological branches, although neither expanding nor publishing prolifically as the Zoological one did under its dynamic Keeper, were receiving notable accessions. Indeed, every year brought more and more material, for which there was less and less space; this process of accretion by 1856 had produced difficulties of storage and display which were felt throughout the Museum. Thus in 1848 and 1849, the enormous Assyrian sculptures excavated by Henry Austen Layard arrived at the Museum and finding room for them raised the question of removing them and other collections, including those of natural history, to another site, a course naturally favoured by Panizzi and naturally opposed by Gray. The formation of the museum complex at Bloomsbury, such as later came into being at South Kensington, was too costly for the Treasury to approve; the land, belonging to the Duke of Bedford which could have been acquired in 1799 for the future expansion of the Museum had by now all been taken. Nevertheless, the inadequacy of space for the growing collections on the Bloomsbury site came home more and more, not only to the Trustees and their staff, but to politicians and the general public.

In March 1847 a memorial to the Prime Minister from the British Association for the Advancement of Science expressed disquiet over the provision for natural history within the Museum, the Trustees of which were considered unable adequately to direct 'the vast and rapidly increasing Natural History departments of the Museum'. This led to a Royal Commission being appointed in June 1847 to enquire in what manner the Museum could be made more effective for the advancement of literature, science and the arts. The Commission's *Report* appeared in 1850 and contains valuable evidence by Brown, Gray and Konig on their respective departments; almost needless to remark, Gray had most to say. The Commission concluded that 'the Natural History Collections are, as a whole, equal if not superior to any in the world'. It did not, however, tackle the problem of housing them. From 1856 onwards the building of a new museum elsewhere as an annexe to Smirke's Bloomsbury one gained powerful advocates (Chapter 5).

4

Richard Owen
Superintendent of the
Natural History Departments

THE PERIOD FROM 1856 to 1883 began with problems of space at Bloomsbury for its library and its collections representing the arts and natural history, and ended with the erection of a new building, the Natural History Museum at South Kensington, and the transfer into it of the natural history collections. The period was one of earnest debate on the aims and methods of a natural history museum. It was a period too of British imperial expansion which brought more and more natural history specimens into the British Museum, but also imposed restrictions by the Treasury on the money available. The Crimean War ended in 1856, with about 4,000 British soldiers killed in action and 20,000 killed by disease, cold and starvation. One of those who suffered was W.H. Flower, a future Director of the Natural History Museum. Income tax had been raised to 1s 4d (7p) in the pound. The Indian Mutiny broke out in 1857 and caused the despatch of 30,000 troops to India. Expenditure on these overseas matters could only be met, without further increase in taxation, by economical measures in Britain and one of them was restraint on the funds available for the expansion of the British Museum. Moreover, conflict in Parliament between William Ewart Gladstone of the Liberal Party and Benjamin Disraeli, later Earl of Beaconsfield, of the Conservative Party adversely affected the Museum's policy and finances.

Two appointments, both unpopular with some members of the Museum staff, made the year 1856 important in its history, namely that of Antonio Panizzi (1797-1879) as Principal Librarian in charge of the whole British Museum and Richard Owen (1804-1892) as Superintendent of the Natural History Departments. The two appointments were connected. The historian Lord Macaulay, sensing the fear by scientists that natural history would be neglected and the library and sculpture galleries unduly favoured during Panizzi's rule, had urged the appointment of the distinguished anatomist and palaeontologist Richard Owen, then Hunterian Professor and Conservator of the Hunterian Museum of the Royal College of Surgeons, partly as a counterpoise to Panizzi, partly to help Owen financially. Panizzi became the sixth Principal Librarian 'to the delight of his many friends and the baffled rage of his equally numerous enemies, both inside and outside the Museum', as Edward Miller has said in his *That Noble Cabinet* (1973). Owen's appointment, although probably not arousing such strong feelings outside the Museum, was certainly unwelcome within it and considered unnecessary by the Keepers of the branches of the Natural History Department, which were now raised to the rank of independent departments, with Geology separated from Mineralogy. All these departments came nominally under Owen's control; their Keepers kept that control nominal.

The management of the natural history collections by Owen had been suggested, probably by Owen, some years earlier. However, a squeamish Trustee quickly crushed a proposal in 1846 to transfer the natural history collections to the Hunterian Museum, where they would be associated with disgusting medical exhibits quite unsuited for the gaze of Victorian mamas and their daughters. Nevertheless, Owen's possible move to the British Museum, following the sudden death of Konig, had become a matter of gossip by 9 November 1851, as is evident from a letter thus dated by T.H. Huxley in London to W. Macleay in Sydney, New South Wales: 'There is a great stir in the scientific world at present about who is to occupy Konig's place at the British Museum and whether the whole establishment had better not, *quoad* Zoology, be remodelled and placed under Owen's superintendence. The heart-burnings and jealousies about this matter are beyond all conception. Owen is both feared and hated'. His brilliant penetrating intellect linked to sly ways of attaining his ends created unease among fellow workers. Huxley further remarked: 'It is astonishing with what an intense feeling of hatred Owen is regarded by the majority of his contemporaries . . . The truth is, he is the superior of most and does not conceal that he knows it and it must be confessed that he does some very ill-natured tricks now and then.'

One of his victims was the distinguished geologist Gideon Algernon Mantell (1790-1852), who regretted in his 'Journal' for 17 December 1845 that 'this highly eminent and gifted man can never act with candour and liberality'. Mantell was ever ready to praise the quality of Owen's work, which he held in high regard. Owen's conduct towards Mantell, when he ventured rightly to disagree with Owen, was indeed 'violent and illiberal' and caused Mantell much pain.

Huxley, whom Owen helped to an appointment, recorded that 'Owen has been amazingly civil to me. He is a queer fish, more odd in appearance than ever and more bland in manner. He is so frightfully polite that I never feel thoroughly at home with him.' Owen had indeed very ingratiating manners for people high and influential in society and particularly for the Royal Family, as also for the young who constituted no threat to him. His scientific contemporaries mostly regarded him with cold admiration for his superb intellectual powers and his remarkable work as a comparative anatomist and palaeontologist, but they distrusted his jealous and devious ways. Panizzi and Gray both regarded Owen's coming to the Museum with misgivings. His post was intended to be a link between the Natural History Departments, the Principal Librarian and the Trustees. In practice it gave him a good salary, little responsibility and much opportunity for research.

However, his perception of the need to move the over-crowded natural history collections from Bloomsbury to a more spacious building elsewhere, and his influential advocacy of this, led ultimately to the creation of the Natural History Museum at South Kensington. He was its first and only Superintendent. Thus it is fitting that Owen's statue stands there in a prominent place on the stairs of the cathedral-like main hall for, even though the 'Index Museum' he envisaged as occupying the bays and central space below has been swept away, remains of the gigantic extinct reptiles, for which he coined the term 'dinosaurs', dominate its vastness.

Richard Owen was born in Lancaster on 20 July 1804, his father, Richard (1754-1809), being a woollen draper and West India merchant, his mother, Catherine, the daughter of Huguenot refugees from Provence. His assertiveness and some less pleasant sides of his character, such as his cunning and jealousy, may well have sprung from ambition, as a fatherless boy, to manifest his ability to the world and outstrip rivals. He was apprenticed to a local surgeon and apothecary, who died, then to another, who joined the Royal Navy, and then to yet another, from whom he learned the art of dissection, before going to the University of Edinburgh in 1824. After studying under John Barclay (1758-1826), he went to London and became an assistant to John Abernethy (1764-1831), a well-known Scottish surgeon at St Bartholomew's Hospital. On 18 August 1826 he was made a member of the Royal College of Surgeons of England and, thus qualified, he set up a private practice near the hospital. Then, through Abernethy's appreciation of his ability, he was appointed in 1827 assistant conservator of the Hunterian Museum, belonging to the Royal College of Surgeons, to help William Clift (1775-1849), who had been John Hunter's assistant. Thus began Owen's long association with museums.

In 1828 he started lecturing to students at St Bartholomew's Hospital on comparative anatomy. The great French anatomist and palaeontologist Georges Cuvier (1769-1832) visited the Royal College's museum in 1830 and Owen, with his good command of French, was given the pleasant task of guiding him around the collection. Evidently impressed by this gifted young man, Cuvier invited him to the Muséum d'Histoire Naturelle which Owen visited in 1831, working there for a short time under Cuvier. Owen may indeed be regarded as the most important of Cuvier's disciples.

Cuvier's influence on Owen through his writings, notably his *Recherches sur les Ossements fossiles des Quadrupèdes* (1812) with the 'Discours préliminaire' translated into English as *Theory of the Earth* (1815), and through personal acquaintance was profound, as Owen acknowledged, above all on account of Cuvier's emphasis upon the interdependence and correlation of separate organs within the same animal body as essential for its way of life, indeed determining this. Thus teeth adapted for grazing vegetation must be associated with a digestive system capable of dealing with such bulky plant food, unlike that of a beast of prey which has a smaller digestive system and sharp cutting teeth for seizing and tearing flesh; many other less obvious correlations link with such major ones. Detailed knowledge of such co-ordination of structure in living animals enabled Cuvier to visualize from an incomplete skeleton the probable shape and habits of the whole animal when alive. He believed that, owing to the close mutual interaction of organs within the body of an organism, none of the parts could change without the others also changing and 'consquently each one of them taken separately indicates and shows the nature of the whole'. He stated that 'the smallest fragment of bone, even the most apparently insignificant apophysis, possesses a fixed and determinate character, relative to the class, order, genus and species of the animal to which it belonged; insomuch, that when we find merely the extremity of a well-preserved bone, we are able by careful examination, assisted by analogy and exact comparison, to determine the species to which it once belonged, as certainly as if we had the entire animal before us'. This Cuvierian method, applied with imagination and insight and backed by a thorough knowledge of anatomy and osteology, proved eminently successful in Owen's hands and enabled him to make spectacular reconstructions of extinct animals known only from a few bones, to resuscitate graphically, as he said in 1844, 'the strangest of the old monsters which it has pleased God to blot out of his Creation'. Such achievements, together with his exact and detailed descriptions, brought him international renown as a palaeontologist.

Within the main groups of the animal kingdom, Cuvier recognized lesser groups exhibiting variations on a basic ground-plan or type. This concept of types underlaid Owen's project for an 'Index Museum', an epitome of natural history, exhibiting the type characters of the principal groups of organisms, when in later years he planned the Natural History Museum. Cuvier rejected Lamarck's views of evolution and Owen followed him in 1868 by dismissing likewise 'the guess endeavours of Lamarck, Darwin, Wallace and others' on the production of species. The work of Cuvier showed conclusively the former existence of creatures no longer living, hence lost to the world, presumably through catastrophic upheavals of the land, followed by new creations. This hypothesis of past world history reconciled science and scripture, and Owen accepted it. Cuvier and Owen had much in common; they united extraordinary scientific ability and achievement with obsequiousness, secretiveness and intellectual arrogance according to the occasion.

Fig. 2. Richard Owen carving a dodo at a dinner with extinct animals he had reconstructed; a note on the table reads 'Please do not eat your bones but save them for Prof. Owen' (from a menu of the Palaeontographical Society).

Owen received for dissection the animals which died in the menagerie of the Zoological Society of London at Regent's Park, as those of the Paris menagerie at the Muséum d'Histoire Naturelle likewise went to Cuvier. Through his papers on these, and also on the pearly nautilus, *Nautilus pampilius,* Owen had become known by 1832 as a capable anatomist. The tragic death of Clift's son, William Home Clift, in September 1832 made Clift's potential son-in-law, Owen, also his obvious successor in the Hunterian Museum. The Royal College of Surgeons raised Owen's salary whereupon he married Caroline Clift. He continued to work on the collections and to publish studies of the anatomy of animals. This led to his appointment in April 1836 as Hunterian Professor of Comparative Anatomy at the Royal College and so began the social climbing so much to his taste.

Darwin brought him fossil material from the voyage of the *Beagle* and turned his attention to palaeontology and the comparative study of teeth. Over the years Owen had acquired a knowledge of the anatomy, including the osteology and odontology, of animals unrivalled in Britain and this stood him in good stead when studying fossils, for he could visualize by analogy with living creatures what shape of animal the fossil bones had supported in life long ago. Owen made his most audacious act of prediction by Cuvierian method in 1839 when a Dr John Rule placed in his hands for examination and purchase a fragment of bone from New Zealand, where the Maoris had a tradition that it belonged to a bird of the eagle kind which had become extinct. This bone, illustrated in *Transactions of the Zoological Society of London* 3: plate 3 (1842) measured only 6 inches (15 cms), with its smallest circumference 5½ inches (14 cms). Owen recognized it as the shaft of a femur with both extremities broken off. He compared it with the femur of man, ox, horse, pig, camel, kangaroo, dog, grizzly bear, lion, orangutan, ostrich, emu, giant tortoise and crocodile, and concluded from the size and structure of this fragment that it represented an ostrich-like bird but 'a heavier and more sluggish species than the ostrich'. No such bird was known to exist or ever to have existed in New Zealand. Nevertheless, at a meeting of the Zoological Society on 12 November 1839, Owen confidently proclaimed that, 'as far as my skill in interpreting an osseous fragment may be credited, I am willing to risk the reputation for it on the statement that there has existed, if there does not now exist, in New Zealand, a struthious bird nearly, if not quite equal in size to the Ostrich' *(Proceedings of the Zoological Society of London:* 175-177, 1840). This was a bold statement indeed to base on a single, incomplete bone only 6 inches (15 cms) long. It was naturally received with scepticism and the Zoological Society had grave misgivings about publication of anything so rash in its respectable *Proceedings* and *Transactions.*

Owen's triumph and a vindication of 'the fruitful principle of physio-
logical correlation' came in 1843, when he received numerous bones
sent from Poverty Bay, New Zealand, by a missionary William
Williams who, quite unaware of Owen's paper, had learned from the
Maoris of an extinct gigantic creature they called 'moa'. On the basis of
this much more complete material Owen defined his new genus
Dinornis with five distinct species 'ascending respectively from the size
of the Great Bustard to that of the Dodo, of the Emu, of the Ostrich,
and finally attaining a structure far surpassing that of the once-deemed
most gigantic of birds' (*Transactions of the Zoological Society of London* 3:
235-275, 1844). Since then abundant remains of these birds, including
a few eggs and feathers, have been found in New Zealand and have
indicated the former existence of at least nineteen species belonging to
six genera, according to the surveys by G. Archey in *Bulletin of the
Auckland Institute and Museum* 1 (1941) and W.R.B. Oliver in *Bulletin of
Dominion Museum, Wellington* 15 (1949).

In 1841, thus shortly after his moa prediction but before its confir-
mation, Owen came into prominence at the eleventh meeting of the
British Association for the Advancement of Science, held in Plymouth,
by an address lasting over two hours on British fossil reptiles. Here he
made another bold proposal, motivated in part, so Adrian J. Desmond
asserts in *Isis* 70 : 224-234 (1979), by opposition to the Lamarckian
evolutionary teaching of a rival anatomist Robert Edmund Grant
(1793-1874). He took three fossil reptilian species, *Megalosaurus
bucklandi, Hylaeosaurus armatus* and *Iguanodon mantelli*, to represent a new
order which he called the Dinosauria and coined the name 'dinosaur'
(from *deinos*, fearful, terrible, wondrous, strange; *sauros*, a lizard).
These species were all then known to him. He described them as terrestrial, egg-laying, cold-blooded devourers of animals and feeders upon
vegetation, 'creatures far surpassing in size the largest of existing
reptiles', yet this was largely speculation. Here again subsequent
discoveries have justified both his concept and his name, for *Tyranno-
saurus rex*, first described in 1905, must surely have been the most
terrible of lizard-like creatures, indeed of any flesh-eating animals. Ten
years later for the Great Exhibition of 1851, with which Prince Albert,
Owen's influential supporter, was so closely involved, Owen supervised stone reconstructions of these gigantic beasts. When in 1854 the
Crystal Palace had been transferred from Hyde Park to Sydenham, a
whole terrifying menagerie of them, made by Benjamin Waterhouse
Hawkins with Owen's help, appeared in the Palace grounds as large as
life at the suggestion of Prince Albert.

Thus Owen grew in reputation and rose in royal favour. Queen
Victoria had provided him in 1840 with a civil list pension, a welcome

supplement to his low Hunterian Museum salary, and with a residence, Sheen Lodge (now totally destroyed), in Richmond Park in 1851. However, these served to increase friction between him and his employers. The trustees of the Royal College of Surgeons viewed with increasing displeasure his participation in activities little connected with the duties for which they paid him as full-time Conservator of their Hunterian Museum, even though some of these, as his co-operation with the great sanitary reformer Edwin Chadwick (1800-1890) and his discovery of the parasitic worm causing trichiniasis, were of public benefit and others, such as his working out of Darwin's *Beagle* material, of great scientific merit; indeed, Darwin frequently quoted Owen's work in *The Origin of Species* (1859). Thus, year by year, hostility grew between the Royal College's board and Owen. It must therefore have been a great relief to him when in May 1856 he received the expected invitation to become Superintendent of the Natural History Depart-

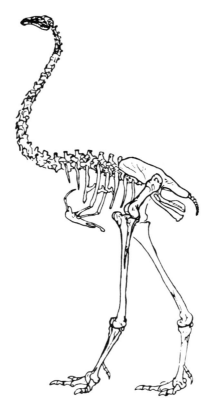

Fig. 3. Skeleton of the giant moa, *Dinornis maximus,* from New Zealand (drawing by Maurice Wilson).

ments of the British Museum with his salary almost doubled. Nevertheless, on promptly resigning as Conservator of the Hunterian Museum, he wrote to the College which knew nothing about his British Museum negotiations: 'I quit the duties which have formed the main labours and pleasure of the last twenty-nine years of my life with unfeigned regret.' Owen's assistant John Thomas Quekett (1815-1861), the quiet, skilful and conscientious microscopist then became Conservator and dissension ceased.

At the British Museum Owen found conditions were very different from those at the Hunterian Museum. He was subject to the authority of Panizzi; in turn he attempted to put restrictions on Gray. Claiming that his duties as Superintendent included supervision and possibly alteration of the publications emanating from the natural history departments, Owen alienated the outside workers, except the least competent, Francis Walker, who were employed by Gray on the catalogues of zoological material, and by 1860 they had withdrawn their help. Thereafter, any proposal by Owen naturally aroused Gray's hostility, which was unfortunate, for, although Owen was sly and self-opinionated, he could be right.

Two years after his Museum appointment, Owen became President of the British Association for the Advancement of Science. He took the opportunity of its meeting at Leeds in 1858 to comment in his Presidential Address (*Report British Association* 1858: xcv, 1859) on 'the present condition of the National Museum of Natural History and of its most pressing requirements'. 'Of them', Owen said, 'the most pressing, and the one essential to rendering the collection worthy of this great empire, is "space". Our colonies include parts of the earth where the forms of plants and animals are the most strange. No empire in the world had ever so wide a range for the collection of the various forms of animal life as Great Britain. Never was there so much energy and intelligence displayed in the capture and transmission of exotic animals by the enterprising traveller in unknown lands and by the hardy settler in remote colonies, as by those who start from their native shores of Britain. Foreign Naturalists consequently visit England anticipating to find in her capital and in her National Museum the richest and most varied materials for their comparisons and deductions. And they ought to be in a state pre-eminently conducive to the advancement of a philosophical zoology, and on a scale commensurate with the greatness of the nation and the peculiar national facilities for such perfection.' After this appeal to British patriotism, Owen continued: 'But, in order to receive and to display zoological specimens, space must be had; and not merely space for display, but for orderly display; the galleries should bear relation in size and form with the nature of the classes respectively occupying them.' Having earlier resented Gray's acquisition of General Hardwicke's collection of skeletons for the British Museum, Owen now stated that 'an osteological collection is as indispensable to the illustration of the Vertebrata as a conchological one is to that of the Mollusca. Nor should the size of any of the skeletons be a bar to the obtainment of adequate space for the Osteological Collection in the National Museum of Natural History. The very fact of the Whales being the largest animals upon the earth, is that which makes it more imperative to illustrate the fact and gratify the natural interest of the public by the adequate and convenient exhibition of their skeletons.' Clearly such space could not be found within the existing British Museum at Bloomsbury. A further statement revealed Owen's belief that there would have to be a separate building for the natural history collections. 'The locality of such an adequately-sized Museum concerns the administrator and the public convenience... I am most concerned in advocating the pressing necessity of adequate space for the National Museum of Natural History, wherever administrative wisdom may see fit to locate it.'

There were, however, grave disadvantages to the creation of a National Museum of Natural History if it involved moving away from Bloomsbury. Thus the Keepers of the Natural History Departments did not want to be handicapped, as they were to be later, by lack of access to the main library at Bloomsbury through removal to another area. In this they were right and they had the support of many eminent naturalists and several Trustees. A memorial addressed to the Chancellor of the Exchequer, then Benjamin Disraeli, in July 1858, stated that 'it is essential that the different classes of natural objects should be preserved in juxtaposition under one roof', in close proximity to the national library and 'associated with the many other branches of human knowledge which are so admirably represented in this great national institution'. On the other hand, land at Bloomsbury for such a building as Owen envisaged had become very costly. No one solution to the congestion within the Museum commended itself to all concerned. There was accordingly occasion for much delay and much debate and Gray and Owen openly opposed one another.

Between 1863 and 1869 Gray and Owen were engaged in controversy over the arrangement of natural history collections within a museum. Gray put forward his views in an address at the meeting of the British Association for the Advancement of Science held in Bath in 1864, printed in *Report British Association,* 1864: 75-86 (1865). Speaking on zoological museums he confessed that he had now 'come to the conclusion that the plan hitherto pursued in their arrangement has rendered them less useful to science and less interesting to the public at large than they might have been made under a different system. Let us consider the purposes for which such a museum is established. There are two: 1st, the diffusion of instruction and rational amusement among the mass of the people; and 2nd, to afford the scientific student every possible means of examining and studying the specimens of which the museum consists. Now, it appears to me that, in the desire to combine these two objects which are essentially distinct, the first object, namely the general instruction of the people, has been to a great extent lost sight of and sacrificed to the second, without any corresponding advantage to the latter.'

Gray accordingly condemned the prevailing custom of putting all the Museum's specimens on public view, because it provided the general visitor with 'little else than a chaos of specimens, of which the bulk of those placed in close proximity are so nearly alike that he can scarcely perceive any difference between them, even supposing them to be placed on a level with the eye'. The deterioration of specimens through exposure to light and the ease of measuring and comparing specimens in an unstuffed or unmounted state made it sensible that for scientific purposes the skins and bones of animals should be stored in boxes or drawers, each devoted to a family, a genus, or a section of a genus, and thereby protected from exposure to light and dust. Specimens in spirit should be kept in dark cupboards, in cool rooms. They should not be in galleries open to the public. Gray concluded that 'a museum for the use of the general public should consist chiefly of the best-known, the most marked, and the most interesting animals arranged in such a way as to convey the greatest amount of information in the shortest and most direct manner, and so exhibited as to be seen without confusion'. He then considered what the display cases should contain and ended by observing that 'such cases would be infinitely more attractive to the public at large than the crowded shelves of our present museums, in which they speedily become bewildered by the multiplicity, the apparent sameness, and at the same time the infinite variety of the objects presented to their view'.

The procedure advocated by Gray of separating display and study material has now become standard museum practice throughout the world. Later and independently William Flower used it at the Hunterian Museum where he followed Quekett as Conservator. It was Flower's lectures, publications and practice, rather than Gray's address, which led to the acceptance of what now seems so obvious and orthodox. Owen then wished, however, to have the major part of the museum collections exhibited, whence the immense area he proposed and whence also the need for a central area containing his 'Index Museum' of selected typical specimens to summarize the whole in a relatively small space.

During the many years that the planning and building of the new museum at South Kensington, described in Chapter 5, occupied the attention of the Trustees, the Office of Works, architects and builders, at Bloomsbury the Keepers of the Natural History Departments and their staff had more than enough to do with the curation, classification, cataloguing and display of their ever increasing material. They had indeed to carry a heavy burden, since lack of space made the incorporation of new specimens in correct taxonomic position ever more difficult and time-consuming, while at the same time they were committed to the research which alone justified the acquisition of such material.

In the 1860s Gray's health began to deteriorate and he broke down completely in 1869; a stroke in May 1869 paralysed his right side and, often frustrated in his activities, he became increasingly irritable and often discourteous. Nevertheless, he taught himself to write with his left hand and produced paper after paper, some, it is said, which would have been better left unwritten. Obstinate as ever, he refused to retire until December 1874. He had worked for fifty years in the service of the Trustees and he died in his apartments of the British Museum on 7 March 1875.

Part II

The Museum at South Kensington

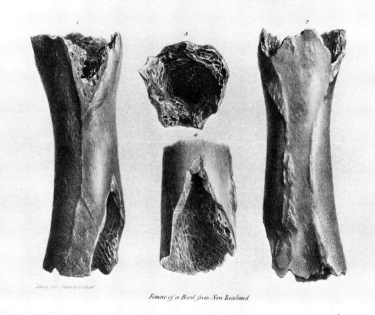

Femur of a Bird from New Zealand

10. The original 6 inch *Dinornis* bone, which Richard Owen
correctly took as evidence of the former existence of giant
flightless birds in New Zealand (from *Trans. Zool. Soc. London* 3: pl.3; 1842).

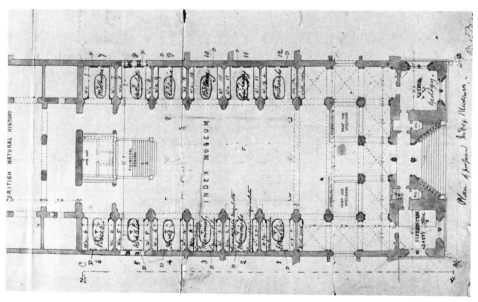

11. Owen's 1879 plan for an Index Museum occupying the main
hall of the Natural History Museum.

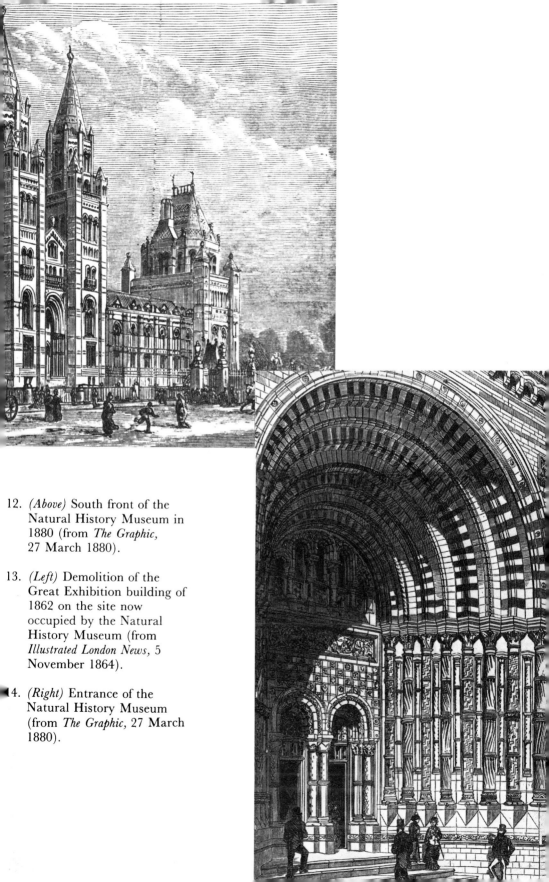

12. *(Above)* South front of the
    Natural History Museum in
    1880 (from *The Graphic*,
    27 March 1880).

13. *(Left)* Demolition of the
    Great Exhibition building of
    1862 on the site now
    occupied by the Natural
    History Museum (from
    Illustrated London News, 5
    November 1864).

14. *(Right)* Entrance of the
    Natural History Museum
    (from *The Graphic*, 27 March
    1880).

A

B

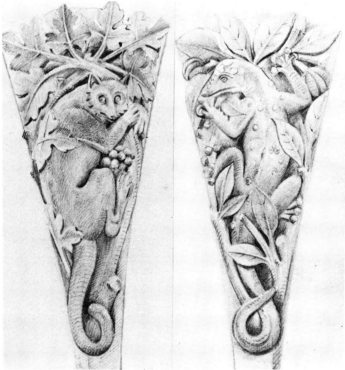

C

15. Pencil sketches by Alfred Waterhouse (1830-1905)
for terracotta ornamentation of the Natural
History Museum.
   a. Passenger Pigeon *(Ectopistes macrourus)*
   b. Common or Greater Rhea *(Rhea americana)*
   c. *(left)* Common Raccoon *(Procyon lotor)*
   (right) Seychelles Gecko *(Phelsuma sundbergi)*

5

The Land and Buildings at South Kensington

T HE PROBLEM OF finding adequate space to house the ever-growing collections and to accommodate the ever-increasing staff and visitors became evident early in the nineteenth century. The acquisition then of a series of bulky antiquities led to the first additions to Montagu House. However, the transformation of the buildings by Sir Robert Smirke and his brother Sydney Smirke during the years 1823-1847 was due to a different acquisition, namely the fine library formed by King George III.

Even this new building proved inadequate. The provision of space for the collections became a matter of public interest and of increasing worry for the Museum's officials. The idea of dispersing part of the collections received attention. Such an idea had indeed been suggested a mere six years after the opening of Montagu House to the public by one Peter John Grosley. Thomas Watts voiced it again in the *Mechanics Magazine* 26: 291-295 (1837): 'The pictures have been removed, why should not the statues follow? The collections at the museum would then remain of an entirely homogenous nature.' However, one Committee of Enquiry after another rejected the suggestion of removing any part of the collections from Bloomsbury.

A memorial by a distinguished list of signatories, Owen among them, in July 1858 protested against the removal of the scientific collections from Bloomsbury, either bodily, or by being broken up among other institutions, and maintained they should be preserved under one roof in close proximity to the national library. However, in February 1859 Owen submitted to the Trustees a plan showing the proportional spaces required for the several departments and classes of a national collection of natural history. This required 5½ acres (2.23

hectares) for a two-storey building, or 11 acres (4.45 hectares) for a single-storey one. Growing concern in April 1860 caused the House of Commons to appoint a Select Committee to enquire into the Museum's requirements. For the Committee's consideration Owen prepared further plans, one being for an extension of the Bloomsbury building, the other for a new building elsewhere. The Committee decided that the natural history collections should remain at Bloomsbury. Much to Panizzi's annoyance, the Committee reported: 'the witnesses examined have almost unanimously testified to the preference over the other collections with which the Natural History Collections are viewed by the ordinary and most numerous frequenters of the Museum. . . It appears, from evidence, that many of the middle-classes are in the habit of forming collections in various branches of natural history and that many, even the working classes, employ their holidays in the study of botany or geology, or in the collection of insects obtained in the neighbourhood of London; that they refer to the British Museum, in order to ascertain the proper classification of the specimens thus obtained.' Nevertheless, Panizzi was firmly resolved to rid Bloomsbury of these collections, their undesirable visitors and their scientific staffs, and Owen now likewise also wanted their removal, though not for the same reasons.

Both were men of great influence behind the scenes. Owen taught the Royal children natural history in Buckingham Palace at Prince Albert's request and the concept of South Kensington as a great museums centre, the future 'Albertopolis', was taking shape in Prince Albert's mind. Moreover, Owen knew Gladstone well and had him as an ally. He delivered a lecture in April 1861 'On the extent and aims of a National Museum of Natural History' which kept his project in view. He emphasized publicly the crowded state of Bloomsbury by deliberately squeezing into the exhibition cases as many stuffed specimens and articulated skeletons as they would hold.

Although disappointed by the Select Committee's rejection of his proposal, Owen remained confident, as always, of the rightness of his views and set to work by inviting Gladstone in October 1861 to explore with him in the British Museum 'every vault and dark recess which had been or could be allotted to the non-exhibited specimens of natural history, i.e. those which it was my aim to utilize and bring to light'. Gladstone gave the same attention to the series selected for exhibition in the public galleries and 'appreciated the inadequacy of the arrangements for that end.' Owen then busied himself with preparing a report on the space requirements of a new museum.

At the end of 1861 the matter again came before a Sub-Committee of the Trustees, this time at the express instance of the Lords of Her

Majesty's Treasury. They reported in January 1862 that 'they have come to the conclusion that it is essential to the advantage of science and of the collections which are to remain in Bloomsbury, that the removal of all the objects of Natural History should take place, and, as far as practicable, should be simultaneously effected.' After considering the relationship of the Department of Botany with the Royal Botanic Gardens at Kew, they recommended 'that all the Natural History Collections be speedily and simultaneously removed'. Owen's plan was ready early in 1862. Gladstone in May 1862 accordingly moved leave in the House of Commons to bring a bill for removal of portions of the Trustee's collections in the British Museum. Thanks to Disraeli's opposition, purportedly on grounds of economy, the House rejected Gladstone's bill. An Irish member of Parliament, William Henry Gregory (1817-1892), best known as the husband of the Irish playright Isabella A. Gregory, expressed regret that a man of Owen's standing should connect himself with a 'so foolish, crazy and extravagant scheme'. However, as Owen himself wrote much later 'neither averment nor arguments in the House on May 18, 1862, had shaken my faith in the grounds on which my Report and Plan of 1859 had been based.' The Act ultimately authorising the removal of Natural History Collections was passed in 1878 (41 and 42 Vict. c 55).

Despite the adverse 1862 vote, the House of Commons approved in 1863 the purchase of 12 acres (4.86 hectares) of land at South Kensington for the new museum, since land was ten times cheaper there than at Bloomsbury. This was part of the 1862 International Exhibition site. Immediately north of this, on land now occupied by the Imperial College and the Royal Albert Hall, stretched the extensive gardens of the Royal Horticultural Society. To the east, on land now occupied by the stately Victoria and Albert Museum, was its predecessor, the South Kensington Museum, consisting of contemporary corrugated iron buildings colloquially known as the 'Brompton Boilers'.

In January 1864 the First Commissioner of Works announced an open competition for the design of the South Kensington museums, then envisaged as being for both natural history and patents. Thirty-two architects contended for the prizes of £400, £250 and £100 offered by the Office of Works. The first prize went to Francis Fowke (1823-1865), a captain of the Royal Engineers and a well-known architect who had designed the Royal Scottish Museum in Edinburgh, the second prize went to Robert Kerr, the third to Cuthbert Broderick. Fowke's proposed building in Renaissance style, using much terracotta, would have covered the whole museum site, as Owen had originally planned. The designs were all based on the proposal made by Owen in 1859. Through the co-operation of Gladstone, Henry A. Hunt of the Office of

Works had put Owen's plans into a workable form in 1862. Hunt's preliminary design included both a circular lecture theatre and a library, neither of which formed part of the building ultimately erected. The Trustees preferred Kerr's design to Fowke's which the competition judges had chosen. Fowke was accordingly requested to modify his design for the Trustees' approval but died before he could make the necessary alterations.

This was but one of the many setbacks in the construction of a new museum, which spread over nearly a quarter of a century. As stated in *The Survey of London* 38: 202 (1975), 'accidental causes were, however, responsible for much of the delay, and the enterprise was sustained by the ardour of Victorian polemic, the boldness of Victorian exploration and the zest of Victorian curiosity'.

Fowke's death endangered execution of his design and the commission for the new building might have passed to Robert Kerr, had not the First Commissioner of Works appointed in February 1866, a rising architect Alfred Waterhouse (1830-1905) to carry Fowke's plan into effect. Waterhouse was born in Liverpool and belonged to a well-known Quaker family, who frowned on his desire to become an artist, but approved a career in architecture. From 1848 to 1853 he was articled to a Manchester architect, Richard Lane, and then travelled widely on the Continent for the study of buildings. Lane favoured a Neo-classical style even for warehouses and somehow caused Waterhouse to react against it. He worked at a time when the designs and writings of Augustus Welby Northmore Pugin and the lectures and writings of John Ruskin, notably his *Seven Lamps of Architecture* (1849), 'preaching salvation through Gothic forms and cursing with ceremony and conviction the classic system of design', to quote John Gloag, had contributed to a turning of public taste away from the austere Neo-classical style, exemplified by Robert Smirke's British Museum and Royal College of Physicians building (now Canada House), by the Fitzwilliam Museum in Cambridge and the Ashmolean Museum in Oxford, towards a revived Gothic style with scope for much elaborate decoration, exemplified by the Oxford University Museum, in which Ruskin was much interested. Ruskin was a hot gospeller for Neo-Gothic. 'It is the glory of Gothic architecture', he proclaimed in 1854, 'that it can do anything. Whatever you really and seriously want, Gothic will do it for you; but it must be a serious want.'

Waterhouse was undoubtedly influenced by Ruskin, although as a practising Victorian architect he could not possibly accept Ruskin's view that 'the use of cast or machine-made ornaments of any kind' was an architectural deceit. In 1859 Waterhouse, then unknown outside Quaker circles and only twenty-nine, won the competition for the

Manchester Assize Courts with a Gothic design. This success led to commissions for buildings in London and elsewhere and he was known as an architect skilled in planning when Fowke's design came into his hands. A few months later Disraeli became Chancellor of the Exchequer and Leader of the Conservative Party in the House of Commons. Money for the building accordingly ceased to be available and its erection was postponed.

Meanwhile Waterhouse studied Fowke's design, concluded that he could not execute it to his satisfaction and in March 1868 put forward a design of his own. To quote his own words, he 'abandoned the idea of a Renaissance building and fell back on the earlier Romanesque style which prevailed largely in Lombardy and the Rhineland from the tenth to the end of the twelfth century'. The term 'Romanesque' covers the round-arched architectural style, with massive vaulting, transitional from Roman to Gothic. Waterhouse apparently adopted it in accordance with Owen's idea of having the architectural decoration of the building associated with the nature of the exhibits; he thought that adornments based on natural history objects would fit in best with a Romanesque style of which his many visits to Germany and Italy had given him a first hand knowledge. He and Owen gave much attention to this ornamentation which is possibly the most notable and unexpected feature of the building.

Fig. 4. Removal of zoological specimens from Bloomsbury to South Kensington as imagined in 1863 (from *The Comic News,* 18 July 1863).

Although the South Kensington site had been bought for the new Museum in 1863, the possibility of putting this on the Embankment delayed its building anywhere until 1870, when South Kensington was finally chosen. Considerations of economy forced upon Waterhouse by the new First Commissioner of Works, the lawyer Acton Smee Ayrton (1816-1886), made him reduce his design, which was achieved by eliminating the intended eastward- and westward-facing side wings parallel with Exhibition Road and Queen's Gate; these omissions were intended to be temporary but unfortunately the side wings were never built. Waterhouse became officially the architect for the building in 1870 and soon had plans ready. These, however, were later modified. There was further delay. By July 1872, when tenders were being invited, building costs had risen, but Ayrton insisted on restricting the money available to that allocated in 1870. Waterhouse now had twice to reduce his design. The contract for £352,000 with the builders Messrs George Baker and Son was signed in February 1873. According to Waterhouse, Ayrton's delaying economic measures added £3,000 to the ultimate cost of the building; they also deprived the Museum for nearly eighty years of an adequate, purpose-built general library and lecture hall.

Waterhouse decided to make extensive use of terracotta on account of its durability and its decorative possibilities, although some have found his use of it harsh and unattractive. Thus Pevsner in 1952 described the Museum as 'covered all over with Waterhouse's favourite terra-cotta slabs, the least appealing of materials, of a soapy hardness and impermeable to weather (durable indeed, as the Victorians intended their expensive products to be)'. There was difficulty in obtaining the immense quantity required for such a large building, on which work began early in 1873. Although construction went ahead, difficulty after difficulty, including alterations of design within the Museum and unreliability of supply of materials, slowed down progress. British iron-founders having priced themselves out of the market, rolled steel had to be imported from Belgium. However, early in 1878 the main roofs had been completed, with slate replacing lead. Unfortunately rising costs and delay in getting materials were ruining the contractors and in 1879 they went bankrupt. Their creditors nevertheless completed the building in 1880. They argued that the alterations to the original plan constituted a breach of contract and, after much negotiation, received an additional £25,000 in 1882, as compensation. In the end the building cost about £412,000, plus Waterhouse's remuneration of £19,730. By 1884 the total expenditure on the Museum, including buildings, fittings and fees, amounted to about £602,000. Further details, together with extensive relevant documentation, will be found in *The Museums Area of South Kensington and Westminster*, forming volume 38 (1975) of the *Survey of London*, edited by F.H.W. Sheppard.

The Museum remains the most impressive of Waterhouse's buildings. His Manchester Court Assizes, Clydesdale Bank, New University Club and St. Paul's Boys School have all been destroyed, but enough of his 200 or so public buildings survive to illustrate his versatility, as is evident from the list by S.A. Smith in *Seven Victorian Architects* (1977). Not one of them is like his Natural History Museum, which *The Builder* of 20 August 1905 rightly said, 'resembles no other building in the world, ancient or modern; its defects may be its own and so also are its merits'.

The façade along Cromwell Road has a length of 675 feet (205 m), with a massive, round-arched central entrance flanked by two high-spired, symmetrical towers rising to 192 feet (58.5 m) with three-storeyed wings on each side, one extending towards Queen's Gate, the other towards Exhibition Road, and both ending in a tower. Waterhouse had planned east and west northward extensions from these towers, hiding from view the one-storey subsidiary brick galleries, but, as mentioned before, these extensions were never built. The major feature inside the building is the vast main hall, 170 feet (52 m) long, with a painted ceiling 72 feet (22 m) high, having bays on each side intended by Owen for his Index Museum and a broad stairway at its far end to the first-floor galleries. These lead southward to an arched bridge, providing access by a stairway to the second floor east and west galleries. The main hall with its stained-glass windows once had so cathedral-like an aspect and a quietness, that respectful visitors have been known to remove their hats on entering this temple of science, 'the animals' Westminster Abbey' according to F.W. Thomas. Although he built the church of St. Elizabeth at Reddish, Stockport, it is the nearest approach that Waterhouse ever made to a major ecclesiastical building. As a Quaker he had, unlike many Victorian architects, no interest in erecting, restoring or architecturally ruining churches and chapels. His activities gave no cause, as did those of his contemporary George Gilbert Scott, for the formation of the Society for the Protection of Ancient Buildings.

The general public admitted in April 1881 was undoubtedly impressed by the grandeur and picturesqueness of the building. The *Saturday Review* called it 'Mr Waterhouse's beautiful Romanesque building'. *The Times* of 18 April 1881, unwontedly effusive, assured Londoners 'that they will now have the opportunity of pursuing the most delightful of all studies in a true Temple of Nature, showing, as it should, the Beauty of Holiness'. Presumably for the benefit of its readers with more secular minds, *The Times* also told them that 'The

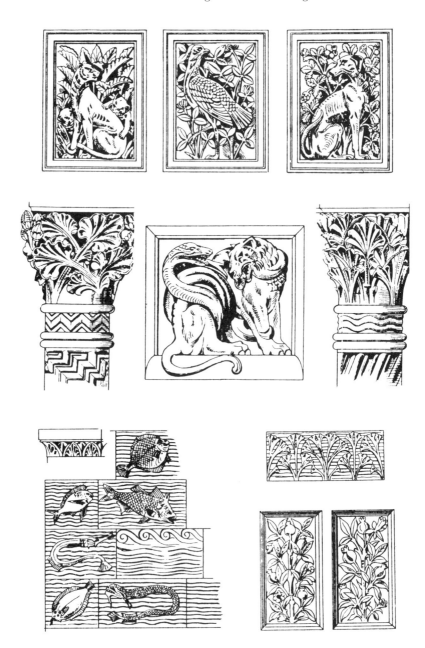

Fig. 5. Some terracotta ornamentation of the Museum (from *The Builder*, 1878).

walls and ceilings are decorated, as befits a Palace of Nature, with all the varieties of animal and vegetable life'. Ruskin had stated in his influential *Seven Lamps of Architecture* (1849) that 'ornament cannot be overcharged if it is good, and is always overcharged if it is bad'. Opinions may differ as to which category of ornamentation the Museum belongs, but there is no escaping its profusion. As indicated above, Owen's insistence on this architectural decoration based upon animals and plants influenced the style of the whole building. The carved stonework on medieval cathedrals and chapels was sometimes both highly naturalistic and elaborate, as at Southwell. This and Worms Cathedral, which Waterhouse studied in 1861, gave precedent for the lavish adornment of Waterhouse's Victorian Romanesque 'Temple of Nature', with innumerable representations of natural objects which would have been utterly incongruous on a Neo-classical temple-like building. The choice of the subject was obviously Owen's; thus he supplied Waterhouse in October 1873 with fifty or so figures of extinct animals. Waterhouse made detailed pencil drawings of these and a French modeller, Dujardin, employed by Farmer and Brindley, produced plaster casts for Owen's inspection before the terracotta slabs and statues were manufactured by Gibbs and Canning of Tamworth, Staffordshire. As Waterhouse's original drawings show, he personally designed them all. The terracotta Seychelles Gecko *(Phelsuma sundbergi)* was based on a specimen in alcohol of what was then a new species; in fact it was not specifically distinguished and named until 1939.

Not everyone approved these embellishments. A writer in *The Field* of 28 April 1881 described the Museum as being 'ornamented — if so it may be termed — both externally and internally with incorrect and grotesque representations of animals, the style of the building being more, much more adapted for a suburban tea-garden than a national museum'. Nevertheless, this terracotta menagerie repays examination; indeed, the more it is studied, the more evident and impressive become its diversity and the painstaking care taken in its creation. The figures on the front of the west wing originally intended for zoology were based on living species, including the conger eel and the ferocious deep-sea stomias fish; those on the east side housing palaeontology represent extinct species; here pterodactyls and sabre-tooths sit high up on pedestals. Over the main entrance are panels representing the American black bear, the great grey kangaroo, the jaguar and the spotted hyena, and a lion in the coils of a snake (Fig. 5), a theme deriving from an exhibit in William Bullock's private museum of 1807-1818 (*Museums Journal* 79: 172-175, 1980). A visitor glancing upwards on entering can see, at the corners whence the arches of the ceiling rise, technically called the springers, representations of the

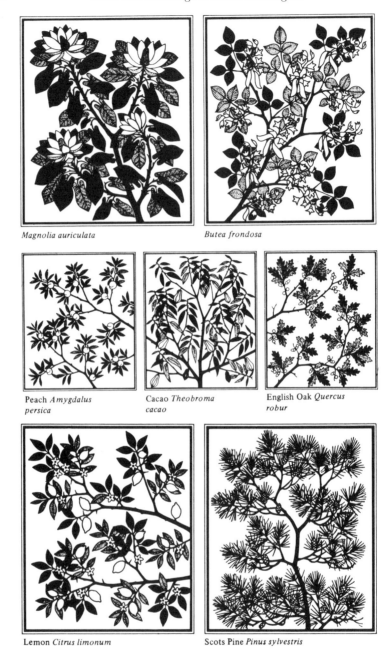

Magnolia auriculata

Butea frondosa

Peach *Amygdalus persica*

Cacao *Theobroma cacao*

English Oak *Quercus robur*

Lemon *Citrus limonum*

Scots Pine *Pinus sylvestris*

Fig. 6.   Some painted illustrations of plants on the panelled ceiling of the main hall.

raccoon, the Seychelles gecko, the banded linsang and the iguana amid foliage. Birds perching or fluttering on leaves ornament the arches of the bays in the main hall. At the foot of the stairway at its north end are panels representing, on the left-hand side, fox and cub, great bustard and snow leopard and, on the right-hand side, demoiselle cranes, greyhound and cormorants; the panels halfway up the stairs represent, on the left-hand side, hare, golden pheasant and cavy and, on the right-hand side, banded stilt, fennec fox and black grouse. At the top of the stairs above the left (west) archway is a large round panel with a pampas deer and similarly above the right (east) archway there is a panel with the rhea. At the other (south) ends are panels representing herons on the west side and ibex on the east. Two dogs, a long-eared owl and a falcon sit on high, just below the stained-glass windows of the restaurant. The pillars by the stairway bridge, spanning the south end of the hall, have monkeys clambering up them to the roof.

The columns at intervals along the front ground and first-floor galleries, which support the floor above, are faced with decorated terracotta slabs on which are represented in low relief a diversity of fish, living and fossil, while above them are panels of stylized plants and then owls, etc., above those. The function of this terracotta facing was not only to conceal the ironwork inside but, more importantly, to insulate and protect it from excessive heat in the event of fire.

The panels on the five columns at the east entrance on the Cromwell Road merit attention, although they pass unnoticed by visitors and staff hurrying into the Museum. Their decorative effect has been gained as elsewhere by stylization at the expense of naturalistic portrayal, but they make an interesting series. The notes on Waterhouse's original drawings establish the identity of the animals which were his models. They include the black-capped capuchin monkey, with tail curling to the left, bushbaby, with tail curling to the right, black rats, weasels, red squirrel, eagle owl, a pair of pied wagtails, a pair of alexandrine parakeets, red-ruffed fruitcrow pecking at a bunch of fruit, hen harrier with outstretched wings, three garden warblers, passenger pigeon with long, pointed tail, as solitary as the last of its species which died in a zoo in 1914, smooth-necked iguana, Egyptian cobra and two entwined snakes of doubtful identity. The inclusion of the American passenger pigeon should prompt reflection on the avarice and thoughtlessness of mankind. The population of this species has been estimated as having been about 3,000,000,000 individual birds in its nineteenth century heyday before human interference: a migrating flock darkened the sky for minutes as it flew over. When the Museum was being built, the species could still be regarded as a representative American bird, numbering hundreds of thousands of individuals, despite the contin-

uous slaughter by shooting, netting and large-scale seizure of young
birds not quite ready to fly and the felling of their nesting woods: it is
now as extinct as the dodo and the great auk, likewise destroyed by
man.

Although Owen was thus primarily responsible for the palaeontological and zoological terracotta reliefs, he obviously left the designs for
the painted ceiling of the main hall to the Keeper of Botany, William
Carruthers. These occupy eighteen major panels, each divided into
nine lesser panels. The two uppermost rows of panels have stylized
paintings merely indicating the vegetable kingdom. The lower panels
represent mostly economic and medicinal plants, i.e. Seville orange,
vine, oak, cocoa, peach, apple, olive, fig, lemon, Scots pine, blue gum,
plum, strychnine, sugar cane, dhat, balsam of Peru, almond, nutmeg,
kokam, purging cassia, quince, maize, sodom apple, gaub, akee,
quassia, aloe, pomegranate and tea, together with ornamental plants
such as banksia, horse-chestnut, magnolia, and dogwood. These were
cleaned in 1973. Before then some members of the Department of
Botany had to study them with field glasses in order to check the
identity of the plants depicted (Fig. 6).

The initial pleasure and pride at the completion of the Museum was
followed by a more critical assessment of its function as a museum
building, out of which it did not come so well. A writer in *Nature* for
16 November 1882 remarked: 'The first point which strikes a visitor at
the present time is that a serious mistake has been made in the erection
of a building with such elaborate and ornate internal decorations for
museum purposes. Now that the cases are nearly all in position and the
specimens are gradually being arranged in them, this incongruity
between the style and objects of the building becomes more and more
apparent. On the one hand, it is clear that the form, position, and illumination of the cases has in many instances been sacrificed to a fear of
interfering with the general architectural effect; and on the other hand
it is equally manifest that it will be impossible to make full use of the
floor space, and especially the best-lighted portion of it, without
seriously detracting from the artistic effects designed by the architect.
Thus we find the beautiful arcade formed by a series of pierced wall-
cases in the Coral Gallery has its effect totally destroyed by the floor-
cases, which it has been found necessary to place along the central line;
and in the British gallery the vistas designed by the architect have been
completely marred by the insertion of large cases in some of the arches.
Again and again we find massive columns, beautiful in themselves perhaps, breaking up a line of cases, or throwing their contents into deep
shade. The peculiar tint of the terra-cotta, too, is far from being suitable for making the objects of the Museum stand out in relief, and this is

particularly manifest in the case of the palaeontological collections, where a great majority of the specimens have a very similar colouring. When an attempt has been made to remedy this by giving the walls near the objects other tints, it is found that such tints do not harmonize well with the general colouring of the building. Nor is the wisdom apparent of bringing into close proximity natural history objects with conventional representations of them adopted by architects. The crowding together, on the same column or moulding, of representations on the same scale of microscopic and gigantic organisms, of inhabitants of the sea and of the land, and of the forms of life belonging to present and those of former periods of the earth's history, seems to be scarcely warrantable in a building designed for educational purposes. Greatly as we admire the spacious hall, the grand staircase, the long colonnades, and the picturesque colouring of the whole building, we cannot but feel that the adoption of such a semi-ecclesiastical style was a mistake... the erection of cases as they may be required in the most convenient and best-lighted situations cannot fail to detract from the striking and pleasing effects of the architecture.'

Generally much admired then as it stood newly-built, with its buff and blue horizontal banding and its ornamentation unsullied, the Museum after some years became more and more begrimed by London soot, its detail obscured and dulled, and it was then regarded as an example of the shocking bad taste of the Victorian period. Thus Augustus J.C. Hare (1834-1903) in his popular guide-book, *Walks in London* (6th ed. 1894) stated that 'facing the Cromwell Road is a huge pile of mongrel Lombardic architecture, an embodiment of portentous ugliness, by Waterhouse, 1873-80, appropriated as the Natural History Museum'.

A gradual change of view, from violent disapproval of the Museum's exterior to cold acceptance, becomes evident in later London guides. Thus Pevsner remarked in 1962 in his Penguin volume: 'The building is of a crushing symmetry... Waterhouse's harsh, logical mind remains in many things a psychological puzzle. The Natural History Museum appears forbidding and terribly serious compared with the almost naughty looseness of Aston Webb's front of the Victoria and Albert Museum', separated from it by Exhibition Road. David Piper in his *The Companion Guide to London* (1964) described it as 'like a chateau in oddly ecclesiastical Romanesque of 1873-81 (by Waterhouse), massive, and with a dour repetition of rounded-headed windows in tough, mottled buff terracotta with chill blue-grey horizontal bands'.

During the years 1974 and 1975, the whole front was carefully and thoroughly washed to remove the accumulated grime of many years, so that externally the Museum now looks almost as it did in 1881. The plainness and dullness of so much modern large-scale building, particularly when this has caused the destruction of the more interesting if less convenient architecture of earlier generations, has made the public look with more appreciative eyes on the wealth of variety in earlier buildings, knowing only too well our incapacity to replace it. The Natural History Museum has come into favour again as an expression of the confident detail-loving Victorian period, arousing interest and also admiration for what *The Builder*, at the time of Waterhouse's death, described as its 'exceedingly florid style' with 'the exterior of the building symbolical of the multiplicity of form and detail in nature'. If Waterhouse carried his love of ornament too far to suit the taste of the early twentieth century, when his architecture was described as 'being deficient in refinement and simplicity', it is welcome now, for, as James Pope-Hennesey wrote in 1941, when so many Victorian buildings had been destroyed and the Museum badly damaged by bombing, 'We have been laughing at the Victorians... The laughter has begun to ring a trifle hollow and we glance back at them with a new respect.'

Mark Girouard's *Alfred Waterhouse and the Natural History Museum* (1981) describes the development of the design of the Museum and some of its most interesting features from the standpoint of an architectural historian.

6

The Move to South Kensington

THE NEW MUSEUM at South Kensington became available for occupation in June 1880. Of those who had been Keepers when the work began, only W. Carruthers (Botany) remained; Gray (Zoology) had died and G.R. Waterhouse (Geology) and M.H.N. Story-Maskelyne (Mineralogy) had retired. The younger Keepers, Günther (Zoology), Lazarus Fletcher (Mineralogy) and Henry Woodward (Geology) had now to do the best they could in a building for whose design they had been in no way responsible. Owen, to whom both the inception and design of the Museum owed so much, remained Superintendent of the Natural History Departments, but the removal and allocation of material was the individual responsibility of the separate Keepers. They did not find the building wholly to their liking; indeed it presented them with many problems, from Fletcher's personal discomfort to Günther's discovery that architectural ornamentation prevented the insertion of some exhibition cases. Moreover, no provision had been made for the lecture hall, the whale room and the general library that Owen had originally wanted or for the spirit collection that was Günther's special interest. The erection of a special building to house some 52,000 glass receptacles of specimens in alcohol, placed away from the main building on account of the fire risk, was accordingly begun in 1881 and was finished in 1883, but addition of the other rooms had to wait for many years.

The planning and preparation of new exhibits had, of course, to be undertaken well ahead of the move. About 1875, Günther set about forming a collection of groups of British nesting birds in their natural surroundings which formed one of the most admired exhibits in the Natural History Museum until its destruction in the Second World War

55

by bombing which severely damaged the Museum on 5 July 1944. Every effort was made to ensure absolute fidelity to nature. As stated by Günther in 1912, 'it was an essential condition that both the parents, with their eggs or the young belonging to the nest, should be taken, and that the actual surroundings which determined the selection of the site by the birds should be preserved.' Lord Walsingham supplied most of the material. To quote Sharpe, 'in each case the scene is as nearly a reproduction of the actual facts as could be attained. The birds that actually built the nest and laid the eggs are there, and the bush or tree, the herbage and the flowers are also reproduced, as they were on the day when the nest was taken, the counterfeit leaves and flowers can scarcely be distinguished from the actual living plants. Dr Günther determined from the first to reproduce nothing but the actual facts, so as to give, as far as possible, a true life picture of the birds as they were in life. Thus specimens in their worn, nesting plumage have not been replaced by handsomer birds which did not belong to the actual nest.' Unfortunately, during the Second World War, it was virtually impossible to evacuate this remarkable and unique collection which occupied 159 glass cases and the world will probably never see its like again. W.R. Ogilvie-Grant's *Guide to the Gallery of Birds* (1905) lists its exhibits in detail.

In July 1876 the Keepers, Günther, Carruthers, Waterhouse and Story-Maskelyne, had received plans of the building detailed enough for them to consider the requisitioning and placing of cases, but in 1879 the Trustees were forced to make urgent demands for these, despite the prevailing financial stringency. Overseas expenditure, caused by such events as the Ashanti War of 1873 to 1874 in Ghana, the purchase of the Suez Canal in 1875, the Kaffir War in 1877, the acquisition of Cyprus in 1878, war with Afghanistan in 1878 and 1879, the Zulu War in 1879 and war with the Transvaal in 1880 and 1881, as well as general colonial administration, competed with expenditure on home affairs and for Disraeli's government a Natural History Museum had low priority.

From the beginning, Owen had cherished the concept of an 'Index Museum' occupying a central position within the Museum as a whole. He described it in his 1859 report as an 'apartment devoted to specimens selected to show the type-characters of the principal groups of organized beings'. It derived from Cuvier's type concept (see p.31), whereby groups of existing organisms could be visualized by a religious mind like Owen's as variations on an archetype, or original model divinely conceived before their creation. Within the 'Index Museum' would be representative specimens of these groups displaying their essential features, 'to show how the mammalian type is progressively modified from the form of the fish or the lizard', which, although strongly reminiscent of the eighteenth-century concept of the Chain of Being, could be interpreted in the later nineteenth century as evidence of evolution. Owen reserved the central cathedral-like main hall of the Natural History Museum for the 'Index Museum' and the architect provided twelve bays 'resembling side-chapels' around it for the groups of the natural world. In 1880 the Trustees requested information on what these bays or recesses would contain and the views of Keepers on the scheme.

Owen outlined his plan of the 'Index Museum' in a *Report by the Superintendent of Natural History on the several Reports of the Keepers of Natural History, 28 July 1880.* The recesses communicating on each side with the central space of the main hall were numbered 1 to 12. They were intended 'to convey an outline, as it were, of the divisions of Natural History, which will be fully and systematically illustrated in the several Galleries of the Museum.' On the one side were recesses 1 to 6 to be devoted to showing 'the principal modifications of the great Vertebrate sub-kingdom. On the opposite side similar elementary illustrations will be displayed of the Invertebrate Animals, of Plants, of Rocks, and of Minerals.'

Owen then dealt with the central space: 'On the floor of the ''Index Museum'' it is proposed to exhibit objects of Natural History exemplifying some prominent quality, as, eg:— the skeleton of a Whale, giving the largest size attained by any aquatic Mammal. The skeleton of an Elephant, showing the greatest bulk known among existing Quadrupeds. The skeletons of the Megatherium, exemplifying the most robust frame in the Animal Kingdom. The skeleton of the Giraffe as the tallest of Mammals. The skeleton of the *Dinornis maximus*, as the tallest and hugest of the class of Birds. A specimen of *Selache maxima*, as the largest of living Fishes. The skeleton of the great Irish Deer *(Megaceros)*, as exhibiting the maximum development of weapons of offence. In the selection and disposition of such specimens the Superintendent will take advantage of the opinion of the Architect in regard to their fitness or harmony with the general character of the ''Index Museum''.'

Carruthers, Keeper of Botany, alone thought it to be 'in every way desirable to carry out the proposal of establishing an ''Index Museum''' as 'a fitting introduction to the collections of the Museum, of much real interest to visitors, and of great educational value to students'. Günther, Keeper of Zoology, considered it not worth having. He regarded it as something of an anachronism in the new Natural History Museum and pointed out that: 'in connection with the British Museum the idea of a separate ''Type Museum'' was started in 1858, that is, at a time when the cases had become crowded with specimens, when the separation of a study series from an exhibition series had only been commenced, when no attempt at descriptive labelling had been made, when heterogeneous objects had to be exhibited in the same room, and when, consequently, the types most deserving of attention were threatened to be lost among a multitude of objects unfit for exhibition.' He thought this stage had passed away: 'for some years past such objects only have been placed in the exhibition series which are required for the study of types, or which contribute towards the instruction of the general public; and such as do not fulfil either of these objects are gradually and steadily withdrawn into the study series.' Günther submitted that the exhibition series in the galleries would better attain the end aimed at by an 'Index Museum'. He recommended moreover the preparation of a new guide in the form of a popular, but systematic, handbook of natural history.

Woodward, Keeper of Geology, likewise objected: 'The recesses, it is to be regretted, are very badly lighted, and but ill-adapted for exhibition purposes. For this reason it would be unwise to place in them any specimens of much value or importance. A very limited series of *duplicates* from the Geological collection, aided by a few diagrams of extinct forms of life and a table of strata, would suffice to fill this recess. The "Index Museum", if carried out thus, would form an "object-guide", "pictorial index", or "hieroglyph", to the galleries of the Museum on either hand. But of course it might be urged, that the same information could be as readily conveyed by a good and cheap illustrated guide-book, giving a general scheme of the arrangement of the Collections, and a key-plan of the Galleries.' He also viewed with some anxiety the prospect that many, if not all, of the choicest specimens now in his geological gallery would be withdrawn to fill the Index Museum and pass out of his full control. He thought that the space reserved for the Index Museum could be turned to better use by being devoted to British natural history 'as a subject worthy of the first and highest place in the New Natural History Museum'.

Fletcher, Keeper of Mineralogy, began his report by stating that: 'The most important of the ends aimed at in the acquirement and exhibition of specimens are the advancement of scientific landmarks, and the instruction of students: to which may be added the awakening of an intelligent interest in the mind of the general visitor. For the first of these an Index Museum would be of no avail, while it would prove attractive to the general visitor only by virtue of its concentration of variety.' Like Woodward, he feared the impoverishment of the galleries resulting from a tendency to accumulate the finer specimens for exhibition in the main hall. He then emphasized the unsuitability of this for 'the unorganized products of nature'. Fletcher summed up his objections to the scheme thus: 'we may say (1), that the selection of indices is probably *practicable* in the case of organized bodies, where the differences of species depend on qualities evident to ocular inspection; but that it is scarcely so in that of unorganized bodies where the differences are molecular; (2), that even if practicable, it is *not desirable* for the purposes of mineralogical study; (3) that the illumination of the recess of the Hall is not as satisfactory for mineral display as is that of the Gallery.'

Such a reception to his 'long-cherished and well-considered elementary, index or type museum', which had so strongly influenced the design of the Natural History Museum as a whole naturally annoyed Owen, who angrily told Günther it would have been as well if his adverse report had not appeared. Owen was now 76, too old to execute his project himself. The Trustees, disturbed though they may have been by the Keepers' reports against it, had little option now but to try and use the main hall for its intended purpose. In 1882 one of the bays was used to display the types of birds, the first zoological exhibit in the new museum, but it remained for Owen's successor, William Flower, a convinced evolutionist, to develop the main hall as an illustration of the diversity of the natural world and it differed greatly from what Owen had devised.

The mineralogical collections were the first to leave Bloomsbury for South Kensington. Lazarus Fletcher (1854-1921), who had joined the Museum staff in 1878, was made Keeper of Minerals in June 1880. In July he had to supervise the removal of his extremely valuable collection. Adequate preparations had been made for packing this at Bloomsbury, but many difficulties faced its reception and re-arrangement in the new Natural History Museum. In 1904 Fletcher wrote: 'Some idea of the nature of this task may be formed if it be pointed out that the cabinets of the table-cases at Bloomsbury were to be made use of in the new Gallery, but that the glazed table-tops were then lying on the gallery-floor at South Kensington, and had as yet no supports; that differences of illumination of the old and new Galleries, and differences of construction of the cabinets, made it necessary that the relative positions of the cabinets in the Gallery at South Kensington should be completely different from the relative positions in the Gallery at Bloomsbury; that every cabinet had for some time to be turned upside down during the process of being fitted to the new floor; that many of them had to be cut in two because of the interference of the structural columns of the Gallery, and new mahogany ends had afterwards to be made and fitted to them. Such a series of operations involves great practical difficulties when the specimens to be removed and arranged are numerous, fragile, and require to be cautiously handled, or are small, portable and of great intrinsic value, and must be kept under lock and key... The transfer of the specimens and the fitting of the cabinets to the floor having been accomplished, the exhibited portion of the systematic collection was increased by the addition of specimens selected from the reserve series in the drawers; the space available for the exhibition of specimens belonging to the systematic collections being one-fourth larger than before. Afterwards, Mr Fletcher conceived the idea of providing both the ordinary visitor and the scientific student with the means of acquiring a systematic knowledge of the contents of the Mineral Gallery... With this end in view, he selected, in the first place, a series of specimens to serve as an introduction to the study of Meteorites, and prepared a corresponding guide-book (1881). This introduction having been found of great service to the public, he continued the work, and by 1884 and 1895 similar series of specimens elaborately labelled, and similar guide-books, constituting introductions to the study of Minerals and Rocks respectively, were completed; these specimens are arranged in the ten window-cases provided in the year 1883 for the northern side of the Gallery.'

Fletcher also referred to other work consequent upon the move to South Kensington:

> 'When the Collection was at Bloomsbury, all the labels were hand-written, and mostly of temporary character; in the course of the re-arrangement at South Kensington, printed labels have been designed and furnished for all parts of the collection, namely species-labels, locality-labels, pseudomorph-labels, and labels for the large specimens and introductory series. There are now nearly 17,000 printed labels exhibited in the Gallery. All the vertical glazed fronts of the table-cases, formerly fixed, were in 1881 made removable, and the ends of the cases have been provided with new fittings. Fittings have likewise been made for the wall-cases, which have themselves been provided since 1880, and specimens have been selected and mounted for exhibition therein. One of the wall-cases now contains a beautiful series of polished slabs of Ornamental Stones; most of the others contain large specimens of minerals and rocks, specially selected and mounted. At Bloomsbury no space was available for the exhibition of rock-specimens; an elaborately labelled series of typical rock-specimens has now been arranged in the eleven window-cases on the southern side of the Gallery.'

The botanical and geological collections were also moved in 1880. They occupied the east wing of the new building, with Geology on the ground floor, Mineralogy on the first floor and Botany on the second floor. The west wing was reserved for Zoology, but was not ready until 1882. The Trustees fixed the date of opening for April 1881, which was a public holiday. The Keepers of the three departments and their staffs worked hard to have exhibits on view for the occasion.

The name of the new building gave difficulty. Officially it housed the Natural History Departments of the British Museum; the historical account published by the Trustees of the British Museum in 1904, 1906 and 1912 was therefore entitled *The History of the Collections contained in the Natural History Departments of the British Museum*. Owen had earlier referred to it as the 'National Museum of Natural History', a designation which failed to convey its subordinate status; indeed he evidently wished it to be autonomous, with himself as its head. The Trustees accordingly called it the 'British Museum (Natural History)', a name which has often been regarded as an anachronism (see p.132ff and p.345ff). *The Field, the Country Gentleman's Newspaper* of 23 April 1881 in reporting the opening of 'the new Natural History Museum at South Kensington' commented that: 'we fail to see the advantage of desirability of terming the South Kensington galleries ''The British Museum''. This name has been long applied to the building in Blooms-bury, and the great confusion can only result by using the same name for two different locations.' *The Field* gave a good account of what could be seen in the Museum and concluded that: 'Opposed as we have been from the first to the dismemberment of our national collection and the removal of the materials of study to a distant suburb, we cannot refrain from expressing our admiration of the manner in which the specimens have been displayed, and the facilities afforded by their arrangement.'

The move of the zoological collections spread over 1882 and 1883. As stated by Günther in 1912, 'the removal was carried out intermittently, the sequence determined by the requirements of the architectural alter-ations in the old buildings as much as by the state of preparations of the new galleries. Towards the middle of 1882 two of the galleries in the new Museum, the western gallery of the second floor and the Cetacean room in the basement, were so far completed that a beginning could be made with the removal of the zoological collections. The osteological specimens, the study-series of Mammalia, the entire collection of Mollusca, with a part of the Corals and Sponges, were the first to be removed and deposited in the galleries destined for their reception. Some other collections which had to be removed on account of building operations in the old Museum, viz. the spirit-specimens of Mammals, Birds and Invertebrates, the dry-specimens of Reptiles and Fishes, had to be temporarily stowed away in the new building until certain rooms were ready for their reception. The part removed in that year consti-tuted about one-fourth of the entire collection. The operations were suspended during the winter months and resumed in March 1883. They continued intermittently to the end of August, when the actual work of removal was completed. This occupied altogether 97 days, on which 354 journeys were made by the vans engaged. The collections were removed, either packed in constructed boxes or trays, to the number of 5,171, or as single specimens, of which there were 1,348. The spirit-collections were contained in 52,635 bottles. The number of cabinets taken with the collection from the old Museum amounted to 350, and that of other pieces of fittings and furniture to 1,348. Excepting an insignificant amount of deterioration, which was unavoidable from so general a disturbance, and which is fully compensated for by the thorough examination to which every part of the collections was subjected in detail, no specimen of any value suffered injury, save a *Pentacrinus* (a fossil sea lily), which could be replaced without great difficulty. A number of very delicate and fragile specimens, which might have suffered by being sent in the vans, were conveyed by hand or in cabs.'

Before the removal, Günther had made detailed plans for the allocation of show-cases and their contents, so that most of the contents of each van-load could be moved into their permanent position, as soon as they arrived at South Kensington, but unforeseen difficulties arose. Repair of the old table-cases for the shell gallery necessitated removal of 3,200 drawers. The impressive collection of skeletons was placed in the second floor of the west wing now occupied by the General Herbarium of the Department of Botany, and with the vaulted room at the western end, now the Botanical Library devoted to the skeletons of elephants. The first floor immediately below was to have housed the bird exhibits but, owing to difficulty with cases, the birds were placed in the ground floor gallery which they still occupy and the mammals placed on the first floor. The north hall behind the stairway of the main hall had been reserved for British animals. Nearly all this exhibition, intended to include all the species of animals found in and around the British Isles, had to be formed anew; the insects and shells were placed in glass-topped cases so that they could be examined with a lens without the cases being opened. Made public in July 1886, it proved extremely popular. There is nothing comparable to it in the Museum today.

With all the collections moved from Bloomsbury to South Kensington by August 1883, Owen felt that his work as Superintendent of the Natural History Departments was done. He had reached his eightieth year and had been in the service of the Trustees since 1856. Although he had exercised little power within the British Museum at Bloomsbury, his period there had been one of fruitful scientific endeavour, and he now saw his long-sustained advocacy of a special museum for natural history specimens vindicated by the grand new building. From the viewpoint of those who had to work within it, the building had drawbacks for which Owen was blamed and the space for the collections, which had earlier seemed excessive to outsiders, filled much more rapidly and inconveniently than had been anticipated. It is possible that congestion at Bloomsbury might have resulted in the dispersal of the natural history collections to a number of institutions elsewhere; research which could only be done efficiently within such a comprehensive institution might never have been undertaken. The collections of the Museum were built up by the Keepers and their staffs; they owed little to Owen himself, but for the creation of a new Museum providing better conditions for display, curation and research on those collections Owen deserves all honour. He retired at the end of December 1883 and was promptly knighted. Honoured as the Grand Old Man of British Science, he died on 18 December 1892.

Part III

The Natural History Museum
1883 - 1949

7

The First Director:
William Henry Flower
1884-1898

R ICHARD OWEN RETIRED in December 1883 as Superintendent of
the Natural History Departments of the British Museum. The
three Principal Trustees of the British Museum, namely the
Archbishop of Canterbury, the Lord Chancellor and the Speaker of the
House of Commons, none of them notable for his scientific knowledge
but probably prompted by T.H. Huxley, Owen's opponent, appointed
William Henry Flower (1831-1899) to replace him. In accordance with
the old regulation to ensure the good behaviour of senior British
Museum officials, presumably considered necessary in the 18th
century, Flower deposited bonds of £2,000, his two guarantors depo-
sited a further £2,000 and he took up his duties on 14 March 1884.
Flower too was an anatomist with a medical background in many ways
like Owen's, having been from 1861 onwards Conservator of the
Hunterian Museum of the Royal College of Surgeons, in succession to
John Quekett, and from 1870 onwards their Hunterian Professor, in
succession to Huxley.

Flower was born at Stratford-upon-Avon on 30 November 1831 and
studied medicine at University College, London, and the Middlesex
Hospital; he became a member of the Royal College of Surgeons in
1854. He promptly volunteered for service as an army surgeon with the
British army going to the Crimea, where it suffered so terribly from
both the harsh climate and inadequate supplies, which together halved
his regiment within four months. During the bitter Crimean winter of
1854 he learned by tragic experience what suffering and death from
cold and starvation were. He served at the battles of the Alma, of
Inkerman and of Balaclava and the siege of Sebastopol, and then had to
be invalided home.

Sometime later he joined the staff of the Middlesex Hospital as Demonstrator in Anatomy and in 1858 became Curator of the hospital's museum. Huxley strongly recommended him for appointment as Conservator of the Royal College of Surgeons' Museum. There in 1861 Flower set about the re-organisation of the Museum's collections with both zeal and originality, paying especial attention to the dentition and osteology of mammals, and he proposed in 1869 a new scheme of classification for the carnivores. His comparative study of the brain in man and apes supported Huxley against Owen and he published in 1865 a reply to a paper by Owen on zoological names of characteristic parts and homological interpretations. He became a convinced evolutionist. All this recommended him to those who were not in sympathy with Owen's views.

Meanwhile, Flower became known to important people. His marriage in 1858 to Georgiana Rosetta Smyth, daughter of the Foreign Secretary of the Royal Society, Admiral W.H. Smyth, placed him at once where the right personal influence counts. As a biographer has said, 'this step in Flower's history had an important bearing on his future success'. He was elected a Fellow of the Royal Society in 1864 at the age of thirty-three. When Huxley resigned from the Hunterian Professorship at the Royal College of Surgeons in 1870, Flower succeeded him. His interests became more and more zoological as Owen's had when occupying the same dual posts of Conservator and Professor, giving likewise special attention to osteology and physical anthropology. Whales were his special subject. He paid, however, much attention not only to research but to the attractive and informative display of exhibits, with results which led the prominent German physician, Rudolf Carl Virchow, to describe Flower as the 'Prince of Museum Directors'.

Flower's work as Conservator of the Royal College's Museum was extremely successful, as the College handsomely acknowledged on his resignation in 1884, by thanking him 'for the admirable care, judgment, and zeal with which for twenty-two years he has fulfilled the various and responsible duties of that office'. There are many testimonies to his success. In 1901, it was stated that his tenure of office 'was a splendid record of original and laborious work, of great administrative capacity, and of unvarying courtesy to visitors. The Museum was most popular under his management... There, amidst the almost unrivalled collections, the tall, fair-haired and earnest worker was daily to be found, minutely studying, comparing and measuring, or giving directions for the extension, arrangement and classification of the varied and valuable contents... His conscientious devotion to duty, his remarkable skill in devising methods of mounting, his artistic eye, his tact with subordinates, and the esteem in which he was held by zoologists and comparative anatomists at home and abroad, give a clue to his subsequent career.' He certainly needed those qualities on moving in 1884 to the much more difficult post of Director of the Natural History Museum.

At the Royal College of Surgeons, although subject to the College's Council, Flower had had complete control over exhibits. He soon found very different circumstances at the British Museum (Natural History). His duties included the care and custody of the Natural History Museum with the superintendence of officers and servants, custody of keys, and engagement of mechanics and labourers, the regulation of the admission of visitors, editing of guide-books and issue of museum publications, etc. for which he was to act as the deputy of the Principal Librarian at Bloomsbury. His duties far exceeded those which had been Owen's as Superintendent of the Natural History Departments at Bloomsbury. The Trustees intended that the new head of the Museum should take a more active and responsible part than Owen had been allowed in its management and, on the basis of these much increased duties, they decided that his official position would be more appropriately designated by the title of 'Director' instead of 'Superintendent'. They stated nothing specifically about the control of exhibits.

Flower, coming to the Natural History Museum as an outsider, had no department of his own, no obvious power base, no allotted territory. He had to create these. It was fortunate for the Museum's future that Flower possessed a courteous and urbane, though strong, personality in addition to his acknowledged scientific eminence and constructive museum experience. No friction marred his relations with Edward A. Bond, the Principal Librarian, of whom he was intellectually and socially the equal, even if technically subordinate; both had for many years held equally responsible positions and they liked and respected one another. Matters were to be far otherwise between their respective, irascible successors, E. Ray Lankester and E. Maunde Thompson.

The Department of Zoology (under Albert Günther), Botany (under W. Carruthers), Geology (under H.B. Woodward) and Mineralogy (under L. Fletcher) had each their public exhibition galleries, their repositories of specimens for research and their departmental libraries. Owen, however, had planned that the high-ceilinged main hall should be an 'Index Museum' but had made little progress in furnishing it with specimens. No Keeper could lay claim to it and Flower accordingly took the main hall as his own exclusive territory. He devoted the bays, the 'side-chapels' of Owen's 'cathedral of science', to exhibits serving as introductions to the specialized galleries of the different departments. His intention was 'to illustrate the leading points in the structure of each large group (such as those to which the term "class" is commonly applied) by carefully selected and prepared specimens accompanied by explanatory descriptions, pointing out the typical form, and the most important deviations from it, and the terms by which these are designated in the literature; corresponding or homologous organs of different animals were to be shown side by side for comparison in a manner not possible in the galleries, where the specimens were necessarily arranged in a systematic, zoological or botanical sequence'. Here Flower's long experience at the Royal College of Surgeons in providing good specimens with clear instructive labels effected almost a revolution in museum display. He firmly believed that a museum should provide both education and entertainment.

Albert Günther, who had been in the service of the British Museum since 1857 and Keeper of Zoology since 1875 and had played so important a part in the development of systematic zoology and especially in ichthyology, retired in 1895. Flower immediately took charge of the Department of Zoology, thus becoming both the Director of the whole Museum and the acting Keeper of a large department, although now aged sixty-four. He set about re-organizing the zoological galleries devoted to mammals and their bones, completing the bird gallery and creating a whale room, as well as carrying on his other duties. He was fortunate indeed in having from 1889 onwards a very efficient Assistant-Secretary, Charles E. Fagan (1855-1921), (p.111).

Flower, by the example of his work and by his influential public lectures, became a missionary for better museum display, but he was also associated with other good causes. 'I wonder what Sir W. Flower's speciality is besides ladies' bonnets', wrote young Miss Beatrix Potter in her secret journal for 13 June 1896; his campaign against feathers on hats had become well known and received further publicity by his letter in *The Times* of 25 June 1896. Earlier in his *Fashion in Deformity* he had campaigned as a medical man and anatomist against the misshaping of women's bodies to meet the demands of a stupid fashion; four of his illustrations dramatically demonstrated the ill-effect of their tight-laced corsets and he likewise emphasized the deformity of the foot resulting from the excessively high heels dictated by another stupid fashion. Now, as a naturalist and humanitarian, he campaigned against the fashion of wearing feathers in their hats. Terns, crested grebes and other British birds were still being ruthlessly slaughtered during their breeding season for the ornamentation of ladies' hats. It was above all the large-scale killing of the parent egrets, the small delicately-plumed white herons of Florida and elsewhere, which caused him to write to *The*

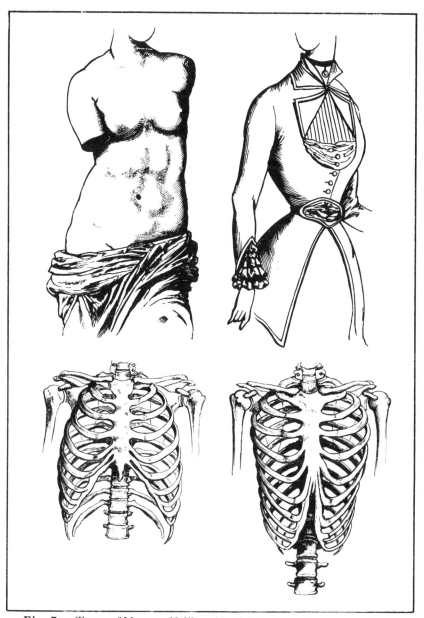

Fig. 7.   Torso of Venus of Milo, *above left*; fashionable wasp-waisted Parisian lady of 1880, *above right;* skeleton of normal female chest, *below left*; skeleton of chest of woman of 23 deformed by fashionable tight lacing to produce fashionable figure, *below right* (from W.H. Flower, *Fashion in Deformity,* 1881).

Times. They were shot as they came to feed their nestlings, which then died of cold and starvation. The cruelty involved in meeting the demands of fashion appalled Flower. 'Notwithstanding all that has been said', he wrote in his letter to *The Times*, 'the garden-party season now beginning shows that this fashion is as prevalent as ever. I have recently noticed many of the gentlest and most kind-hearted among my lady friends, including some who are members of the Society for the Protection of Birds, and who, I am sure, would never knowingly do any injury to living creatures, adorned with these very plumes . . . the purveyors of female raiment, to salve the consciences of their customers, have invented and widely propagated a monstrous fiction, and are everywhere selling the real feathers warranted as artificial! Within the last few days I have examined numbers of plumes, the wearers of which were priding themselves on their humanity, relying upon the assurances of the milliner that they were not real egrets' feathers, but manufactured. In every case it did not take a very close scrutiny to ascertain that they were unquestionably genuine. The only ''manufacture'' consisted of cutting the plume in two, and fixing the upper and lower half side-by-side, so that a single feather does duty for two in the "brush". Thus one of the most beautiful of birds is being swept off the face of the earth under circumstances of peculiar cruelty, to minister to a passing fashion, bolstered up by a glaring falsehood.'

According to R.W. Doughty, *Feather Fashions and Bird Preservation* 74 (1975) between 800 and 1,000 snowy egrets had to be killed to provide one kilogram (2.2 lb) of their feathers; thus millions must have been slaughtered to supply the quantity indicated by import and export statistics. Representatives of the Natural History Museum took part in steps to prohibit the importation of such plumage and to protect birds within the British Isles and the British Empire, but the feather trade was then firmly entrenched. Lord Avebury (earlier John Lubbock), a Trustee of the British Museum, introduced a Bill into the House of Lords to prohibit the importation of the skins and plumage of wild birds in May 1908, which the House of Lords passed, but which the House of Commons rejected in July 1908 (p.105).

Flower, who was twenty-eight in 1859 when Darwin published his *Origin of Species by Means of Natural Selection* and also by then a friend of T.H. Huxley, early became a convert to the theory of evolution by natural selection. Evolution is a slow process and a careful systematist dealing with present-day organisms becomes more impressed by the constancy of characters and the distinctness of existing species than by their hypothetical past divergence from a common stock. Thus Flower's contemporaries at the British Museum, Owen, Gray and Günther, were not convinced and they maintained an agnostic attitude

16. Sir William Henry Flower (1831-1899), anatomist and
zoologist, Director 1884-1898.

17. Geological gallery in 1892, with skeleton of Mastodon.

18. Osteological gallery in 1893.

19. Albert Günther (1830-1914),
    Keeper of Zoology 1875-1895.

20. William Carruthers (1830-
    1922), Keeper of Botany
    1871-1895.

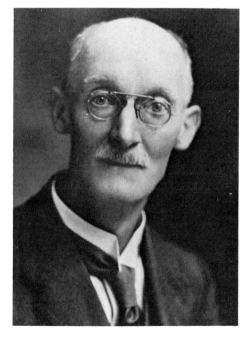

21. Henry Woodward (1832-
    1921), Keeper of Geology
    1880-1901.

22. Charles Joseph Gahan
    (1862-1939), Keeper of
    Entomology 1913-1927.

23. The Natural History Museum's housemen, cleaners etc. assembled outside the Museum for an outing in the 1890s.

24. Senior Museum staff in June 1907: *left to right* R. Bowdler Sharpe, G. A. Boulenger, A. Smith Woodward, C. E. Fagan, E. A. Smith, F. D. Godman (visitor), J. J. Parkes, F. Jeffrey Bell, M. R. Oldfield Thomas, A. B. Rendle.

towards the theory of evolution. Thanks to Owen, a figure of Adam stood high above the entrance to the Natural History Museum when completed in 1880, defiant of those who would deny his existence; indeed, the second and fatal fall of Adam was simply an accident of the Second World War; he crashed from his pinnacle in 1941. Under Flower's directorship — it would have been unthinkable under Owen's — a large marble statue of Darwin by J.E. Boehm R.A. was installed at the head of the stairs at the rear of the central hall. An appeal to the public raised £4,500, of which 2,296 subscriptions came from Sweden, some from quite humble people; the statue itself cost £2,000. On 9 June 1889 the Prince of Wales, later King Edward VII, formally received it for the Museum after Huxley had made an eloquent address. Two admirals represented the Royal Navy, Admiral Sir Bartholomew James Sullivan and Admiral A. Mellersh, at the ceremony and both had served with Darwin on the voyage of the *Beagle* in 1831-36. In 1900

Precocious Child (in front of Darwin's Statue at the Natural History Museum). And is this a fossil monkey, ma?

Fig. 8. Statue of Charles Darwin (from *Larks,* 14 October 1893).

the Prince of Wales unveiled a companion marble statue, that of Huxley himself, by Onslow Ford, R.A. likewise paid for by public subscription.

There were a number of widely-held beliefs regarding the requirements of the Natural History Museum which Flower had to counter by letters to the press. One was that the Museum would pay £10,000 for a tortoise-shell tomcat, another that it would pay £100 for the intact ash of a smoked cigar. Concerning the last *The Star* newspaper obligingly stated that 'unsmoked Havanas may be sent to *The Star* office, carriage paid, and the ash preserved without charge'. Important matters of all kinds exercised the Trustees during these years. In December 1895 they appealed to the Treasury that four 'umbrella-takers' in the Museum could be allowed two pairs of trousers a year instead of one. On 9 January 1897 the Prince of Wales, the Bishop of Winchester and others had to consider the appointment of charwomen. Because in January 1885 narrow-minded fanatics of the type common in the modern world had tried to dynamite public buildings in London, the Trustees had to order the examination of the belongings of visitors as they entered the Museum; ten plain-clothes policemen roamed through the galleries.

In 1896 the long-standing problem of opening the British Museum to the public on Sunday came to a head. The Trustees approved Sunday opening, but could do nothing without the approbation of Parliament. From 1850 onwards, the National Sunday League had campaigned for the opening of botanic gardens, public parks and art galleries. Understandably, working-class men feared that these proposals, however innocuous, might lead to a 'Continental Sunday' and themselves working seven days a week, instead of six. Many people had strong religious objections to Sunday being other than a day of religious observance and rest, except, of course, for domestic servants. Outside London such objections were overcome in various ways; Liverpool, for example, employed Jews on Sundays. In Scotland, where it was said to be 'better to steal on Saturday than smile on Sunday', the Sunday opening of the Royal Botanic Garden had not had a demoralizing effect according to the member of Parliament for Lanark, himself a working man, and anyway courting in a public garden was better than in a closed house on the high street. Thus Mr Holborn edified his fellow M.P.s when in March 1896 the matter of the Sunday opening of the British Museum came once again before Parliament. Over the years, public opinion had changed and by then there was little new which could be said for or against. The bill introduced by Massey-Mainwaring permitted the Museum to be open from 2 p.m. to 6 p.m. on Sundays; no man would be required to work more than six days a week and any who had conscientious objections would be exempt from Sunday duty. Some 109 London trade unions had petitioned that reasonable concessions should be made to working men in the matter of Sunday opening. The House of Commons undoubtedly reflected general public opinion when on 10 March 1896 it passed the bill by 178 votes to 93. The Sunday attendance in 1896 was 36,923, rising to 70,084 in 1905. In 1979 it was 485,978.

Flower's influence on museum display was so far-reaching and persuasive, his advocacy and practice so convincing, his principal methods later so generally accepted as to seem obvious and commonplace, that it is difficult now to appreciate their originality and importance. His part in the history of museums is well stated by his successor, E. Ray Lankester, in *Nature* on 13 July 1899: 'There can be no doubt in the mind of any man who is acquainted with the present condition of the public galleries of the great museums of natural history in Europe, and with the condition which characterised those of similar institutions in Great Britain previously to the year 1864, that a very great and important change for the better was effected by Flower, who deserves to be considered as an organiser and inventor in museum-work. His methods have not only met with general approval, and their application with admiration, but they have been largely adopted and copied by other curators and directors of public museums both at home and abroad. But the work of the museum curator consists not merely in framing theories in museum organisation and arrangement: the more important part of his work is the putting of such theories into practice. To do this, energy and patience in the surmounting of obstacles are necessary, and perhaps as much as or more than any other quality — the artistic sense. Sir William Flower possessed this last quality in a remarkable degree. No pains were spared by him in selecting the proper colour for the background or supports of the specimens exhibited in a case, or in effectively spacing and balancing the objects brought together in one field of view. He took the greatest pains to make the museum under his care a delight to the eye, so that the visitor should be charmed by the harmony and fitness of the groups presented to his notice, and thus the more easily led to an appreciation of the scientific lessons which each object has to tell... The first great principle upon which Sir William Flower insisted was that the possessions of a great museum of natural history must be divided into two distinct parts — to be separately dealt with in almost all respects — viz. the public or show-collection, and the special or study-collection, not exhibited to the general public, but readily accessible to all investigators and specially-qualified persons. The latter collection, he insisted, should have at least as much space devoted to it as the former.

In this way the public galleries would (he showed) be cleared of the excess of specimens which, nevertheless, the museum must carefully preserve for the use of specialists. Then, further, Flower held that every specimen placed in the public or show-collection should be there in order to demonstrate to the visitor some definite fact or facts, and so should be most fully visible, isolated rather than obscured by neighbouring specimens, and ticketed with an easily-read label stating clearly and simply the reason why it is worth looking at — that is to say, what are its points of interest. He would thus have reduced very much in *number* the specimens commonly exhibited in natural history museums, and have increased the *interest* and *beauty* of each specimen selected for the public eye. Another principle which he often insisted upon ... was that in public galleries the visitor should see, side-by-side, the stuffed or otherwise preserved animal (mammal, bird, reptile, fish, mollusc, insect, worm or polyp) and its skeleton and important parts of its internal structure and the remains of its extinct allies.'

Unhappily, his heavy commitments proved too much for Flower's by no means robust constitution, impaired as it had been by his Crimean War service. He collapsed in October 1897, resigned in August 1898 and died on 1 July, 1899, at the age of sixty-seven. From 1879 until his death, he was President of the Zoological Society. Many honours justly came to him, among them a knighthood (K.C.B.) in 1892, honorary doctorates from Edinburgh, St. Andrews, Dublin (Trinity College), Cambridge, Durham and Oxford, and the then most esteemed of all, the Royal Prussian order 'Pour la Mérite'.

A fitting tribute to Flower's work was the *The Times* obituary notice on 3 July 1899, which stated that Sir William Flower was much and justly esteemed by scientific men all over the world. 'The kindness of his nature, his unwearying sympathy and the patient attention which he gave to every matter brought under his notice, endeared him to friends and colleagues. He worthily maintained the courteous attitude to the public which has become an honourable tradition in the British Museum.' *The Times* did not, however, state that he had effected two major changes, apart from exhibits, within the Museum. He had given his office as head of the Natural History Departments an authority such as Owen had never been allowed and he had brought exposition of the theory of evolution into the scope of the Museum, which Owen would not have done. For his work at the Royal College of Surgeons and the British Museum (Natural History), for his clear enunciation of the functions of museums and his practical exemplification, he stands as one of the greatest of museum administrators.

8

A Period of
Dissension and Growth
1898 - 1907

EDWIN RAY LANKESTER (1847-1929) was Director of the British Museum (Natural History) from 1898 to 1907, during which period he became much embroiled in disputes with the Principal Librarian and Director of the British Museum, Sir E. Maunde Thompson (1840-1929) at Bloomsbury and with the Museum's Trustees. His appointment, reign and compulsory retirement aroused much controversy and some ill-feeling among British scientists; these events reflect personalities of the time and the astute manipulation of an influential and well-known, elitist corporation, the Royal Society.

The ill-health of William Flower in 1897 and 1898, and his impending resignation as Director, made the appointment of his successor a question of deep concern to many beyond the Trustees and Principal Trustees of the British Museum. The rumour spread that they intended to make the next Director of the Natural History Museum at South Kensington 'a kind of lieutenant to the Principal Librarian at Bloomsbury'. It led to protests in the *Daily News*, *The People*, *The Medical Press* and *The Times*, and most notably a memorial to the Trustees by twenty-three Fellows of the Royal Society headed by Lord Kelvin and eight other distinguished men in July 1898. Their main contention was that, in the interest of the welfare of natural history, 'the principal official in charge of the national collection relating to the subject should not be subordinate in authority to any other officer of the Museum'. It is not known who drafted this seemingly reasonable and innocent document: Lazarus Fletcher, its victim, later suspected Michael Foster, Secretary of the Royal Society, E. Ray Lankester (who did not sign it) and W.F.R. Wheldon as probable authors.

The Times on 9 July 1898 published a long leading article in support of this high-minded group of signatories. It immediately led to a letter from Thompson on behalf of the Trustees, stating that the signatories were under a misapprehension, and emphasizing his own supreme position: 'The Trustees have no intention of abolishing the office of Director of the Departments of Natural History, or of imposing any new limitations on the duties of that office; nor do they contemplate any change in the constitution of the British Museum. The two Museums at Bloomsbury and Cromwell Road are, and always have been, under one administration; they are supported by one Parliamentary vote; and the Director and Principal Librarian is, and always has been, the accounting officer and the chief executive officer of the entire British Museum.' Flower himself wrote that 'if there were any question of undoing, or in anyway impairing, the work at which I have laboured incessantly for the last fourteen years, I should be the first to protest against such a course, but I am unaware that any change is contemplated that would have this effect'. He then stated that the progress at South Kensington which the memorialists had praised had been greatly due 'to the wise administration of the Trustees and to the constant support and sympathy of two successive official heads of the whole establishment, the late Sir Edward Bond and Sir Edward Maunde Thompson'. He feared that, while the result of severance of the Natural History Museum from the remainder of the establishment could not be forecast, 'it might lead to disaster'.

E. Maunde Thompson was a very distinguished palaeographer, born in Clarendon, Jamaica, but educated at Rugby in England. For financial reasons he had to leave University College, Oxford, without taking a degree, and in 1861 he entered the British Museum as an office assistant, but was soon moved to the Department of Manuscripts of which he became Keeper in 1878: he became Principal Librarian in 1888, succeeding the genial Sir Edward A. Bond. Edward Miller, the historian of the British Museum, states that 'as with Panizzi, stories of him, especially of his temper and ruthlessness towards his unfortunate subordinates, continued to circulate for many years after his retirement in 1909 and, for the most part, depicted him as a savage and vindictive tyrant'. Formidable and masterful as an administrator though he was, Thompson wisely never showed that side of his character to Flower; it was in store for Flower's successor.

More lay behind the memorial to the Trustees than many of its signatories knew. On 11 June 1898 Flower informed the Keeper of Mineralogy, Lazarus Fletcher, of his intent to resign and on 25 June 1898 he invited him to become a candidate for the directorship. The British Museum's Standing Committee of Trustees, which included

naturalists and men of affairs as eminent and practical as Lord
Avebury, Lord Walsingham, Frederick Ducane Godman and Sir John
Evans, met on 2 July and unanimously recommended Fletcher's
appointment. There would appear to have been no doubt as to his competence and suitability; he was, however, a mineralogist and E. Ray
Lankester, Linacre Professor of Comparative Anatomy at Oxford, and
in 1896 Vice-president of the Royal Society, coveted the position. The
news of the Trustees' decision leaked out, whereupon Lankester's
friends went quickly into action. On 5 July they prepared a memorial to
the Trustees for signature by Fellows of the Royal Society. The Council
of the Society met on 7 July, an impressive number of signatures were
obtained, and the memorial was taken to *The Times* for immediate publication. Lankester's name nowhere appears in it, yet he himself
brought it to John Murray for signature and, according to Fletcher,
was a principal canvasser. In consequence, on 11 July 1898, Flower
asked Fletcher to withdraw his candidature, even though Lord
Avebury saw no reason why a mineralogist should be debarred from
the directorship. That was, however, the intent of the memorial. A
person hiding his identity under the designation 'One of the original
signatories' stated in *The Times* of 14 July that 'There was no misapprehension amongst those who drafted the memorial... The memorialists
did not think it proper or necessary to state explicitly the details they
had ascertained... They objected chiefly to the proposal made by the
Standing Committee of the Trustees on 2 July, to use the Directorship
of the Natural History Museum as ordinary promotion for the existing
staff of the museum, and to the formal recommendation, made at the
same time, of one of the museum staff for that post, who, although an
able and meritorious worker in a special branch of science, is not a
naturalist... Fortunately the proposals of the Standing Committee of
the Trustees are not necessarily accepted by those whose duty it is
actually to make the appointment.' That was plain enough. It was to
exclude Fletcher and prepare the way for the appointment of the
zoologist who wanted the post, indeed to force this, in defiance of the
Museum's competent Trustees. Responsibility for appointment of the
Director lay with the three Principal Trustees, namely the Archbishop
of Canterbury, the Lord Chancellor and the Speaker of the House of
Commons, and as non-scientists they could hardly be expected to defy
the wishes of the Royal Society so effectively publicized, especially as
Lankester personally knew the Speaker and apparently had made it
clear to him in 1896 that he wanted the post. On 3 August 1898 they
nominated and approved the appointment of Professor Edwin Ray
Lankester, F.R.S., to be Director of the Natural History Departments
of the British Museum (Natural History) and 'to hold, enjoy and

execute the said employment and service'. With this, as during Flower's last years at the Museum, was combined the post of Keeper of Zoology. He resigned his Oxford professorship and took up his duties at the Museum in October 1898. His concept of those duties did not always tally with that of the Trustees.

On learning of Lankester's appointment the Standing Committee of the Trustees had necessarily to acquiesce but were angry all the same. They drafted a resolution for communication to the Principal Trustees: 'Resolved, That the Trustees composing the Standing Committee of the British Museum, while fully recognising the force and bearing of the Statute which vests the nomination and appointment of the Museum staff in the hands of the Principal Trustees, are of the opinion that the time has now arrived when it is in the interests of the Public Service that a change should be made in the Statute. Having regard to the fact that the Standing Committee is the body responsible for the orderly and efficient working of the Museum, they desire to place on record their judgement that the practice of filling the higher posts in the Museum without consultation and concurrence with the Standing Committee is contrary to the interests of good administration.'

Lankester thought otherwise, but he began his reign in an atmosphere hardly of goodwill. He was an outstanding zoologist, who made many and important contributions to the knowledge of the morphology of fossil fishes, Oligochaeta, Mollusca, Arthropoda and Protozoa. As early as 1871, he described protozoan parasites in the blood of vertebrate animals. Indeed, he left the mark of his originality on almost all the subjects he investigated, and they were many. In 1884 he played an important part in the founding of the Marine Biological Association and later in the erection of its Plymouth Marine Laboratory. His career before entering the Museum had been continuously successful. He was born in London on 15 May 1847, the eldest son of the physician and microscopist Edwin Lankester, and as a boy he met Darwin, Huxley and other scientists in his father's house; he thus became known to influential people from the start and learned how to use them. He spent his first university year in Cambridge, then moved to Oxford, and in 1871-2 studied in the celebrated marine laboratory (Stazione Zoologica) at Naples. He was Jodrell Professor of Zoology at University College, London, from 1874 to 1891 and was elected to the Royal Society in 1875 at the age of twenty-seven. From there he returned to Oxford as Linacre Professor of Comparative Anatomy, a post he held until becoming Director of the British Museum (Natural History). One of his tasks at Oxford was to re-organize the zoological exhibits of the Oxford University Museum, which he did with his customary efficiency, and it brought him into contact with Flower.

A magazine, aptly called the *Candid Friend*, said of Lankester in May 1901 that 'His own head is shaped like a benevolent biscuit-tin and is packed as full of knowledge as other people's eggs are full of meat . . . the only thing that moves the excellent and bulky biologist to unmitigated wrath is a real idiot. He refuses to suffer fools gladly, and the majority of his official comrades throughout his life have therefore missed the finer qualities that distinguish a particularly attractive and many-sided nature. At Oxford he was perpetually battling with the Idiot Incarnate.'

Tall, massive and paunchy, endowed with a booming voice and a superb intellect marred, however, by an impetuous temperament, Lankester could both over-awe and endear himself to academic colleagues and students, but not to the Trustees of the British Museum. Trouble began early. Cool relations and conflict with the Principal Librarian, E. Maunde Thompson, at Bloomsbury became evident one year after Lankester's appointment at South Kensington when Thompson wrote to him on 14 October 1899: 'I have also, with reluctance, to note the long time you have been absent on vacation, far longer than by the rules you were entitled to. I would be glad if, in future, you would kindly let me know when you go away on vacation for any long period of time. Yours very truly, E. Maunde Thompson.' To this Lankester replied on 17 October 1899: 'With regard to the suggestion with which your letter concludes, I may say that I shall always be glad to meet your convenience, so far as possible, in regard to the business in which we are both concerned; and that during any prolonged absence from London I will leave an address here to which you can write, should you desire to consult me. You, I hope, will oblige me in the same way.' That was not the subservience Thompson expected. He replied on 21 October 1899: 'I have to acknowledge your letter of 17th instant. It seems to me that you wrote this letter under a misapprehension of the relative positions of the Director and Principal Librarian of the British Museum and the Director of the Natural History Departments. On reconsideration you will, I hope, recognize that the tone of equality you have assumed is incorrect . . . I have to remind you that it is my duty to see that officers of the British Museum Establishment give full attention to their duties. Under the provisions of the Order in Council of the 15th August 1890 your vacation during the first ten years of service is limited to thirty-six week days. I must ask you to let me have a return of the number of days you have been absent on vacation during the current year, setting out separately the special leave of absence that was allowed you by the Trustees.' Bond, and indeed Thompson himself, would never have addressed Flower in this way. Lankester replied simply on 25 October 1899: 'I have to acknowledge the receipt of your letter of October 21.' Thompson countered next day: 'I have duly received your letter of yesterday acknowledging mine of the 21st. Will you be so good as to inform me if that is the only reply I am to receive. Yours faithfully, E. Maunde Thompson.'

Lankester, however, was just as self-righteous and conscious of his dignity as Thompson; he had given up his Oxford professorship to come to the Natural History Museum and he was a Fellow of the Royal Society. He replied on 27 October: 'Dear Sir Edward, Your view of our official relationship differs, I am very sorry to be obliged to say, from that which, I think, is warranted by the instructions and information furnished to me by the direction of the Trustees. . . I believe I am not mistaken in thinking that you did not consider it your duty to ask my predecessor, Sir William Flower, to report to you concerning his vacations, and that neither you nor your predecessor in office ever did so. I have regarded the position to which I was appointed at the Natural History Museum as identical with that held by Sir William Flower, and have, to the best of my belief, conformed to his practice in regard to vacations, whilst allowing nothing to interfere with the full discharge of my work at the Museum. I am, of course, ready now and at all times to make such a statement with regard to my vacations as is possible, and of the reasons for them, to the Trustees should they wish me to do so. I think that I should be wrong to acquiesce in the new departure which it seems to me that you propose in regard to the relationship of the Director and Principal Librarian and the Director of the Natural History Departments. . . When you received the title of ''Director of the British Museum'' there appears to have been no extension made by the Trustees in your duties as to give you control of the Director and officers of the Natural History Museum. . . I am obliged with great reluctance to object to your belief that I should report to you. I am under the belief that I should report directly to the Trustees and not to you.'

This correspondence led to a direction by the Standing Committee on 28 October 1899 that Lankester should prepare and send to each member a statement of the view which he took of the official relationship between the Director of the Natural History Departments and the Director and Principal Librarian of the British Museum. This he set out in a well-argued memorandum of eight printed folio pages.

Legally Thompson was right and the Trustees were in no mood to support Lankester against him; in a resolution of 11 November 1899 they concluded that the Director and Principal Librarian was justified in asking for a report of the holidays of all the officers of the Natural History Museum. For Lankester all this discussion of his conduct by the Trustees was very humiliating.

The time had come once again to mobilize the victorious Royal Society regiment for action against the Trustees. On Lankester's behalf, but without mentioning his name, a memorial was accordingly drafted hastily in May 1900 and circulated widely for signature before submission to the President and Council of the Royal Society for endorsement. It violently attacked the management of the Natural History Departments of the British Museum, which of course included Mineralogy and Botany, and referred to the deplorable condition of the Museum. The Trustees had, however, two able and loyal servants in their keepers, Lazarus Fletcher, who had been denied the directorship through Royal Society pressure in favour of Lankester and, having served on the Society's Council, knew how such matters were managed, and George Murray, who was well aware of Lankester's desire to transfer the Department of Botany to Kew under his friend Thiselton-Dyer (p.296). Both were Fellows of the Society. They accordingly launched a counter-attack. In July 1900 they printed and circulated a long shattering memorandum to the Society's President and Council, the more effective because their Departments were known to be efficiently run. The memorial concerning the alleged mis-management had been circulated by E.B. Poulton, Professor of Zoology at Oxford. It was at once obvious, said Fletcher and Murray, that 'though he was himself doubtless acting with good faith. . . he was merely an instrument in the hands of more astute persons to whom anonymity is for the moment an advantage.' We have now good authority for asserting that one of the parties to the drafting of the Memorial is Sir Michael Foster,' a senior Royal Society secretary, who being precluded by the wording of the Memorial from signing it could thus conceal his connection with it from the President and Council. 'Of course,' they continued, 'Sir Michael has a perfect right . . . to shoot from behind a boulder, if he is of the opinion that such a method of attack is the safest and most likely to be successful; but we submit that there is a great lack of candour and fair play in this matter of dealing with the Royal Society Council and in this mode of attempting to secure the official help of the Royal Society in support of an attack on the Trustees of the British Museum or on ourselves.' Fletcher and Murray then referred to methods by which signatures had been obtained and noted that there was scarcely a single signatory 'to whom the Royal Society itself would turn for guidance in an attempt to manage a Natural History Museum. . . the Standing Committee of the Trustees of the British Museum is at least as capable as the Council of the Royal Society of satisfactorily advising the Government on the difficult prob-lems involved in the proper management of a large Natural History

Museum.' The memorialists had asked for an enquiry. Fletcher and Murray shot back: 'we therefore, in our turn, ask for a searching enquiry to be made, also without delay, by the President and Council of the Royal Society into the origin, names of the drafters of the Memorial, the good faith and the methods used in obtaining signatures, in the case of both this Memorial and the allied Memorial signed by upwards of eighty Fellows of the Royal Society and presented to the Trustees of the British Museum in the year 1898. The first signatory of the Memorial of 1898, was Sir Michael Foster and he is therefore responsible for the character of the statements made in it.' That was the memorial which had gained Lankester his appointment. Fletcher and Murray thus hit the target with devastating effect. The Council of the Royal Society was now embarrassingly placed; such an enquiry would have incriminated too many of its Fellows. It wisely rejected both the proposed memorial and the proposed enquiry. Fletcher and Murray had known that such an exposure might, in Fletcher's own words, bring upon themselves 'the personal emnity of a powerful group of men whose methods of working had been, and might continue to be, of an underground and therefore particularly dangerous character', but they stuck to their guns. The attack on the Trustees by a letter to *The Times*, backed by the President and Council of the Royal Society and by scores of prestigious signatures, as intended by Lankester and his supporters, had been defeated. It was to be nearly twenty years before another was launched from Burlington House.

Fletcher noted that the memorial of 1898 certified the high degree of efficiency of the Museum and its excellence of management then and the memorial of 1900 certified a deplorable condition within the Museum and the faultiness of its system of management, but no change whatsoever had been made during the two years. Nevertheless, twenty-two distinguished men of science, nineteen of them Fellows of the Royal Society, had either drafted or signed both memorials. Since they had certified the excellence of the system of management in 1898 and the badness of the same system in 1900, Fletcher concluded that 'their signatures are only of value as showing the readiness of these distinguished men to become signatories of memorials'.

In 1901 Lankester came into opposition with an important Trustee, Thomas de Grey, Sixth Baron Walsingham (1843-1919), which was unwise. For his fellow aristocrats Lord Walsingham's wealth, possessions and sporting prowess doubtlessly compensated for the eccentricity of his devotion to entomology; he boasted in *Who's Who* of owning about 19,200 acres and of shooting 1,070 grouse in one day on his Blubberhouses Moor. From 1876 onwards, Lord Walsingham was an assiduous Trustee of the British Museum. In July 1901 he made a deed of gift of his superb collection to the British Museum. The terms of this transfer did not satisfy Lankester, who advised against acceptance primarily on the grounds that the value of the collection had been over-rated and the annual expenditure on its upkeep would be too high. When on 26 May 1906 the Trustees decided that Lankester should be compulsorily retired after reaching the age of sixty (instead of seventy as he had contemplated), Lord Walsingham personally announced their decision to Lankester. Receipt of the Walsingham collection was delayed until 1910. Meanwhile Lankester's relations with the Trustees deteriorated and in 1904 they appointed a Sub-Committee to enquire into the present working of the Natural History Museum. Part of their report reads:

'Your Sub-Committee have held five meetings at the Natural History Museum since their appointment. They have had the advantage of having before them the Directors of the Museum at Bloomsbury and of the Natural History Museum, the Keepers and Assistant-Keepers of the various Departments at the latter Museum, and of hearing their statements on the subjects referred to the Sub-Committee. They have also had interviews with Mr. Fagan, the Assistant-Secretary.

'When Sir Richard Owen was appointed as head of the Natural History Museum he appears to have regarded the post as being in the nature of a reward for scientific eminence, while adminis-tration and superintendence were to occupy a secondary position. Sir W. Flower exercised a closer and more systematic superin-tendence over the Museum than had been the practice of Sir R. Owen. Prof. Lankester appears to take the view that his duties and functions are such as were undertaken by Sir R. Owen, rather than those fulfilled by Sir W. Flower. He disclaimed res-ponsibility for the proposal of purchases, except in the Zoological Department, nor do the Keepers consult him as to purchases. He further told us explicitly, in various forms, that he does not con-sider regular and systematic inspection of the Museum as a whole to be part of his duty. On this principle he appears to act. One effect of the Director's view of his duty has been to throw upon Mr Fagan an additional amount of work for which he is not adequately remunerated.

'We fully recognise the great value of the scientific researches prosecuted by the Director, but at the same time we are strongly of opinion that in the interests of the Museum the duties as laid down by the Statutes should be strictly carried out in future, in respect of attendance and otherwise, in conformity with the practice usual in the case of other Civil Servants.

'The Statutes and Rules of 1898 are to the effect that he should perform the same duties connected with custody and superintendence at the Natural History Museum as those discharged by the Director at the Museum at Bloomsbury. Among these duties as laid down in Section 2 of Chapter II is that he shall exercise a general superintendence over all the Departments; and shall take care that the officers, assistants, attendants, and servants be regular in their attendance and perform their proper duties; and shall report every omission in this respect to the Standing Committee.'

To this Lankester replied:

'The Director of the Natural History Departments has been invited by the Trustees to make a statement with reference to the Report of the Sub-Committee submitted to the meeting on July 9th, 1904.

'He begs to say, in the first place, that he is most willing and anxious to carry out the wishes of the Trustees, and to act upon any recommendations made by them for improvement in the administration of the Natural History Museum as a whole or of any of its Departments. He has no other aim in life than the maintenance of the Natural History Museum as the greatest scientific institution of its kind in existence. His whole time and strength are absolutely devoted to its working as a place of scientific study, of popular edification, and of imperial service.

'The concluding paragraph of the Sub-Committee's Report is as follows:—

"With respect to the general working of the Museum in its various Departments your Sub-Committee have no special recommendation to make. From their interviews with the Keepers and Assistant-Keepers they have received a highly satisfactory impression as to the manner in which their several duties are performed."

'The Director trusts that he may regard this as an expression of general approval of the results of his administration as Director and as Keeper of Zoology during the six years in which he has held those posts.

'At the same time the Director would have been glad if the Report had taken notice of the long list of administrative work in the public galleries, in the store-rooms and basement of the Museum, in the preparation of guide-books, reports, and monographs, and in many other directions carried out by him, submitted in his printed memorandum to the Sub-Committee. These matters have chiefly occupied the Director's time and energy, and he ventures to hope that the large amount of administrative work done by him tending to the increased value of the Museum as a public scientific institution is regarded with approval by the Trustees.

'The Director was not aware that regular and systematic inspection of the whole Museum by him at fixed intervals was desired by the Trustees. He had himself thought that occasional but frequent visits by him to the various departments of the Museum formed the best method of inspection, and has carried out that method effectively; but he will gladly modify his practice in this matter, and the expression of the wishes of the Trustees will be of material assistance to him in so doing.

'The statement in paragraph No. 2 that, in consequence of the present Director's taking a view of his duty differing from that taken by Sir William Flower, an additional amount of work has been thrown by him upon the Assistant Secretary, Mr Fagan, is due, he ventures to suggest, to a misapprehension as to the difference between the work done by Sir William Flower when he was Director only (1884-1895) and that which he deliberately arranged for himself and his assistants, with the formal approval of the Trustees, when he became Keeper of Zoology as well as Director in 1895.

'It is, however, necessary to reckon with the fact that the amount of work falling upon the Director and his office has increased, and must further increase, with the expansion of the Museum and the growing demands made upon the administration for advice and information, not only by the public, but by various Government Departments.

'The reason (in addition to that arising from this necessary increase of the Museum's activity) given by the Director a year ago to the Trustees for asking the Treasury for an increase in Mr Fagan's salary was that Mr Fagan had been led nine years ago to expect it, when Sir William Flower, with the assent of the Trustees, did, in the re-arrangement of work, add to Mr Fagan's responsibilities.

'In the third and fourth paragraphs of the Report the Statutes are cited, and it is stated that they should be strictly carried out by the Director in future. The Director, in his memorandum addressed to the Sub-Committee, stated that he regarded the Statutes as the rule and indication of his duty, and he is not aware of any omission of his to carry them out.

'The Director begs to assure the Trustees that it will be his constant endeavour to carry out the Statutes strictly, and to see that they are strictly carried out in future by the staff of the Museum in accordance with the direction of the Trustees.

'The fact that the Sub-Committee state that they have received a highly satisfactory impression of the general work of all the Natural History Departments over which the Director exercises superintendence, and that after their inquiry they state that they have no special recommendations to make in regard to the working of the Departments, leads him to hope that there has been no serious neglect hitherto in this respect.'

The strain of this investigation was more than Lankester could stand and he had to be granted two months of sick leave for complete rest.

There for the time being the matter ended. It came to a head again in May 1906 when the Standing Committee of the Trustees forwarded to Lankester an official document stating that, in conformity with a clause in the Civil Service Superannuation Act which empowered the head of a department to call upon any officer in his department to retire at the age of sixty, they called upon him to retire from the post of Director of the Natural History Departments in May 1907 on such pension as he was by regulation entitled to receive. It was a terrible blow to both Lankester's self-esteem and his financial standing. On 8 August 1906 he published a long letter in *The Times* stating that, 'The decree of the Trustees simply amounts to this — they propose to remove me from a post of which the salary is £1,200 a year and to leave me unemployed and without possibility of employment at the age of 60 on a pension of £300 a year. This sum is the *maximum* which the Treasury can pay as a pension.' Lankester fought back, challenging the power of the Trustees to remove him, and in *The Fortnightly Review* of December 1906 (pages 1039-1054) under the title 'Eight years at the Natural History Museum' he published a detailed justification of his activities within the Museum. The Law Officers of the Crown, to whom the question was referred, then ruled in March 1907 that he was removable at the pleasure of the three Principal Trustees. One of them, the Archbishop of Canterbury, suggested that he should be given a Civil List pension of £250 in addition to his normal Treasury pension of £300, the two amounting to almost half of his full salary. Accepting this and a knighthood (K.C.B.), Sir Edwin Ray Lankester ended his controversial tenure of office on 31 December 1907. The Linnean Society of London awarded him the Darwin-Wallace medal in 1908 and the Royal Society the Copley medal in 1913. He added to his income by high-class scientific journalism, contributing well-written and well-informed popular essays to *The Daily Telegraph* and elsewhere which were reprinted and revised as *Science from an Easy Chair* (1910), *More Science from an Easy Chair* (1912), *Diversions of a Naturalist* (1915), *Secrets of the Earth and Sea* (1920) and *Great and Small Things* (1923). He died in London on 13 August 1929, highly respected for his scientific achievements and mourned by a wide circle of friends, his troubles at the Natural History Museum now forgotten.

In many respects Lankester was his own worst enemy. As the writer of a highly sympathetic obituary notice, P. Chalmers Mitchell, said in *The Times* of 16 August 1929, he had 'a genius for putting himself in the wrong by explosive and unconsidered action in a just cause, or at least in an otherwise completely tenable position. The mistake once committed, Lankester would concentrate his attention exclusively on the justice of his cause, while those who were opposed to him would see nothing but the violence of his conduct. His misunderstanding with the University of Edinburgh, his brush with the police in Piccadilly, his relations with the Standing Committee of the Natural History Museum, and many minor events in his career were variants of the same theme. His character, his intelligence, and a really high conscientiousness made it practically certain that in any real dispute he would be on the side of real justice and wisdom; but if there were any way of proceeding impulsively and imprudently he was more likely to stumble into it.'

Fig. 9. The okapi, *Okapia johnstoni;* (drawing by H.H. Johnston in *McClure's Magazine*, September 1901).

This belligerent side of Lankester's character tends to obscure the solid contribution which he made to the progress of the Natural History Museum during his directorship. Zoologically the most exciting event of his period was the discovery and description of the okapi. The existence of this large and very remarkable forest-dwelling mammal became known to Sir Harry Johnston through two waist belts of striped skin which he obtained from natives of the eastern Congo forest near the Semliki river, who called the animal okapi or 'o'api'. These he sent to the Natural History Museum, which considered them to represent a new species of zebra. Later Sir Harry obtained a complete skin and two skulls which were received at the Museum on 17 June 1901. From this material it was evident that the okapi belonged to the giraffe family (Giraffidae), of which it was a very primitive member, its closest relatives being genera only known in a fossil state; and thus it

Fig. 10. Bands of skin of the okapi, on which the first scientific description of the species, as *Equus johnstoni*, was based (from *Proceedings of Zoological Society*, 1901).

represented a genus new to science. Lankester wrote at once to *The Times* reporting its arrival and it was also widely featured in the popular press. In 1907 the Museum purchased a skeleton for £200.

The gift of a cast skeleton of *Diplodocus carnegii* by the Scottish American industrialist, Andrew Carnegie, in 1905 also aroused considerable public interest. This huge dinosaur up to eighty feet (24.3m) long and estimated to have weighed twenty tons (20.3 tonnes), flourished in Jurassic times about 150 million years ago. King Edward VII when Prince of Wales had been a keenly interested and conscientious Trustee of the British Museum (p.99) and he retained this interest after his resignation upon becoming King. Carnegie had shown him an illustration representing this remarkable beast which had been based on the very impressive skeleton, excavated in Wyoming, and mounted in the Carnegie Museum, Pittsburgh. The King, who was a guest of Carnegie, suggested that a reproduction of it would be welcome for the Natural History Museum. Carnegie accordingly offered in 1903 to have casts made at his own cost, even then about £2,000. They arrived at the Natural History Museum in thirty-six cases in February 1905 and the Director of the Carnegie Museum and an assistant came over in April to mount them. The ceremony of presentation took place on 12 May when Lord Avebury formally accepted it from Carnegie on behalf of the Trustees, with 300 persons present. It remains one of the most sensational exhibits in the Museum and the joy of cartoonists and children (Figs 12-14).

Lankester was a hard-working and conscientious Director with far more routine tasks falling upon him than he had ever had at Oxford. Since the Trustees, and still less the general public, had little concept of what they involved, he set out to teach them in his *Fortnightly Review* article:

> 'On entering upon my duties, I found that there was a definite amount of routine work which must occupy a portion of the Director's time every day. Letters asking for information as to the gift or purchase of specimens, as to guide-books, as to collecting, as to identification of specimens sent, applications for posts in the Museum, for permission to draw or study, and so on, arrive every day. Answers to these had to be dictated or indicated, and other letters from Colonial governors, British and foreign officials, to be answered by the Director himself. Letters of thanks for gifts had to be signed, and written orders signed and sent to the staff. Every bill from every department, from that for a stuffed elephant to that for washing dusters or printing a monograph, had to be examined and signed or initialled by the Director, and often inquiries directed in order to make sure as to the correctness of the account.

The reports of the entire staff, and more especially of the Zoological Department, as to illness, absences, increase of pay, etc., had to be examined, the complaints, suggestions, and inquiries of the members of the staff attended to by personal interview or memorandum, and directions and decisions of the most diverse kind to be given, the latter involving such questions as the discharge of a servant, the immediate purchase of a rare specimen, purchases to be recommended to the Trustees, the colour to be used in painting the ceiling of a gallery, the pose to be given to the skeleton of an extinct reptile, and the quality of type and paper to be used in a guide-book. The agenda for the monthly meeting of the Trustees had to be prepared, the reports of the keepers verified and epitomised, the assistant secretary drafting the several items. In autumn the budget for the year, dealing with a proposed expenditure of over £50,000, had to be set out in detail. Besides this, visitors sent in their names continually, and had often, from lack of time, to be refused an interview, whilst persons of official or scientific importance had to be conducted over the Museum. Then came consultations with the keepers, inspection of works in progress in all parts of the Museum (heating, lighting, ventilating, building), of the taxidermists' room, of the modellers' studio, of new specimens in course of being unpacked, of new

Fig. 11. Edwin Ray Lankester, Director of the Museum, riding an okapi (cartoon from *Punch*, 12 November 1902).

cases, of the work-rooms and studies and the staff of keepers, assistants, and voluntary workers busy in them. This makes up a formidable list, but a good administrator with an intelligent and trustworthy staff can'put through an immense amount of merely mechanical work in the course of a few hours. What is fatiguing in such work is the necessity of continually exercising choice and deciding alternatives in very different and varied classes of business. Whilst regularly discharging this routine work day by day, I gave the best part of the time and energy which remained to me to several larger matters of administration having reference, on the one hand, to the scientific work of the staff and, on the other, to the improvement and development of the exhibition galleries so as to increase their scientific value and their suitability for giving pleasure and instruction to the public.'

Lankester certainly gave much attention to the exhibits in the public galleries. 'There are few museum directors who have corrected and re-written so many labels as I have', he said. 'Young curators will either write too long and learned a label, or shrink to the opposite extreme and jerk out an unintelligible sentence with few words and less sense'. He himself painted on the specimen of the python the iridescent bloom of a

Fig. 12. W.J. Holland, *right*, from the Carnegie Museum, Pittsburgh, supervising assembly of casts of skeleton of *Diplodocus carnegii* at South Kensington (from *The Graphic,* 5 May 1905).

blue colour which shows on the black scales! Old exhibits were improved and new ones introduced. The preparation of specimens for a remodelled fish gallery took much time, labour and skill: prepared skins were given their true colours by painting them either from fresh specimens or good original drawings, or else casts or models were made and coloured as in life. To everything within the zoological galleries Lankester gave constructive attention.

An enquiry into the number of named and unnamed specimens in each group of animals within the Museum made him especially aware of their historic importance. He accordingly obtained the sanction of the Trustees for the preparation and publication of *The History of the Collections contained in the Natural History Departments of the British Museum.*

Fig. 13.   Andrew Carnegie, *standing*, officially presenting *Diplodocus carnegii* to the Museum; seated, *left to right*, E. Ray Lankester, Lord Avebury and W.J. Holland.

Volume 1 (442 pages), dealing with the Libraries and the Departments of Botany, Geology and Minerals, was published in 1904, volume 2 (782 pages), with separate accounts of the collections within the Department of Zoology, in 1906, and an Appendix (109 pages) by Albert Günther, giving a general history of the Department of Zoology from 1856 to 1895, in 1912. These are especially valuable for the alphabetical lists of collectors and donors of collections of specimens.

Another important innovation by Lankester was the loan of specimens for study and identification by specialists in other institutions. The enormous quantity of unnamed insects which had accumulated over the years presented a major problem, since the entomological staff was much too small to cope with it. Thus in 1904 the unidentified insect material included 15,000 specimens of Diptera, 22,000 of Lepidoptera, 17,300 of Rhynchota, 130,000 of Coleoptera, 34,000 of Hymenoptera, 1,200 of Neuroptera and 3,200 of Orthoptera. Since the number of insects is so immense and their taxonomy so complicated, a single entomologist can efficiently deal with only a minute fraction of the teeming whole. As Lankester emphasized, 'an expert is, as a rule, an expert only for a small family of insects. He can readily name horse-flies, but cannot without long study name gnats; another may be skilled in dung-beetles and scarabs, but cannot help you with weevils.' Lankester's enquiries in France, Belgium and Germany led him to the conclusion that 'a staff capable of dealing effectively with all groups of insects would have to consist of no fewer than 102 specialists, each taking a separate section. So large a staff is beyond the finances of any museum.' Indeed at this time the entire staff of the Natural History Museum, including not only scientists but attendants, police, artisans, etc., was only 143 persons. On the continent of Europe the system of forwarding material for study to specialists in other institutions was well-developed. Thompson at Bloomsbury knew so little about the need for such co-operation that he characteristically took Lankester to task for even enquiring about it without his authority. Lankester, however, realized that this was very important both for the benefit of the Museum and science generally. His first attempt to get permission to send out unstudied specimens for examination by specialists elsewhere failed: it was held to be contrary to the direction in the 1753 Act that the collections 'shall remain and be preserved in the Museum for public use to all posterity'. Four years later a great legal authority informed Lankester that in his opinion these words had not the restrictive sense which had been attributed to them, and that it was not only within the power of the Trustees to allow specimens to be sent out for identification but actually their duty to do so.

Fig. 14. A suggested use of the *Diplodocus* skeleton (from *Snaps*, 3 May 1905).

Lankester accordingly brought up the matter of loans again. In a ruling of November 1902 the Lord Chancellor approved the lending of material for identification and the Trustees happily assented. This did not cover the loan of types or unique identified specimens, but proved nevertheless one of the most beneficial of Lankester's services to the utility and prestige of the Natural History Museum as an international scientific institution.

When Lankester left the Museum so unhappily, he could, nevertheless, look back upon a period of much achievement under his direction; the work of re-organization begun by Flower had been virtually completed, the exhibits throughout were displayed in a pleasing and instructive manner, special effort had been made to obtain representative specimens of breeds of domesticated beasts and birds which by their diversity provided important evidence for the theory of evolution, notable publications had been issued, the collections for study had grown continuously.

9

Peace and War
1908 - 1919

NEITHER BEFORE NOR immediately after the departure of Sir Ray Lankester on 31 December 1907 did the Principal Trustees of the British Museum venture to appoint a new Director of the Natural History Museum. Under the general and largely nominal supervision of the Director and Principal Librarian at Bloomsbury, for a year and a half the South Kensington Museum's highly efficient Assistant Secretary, Charles Edward Fagan (1855-1921), the Keepers of the Departments and the Standing Committee of the Trustees kept their directorless Museum running satisfactorily. A question was raised in Parliament on 24 November 1908 regarding the vacant directorship, but still the Principal Trustees took no action; maybe they remembered the tart response of the Standing Committee of the Trustees to their appointment of Lankester under Royal Society pressure. The Trustees had decided meanwhile to separate the posts of Director and of Keeper of Zoology which Lankester had held simultaneously. At Bloomsbury Sir E. Maunde Thompson, who had been such a thorn in the flesh for Lankester and even more so for his Bloomsbury staff, retired as Director and Principal Librarian; in July 1909 Frederic George Kenyon (1863-1952), likewise from the Department of Manuscripts, was appointed in his stead.

A letter to *The Times* on 19 April 1909 calling for a Royal Commission to enquire into the administration of the Natural History Museum brought matters to a head. The Trustees on 24 April 1909 thereupon requested the Principal Trustees 'to appoint a Director of the Natural History Departments'. Accordingly, on 3 July 1909 they appointed Lazarus Fletcher (1854-1921), Keeper of Mineralogy, who had been pushed aside in 1898, purportedly because he was a mineralogist and also a member of the Museum staff. Relations between the newly-appointed heads of the Bloomsbury and South Kensington museums now became as cordial as they had been in the happy days of Bond and Flower. Another significant change of position was the transfer of Basil Harrington Soulsby (1864-1933) from the Department of Printed Books at Bloomsbury to the Director's Office, and thence to the General Library at South Kensington. Fagan received a well-deserved increase of salary to £700 a year.

Lazarus Fletcher joined the staff of the British Museum in 1878. He was born on 9 March 1854, at Salford, on the outskirts of Manchester, of humble parentage, and was the eldest of eight children. Someone perspicacious had brought him as a promising boy to the notice of the equally discerning High Master of the Manchester Grammar School, who had given him a place in the school and compensated his father for loss of the boy's earnings, had he been employed as a factory lad, by paying him the same amount. The grammar schools of England have always provided an educational way upward for talented boys with poor parents and Fletcher certainly justified his free schooling by his subsequent career of fruitful scientific endeavour. He had a brilliant school and university career, distinguishing himself in mathematics and natural science, gaining an open scholarship to Balliol College, Oxford, and becoming a demonstrator in physics at the Clarendon Laboratory, Oxford, in 1876. Here a knowledge of German decisively influenced his career. He read Paul Heinrich Groth's *Physikalische Krystallographie* (1876) and thereby much impressed Professor R.B. Clifton, Head of the Clarendon Laboratory, who accordingly brought the unusual young man to the attention of a colleague, Professor Mervyn Herbert Nevil Story-Maskelyne (1823-1911), a mineralogist of great ability, whose duties at Oxford rested so lightly upon him that he managed to be Professor of Mineralogy at Oxford from 1856 to 1895 and also Keeper of Minerals at the British Museum from 1857 to 1880, when he resigned on inheriting the family estates in Wiltshire and became a Member of Parliament. Also impressed by Fletcher's knowledge, ability and enthusiasm, Story-Maskelyne had appointed him as his principal assistant in 1878. Two years later, Fletcher had succeeded Story-Maskelyne as Keeper of Minerals. The major task which had confronted him at Bloomsbury was the packing and dispatch to South Kensington of thousands of mineralogical specimens, including gemstones of very high value, and their display in an attractive and informative manner in their spacious new abode, for which he had designed new show cases. When the new museum opened in April 1881, they had been on exhibition; none had been lost or stolen. He prepared handbooks manifesting 'unrivalled powers of elucidation and exposition', which fellow mineralogists have described as 'models of simplicity and accuracy', and his *The Optical Indicatrix and the Transmission of Light in Crystals* (London, 1892), translated into German as *Die Optische Indicatrix* (Leipzig, 1893), brought him international renown. In addition to crystals, he gave special attention to the analysis of meteorites. He became a Fellow of the Royal Society and was a member of the Society's council from 1895 to 1897, and from 1910 to 1912; from 1888 to 1909 he was General Secretary of the Mineralogical Society. When the Trustees agreed in 1898 to appoint Fletcher Director of the Natural History Museum, they knew well of his administrative and research capabilities, intellectual powers, and consideration toward others. However, the more aggressive and assertive Ray Lankester called to his support a group of lobbying zoological friends more numerous and influential than Fletcher could have mustered even had he been so inclined. Thus his appointment as Director was delayed until 1909 and apparently the objection, purportedly decisive in 1898, that he was a mineralogist no longer held good.

Unfortunately, when Fletcher became Director at the age of fifty-five, he had been much afflicted by illness and anxiety, for his wife was many years an invalid, and he himself had had a bad breakdown in health in 1906, from which he never completely recovered. The dynamism of his early years had gone. Luckily there was always the dependable competent Charles Fagan at hand. Indeed, it is doubtful if Fletcher could have stood the strain of the difficulties besetting the Museum during the 1914-1918 World War, but for Fagan's unostentatious management of affairs and his deep fund of common sense, especially as illness often kept Fletcher away from the Museum.

Among the events of 1910, Fletcher's first full year in office, were the visit of Theodore Roosevelt in May; a meeting of representatives of the Natural History Museum and the Colonial Office to prevent the discriminate slaughter of birds for the plumage trade; and the death of King Edward VII, a very good friend of the Museum (p.91). As a Trustee, when Prince of Wales, he had diligently attended board meetings and had found in the business of the Museum a satisfying variant to the travel, sport, philandering, and lavish eating with which his exclusion by Queen Victoria from governmental matters had made him fill his seemingly aimless life. It was indeed to counteract this exclusion that Gladstone brought about his appointment as a Trustee in 1881. He used to walk round the galleries with Flower and, when the latter wished to replace the badly-stuffed British mammals brought from Bloomsbury, he gave instructions to the royal game-keepers at Sandringham to trap rats, rabbits, etc. for the Museum. He participated in public ceremonies, such as unveiling the Huxley statue, and presented specimens, the most notable in 1910 being the skeleton of his celebrated horse 'Persimmon', winner of the Derby race in 1896.

Lankester in *The Daily Telegraph* of 21 May 1910 paid King Edward VII a warm tribute: 'When I became Director of the Natural History Departments of the British Museum, in 1898, I constantly met King Edward, who was then the Prince of Wales, at the meetings of the Standing Committee of the Board of Trustees. He was one of the most regular attendants at the meetings, and evidently took great pleasure in the discharge of his duties as a trustee. When he came to the throne he was most anxious, if possible, to remain a trustee, and it was only after some consideration that he came to the conclusion that it was not possible for him as Sovereign, to continue to act as a member of the board. On several occasions I had the honour of conducting him alone to inspect some of the additions to the collections, and he not only was always kind and gracious in manner, but showed a keen enjoyment in natural history and a remarkable personal sympathy with the interest taken by the others in the rarities and beauties of the animal world . . . The chief and most abiding impression that King Edward made upon me was that he was actuated by a vivid sense of public duty, and that he discharged his duties in no grudging way, but with a keen enjoyment of them, and in a happy spirit, which communicated itself to those around him. He must sometimes have been bored, even tired out, but he never allowed a trace of such condition to appear in his voice or manner.' For an intelligent and able man such as King Edward VII, to whom over many years when Prince of Wales the pursuit of pleasure gave the main outlet for his energy and interest, the contact with the cultivated and learned men working as fellow Trustees of the British Museum was evidently welcome, as his conscientious attendance at their meetings demonstrated. Thus at the Natural History Museum his death on 6 May 1910 occasioned mourning that was genuine and not merely formal.

It was also in 1910 that Lord Sudeley (1840-1922), at the age of seventy, with the effective help of *The Times,* began a campaign for the better educational use of museums and art galleries. In a letter to *The Times* of 10 October 1910 he remarked that no one who 'has observed the listless demeanour of a great number of those who visit and wander about our museums but must come to the conclusion that there is something gravely wrong, and that the reason why so many (often estimated at three-fifths) appear so little interested is due to some cause not difficult to discover, and which should be remedied if possible. Those who have had the advantage of going through a museum with distinguished personages when attended by a head of the department can realize the wealth of information which is imparted in a short time. Many also can remember their appreciation of those delightful Sunday afternoons spent with the late Sir W. Flower in the Natural History Museum, when, with a select body of friends, he took the trouble to walk through his beloved Museum and to explain in his marvellous, simple and charming manner various points of thrilling interest and of mysterious evolution which everywhere presented themselves, from embryo legs in the mighty whale down to the eccentricities of the smallest insect.' Lord Sudeley accordingly advocated the employment of special, well-informed guides to make known such matters of interest not simply to the privileged friends of a great director, but to average visitors. 'Such "guide demonstrators" should, of course, not be of the usual race of "parrot guides", but must be intelligent people of either sex, attached to the staff, proved thoroughly competent, after proper examination, to explain in a pleasant manner the history, value, and matters of interest connected with each specimen. I am assured by those best able to judge that such people could easily be obtained. In any event, why should not an experiment be made of, say, six of such "guide demonstrators" in the British and also in the Victoria and Albert Museums, and, perhaps, a few in Kew Gardens?' *The Times* backed up this suggestion with a long leading article on 'Museums and the public'.

Such advocacy convinced the Trustees of the British Museum and they instituted demonstrations by guides at Bloomsbury in 1911. Their success made Lord Sudeley return to the fray. In *The Times* of 21 October 1911 he asked 'whether, now that the experiment has been tried with such marked and undoubted success, steps should not at once be taken to extend largely the system to all museums, galleries and public gardens (especially at Kew), not only in London, but also in the provinces. The Natural History Museum, a department of the British Museum, would seem specially marked out for the adoption of this system.' Once again the Trustees responded sensibly to a sensible proposal. They appointed John Henry Leonard (1864-1931), a science graduate (B.Sc) with teaching experience, as guide demonstrator at the Natural History Museum and he began his duties on 26 May 1912, daily making one tour of about an hour's duration at 11.30 a.m., and another at 3 p.m. He was knowledgeable and enthusiastic. Crowds of both the young and the old followed him around the Museum and his talks as he led them from one interesting exhibit to another gave a new educational dimension to the Museum. In the course of his service, from 1912 to 1931, he became the best known and most popular member of the Museum staff (p.136).

On 29 April 1914 the First Commissioner of Works, Earl

Beauchamp, stated to the House of Lords: 'My Lords, I am happy to inform the noble Lord [Sudeley] that the system of appointing an official paid guide demonstrator has been tried in several cases with great success . . . The authorities of the Natural History Museum appointed a guide demonstrator in May 1912 and 7,392 people went round with the guide in that year. Last year the number rose to 17,022 . . . At the three museums a total of 84,465 has been shown the collections since the guide demonstrators were instituted . . . I should also like to take this opportunity of expressing our deep sense of obligation to the noble Lord who has given so much time and energy to forwarding this movement.' Lord Sudeley's part in thus extending the educational facilities of museums has long been forgotten, but it demonstrates nevertheless the importance of an enterprising, persistent, well-informed private individual in battling for the public good against opposition and inertia.

A dispute over encroachment upon the Natural History Museum's land brought much anxiety to Fletcher and the Trustees in 1911. The Science Collections and the Art Collections, which together originally formed the South Kensington Museum, were put under separate directors in 1893, but remained on the east side of Exhibition Road. The Natural History Museum is on the west side of Exhibition Road. In 1898, a Select Committee recommended that the Science Museum (as the Science Collections had been renamed in 1885) should be transferred to a new building on the west side of Exhibition Road behind the Natural History Museum and a boundary line between them was agreed in 1899 by the Treasury and the Office of Works. This ran from Exhibition Road to Queen's Gate and involved the loss of some land earlier allocated for expansion of the Natural History Museum. Immediately to the south of this boundary and deliberately separate, on account of fire risk, from the main Natural History Museum building was the Museum's Spirit Building. This one-storey building housed thousands of zoological research specimens preserved in bottles of alcohol and formalin, notably specimens of snakes, frogs, fishes, crustacea, worms and other invertebrates. It had cost some £20,000 to build and equip. The completion in 1909 of the splendid building for the Art Collections, which Queen Victoria had decreed should be called the Victoria and Albert Museum, brought up the need for the proposed Science Museum building behind the Natural History Museum. The scientific exhibits had never been adequately housed; Stephenson's 'Rocket' is said to have stood for years in the open 'like a broken-down traction-engine'; much valuable and irreplaceable material was stored in temporary sheds and the galleries of the old building were very vulnerable to total loss by fire. There was no dispute over the desirability, indeed the urgency, of 'a dignified and ample home' for its primarily engineering and industrial material and also for a geological museum as part of, or in proximity to, it. The difficulty arose over the limited area now available for all this and for the future expansion of the Natural History Museum. The Office of Works, being responsible for the new buildings of the Science Museum, eyed covetously the land within the Natural History Museum's 1899 boundary. The Trustees anxiously resolved to maintain their right to it. Both sides had justifiable claims and did not want to oppose each other, but were forced to do so.

In June 1910, after an offer of £100,000 towards the cost of the Science Museum building by the Board of Management of the Royal Commission for the Exhibition of 1851, which had surprisingly large financial resources, the First Commissioner of Works, through Sir Schomberg McDonnell, wrote to the Director of the Natural History Museum stating that it was proposed to demolish the Museum's Spirit Building and erect a new building to the west of the Museum, between it and the Queen's Gate road, to construct the Science Museum on the ground immediately to the north of the Natural History Museum and put a private road between them to act as a safeguard against fire. The Trustees naturally objected strongly to this proposed violation of the 1899 agreement. They had lost land already; what they now had was requisite for their future needs and accommodation was already becoming cramped. On 22 March 1911 the Trustees repeated their objections and noted that 'the proposed scheme involves the demolition of buildings specially constructed during the last twenty-eight years, upon which (and their fittings) the large sum of £38,000 has been spent out of funds voted by Parliament. The Trustees cannot be a party to what they consider an indefensible waste of public money.' The First Commissioner of Works evidently thought the matter settled against the Trustees when he informed them on 6 April 1911 'His Majesty's Ministers have decided that such a revision cannot be avoided in view of the urgent necessity for the building of a Science Museum'.

Meanwhile, the danger to the future of the Natural History Museum had become widely known. Sir Henry Roscoe wrote to *The Times* on 8 May 1911 suggesting that the Natural History Museum's spirit collections should be removed to a cheaper and less dangerous site elsewhere. His letter prompted a letter in *The Times* of 13 May 1911 from A.E. Shipley, Master of Christ's College, Cambridge, who emphasized that 'the specimens in spirit are an integral part of the entire collection and that a natural history collection of which the spirit-collections are kept elsewhere would be about as useful as a library from which all books of reference had been banished. The spirit-specimens are absolutely essential for the normal, every-day work of the Museum.' *The Times, The Morning Post, The Daily News, The Westminster Gazette* and *The Saturday Review* all took up this controversial matter. 'Hands off the Natural History Museum', wrote the editor of *The Saturday Review* on 13 May 1911. 'This, we are sure, will be the feeling of the public the moment it gets wind of the nefarious design to grab a portion of the Museum gardens — a design approved of course by the Office of Works . . . Why all this secrecy? Why this hurry? The Natural History Museum is in possession. The ground debated is its rightful property. The so-called "Science" buildings are mere squatters, allowed, foolishly perhaps, by the Trustees but without any title or claim to ownership, still less to expansion. The Natural History Museum is a great and growing national work — it wants room, and room it must have . . . Better have no "Science Museum" than that the Natural History should suffer.' The same issue of *The Saturday Review* carried a more temperate, well-informed and fair review of the situation entitled 'The trespass on the Natural History Museum'. A letter of the same quality from N. Charles Rothschild, Chairman of the Sub-Committee A of the Colonial Office Entomological Research Committee, argued in particular for the increased space needed not only for its stuffed animals and skeletons, but for a considerable expansion of its entomological department already too cramped and unable to meet the ever-increasing public demands upon it by stock-breeders, doctors, agriculturists and others. Mr. Asquith, the Prime Minister, can hardly have expected then to receive on 29 May 1911 a memorial signed by nearly 600 members of scientific societies, the Royal Society prominent among them; there were also those of the general public collected independently by the members and subscribers of Lloyds, probably at Charles Rothschild's suggestion. These signatures, numbering in all about 830, certainly testified to the live and widespread national interest: they included those of such venerable figures as Sir Joseph Hooker, Alfred Russel Wallace and Sir Archibald Geikie. The memorial concluded that 'the experience of the last thirty years proves beyond a shadow of doubt, in our opinion, that the whole of the unoccupied part of the site which has hitherto been reserved for the Natural History Museum is barely sufficient for the extensions which will be required in a future which is by no means remote . . . the maintenance in its integrity of the site which was secured to the Natural History Museum by the delimitation of its northern boundary by the Treasury and the Office of Works in 1899 is of vital importance to the future efficiency of that Museum.' There were also resolutions in May 1911 from the Zoological Society, the Linnean Society and the Challenger Society, against the alienation of Natural History Museum

25. Sir Edwin Ray Lankester (1847-1929), zoologist,
    Director 1898-1907.

26. Old-style museum display case in main hall in 1914
exhibiting natural history material from the tragic Antarctic
expedition of Captain Robert Falcon Scott (1868-1912) with
his widow Lady Scott (later Lady Kennet) and their son
Peter (later Sir Peter Scott) viewing this (from *The Bystander*,
21 January 1914; drawing by Arthur Wall).

27. The fish gallery in the evening lit by electric light in 1911.

28. Formal presentation of cast of skeleton of *Diplodocus carnegii* by Andrew Carnegie (1835-1919) on 12 May 1905, Lord Avebury speaking.

29. Sir Lazarus Fletcher (1854-1921), mineralogist, Keeper of Mineralogy 1880-1909, Director 1909-1919.

land. This safeguarded it for the time being and the site controversy ended in July 1911. The difficult situation within the Science Museum itself was partly relieved towards the end of 1911 by Imperial College giving up some accommodation; about 16,000 square feet (1,472 sq m).

The year 1912 was not without its crisis. The Museum was closed for a short time owing to the activities and threats of suffragists which continued into 1913: muffs, parcels and umbrellas, their usual weapons, had to be left with the cloakroom attendants. A sensational end to the year was the beginning of the long-standing controversy over the Piltdown skull (p.235).

The noted taxidermist James Rowland Ward of Piccadilly, who died at Boscombe on 28 December 1912 aged sixty-four, bequeathed an annual income of £500 for ten years to be used by his trustees out of the residuary estate for the purchase of specimens to be presented to the Natural History Museum. He had been engaged in taxidermy since 1862 and many of the exhibits at South Kensington and Tring had been done by him. On the death in 1951 of Mrs Lina Ward, James Rowland Ward's widow, the duty of distributing the residuary estate fell upon the Rowland Ward Trustees. They suggested to the Museum that its share should be used for groups of animals with appropriate backgrounds to form a Rowland Ward Memorial Exhibit. A position in the main hall being unsuitable, the Rowland Ward Trustees ultimately provided the superb groups of African mammals at the end of the west gallery on the first floor, which was completed and opened to the public in 1960.

In 1914 the Importation of Plumage (Prohibition) Bill was presented to Parliament. The Trustees welcomed this new attempt (p.72) to suppress the plumage trade which inflicted so much cruelty and was bringing so many beautiful birds nearer to extinction and they resolved to give it their hearty support. The plumage trade was, however, profitable. The opponents of the Plumage Bill, then before Parliament, accordingly convened a meeting at Burlington House, Piccadilly, against the proposed legislation. At this meeting C.E. Fagan, Assistant Secretary of the Natural History Museum, Sidney Harmer and Ogilvie-Grant represented the Museum's Trustees in their attempt to prohibit the import of feathers. Rather surprisingly, Dr (later Sir) Peter Chalmers Mitchell (1864-1945), Secretary of the Zoological Society of London, chose to appear on the platform in support of the plumage traders and, by reason of his office, thereby implied that the Zoological Society likewise supported them against the Natural History Museum and the bird protectionists. Fagan therefore requested Mitchell to state publicly before he addressed the meeting whether he was about to speak in his official capacity as representing the views of the Zoological Society's Council in opposition to the Bill, or whether he was about to express his own personal opinion. Being pressed for a definite and unequivocal reply, he was forced to admit that he had no mandate from the Zoological Society and attended merely in a private capacity. This was all the Museum representatives wanted. An eye-witness recorded that 'after the meeting Mitchell, livid with rage, stepped down from the platform and, coming up to where we were sitting, stopped in front of Fagan and positively hissed out "I demand of you a public apology!" He got an appropriate reply but no apology, public or private'. Thereafter Mitchell refused to shake hands or even to speak to Fagan. The retirement of Fletcher in 1919 as Director provided the opportunity of revenge (p.113). The Plumage Bill did not, however, receive royal assent until 1921 and not until 1922 did it become operative.

The outbreak of war in August 1914 suspended many activities as members of the staff belonging to the Territorial Army or the Reserve were called up for military service; others volunteered or were transferred to the clerical staffs of the Admiralty or the War Office. In the first month of the war, fifteen men left for the army and six were moved elsewhere. In October, fifteen more of the staff joined the forces. This depletion of staff continued until by July 1916 there were only twenty-six men of military age left, some of them active as members of the Anti-Aircraft Observer Corps or of the Red Cross ambulance service, and fourteen of these had been rejected on medical grounds. Lectures to soldiers of the Royal Army Medical Corps and the Royal Veterinary Corps on the anatomy of the horse, on army biscuits, and noxious insects were given in the galleries; and exhibits of special war-time significance were mounted, including large models and specimens of malarial mosquitoes, tsetse fly, plague flea, clothes' moth, louse and house fly.

Some of the galleries had been closed for use by a government department, but in January 1916 the Government decided to close totally the British Museum at Bloomsbury (except the Reading Room), the Natural History Museum, the Science Museum, the Tate Gallery, the National Portrait Gallery and the Wallace Collection. The closing of these national museums for a year, it was calculated, would pay for the war for a quarter of an hour. This decision naturally aroused strong public protest. The museums were being visited by many soldiers in London from overseas and, the Natural History Museum in particular, by wounded soldiers from convalescent homes in South Kensington. *The Weekly Dispatch* for 30 January 1916 stated that 'By closing the museums of London we shall save almost exactly one-fifth of the sums paid to members of Parliament for agreeing to agree with each other, whether right or wrong. Meanwhile the Jockey Club is going to ask the Government for more racing facilities... The Premier himself has gravely warned us about the urgent need for thrift. Anyone who saw him at his niece's wedding last Thursday would have been inclined to agree with him.' The newspaper then described the masses of floral decorations at St. Margaret's church, Westminster, and the bride's sumptuous, satin dress.

In defending the closure of the British Museum, the Speaker of the House of Commons spoke in a derogatory manner of 'deciphering hieroglyphs or cataloguing microlepidoptera' in war-time, but his second example of remoteness from actuality was certainly ill-chosen. Hermetically-sealed tins of army biscuits for troops in South Africa, Ceylon, the Sudan, Mauritius, Malta and Gibraltar were found, on

THE PRIME MINISTER: "M'yes, most interesting in peace time. Full of ancient survivals and funny old relics of bygone times, but a most expensive and extravagant luxury in time of war, you know!"
COLONIAL (in London for the first time): "*I see, Sir. Very much like the House of Commons, eh?*"

Fig. 15. Herbert Henry Asquith, Prime Minister 1905 to 1916, jovially justifying closure of the British Museum to an Australian soldier (from *The Passing Show*, 12 February 1916).

opening, to be alive with fat white maggots. Investigations of these by John Hartley Durrant (1863-1928) of the Natural History Museum in association with the War Office identified the culprits as the larvae of three species of flour moths (microlepidoptera) and two of beetles. Ironically Durrant was the officer appointed to the Museum to take charge of the Walsingham collection (p.85).

This naturally led to correspondence in *The Times*. One writer on 4 February 1916 referred the Speaker, as a Principal Trustee of the British Museum, to the Museum's own reports on research: 'Here it may be enough to mention assistance to the Admiralty in connexion with damage by insects to the envelope of an airship and a balloon; protection of aircraft and telephone apparatus against white ants; treatment of body vermin, with special reference to troops in the field; defence against locust plagues, against wood-eating ants and saw-flies, against numerous agricultural pests, cotton pests in Egypt, etc; assistance to governments, commercial companies, and individuals in British Possessions all over the world. Other departments take their share; one picks at random — study of anthrax-bearers in camels, disease-transmitting crustaceans in Egypt, parasitic worms in Gold Coast, Nyasaland, and West Indies, slugs devastating rubber plantations in Jamaica, fisheries of Britain, Lagos, the Cape, and elsewhere. Quite recently, I am told, the Botanical Department has given advice on woods suitable for aircraft and has reported on samples of fodder submitted by military authorities. These few instances are enough to show not merely the Imperial but the direct military value of the work being carried on by gentlemen whom our economists would take away to copy documents and add up figures. Even if the help were not so immediate, the work would be no less valuable. It would take too long to explain to politicians what men of science understand well enough, that the systematic study of "cataloguing" of the varied forms of life, even the minutest, constitutes the indispensable foundation for all this economic knowledge.'

Under the heading 'A voice from the Museum' *The Evening News* of 1 February 1916 printed another kind of protest:

> 'Said the bones of the sabre-toothed tiger
> To the Ichthyosaurus's cast,
> "How long do you think, my dear sir,
> This bally old war will last?
> I have watched for the past decade
> In seemingly endless parade,
> These human specimens pass my case,
> Do you think an end has come to their race —
> That their steps no longer re-echo the hall

Or their gibbering questions, that well recall
The voices I heard as my spirit left
Sped by the flint when my skull was cleft?''
The mammoth's head that hangs by the wall
His wide ears opened and heard it all,
And thus spake out with a trumpet call:
''The war is not over nor is man dead
(As they pass in the street I can see each head)
But the war will last, so I'll be bound,
As long as they think the policy's sound
To save the halfpence and waste the pound.'

These protestations had a surprising effect. The Natural History Museum was never completely closed, its attendance remained high, always above 400,000 visitors a year, and the guide-lecturer was kept busy all the time, explaining the exhibits to convalescent and overseas soldiers, and to the public in general. By the end of 1916, fifty-nine men of the Museum staff were serving in the Armed Forces and only one man of military age and passed as fit for service remained, and he had been exempted as indispensable; the elderly and the unfit not only maintained the collections and dealt with enquiries, but also served as special constables and ambulance workers.

A serious threat came early in 1918. By now the army of clerks necessary to keep men fighting elsewhere had grown so luxuriantly that the Government proposed to take over both museums at Bloomsbury and South Kensington and dismantle the exhibits for their accommodation. This frightening prospect caused the Linnean Society of London to summon a special meeting on 7 January 1918 and to adopt unanimously the following resolution for transmission to the Government:

'The Fellows of the Linnean Society in Meeting assembled desire to place upon record:— Their profound astonishment and alarm at the reported intention to dismantle the British Museum, including the Natural History Museum, in order to use it for Government offices: their emphatic protest at a procedure which must endanger priceless and irreplaceable possessions acquired at great cost and infinite labour during the last two hundred years, constituting the most splendid museum in existence and the recognised centre of systematic scientific research: their dismay at a resolution which may paralyze scientific activities that during the past three years have been devoted to work intimately connected with the prosecution of the war; and at the expenditure of a large sum in adapting unsuitable buildings, whilst other and more suitable accommodation might be provided at much less cost: and finally to emphasize the disgrace which must accrue to the Nation in the eyes of the world, by the evidence thus afforded of the inability of the Government to appreciate the essential value to the Nation of scientific assistance such as the British Museum has rendered and is capable of rendering.'

This, and representations from elsewhere, held back the Government's grasping hand.

By no means everyone sympathised with the Museum's plight. One gentleman had protested in *The Daily News* of 10 January 1917 against the Government's requisition of Hotel Cecil 'thereby liquidating an apparently sound and prosperous business proposition' and suggested that 'consideration be given to the advisability of utilizing our very extensive museums for war purposes rather than the closing down of flourishing enterprises . . . the deprivation of a visit to a museum is not so urgent as the preservation of established business concerns'.

The major event of 1918 was, of course, the end of the First World War. The armistice of 11 November brought relief at last to the suffering war-wearied peoples on both sides, and on 28 November the Natural History Museum flew its Union Jack in celebration. On 16 December the whole Museum was re-opened to the public. It had come through the war unscathed; sixty-five members of its staff had served in the Armed Forces, E.E. Austen gaining a D.S.O., W. Campbell Smith and A.K. Totton the Military Cross, but thirteen had been killed. Gradually the staff returned and set to work on the accessions of specimens which, despite the war, had continued to crowd into the Museum.

By the death on 19 February 1919 of Frederick Ducane Godman (1834-1919) in his eighty-sixth year, the Museum lost a generous bene-factor who had served it well as a Trustee since 1896. A man of wealth, he had spent most of his life in studying the birds and insects of Mexico and Central America and, together with his friend and collaborator Osbert Salvin (1835-1898), had given the Museum the enormous zoo-logical collections they had assembled and used for their *Biologia Centrali-Americana: Zoology, Botany and Archaeology*, published at their own expense in 215 parts or 63 volumes with 1,677 plates (900 coloured) between 1879 and 1915. This contains descriptions of more than 19,000 species of insects new to science. Their collections received by the Museum included some 520,000 bird skins, more than 100,000 specimens of Lepidoptera and 82,000 specimens of Coleoptera, as well as hundreds of specimens of other insects, very many of them type-specimens, for neither before or since has there been such extensive natural history investigation of this rich, diversified area.

Shortly after Godman's death, his friends formed a memorial fund committee to commemorate visibly within the Museum Godman's and

Salvin's contribution to science, intending that the balance of any money collected should serve as the nucleus of a fund to provide the Museum with specimens by promoting biological exploration. In 1891 he had married Mary Alice Chaplin, who greatly encouraged him in his endeavours. Dame Alice Godman and her two daughters offered the Museum £5,000 as capital to establish a Godman Memorial Exploration Fund. The Trustees much appreciated this generous act and likewise, one trusts, have the many young naturalists whose travels have been supported from it. The committee, with Lord Rothschild (Walter Rothschild) as chairman and the efficient, indefatigable Charles E. Fagan as honorary treasurer, commissioned Sir Thomas Breck to design a mural tablet, which after his death was completed by Arnold Wright and set in the wall of the main hall central staircase.

Care-worn and often ill, Fletcher, who had been knighted in 1916, was happy to retire on 3 March 1919. On 24 February 1919 he wrote rather sadly to Sir Frederic Kenyon, Director of the British Museum, that 'as for the last ten years, there is nothing to show except the keeping of the peace, and keeping people at peace with each other so far as that is possible. I was anxious to keep going till the end of the war, for it was obvious that difficulties were likely to arise; now and then it seemed impossible that I could do so; if you had not been at hand, always ready to give a helping hand, I should have despaired.'

Now all he wanted to do was to glide away to a quiet retirement in Westmorland, but he did not long enjoy even this, for he died on 21 January 1921. It is evident that the patience, care and consideration Fletcher gave to everything caused him to be as well-liked for his character as he was esteemed for his intellectual standing and achievements. An obituary recorded that 'his simplicity and consideration for others gave him a charm of character which made him beloved by all who knew him. Nothing could exceed his sympathy and loyalty in friendship. . . Himself the soul of truth and honour he could not bear dishonesty or lack of straightforwardness on the part of others and any contact with unscrupulous or underhand action caused him intense pain and distress.' Knowing the Royal Society background to the three memorials, signed by eminent scientists, relating to Museum appointments and the conduct of the Trustees, he must have suffered indeed.

However, the main and often the whole burden of administration had been carried neither by Fletcher nor by his predecessor Lankester, but by the Museum's Assistant Secretary, Charles E. Fagan (1855-1921) (p.97). Flower himself had said without Fagan's assumption of the administrative duties he could not have carried on his own work in the Museum. As *The Field* said after his death, 'Directors came and went but Mr Fagan remained as the capable business member of the permanent official staff, organising everything, supporting and carrying projects to completion, consulted, trusted and liked by everybody' except, it may be added, by the Secretary of the Zoological Society after the 1914 Plumage Bill incident (p.105). He had two years to serve before retirement. A capable administrator being needed for the difficult period of post-war reconstruction, the Trustees and in particular Lord Rothschild thought it just and appropriate to appoint Fagan as Director for his last two years. He had, however, the wrong background. His life had been devoted not to scientific endeavour, but to promoting the scientific endeavours and reputations of others. He was the youngest son of George Fagan who had been H.M. Minister at Caracas, Venezuela, and the grandson of Robert Fagan, H.M. Consul General for Sicily. In his youth he had thus become acquainted with the Italian exiles Mazzini, Garibaldi and Panizzi, and it was probably through Panizzi's influence that he entered the British Museum in 1873 at the age of eighteen as a clerk. From Bloomsbury he was transferred as a clerk to South Kensington and, being so obviously a talented methodical reliable administrator, he was promoted to Assistant of the First Class in 1887 and then to Assistant Secretary in 1889, rises both merited and welcome, for his salary had been disgracefully low. Thereafter he managed the Museum for Lankester and Flower, served as honorary treasurer to various committees and became British representative on the International Commission for the Protection of Nature. He never pretended to be a scientist but he certainly came to possess a wide general knowledge of scientific matters.

The probability of Fagan's·appointment as director of the institution to which he had given such long, dedicated and fruitful service brought forth the predictable reaction, a memorial from Fellows of the Royal Society to prevent it and to limit the freedom of action of the Trustees of the British Museum. Already in January 1919 the interested group had brought their influence to bear upon the President of the Royal Society, Professor J.J. Thomson (1856-1940), Master of Trinity College, Cambridge. Thomson was a very distinguished physicist, who as President during the war had nobly defied those Fellows keen to evict their fellow-members of German descent from the Society and his reputation stood high, but he had no particular interest in natural history or knowledge of the British Museum. In view of the representations made to him, he accordingly wrote to Sir Frederic Kenyon that 'I think it is my duty, as President of the Royal Society, to let you know there is the strongest possible feeling among men of science that it is necessary for the progress of Natural History in this country that this important post should be filled, as it has been in the past, by a man of the highest possible distinction; they would regard it as a calamity if this tradition were broken'. Fagan himself soon learned what was afoot, for he had many friends and only one enemy. On 13 February, 1919, he wrote to Kenyon that, 'I hear that Chalmers Mitchell, Secretary of the Zoological Society, who, by the way, is shortly resigning the post, is actively interesting himself against me in the matter of the Directorship' (p.106).

By 27 February 1919, enough impressive signatures had been gathered for a memorial to be published in *The Times*, the same method as had been used to prevent initially the appointment of Lazarus Fletcher in 1898.

'To the Editor of *The Times*:

Sir, The Director of the British Museum (Natural History) is about to retire, and we learn with deep apprehension that the principal trustees, with whom the appointment rests, have received, or are about to receive, from the general body of trustees a recommendation to pass over the claims of scientific men and to appoint a lay official, who is at present assistant secretary. The former directors, Sir Richard Owen, Sir William Flower, and Sir Ray Lankester, like the present director, Sir Lazarus Fletcher, were all distinguished scientific men. The Natural History Museum is a scientific institution. There is a large staff of scientific keepers and assistants. The director has to represent natural history to the public, to other scientific institutions at home, in the Dominions and colonies, and in foreign countries, and to the many Government Departments with which the Museum has relations. He must represent it with knowledge and authority. There are few posts with such possibilities of advancing the natural history sciences, of making them useful to the nation, and of interpreting them to the public. The existence of the post is a great stimulus to the zeal and ambition of zoologists and geologists.

The argument alleged in favour of the recommendation are trival. It is stated that a former director was allowed by the trustees to leave the administrative details to the member of the clerical staff whom it is proposed to promote, that he performed these duties with ability, and during the tenure of the present director retained and extended his powers. It is urged that the tenure of the new director would be short, as he would have to retire in two years under the age limit. It is pleaded that promotion would entitle him to a larger pension and that he need not be called director, but only acting-director.

Plainly, if the assistant secretary be the only man who knows the details of administration it is important that the permanent director should be appointed at once, in order to have the opportunity of learning them before taking them over. In actual fact there is nothing in the administrative work of the directorship that could not be learned in a few weeks or months by any person of ordinary intelligence. At least two of the present keepers are eligible for the vacancy, have attained the necessary scientific standing, and have ample experience of the Museum itself. To pass over these or several eminent and eligible men not on the staff in favour of one of the ordinary office staff would be an affront to scientific men and of grave detriment to science.

W. Boyd Dawkins F.R.S., Manchester
J. Cossar Edwart F.R.S., Edinburgh
F. W. Gamble F.R.S., Birmingham
J. S. Gardiner F.R.S., Cambridge
Walter Garstang D.Sc., Leeds
E.S. Goodrich F.R.S., Oxford
W.A. Herdman F.R.S., Liverpool
S.J.Hickson F.R.S., Manchester
J.P. Hill F.R.S., London
W.E. Hoyle D.Sc.

Arthur Keith F.R.S.
J. Graham Kerr F.R.S., Glasgow
E.W. McBride F.R.S.
W.C. McIntosh F.R.S., St Andrews
J.E. Marr F.R.S., Cambridge
P. Chalmers Mitchell C.B.E. F.R.S.
E.B. Poulton F.R.S., Oxford
R.C. Punnett F.R.S., Cambridge
A.E. Shipley F.R.S., Cambridge
W.J. Sollas F.R.S., Oxford
Jethro J.H. Teall F.R.S.
J. Arthur Thomson LL.D., Aberdeen'

This letter gave the Principal Trustees no option but to reject Fagan. Fletcher wrote to this effect on 3 March 1919 to Kenyon and remarked that 'The present agitation is probably being stirred by Chalmers Mitchell who is very skilled in the memorialistic method and knows by experience and success all its possibilities. He got his own post by a successful use of the method. Nearly all the signatories have attacked the Trustees in the same way again and again. . . I have been a Fellow of the Royal Society for thirty years and know the line the Fellows will take'. He wrote this at 10pm on 3 March. It was his last act as Director, for his directorship ended at midnight. There were plenty of distinguished men who would have challenged on Fagan's behalf the statements in this letter, but Fagan dissuaded them. He told Kenyon:

'I am receiving many letters from scientific and other friends offering to reply on my behalf and sending me the draft of what they propose to say. I am strongly discouraging such action out of a sense of loyalty to the Trustees... You will realize that it is hard for me to have to submit to a malicious and unjust attack without my being free to expose it in a manner which would place a very different complexion on the whole matter.'

The Times letter did not, however, go completely unchallenged. Thus Sidney Harmer, Keeper of Zoology at the Museum, wrote to *Nature* that Fagan's work 'has been essentially scientific, and that his services in rendering the national museum a scientific institution had been exceptionally great'. W.R. Ogilvie-Grant wrote to *The Times* that the Trustees 'might certainly be supposed to know better what is for the benefit of the Museum than a number of university professors who, however individually able, deal with a side of natural history which has little or no connexion with the making and improvement of museum collections ... I served under Owen, Flower, Lankester, and Fletcher, and have had more than thirty years' experience of Mr Fagan as an enthusiast for the Museum, an encourager of scientific work, and as an administrator, and I should most warmly welcome his promotion to the post of which he has already done so much of the work.'

Harmer also strongly supported Fagan in a letter to a signatory of *The Times* letter. This was a generous tribute and all the more so because it came from a man who stood most to gain by Fagan's disappointment. In fact, Harmer behaved most honourably throughout. Unaware that Fagan would like to be considered for the directorship, he had put himself forward as a candidate in December 1918. Fagan, not knowing this, asked Harmer whether he and his colleagues would be willing to serve under him. Harmer informed Kenyon that on this matter he could only speak for himself, but that his relations with Fagan throughout had been most cordial, 'that I have invariably found him helpful in counsel and that I have a high admiration for his character, and administrative ability, which is exceptionally great'.

On 8 January 1919 he wrote to Fagan himself:

'After full consideration, I have decided that I do not wish to be regarded as a candidate for the office as against you. I suppose there can be no doubt that with the end of the war the recovery of normal conditions, reconstruction and new developments will be matters to which the new head of the Museum will have to give his special attention. The qualifications which appear to me necessary for this work, so important for the general welfare of the Museum, are long experience, involving an intimate practical acquaintance with all details of administration, conspicuous tact and *savoir faire*, and unerring judgment. All these are your special possession, and I believe there is no-one so well fitted as yourself to take charge of the direction of affairs at a time when matters so important for the future of the Museum are likely to come up for settlement. The great services you have rendered during your long period of office are too well known to need further comment from me than the remark that, with your other qualifications, they appear to me to establish a claim which it would give me sincere pleasure to see recognized by the Principal Trustees.'

The hands of the Principal Trustees had been fettered, however, by the letter to *The Times* in 1919 as they had been in 1898. There were several scientifically distinguished applicants for the directorship, among them D'Arcy Wentworth Thompson. Unable now to appoint Fagan, the Principal Trustees chose Harmer, but Fagan's merits were recognized by a rise of status from Assistant Secretary to Secretary and an increase of salary. Harmer became Director on 12 March 1919 but decided to retain his position as Keeper of Zoology. Fagan's relations with the new Director remained as friendly and helpful as ever, but he became seriously ill late in 1920. He officially retired in mid-January 1921 but, alas, he had only two weeks more to live. He died on 1 February 1921. The Natural History Museum can never again have so long-serving an official and never one more dedicated to its interests and successful in achieving them.

10

Between the Wars
1919 - 1938

SIDNEY FREDERIC HARMER (1862-1950) had had a distinguished academic career in Cambridge before being appointed Keeper of Zoology at the Natural History Museum in 1907 and a period of fruitful service in the Museum before becoming Director in 1919. He belonged to an old East Anglian family and was born in Norwich on 9 March 1862. His father Frederick William Harmer (1835-1923), a wool merchant, gained renown as a keen amateur geologist and wrote *The Pliocene Mollusca of Great Britain* (1914-1925). After studying at University College, London, from 1878 to 1881, and qualifying there for the degree of B.Sc. (London), Harmer entered King's College, Cambridge, in Michaelmas 1881, gaining part 1 of the natural sciences tripos in 1883 and part 2 in 1884. He was awarded the degree of Sc.D. in 1897. In 1892 he became Superintendent of the Cambridge University Museum of Zoology, a position which gave him considerable experience in the administration of a zoological museum, and, although his own research was primarily on Polyzoa his zoological interests extended widely enough for him to edit, with A.E. Shipley, *The Cambridge Natural History* (10 vols, 1895-1909). His duties at Cambridge as Superintendent included the general management of the museum, the registration of all specimens received, the preparation of catalogues, the care of stores and of the museum library, and the preparation of annual reports. Before 1909, he had visited the principal museums of natural history in the United States of America, notably those of New York, Washington, Philadelphia, Yale University, Pittsburgh and Chicago, several on the continent of Europe and also those in South Africa at Cape Town and Pretoria. In 1904 he was President of the Museums Association. This background of museum

117

-experience, added to his zoological eminence, obviously convinced the Trustees and he was appointed Keeper of Zoology in 1907 following the retirement of Ray Lankester. During the succeeding years, his recommendations came frequently before the Trustees and gained their approval and confidence; he evidently impressed them as sound, steady-going and enterprising. Moreover, his appointment as Director restored the so often maligned Trustees to the favour of the lobbying zoological world.

As W.T. Calman said in an obituary of Harmer (*Obituary Notices of Fellows of the Royal Society* 20: 359-371, 1951) about his move from Cambridge to South Kensington, 'it may easily be supposed that he found the atmosphere of his new post very different from that of the one he had just left. In the first place, he was required to attend to a vast amount of trivial administrative detail (not that this had been entirely absent at Cambridge) with completely inadequate clerical assistance, or with none at all. In the second place, the junior staff of the department, few of whom had any university training, were mostly narrow specialists, quite satisfied to ignore all the broader aspects of zoology, but yet all too ready to resent any of the higher posts being filled otherwise than by promotion from the lower grades. On the other hand the academic zoologists of London, very few of whom ever entered the Museum building, remained ignorant of its work and even thought that it contained nothing beyond the specimens exhibited in the public galleries. There were thus ample opportunities for the exercise of tact both within the Museum and outside, and no one could ever accuse Harmer of any deficiency in this respect.'

Through Harmer's initiative, when Keeper of Zoology, the Natural History Museum became the major centre of whale research. The Cetacea, i.e. whales, porpoises and dolphins, had been a special interest of William Flower's from at least 1864 onwards. When Director, he had been able to add a whale room, a temporary structure of galvanised iron, into which the specimens of Cetacea, originally inconveniently located in the basement, were moved for exhibition. This was opened to the public on Whit Monday 1897. Thereafter, work on the Cetacea stayed for some years in abeyance. Harmer's interest had been even longer in abeyance, in fact since 1893 when he and Thomas Southwell had published notes on a specimen of Sowerby's Beaked Whale, *Mesoplodon bidens*, stranded on the Norfolk coast. Now Keeper of Zoology, he set about replacing the skins of dolphins in the whale-room by plaster casts as specimens became available. The stranding of a Lesser Rorqual, *Balaenoptera acutorostrata*, in September 1911, at Aberystwyth and the appearance soon afterwards off Penzance of a shoal of Pilot Whales, *Globicephala melaena*, and the stranding of one, brought them to his special attention; but he learned of these events only through newspaper notices and much time was accordingly lost before specimens were obtained for the Museum through the Board of Trade. Harmer, however, lost no time in informing the Trustees.

Since the fourteenth century, if not earlier, whales, porpoises and dolphins have been recognized in the British Isles as Royal Fish or Fishes Royal. In a statute enacted in the seventeenth year of the reign of Edward II, *De Praerogativa Regis*, the sovereign's entitlement to whales and the sturgeon was established and it covered stranded animals and those caught near the coast. Along certain stretches of the coastline the right to Fishes Royal has passed from the crown to landowner, corporation or holder of a crown appointment. One such stretch, from the Naze, Essex, to a point near Newhaven, comes under the Lord Warden of the Cinque Ports. Scottish law, likewise recognizes the right of the Crown to Royal Fish, although its provisions are such that most

Fig. 16. Portrayal of a distressing incident on the Welsh coast as reported in September 1953 by telegram from H.M. Coastguard at Fishguard, Dyfed, South Wales: 'Countess of Wales in advanced state of decomposition stranded at Fishguard Pembrokeshire... upside down in deep water between rocks accessible only by boat and with difficulty'. This cartoon by Peter Green put on the Museum notice-board illustrated the lady's plight. The Countess proved to be the carcase of a whale, the Lesser Rorqual, *Balaenoptera acutorostrata*. There was no obituary in *The Times*.

cetaceans of a length less than 25 feet (7.6m) cannot be claimed on behalf of the Crown. On this medieval legal foundation has been built much of the present knowledge of the distribution and movements of Cetacea around the British Isles. F.C. Fraser (p.190) summarized some results obtained from the availability of stranded specimens in his historical paper on 'Royal fishes: the importance of the dolphin' in R.J. Harrison's *Functional Anatomy of Marine Mammals:* 1-44 (1977).

At Harmer's instigation, the Trustees on 28 October 1911 approved the suggestion that the Board of Trade should be made aware of the desirability of early information being given to the Museum about stranded Cetacea. The original intent was simply to obtain specimens. Harmer soon realized the possibility of gaining general information by the assistance of the Board of Trade and the Admiralty. These bodies readily co-operated. In June 1912 the Board of Trade informed the Museum that a circular would be issued to all Receivers of Wreck instructing them to telegraph direct to the Museum particulars of stranded whales with a view to affording the Museum an opportunity of securing specimens before the carcases were buried. The Trustees then applied to the Treasury for permission to buy a pair of whalers' overalls! Harmer, with Lydekker's help, prepared a pamphlet describing the different kinds of whales and by 1913 some 1,500 copies had been printed and sent to the Board of Trade for distribution among Receivers of Wreck.

The information gathered this way enabled Harmer to publish the first issue of a *Report on Cetacea stranded on the British Coasts during 1913* (1914), the first of several reports. As Director, Harmer maintained the same interest as he had shown as Keeper of Zoology. It was fortunate, therefore, that his retirement meant only a change of personnel, not of policy, as regards the recording of information on stranded Cetacea. Francis Charles Fraser (1903-1978), then an Assistant Keeper in the Department of Zoology, later Keeper, took over the compilation of Reports, which are still issued.

The pamphlet by Harmer and Lydekker has passed through several editions, two of which included a section on turtles. The latest edition, the fifth, was published in 1976 as *British Whales, Dolphins and Porpoises*. This records that by the end of 1974 a total of 1,810 identifications of stranded Cetacea had been made.

Harmer did not, however, limit his attention to British Cetacea. In a lecture on 'Whales and Whale Fisheries' delivered at the Royal Colonial Institute in January 1885, Flower had pointed out how excessive whaling in the North Atlantic had destroyed the once profitable whale fisheries and had been followed by the extermination, in a very cruel, avaricious and short-sighted manner, of the whales breeding on the New Zealand and Australian coasts, thus destroying another profitable whale industry. The situation had become far worse when Harmer turned his attention to whales and whaling.

In 1911 he directed the notice of the Trustees to the immense and unrestricted slaughter of whales in Antarctic seas, which could not go on for long without endangering the existence of the species; during the 1910-11 season 9,500 whales had been killed. The Trustees accordingly made representations to the Colonial Office for calling an international conference on measures to protect them against this excessive and alarming exploitation. In 1913, the Trustees again gave attention to the protection of Antarctic whales and dispatched Major G.E.H. Barrett-Hamilton with the Museum taxidermist, P. Stammwitz, to South Georgia for an enquiry in October 1913, but unfortunately Barrett-Hamilton died suddenly of heart-failure on 17 January 1914 after only nine or ten weeks of investigation and observation. In 1915 Harmer put before the Trustees an analysis of Antarctic whaling statistics which showed that since 1904 the Humpback Whale, *Megaptera novaeangliae*, which had then provided 90% of the whales killed, had meanwhile so declined as to raise anxiety about its likely extinction and that in consequence the whalers had now engaged in the large-scale destruction of the Fin Whale, *Balaenoptera physalus*, and the Blue Whale, *Balaenoptera musculus*. In 1919, with the First World War now ended and the need for protection of the Humpback, and probably the Right Whale, increasingly urgent, the Trustees again made representation to the Colonial Office for international action. They welcomed the Colonial Office regulation in 1920 for a close season from 1 June to 15 October every year at South Georgia. The preservation of these grand, endangered animals and the investigation of their structure and habits have continued to be major fields of interest and action for the Natural History Museum. To Harmer especially belongs the credit for initiating and then sustaining them.

During Harmer's first year as Director, the Museum received the Selous collection of big game trophies shot and preserved by Frederick Courteney Selous (1853-1917). Although he had made his livelihood by killing African big game as a hunter and by writing about his prey as a naturalist and traveller, F.C. Selous was far from being an indiscriminate, commercial killer; he was scientifically interested and keenly observant and, had he lived later, would probably have preferred the camera to the gun. From the age of nineteen, when after schooling at Rugby he went out to Africa to become an elephant hunter, until his death in battle at the age of sixty-four in German East Africa (now Tanzania), his life continually embraced adventure, hardship and danger and when these were lacking, he sought them.

Charles Fagan had written in *The Field* of 13 January 1917 that 'Nowhere outside his home circle will this great and chivalrous hunter and field naturalist be more missed or mourned than at the Natural History Museum, where he was wont to spend a great deal of his leisure time and where he had many friends always ready to welcome him cordially. His association with the museum started so long ago as 1881, when he sent to the Department of Zoology, which was then in course of being removed from Bloomsbury to South Kensington, a series of 144 mammals from Rhodesia. Since that year, he kept up a regular intercourse with the authorities.' Fagan then listed some of the more notable specimens with which he had enriched the museum. They included fine specimens of the greater kudu *(Tragelaphus strepiceros)*, white-tailed gnu *(Tragelaphus gnou)*, springbok *(Antidorcas marsupialis)*, bontebok *(Damaliscus dorcas dorcas)*, blesbok *(Damaliscus dorcas phillipsi)*, nyala *(Tragelaphus angasi)*, sable antelope *(Hippotragus niger)*, and Osborn's caribou *(Rangifer tarandus osborni)*, several mammals, notably the Selous sitatunga *(Tragelaphus spekei selousi)*, and the Mashonaland eland *(Tragelaphus oryx livingstonei)* were named in his honour.

Friends of Selous immediately thought that so brave, modest, kind-hearted and successful a naturalist, pioneer, sportsman and explorer should be nationally commemorated and nowhere better than in the Natural History Museum. By June 1917 the Selous Memorial Committee, with E.S. Montagu as chairman and, of course, the trustworthy Charles Fagan as honorary treasurer, had decided to erect a bas-relief in the Natural History Museum, the Trustees having gladly given permission. They commissioned William Robert Colton (1867-1921) to sculpture it. His memorial took the form of a life-size bronze bust of the great hunter. Kensington Boy Scouts and ex-service men from Selous's own Legion of Frontiersmen formed a guard of honour on the stairway when on 11 June 1920 E.N. Buxton unveiled it in the presence of a very distinguished gathering, including Viscount Grey of Falloden, who accepted the memorial on behalf of the Trustees, Lord Rothschild and Sir Robert Baden-Powell the Chief Scout. Grey and others spoke movingly from their personal knowledge of Selous: then all stood silent and through the stillness of the great hall there rose and fell, loud and vibrant, the unforgettable notes of the British Army's farewell to its valiant dead, the 'Last Post' sounded by two buglers of the Legion of Frontiersmen.

In 1923 Stanley Baldwin, as Chancellor of the Exchequer in the Conservative Government, introduced a bill for charging admission to Museums. The Fees Increase Bill passed its second reading. It led, however, to protests by Muirhead Bone, Sir Arthur Evans, John Galsworthy, H.A.L. Fisher, Ralph Hodgson, R.B. Cunningham

Graham, J. Graham Kerr, E.W. Macbride, Cecil Roberts, George Bernard Shaw and others, and a leader in *The Times* of 20 March 1923. Mr Punch K.C. had himself portrayed on 21 March 1923, in *Punch* of course, tearing up the admission charge poster. The same journal carried a report by E.V. Lucas of the trial of Mr Stanley Baldwin, Chancellor of the Exchequer 'for his murderous attack on the liberties

A CONTEMPTIBLE ECONOMY.

Fig. 17. Mr Punch demonstrates his opinion of the proposed entrance fee for the British Museum (from *Punch*, 21 March 1923).

of the English nation... The accused man had borne an excellent character for many years and was the author of the statement, now famous, that the salvation of the world lay in respecting words of one syllable — Faith, Hope, Love and Work. It was not so much the character of this aphorism, as the fact that it was uttered in the House of Commons, that made it remarkable... The British Museum belonged to Britons, and, having always been free, should be free for ever.' However, it was not Mr Punch's eloquence that determined the issue. The most decisive factor was probably the cost of installing turnstiles and modifying entrances, estimated at £500 a time, and the wages of extra attendants, thirty-two shillings (£1.60) a week plus bonus; on 23 March 1923 the Government withdrew the bill.

Among other matters concerning the Museum in 1923 were: an arrangement with the British Broadcasting Company permitting museum staff to broadcast; the dispatch of an expedition under the polar explorer and naturalist Captain (later Sir) George Hubert Wilkins (1888-1958) to tropical Australia, to procure specimens of its vanishing fauna, the subject of his book *Undiscovered Australia* (1928); the unveiling of the memorials to Frederick Ducane Godman and Osbert Salvin (p.111), and a memorial portrait of Alfred Russel Wallace (1823-1913); and the death of Charles Rothschild (p.140), known to the world in general as a public-spirited and able financier, but esteemed in the Museum as an authority on fleas (Siphonaptera) and a promoter of nature reserves. Rothschild's assets were valued at probate as £2,250,000, upon which death duties of £915,000 were paid. He had already made a deed of gift of his collection of Siphonaptera. He then bequeathed £10,000 to the British Museum upon trust to provide income in perpetuity for the salary of a proper custodian of his collection of Siphonaptera, and other parasitic insects, which, received in 1923, contained at least 250,000 specimens. Carl Jordan (p.140), his collaborator at Tring, received £3,000.

Harmer's last year of office was 1926. A matter for pride was an exhibit in the main hall of African elephants forming a habitat group within a bay on the east side, for which trees and vegetation had been specially brought from East Africa. To a young person, it was one of the most dramatic and impressive sights in the Museum. It cost a very large amount of time and money and in due course was swept away during one of the periodic drastic alterations and removals to which the main hall exhibits are still subjected.

One of Harmer's last acts as Director was the founding of a quarterly Natural History Museum periodical of a popular, but scholarly, character, *Natural History Magazine*, emulating the *British Museum Quarterly* founded by Kenyon at Bloomsbury in May 1926. The first number appeared in January 1927. Thereafter, responsibility for its publication rested upon Harmer's successor, C. Tate Regan, who brought it to an end in October 1936, with its fortieth number completing volume five. It had not been a financial success.

Sir Sidney Harmer, who had been knighted in 1920, ended his museum service by retiring at the age of sixty-five on 9 March 1927. He returned to Cambridge, where he had been made an Honorary Fellow of his old College, King's, and died there on 22 October 1950 at the age of eighty-eight. He had seen the Museum develop smoothly through a very difficult time, without having made any marked changes, and there had been no friction between him and the Trustees. He had revived the Museum's interest in whales and their preservation and had induced the British Government to send out the *Discovery* Expedition, so important to Antarctic zoology. C. Tate Regan, who had succeeded him as Keeper of Zoology, now succeeded him as Director.

Temperamentally the two, although equally eminent intellectually, diverged remarkably and the Trustees probably soon noticed the difference between the East Anglian equanimity of Harmer and the more Irish volatility of Regan, who suffered far from gladly much frustration in his plans for the Museum owing to financial stringency.

Charles Tate Regan (1878-1943) was the first Director to have spent his whole scientific life in the Natural History Museum; he was also the first never to receive the customary knighthood. Other honours, however, came to him as tributes to his zoological eminence and industry and were indeed more appropriate. Although of Irish descent, he was born at Sherborne, Dorset, on 1 February 1878, his father being then a music master at Sherborne School. He went to school at Derby, where his ability and his enthusiasm for natural history led his science master to suggest that, after a training in biological science, he should seek employment in the Natural History Museum. This suggestion determined his whole career; he might otherwise have devoted his life to music as his parents had. In 1897 he entered Queen's College, Cambridge, studying there under two stimulating zoological teachers, Adam Sedgwick and J. Stanley Gardiner, and graduated in 1900. Next year he was appointed as an Assistant in the Department of Zoology at the Natural History Museum. The acting Keeper, Ray Lankester, placed him under Georges Albert Boulenger (1858-1937) to work on fishes and that determined the nature of his research for the rest of his life. Boulenger, a Belgian-born zoologist who specialized in amphibia, reptiles and fish and, after his retirement, on roses, was a prodigious worker with high standards, which he impressed upon his young assistant. Regan too became a brilliant systematist, with approaching 250 papers on fish to his credit as well as the then standard book, *The*

Freshwater Fishes of the British Isles (1911). Thus he justly deserved election to the Royal Society in 1917 at the age of thirty-nine, which is early for a taxonomic worker, followed by an honorary D.Sc. from the University of Durham in 1929. He attained the rank of Assistant First Class (later termed Assistant Keeper) in 1907, and became Deputy Keeper of Zoology in 1919 and Keeper in 1921.

Whilst Keeper, Regan had become acquainted with the pressing problem of finding storage space for the continually growing collections in the Museum. Indeed, most of the zoological material which interested him had necessarily to be preserved in alcohol. Thus a new building for such specimens became his special concern and the final design for the New Spirit Building, erected between 1920 and 1930, to the north-west of the Museum, was largely of his making. He regarded this as his most important service to the Museum. Preoccupation with the problems of securing new accommodation and renovating old was to be with him throughout his directorship. Certainly conditions had become inconvenient for those trying to work on the collections, especially for the entomologists, whose work on insects of economic importance was important to the Empire Marketing Board. According to N.D. Riley, the turning point came when two Trustees, a Prime Minister and an ex-Prime Minister, on a tour of inspection, became wedged in a narrow passage between cabinets and work-tables, and readily agreed that things really were becoming intolerable. The figurative turning point was literally the lack of one.

Already in January 1927 J. Stanley Gardiner, Professor of Zoology in the University of Cambridge, had called public attention, by a letter in *The Times*, to the gross overcrowding of specimens in the Museum, of which the staff and the Trustees were painfully aware. Galleries suitable for exhibition purposes had to be used instead for storage, because there existed no room elsewhere. It posed a major problem for all concerned. They accordingly welcomed the setting up of a Royal Commission on National Museums and Galleries in 1927 which issued an interim report in 1928, recommending immediate expenditure on new buildings of £183,000 and further expenditure of £124,000 on buildings less urgently required. Work on the new building they recommended did not, however, begin until 1934 and was only partly finished in 1938 when Regan retired.

In July 1927 the Trustees asked the Office of Works to make provision in their 1928-29 Estimates for the New Whale Room, additional accommodation for the Department of Zoology, a lift in the Department of Geology from basement to ground floor, new ladies' lavatories, etc., but all concerned had to wait a long time. However, by October 1927, the Treasury had decided that it would allow the

Museum authorities to accept an offer from the Empire Marketing Board to pay for a new building to house the inconveniently over-crowded entomological collections (p.218); these, of course, were needed, often urgently, for consultation in campaigns against insect pests throughout the British Empire.

The Trustees had long been aware of the unfortunate and frequently costly results of introducing animals for commerce or sport into areas where they are not native. Thus, when informed in March 1929 that an assistant game warden in Kenya proposed to introduce the American black bass fish into Lake Naivasha, they disapproved the proposal and told the Colonial Office that they deprecated all such introductions of exotic animals and plants, at least until a thorough survey of the native fauna and flora had been carried out. The black bass was nevertheless introduced into Lake Naivasha and the Governor of Kenya Colony replied that 'the fauna of the lake previously consisted of a single species of fish'! A protest by the Trustees in 1936 against the proposed intro-duction of crayfish into Kenya as being deplorable zoologically, and possibly harmful economically, was equally ineffective.

The usual history of the introduction of exotic mammals for fur-production is that some private individuals initially reap a good profit and then leave to the general public the heavy burden of expenditure on exterminating or controlling those which have escaped; this far exceed-ing in public cost the private profits made. From 1930 onwards the Trustees successfully urged upon the Ministry of Agriculture and Fisheries the need to exterminate the recently introduced muskrat or

Fig. 18. Muskrat, *Ondatra zibethica* (engraving in J.G. Wood, *Illustrated Natural History*, 1865).

musquash, *Ondatra zibethica*, and later but unsuccessfully the coypu or nutria, *Myocastor coypus*, before they became pests beyond control. The moving force behind this was Martin Alister Campbell Hinton (1883-1961) (p.186).

The fur of the muskrat is thick, soft and glossy, being admirably suited for its aquatic life, and so highly esteemed that enormous quantities of skins have for many years been imported into Europe from North America, where it is widespread. Thus the introduction and breeding of muskrats in Europe seemed to offer an opportunity of sharing in the profits of this lucrative fur trade. In 1905 a Bohemian nobleman turned loose on his estate at Dobris (Dobrisch), about 25 miles (40 km) south-west of Prague, Czechoslovakia, two male muskrats and three females imported from Alaska. They bred swiftly and prolifically and spread widely. Now, despite continuous warfare against them, the descendants of those five muskrats at large in Europe number more than a hundred million. They burrow into the banks of rivers, canals, railway embankments and streamside roads, causing flooding and collapse, and they destroy aquatic vegetation; their control and the repair of damage annually cost enormous sums. Up to 1932 muskrats could still be imported into Britain under licence; from 1927 onwards numerous fur farms were set up to provide breeding stock at £10 a pair and before long, many individuals had escaped and were forming wild colonies. Unchecked, they would probably have increased to many thousands by 1936 and the cost of controlling them would undoubtedly have risen to thousands of pounds annually. Hinton apprehended the danger clearly. On 20 December 1929 he urged at a Ministry of Agriculture conference that the breeding of muskrats in Britain should be totally prohibited. The Trustees of the Museum accordingly informed the Ministry of Agriculture in January 1930 that they viewed with the gravest apprehension the possible results of breeding muskrats here and offered the help of their scientific staff and support for any legislation to prohibit the introduction of any animal or plant which could be shown on scientific grounds to be undesirable. Hinton and E.C. Read, of the Ministry of Agriculture, accordingly prepared a memorandum summarizing the available information. On 22 March 1930 the Trustees again informed the Ministry of their disquiet. They found great difficulty and many delays in impressing upon the Ministry the urgency of the situation. Indeed, the Ministry did not issue an order until March 1933 totally prohibiting the importation and keeping of muskrats, a measure the Trustees had urged upon them exactly three years earlier. However, the Destructive Imported Animals Act became law in 1932 and the campaign against the muskrat began in earnest, some 1,531 being killed that year and

1,054 in 1934. In 1939, in both England and Scotland, extermination was complete. This success cost much money and the Museum lost the services of Hinton for much of 1932, but Museum time was never better spent; more than any other individual, he had alerted the country to its danger and he had taken an active practical part in saving it. As a biographer remarked, the country never gave any recognition to its Pied Piper. Certainly, it never realized the influential backing of the Natural History Museum's Trustees.

The Natural History Museum was able to instigate a campaign of extermination against the muskrat in Britain, because of its known costly depredations elsewhere. No such evidence was available in 1932 against the potentially dangerous coypu, which has since become a costly pest. The warnings of the Trustees accordingly passed unheeded until the opportunity for effective action had passed, but they merit notice. The coypu is a South American aquatic rodent with a soft grey fur, known as 'nutria', under a covering of coarser hairs. Like the muskrat, it seemed to provide fur-breeders with an opportunity of getting rich quick. Three pairs at £40 a pair were bought from France in 1930 by one importer. In 1932 the Trustees proposed that the coypu should be scheduled under the Destructive Imported Animals Act of 1932. This led to protests to the Ministry of Agriculture by fur-breeders and farmers, who were then getting from £15 to £20 a pair and claimed that the coypu was a harmless animal, since no evidence could be produced of its doing any serious damage or of maintaining itself in a wild state. The Trustees nevertheless on 26 November 1932 restated

Fig. 19.   Coypu, *Myocastor coypus* (engraving in J.G. Wood, *Illustrated Natural History*, 1865).

their opinion that it should be scheduled under the Destructive Imported Animals Act, even if no evidence as yet could be produced against it. The Ministry stated then that, if the Trustees adhered to this opinion, they should furnish a considered statement including evidence as to the destructive habits of the animal when at large. By 1939, however, almost all the fifty initially profitable coypu farms had closed down and the coypu, left unchecked, was gradually establishing itself as a feral beast. A skin of an escaped coypu was received at the Museum as early as May 1933. The Trustees informed the Ministry in July 1933, that they considered this incident justified the warnings they had already addressed to the Ministry. In 1962, when the evidence from damaged dyke banks and river walls, destroyed agricultural crops and native vegetation was all too apparent, the coypu was at last scheduled as the Trustees had proposed thirty years earlier. By June 1979 when the annual cost of coypu control had risen to £84,000, some 220,050 coypus had been killed during the last sixteen years and its extermination was estimated as likely to cost between £1,400,000 and £2,300,000 according to the 1978 Report of the Coypu Strategy Group, set up by the Ministry of Agriculture, Fisheries and Food. Worthy of note is the Group's statement that 'we share the anxiety, expressed by some of our witnesses, lest the arrival, escape or release of other non-indigenous species may give rise to problems and expense comparable with those involved in dealing with the coypu'. It was an anxiety the Trustees had expressed for half a century.

In October 1927 a school of false killer whales, *Pseudorca crassidens*, numbering 126 individuals, had the misfortune to get stranded on the north-east coast of Scotland at Dornoch Firth, Sutherland. The Receiver of Wreck at Invergordon immediately telegraphed the Museum about these 'Royal Fish' (p.119) and, since they provided a most unusual opportunity of studying a school of whales, Martin Hinton, the Museum's taxidermist, and preparator Percy Stammwitz and a friend, set off at midnight that very day for Sutherland. The dead whales were scattered over some thirty miles (48km) of coast. Getting them together, by towing carcasses to a convenient place, and assembling and training men to cut them up, packing a gutted female weighing 22 cwt (1,117 kilos) and a gutted male weighing 34 cwt (1,727 kilos) for transport to the Museum as well as the preparation of 124 skeletons, kept Hinton and his helpers frantically busy from 25 October to 5 December. The false killer is a comparatively rare whale and the collection of so much material all at once remains unique. It brought again to notice the need for the proposed New Whale Hall at the Museum.

The designing of a New Whale Hall then went ahead and two plans were available for consideration by the Trustees in October 1929. They approved one prepared by John H. Markham. The original intent was to have natural lighting by using the maximum of glass surface — at one time a roof entirely of glass was envisaged — but the Keeper of Zoology, W.T. Calman, objected to this because 'the large, suspended skeletons viewed from the ground would be silhouetted against the glare of light which would have made it difficult to view them properly and with reasonable comfort.' Markham accordingly changed the design; he aimed at the maximum of simplicity, so as not to detract from the exhibits, with a colour scheme suggestive of their marine origin. The steel framework had to be exceptionally strong in order to carry heavy specimens suspended from the roof, but it was cased and the internal surfaces were finished with plaster, which is more pleasing than exposed steel girders. It was now possible to exhibit for the first time the skeleton of a large blue whale, *Balaenoptera musculus*, which had remained in store for forty-two years from lack of space for exhibition. The animal, believed to be a female four or five years old, became stranded on a sandbank at Wexford Bay, south-east Ireland, in March 1891 and measured about eighty-two feet (25 m) in length. The suspension of its skeleton weighing not less than ten tons (10,160 kilos) presented many difficulties all successfully overcome by the Museum's general foreman, W. Sanders, and picked members of the Works staff. By 24 February 1934 it hung in its permanent position, rightly to become a source of wonder for generations of school children and a reminder to adults of what the world stands to lose from excessive whaling.

During 1937 and 1938 the New Whale Hall provided the general public with the dramatic opportunity to witness the construction of a life-sized model of the blue whale. Calman proposed in July 1933 that a cast of a large whale should be made for exhibition, but the Treasury refused to sanction the estimated expenditure. The Museum's taxidermist, Percy Stammwitz, suggested in 1937 that, using the detailed information available, a life-size model, instead of a cast from an actual specimen, could be made from start to finish within the Whale Hall itself. Work began that summer, much of it being done by Percy Stammwitz and his son, Stuart, in collaboration with F.C. Fraser as scientific supervisor, together with joiners constructing the wooden framework. They made a preliminary model in clay on a scale of one inch to a foot, the full-size model to be 93 feet (28.3 m) long, and took a plaster cast from this, which enabled them to work out the dimensions of the full-size model. Large paper patterns, showing the shapes of transverse sections of the animal's body at three foot (0.9 m) intervals, were then cut and these were then copied by the joiners in wood and fastened together at the correct intervals and sequence by slats. This huge framework with a surface area of about 300 square yards (250 square m.) was then covered with small-mesh wire netting; plaster was imposed on this. Thus the animal gradually took shape. A trapdoor left open on the stomach enabled the workmen to climb inside for secret, and probably forbidden, smoking; Jonah in the belly of the great fish could not have been so comfortable. Before the trapdoor was sealed and plastered over, a telephone directory and some coins were left inside. The model completed, there remained the question of colour. On this, Fraser and Stammwitz violently disagreed. Ultimately it was painted a bluish steel-grey, with a number of pale or white flecks. Although weighing between six and seven tons (6,080-7,110 kilos), the model swayed gently as the workmen painted and they could only work for short spells before feeling sea-sick! The work was finished in December 1938. At the time it was the largest model of a whale in any museum, but the templates and details of construction were later lent to American museums which naturally made their models a little longer.

The second part of the final report of the Royal Commission on National Museums and Galleries became available in January 1930. For the Natural History Museum this was an important document. It recommended that the Museum's Director should be made wholly responsible for the care and custody of the collections housed therein and thus not subordinate to the Principal Librarian and Director at Bloomsbury, a position which had so irked Ray Lankester; that structural altertions should be completed at an early date and that a lecture hall, which the Museum had needed from the beginning, should now be made available. It also revived an old, controversial matter by stating that 'a combination of the Royal Botanic Gardens, Kew, and the Botanical Department of the Natural History Museum represents the aim which should be aimed at.'

An Act of Parliament in 1930 then made the two directors independent. The Natural History Museum, with its Director as its accounting officer, thus became an autonomous institution after nearly fifty years of legal but, in fact, mostly nominal subordination to Bloomsbury; both museums remained, however, under the control of the same body of Trustees (p.16). The official title of the South Kensington Museum, i.e. British Museum (Natural History), remained unchanged, although Tate Regan tried to get it made more in keeping with English grammar and usage and with the Museum's status, by proposing that the name should be amended to 'British Museum of Natural History'. Uncertain of the legality of such an improvement, the Trustees referred the matter to the Treasury Solicitor. He replied that 'the adoption of the distinctive title ''British Museum of Natural History'' seemed to him a matter within the general powers of the Trustees of the British Museum'; such a change implied no variation in the terms of their Trust. The Trustees then postponed consideration of the matter. Brought before them on 13 December 1930 they once again postponed it: 'although not objecting in principle to the proposed title (''The British Museum of Natural History''), the Trustees were of the opinion that the time was inopportune for making such a change, and deferred consideration till a later date.' What made it inopportune is obscure. Six years later, on 24 October 1936, the Director reminded the Trustees that in 1930 he had brought before them the question of changing the designation of the Museum from the inconvenient

Fig. 20. The main hall of the Museum in 1929 (from a London Underground railway advertisement in *Evening News,* 13 February 1929).

'British Museum (Natural History)' to 'British Museum of Natural History' and that in their opinion then the time had not been opportune for making such a change although there was no objection to the proposed title. After some discussion, the Trustees agreed that the title proposed by the Director be adopted. Their printed minutes were accordingly headed 'British Museum of Natural History'. They then had second thoughts.

Shortly afterwards, the Trustees decided that no effect should be given to their resolution until the matter had been considered and reported upon by Lord Macmillan and the Master of the Rolls, Lord Wright. These law officers replied by 16 December 1936, that the proposed change was not illegal; after considering the relative Acts of Parliament, the change of designation could be readily made without affecting the substance of the Statutes and Rules. At the Trustees' Meeting of 16 December Tate Regan the Director, invited by the Chairman to comment on this report, 'stated that it appeared to confirm the information he had given to the Trustees on 24 October, namely, that the proposed title was legal and that it had no substantial effect on the Statutes. He expressed the view that the words "British Museum" in their original sense meant all the collections that formed the Trust. If used in this sense, there had been since 1 January 1931 two Directors of the British Museum; one responsible for the humanistic collections, the other for the natural history collections. The words "British Museum" were, however, generally used for the humanistic collections and the building that contained them, and the natural history collections and building were known as the "Natural History Museum". The title "British Museum (Natural History)" was used only in official documents; it was inconvenient and would never come into general use, and the Director thought it misleading, so long as the words "British Museum" were used for the building and collections at Bloomsbury. The two museums governed by the Trustees had similar aims, methods, and traditions, and he valued the connexion between them; this was why he had hoped to adopt a title that could be generally used in place of "Natural History Museum" and that indicated this connexion.' Tate Regan's proposal was intended to carry to a logical conclusion the Act of 1930, which had made the two Directors independent of each other. Had the Trustees in October decided to retain the title 'British Museum (Natural History)' he would have accepted their decision without question; but to allow him to use another title for twenty-six days, then suspend its use, and perhaps finally revert to the old one, placed him in a most difficult position. The Director added that he was quite in the dark as to the real reasons for reconsideration of this matter, but was ready to answer any questions relating to them.

The Trustees decided (Sir Henry Miers dissenting) that it was inexpedient to adopt the title 'British Museum of Natural History' and they accordingly resolved to rescind their Resolution of 24 October on the subject. They further decided that the present title 'British Museum (Natural History)' be retained without prejudice to future consideration of an alternative should circumstances render such a course desirable. The matter was again to be debated in 1963 (p.345) with the same negative result — a striking testimony to British conservatism. Outside Britain it is commonly known as the 'British Museum of Natural History'.

The fiftieth anniversary of the opening of the Natural History Museum to the public in 1881 came on 18 April 1931. The quinquagenary or jubilee celebration was, however, postponed to 29 September 1931 to coincide with the centenary meeting of the British Association for the Advancement of Science held in London from 23 to 30 September. The year 1931 proved, however, one of financial difficulty and political tension in many parts of the world, notably in Austria and Germany, where so much British money was invested that Britain had later to borrow from France and the United States. A run on the pound began in July and the Labour Government was replaced in August by a National Coalition Government under Ramsay MacDonald, which immediately brought in an economy budget raising taxes and cutting the allowances of the unemployed, and the wages and salaries of state employees by 5% to 15%. In A.J.P. Taylor's opinion 'September 1931 marked the watershed of English history between the wars'. It was thus a most unfavourable month for the Museum's intended celebrations, as also for airing plans of expansion, and these were adversely affected. Nevertheless, over a hundred representatives of museums and learned societies from Britain and abroad attended a reception in the Museum and were welcomed by the Earl of Crawford and Balcarres on behalf of the Trustees, and by Tate Regan as Director on behalf of the Museum's scientific staff. Regan's address contained remarks obviously intended not only for the ears of the delegates: 'The Museum is old-fashioned: it was built too soon, and we have to make the best of it. One aim of the Museum is to interest and instruct the public by means of the exhibition galleries. In the fifty years we have made slow but steady progress; we have only a few preparators; we have not much money to spend; we are hampered by the fact that many of the galleries serve for storage as well as exhibition, and one full of table cases or cabinets of drawers, for which we have no room anywhere else... The other main business of the Museum is to form collections of all natural objects, to classify them, describe them, and arrange them, so that they are available for

study. . . The collections that were transferred from Bloomsbury fifty
years ago were already important; now they are at least six times as
large. The insects have increased from one million to eight million, the
birds from 60,000 to 600,000, the fishes from 40,000 to 175,000, and
other collections have grown at the same rate. We have found room for
these by utilizing the basement, by cutting off exhibition galleries from
the public, and by a certain amount of new building.' In the evening
the Government gave another reception in the Museum, the guests
being received by the Prime Minister, The Rt. Hon. J. Ramsay
MacDonald, and his daughter, Miss Ishbel MacDonald.

On 4 December 1931, the Museum lost by death the best known and
most popular member of the staff, its first guide lecturer, John Henry
Leonard (1864-1931). From his appointment on 20 May 1912 until his
illness in October 1931, he conducted thousands of visitors around the
Museum, taking them from exhibit to exhibit and clearly and enthus-
iastically explaining matters of special interest which might otherwise
have passed unnoticed; thereby he amply justified Lord Sudeley's
campaign (p.100) for thus increasing the educational and recreational
use of museums. *Punch* on 6 January 1932 paid him a fitting tribute:
  'From auk to zebra, from white Pole to Pole,
  Bird, beast and man himself he brought to men;
  Gave back to each dead specimen the soul
  And made it live again.
  As from a chrysalis
  The moth unpacks its powdered wings and flies,
  So he unpacked his learning store of gold,
  Till all, it seemed, on earth that's born and dies
  Was ours to have and hold.'

The lack of adequate accommodation in the Natural History
Museum had become so grave by October 1936 that the Trustees drew
the attention of the Office of Works to the urgent necessity of providing
additional buildings without delay, if the efficiency of the Museum was
to be maintained. After exhaustive enquiry and discussions with the
Director and the Keepers of several Departments, they could
recommend no temporary measures of any avail. They needed a bold
scheme of building to provide the requisite space for storage of
specimens, for studies and for workshops. This essential additional
accommodation could be provided by the completion of the existing
west and north blocks which, according to a proposal of the Royal
Commission on National Museums and Galleries in 1928, should have
been done by 1933.

The Trustees supported their request by a general statement:
  'The conception of the function of a great national collection such

30. Sir Sidney Frederic Harmer
    (1862-1950), zoologist,
    Keeper of Zoology 1909-
    1921, Director 1919-1927.

31. Charles Tate Regan (1878-
    1943), zoologist, Keeper of
    Zoology 1921-1927, Director
    1927-1938.

32. Sir Clive Forster-Cooper
    (1880-1947), zoologist,
    Director 1938-1947.

33. Sir Norman Boyd Kinnear
    (1882-1957), zoologist,
    Keeper of Zoology 1945-
    1947, Director 1947-1950.

34. Botanical gallery, Department of Botany, in 1911.

35. Taxidermists' room in 1902, with T. Sherrin and C. E. Seimund.

36. Taxidermists' room in 1926, with Percy Stammwitz and Stuart Stammwitz.

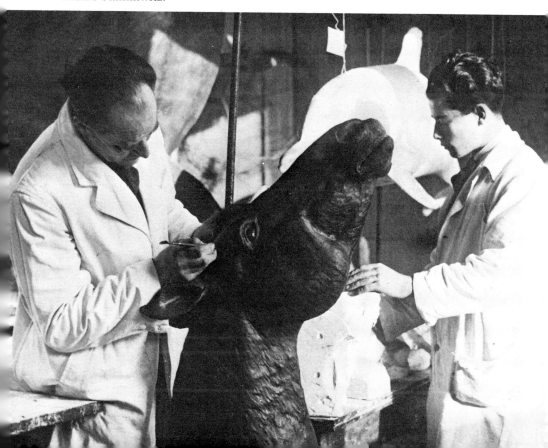

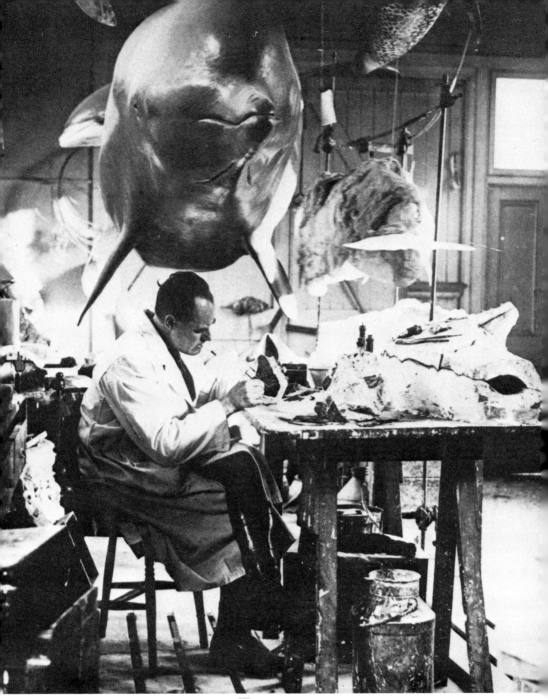

37. Percy Stammwitz (1881-1954), taxidermist and modelmaker, in the workshop, c.1926.

as is housed in the Natural History Museum has greatly widened since the present main building at South Kensington was completed in 1880, more than half a century ago, and one of the chief difficulties which have embarrassed the Trustees is the fact that the premises then provided were designed without appreciation of the purposes which the Museum has now to serve. The Museum is a place of deposit for the national collections of natural history, but the mere amassing and warehousing of the material collected is only the first step. It is the utilisation of the collections for the advancement of knowledge and for public instruction that is the justification of the enterprise. But even the safe housing of the material which is constantly accumulating, apart from the problem of making it available to the student and to the public, has become a matter of difficulty through lack of space. The statistics are instructive. In round figures the specimens now contained in the Museum number as follows:—

> Zoology 2,750,000
> Entomology 8,000,000
> Geology 1,700,000
> Botany 4,000,000
> Mineralogy 250,000

Several million Protozoa, Diatoms, etc., mounted on thousands of microscope slides, are not included in these figures.

The extent of the accessions in the ten years 1926 to 1935 is as follows:—

> Zoology 360,000
> Entomology 3,200,000
> Geology 160,000
> Botany 665,000
> Mineralogy 30,000

a total of 4,415,000 specimens. The collections must continue to grow, for they are still far from complete in many departments. Thus the collection of insects is estimated to contain representatives of only about 55 per cent of the known species. Even to store this vast and growing mass of immensely valuable national property under safe conditions requires ample accommodation. But to deal with it so that it may serve the purposes for which it has been accumulated necessitates a great deal of additional space. There must be workrooms in which the material can be unpacked, classified, prepared, and mounted; the scientific members of the staff must have rooms for study and research, in which they can carry out the investigations that they are called upon to perform, and accommodation must be provided for the numerous visitors from Britain, from the dominions and colonies, and from foreign countries, who come to study the collections. These things are essential if the Museum is to make its due contribution to the advancement of scientific learning.

But there is the other and in its own way not less important aspect of the Museum to be considered, its social value as a place of valuable and interesting instruction for the general public. This necessitates the selection and exhibition of specimens so that they shall be at once educative and attractive. Owing to the large number of accessions in recent years the space available for exhibition has had to be increasingly encroached upon for storage purposes, with the result that as the collections have grown in value and interest the means of exhibiting them has diminished. Yet in spite of this the public appreciation of the Museum has shown a steady increase, the last four years having shown record numbers of visitors. To do justice to this growing interest the Trustees desire that all the Galleries should be cleared, reorganised, and re-equipped so that they may to their full extent serve the purpose of exhibition. This cannot be done unless the additional accommodation now sought is provided.'

In 1938 work began at last on the completion of the west block for the congested entomological collections, but the outbreak of World War II in September 1939 stopped it all and the building was not ready for occupation until 1952 (p.218).

The major event of 1937 for the Museum was the bequest by Walter Rothschild (1868-1937), second Baron Rothschild, of his private Museum at Tring. The Zoological Museum, Tring, owes its existence to the enthusiasm for natural history of its founder and the financial acumen and competence of his banking relatives who supported him: it may owe its continuance to his weight which became too great for a cavalry horse to carry into battle and saved him from becoming a target for Boer marksmen in the South African war.

In 1872 Nathaniel Mayer Rothschild (1840-1915), first Baron Rothschild in the United Kingdom, bought Tring Park, once the home of Nell Gwynn. He was a great grandson of Mayer Amschel Rothschild (1744-1812), the astute and far-sighted financier of Frankfurt am Main, who began the family's fortune. His eldest son, Lionel Walter Rothschild, became deeply interested in zoology when a boy. In 1881, at the age of thirteen, he met the British Museum's Keeper of Zoology, Dr Albert Günther, who had noticed the boy looking intently at cases of zoological specimens not yet moved from Bloomsbury. Thus began a friendship which lasted until Günther's death some thirty years later. Günther became a zoological father-figure for young Walter

Rothschild, who began early to collect and buy zoological specimens, mostly of butterflies, moths and birds, and to form an associated library, being much more liberally supplied with money than many young men and devoting it to science more zealously than most of them would have done, although such spending habits later brought him near to disaster. After a period in Germany at Bonn, which doubtlessly strengthened his respect for German science already infused by Günther, he entered Magdalene College, Cambridge, as an undergraduate to study for the natural sciences tripos. Here he became friendly with the zoological professor, Alfred Newton (1829-1907), who used every Sunday to welcome students at his rooms in Magdalene College. Newton was primarily an ornithologist and later responsible for the monumental *Dictionary of Birds* (1893-1896). Never before had a student possessing 38,000 Lepidoptera and 500 birds come to Cambridge. Rothschild continuously made use of Günther's wide expert knowledge and wise advice. As his collections grew, they had to be stored in sheds and rented rooms in Tring which hindered access and rendered them liable to damage. Accordingly, when he came of age, his father gave him a piece of land on the outskirts of Tring Park and, after discussions with Günther, built there a private museum to display his mounted specimens and store his other specimens and library and also erected a house for a caretaker.

Two appointments greatly influenced the scientific future of this museum and quickly brought it international standing. Count Hans von Berlepsch (1850-1915) was an amateur German ornithologist who visited the British Museum in 1879, thus becoming known to Günther, and who built up a big private collection of bird skins at Münden. Among those who studied his material was Ernst Johann Otto Hartert (1859-1933), likewise a German ornithologist, who had already travelled widely in Nigeria, Malaya, northern India and the West Indies. Bowdler Sharpe met him in May 1891, at an ornithological congress in Budapest and, on his recommendation, Günther invited Hartert to London to prepare Volume 16 of the British Museum *Catalogue of Birds.* Rothschild engaged him as his museum curator and he remained at Tring until his retirement in 1930, when he returned to Germany. His introduction into British ornithology of the concept of subspecies designated by trinomials, e.g. *Loxia curvirostra scotica* Hartert for the Scottish crossbill, at first aroused strong opposition, but has subseqently become generally accepted. Contemporaries reputed Hartert to possess a wider knowledge of the world's birds than probably any other ornithologist, a significant part of which he made available in his monumental *Die Vögel der Paläarktischen Fauna* (1903-1922).

Rothschild's other significant appointment was that of Dr Heinrich

Ernst Karl Jordan (1861-1959) again through Count von Berlepsch at Münden. He came of Hanoverian peasant stock and was the youngest of seven children; his father died when he was five years old but, thanks to an uncle, he received a good schooling in Hildesheim, then studied botany and zoology at the university of Göttingen, where he received his Ph.D. degree, and then became a school teacher at Münden for five years. The young man's enthusiasm and knowledge had evidently impressed von Berlepsch. Walter Rothschild invited Jordan to Tring in 1892; he arrived in 1893 and worked there for the rest of his life, publishing, so it is said, the finest of his many publications in his eighties and nineties. Jordan worked at many groups, but his most important research was on fleas (Siphonaptera) in association with Nathaniel Charles Rothschild (1877-1923), Walter's younger brother. Charles was as interested in natural history as his brother but, unlike him, possessed good business ability and earned his father's approval by working diligently and successfully in the Rothschild bank at New Court. In 1912, he founded the Society for the Promotion of Nature Reserves. His major scientific interest was in fleas, which, unlike his brother's pet groups, require little storage space but close study under the microscope for their understanding.

Unfortunately, Charles Rothschild fell a victim to the epidemic of the mysterious 'sleepy sickness', *encephalitis lethargica*, which suddenly became widespread towards the end of the First World War and then completely vanished about 1923. It was incurable and in despair, at the age of forty-six, he took his own life, a sad end indeed for one so gifted, generous and public-spirited. His collection of fleas, the most comprehensive in the world, passed to the British Museum (Natural History) to which he had made a deed of gift in 1913; Jordan continued to work painstakingly at the group long after his retirement, 'seated at a desk that was to him in perfect order, but to everyone else looked like chaos'. The monument to their work is *An illustrated Catalogue of the Rothschild Collection of Fleas (Siphonaptera) in the British Museum (Natural History)* by George H.E. Hopkins and Miriam Rothschild (daughter of Charles Rothschild and niece of Walter Rothschild) in five bulky volumes (1953-71). Jordan provided the classification adopted.

The Rothschild Museum was founded at a time of rapidly expanding biological exploration in little-known tropical regions, when almost every collection of plants and animals from the tropics included species hitherto unknown. Anticipating the flow of new species into the Tring collections and the reluctance of existing periodicals to provide enough space for their publication, Günther suggested that the Rothschild Museum should publish its own journal *Novitates Zoologicae*, which Rothschild wealth enabled it to do. The first part of volume 1 appeared in January 1894, the last part of the volume 42, which ended the series, in March 1948, ten years after the Museum's affiliation with the British Museum (Natural History). No British zoological periodical excelled it in style; it was of quarto size and many papers were illustrated with hand-coloured lithographs. Many distinguished zoologists contributed papers.

The upkeep of the Museum made heavy demands on Walter Rothschild's income and several times brought him near to ruin. Although a member of the Rothschild banking house, he possessed little business ability, unlike his brilliant father and brother, and after a gallant attempt at learning international finance and after constant rows with his uncles, he left the bank in 1908. Thereafter, he devoted himself to the affairs of his own Museum and of the British Museum, of which he had become a Trustee in 1899, and to travel. Elected a Member of Parliament from 1899 to 1910, he consistently neglected his parliamentary duties in order to visit the Natural History Museum.

In 1910 and 1912 Walter Rothschild added two wings to the Museum to house his collection of birds and insects. On the death in 1915 of his father, who had disinherited him after the 1908 row in favour of his younger brother Nathaniel Charles, he succeeded to the title. Although reputed to have the fashionable Edwardian interest in chorus girls, he never married and on his death in 1937 the title passed to his nephew Nathaniel Victor (b. 1910), the present Baron Rothschild.

Unfortunately Walter Rothschild's debts mounted. However, before then he had sold his huge collection of beetles, to which Jordan had devoted so much care, because they were too much to manage. The crowning blow came in 1931. Having large debts, he decided to pay them by selling his collection of birds, on the study of which Hartert had spent so much of his life. It was packed and sent to the American Museum of Natural History in New York in 1932. This sale caused much dismay among British ornithologists, who considered that the British Museum should have purchased it. Lord Rothschild suffered much criticism as a result of this loss to Britain. Indeed, the loss of this treasured collection played upon his mind. He became an invalid through breaking his leg and, subsequently developing cancer, he died on 27 August 1937.

His Will of 19 November 1923 with a Codicil of 25 July 1937 bequeathed to the Trustees of the British Museum the building and contents of the Tring Museum and a house used as a laboratory, provided that the Trustees used this Museum in a modified form for zoological research. The collections included more than 2,000 mounted mammals, about 1,000 reptiles and amphibians, more than

2,000 mounted birds and twice as many skins, despite the sale to the American Museum of Natural History, and a vast collection of insects, among them nearly 30,000 Lepidoptera. In the library were nearly 30,000 primarily zoological volumes. A survey by the Office of Works indicated that much expenditure was needed on renewal of the electric lighting and the heating system, together with redecoration, but this in no way diminished the Trustees' appreciation of Lord Rothschild's superb bequest. In July 1938 a British Museum Bill enabling the Trustees to accept the bequest passed both Houses of Parliament. It was just in time. During February 1937, precautions against air-raids (later designated A.R.P.) for the Museum were already being discussed in view of the worsening political situation and plans for the evacuation of part of the collections to the Tring Museum formed an essential part of these.

After Hartert's retirement in 1930, Jordan took charge of the Tring Museum until his own retirement. T.C.S. Morrison-Scott (later Director of the British Museum (Natural History)) from the Department of Zoology, then became officer-in-charge from 1938 to 1939 and, when he left on war-service, was followed by J.R. Norman until 1944 and then by J.E. Dandy from the Department of Botany. During the period 1969-71, the public galleries were modernized, and a new building was erected to accommodate the national collection of bird skins and skeletons, which was transferred from South Kensington, and it became the Sub-Department of Ornithology.

Regan's sixtieth birthday came on 1 February 1938. He had indicated in February 1937 his personal wish to remain in office beyond the age of sixty, but the Trustees decided that they could not press him to undergo the strain on his health which the continuance of his duties would involve and expressed their regret that he had not availed himself of the option open to him of retiring voluntarily. His health had indeed been bad and, although this could little be foreseen at the time, the strain of coping with Museum conditions in the war years would have wrecked him. He had served the Museum loyally and efficiently for thirty-seven years. By the study of its collections he had made impressive and lastingly valuable contributions to ichthyology. His tenure of office had seen the nation saved from the menace of the musk-rat. In the Museum, the collections had immensely increased both in size and scientific importance and, although accommodation for them had not correspondingly expanded, this was not for want of urging on his part. A notable event of his directorship was the first appointment of women as permanent scientific members of the Museum staff. As his biographers, R.H. Burne and J.R. Norman, stated in *Obituary Notices of Royal Society* 4: 414 (1943), 'reconstruction was sadly hampered by the financial conditions of the country around 1931. This meant the abandonment, temporarily at least, of some of his cherished ideas, and was a disappointment to him. It will be apparent that a scheme of reorganization on the scale that Regan had in mind, involving considerable expenditure and dependent on the co-operation of more than one authority, requires for its smooth development exceptional gifts in the art of meeting and overcoming difficulties with patience and methods of gentle persuasion. To one of Regan's highly strung, eager and outspoken temperament, such an art did not come naturally or easily, and it seems probable that in his relations with other authorities he made for himself worries and difficulties that might have been avoided by one of a more equable nature.' He died on 12 January 1943.

11

The Second World War
and its Aftermath
1938 - 1949

T HE YEARS 1938 to 1947 during which Clive Forster-Cooper (1880-1947) was Director of the Natural History Museum included the most anxious, difficult, mentally and physically demanding period faced by any of its directors — the wartime period of danger and frustration during which the Museum stood in peril of destruction and sustained grave damage, when many of its normal functions had had to be suspended, its collections dispersed, its staff cut to the minimum. No-one could foresee all this when Forster-Cooper took office in February 1938, coming from Cambridge ambitious to modernize exhibits as he had done there and to organize large-scale expeditions such as some great American museums did. However, the wrecking of these aspirations forms a very minor part indeed of the tragedy of those years. Although Germany, Italy and Japan as aggressive totalitarian states had united themselves by an ominous pact in November 1937 and the rising military power of Germany was increasing fear in all its neighbouring countries, hope of peace in Europe still remained, flickering but not yet extinguished. Nevertheless Forster-Cooper's appointment evoked surprise. He was fifty-eight, only two years younger than Regan who had been forced to resign at sixty purportedly for health reasons, and his health, like Regan's, was not sound; he had had no previous close association with the Museum. Presumably he knew the right people. Apart from age and health, he possessed good qualifications for the post of Director: he was a distinguished Cambridge zoologist and a Fellow of the Royal Society, he had travelled widely and had gained museum experience both by seeing museums abroad and by re-organizing the Cambridge University Museum of Zoology for university teaching of vertebrate development, he had been bursar of Trinity Hall, Cambridge, chairman of the University Buildings Syndicate and director from 1914 to 1947 of the Museum of Zoology, whence Sidney Harmer had come to the Natural History Museum in 1909. He had proved himself a capable administrator. Now, unfortunately, adverse circumstances restricted to the end the full exercise of his talents and experience.

Clive Forster-Cooper was born at Hampstead on 3 April 1880, and educated at Rugby School and Trinity College, Cambridge, graduating in 1901. While he was still an undergraduate his zoology professor, J. Stanley Gardiner, invited him to come on an expedition to the Maldive Islands in the Indian Ocean in 1899. Gardiner becoming ill, Forster-Cooper, just twenty, had to take over full responsibility for the ship and its scientific work, which he did so competently that when Gardiner organized in 1905 an expedition funded through the bequest of Constance Sladen, wife of the wealthy naturalist Percy Sladen (1849-1900) to the Indian Ocean in H.M.S. *Sealark*, he again asked young Forster-Cooper to accompany him as his scientific assistant. In 1907, when working in the United States, Forster-Cooper's interests switched from marine biology to vertebrate palaeontology. He made in 1910 and 1911 two very successful fossil-hunting expeditions to the Bugti beds in Baluchistan, which yielded among much else, bones of *Paraceratherium* [*Baluchitherium*], a gigantic extinct rhinoceros, which may have been the world's largest land mammal.

The 1914-1918 World War diverted him from the study of such extinct giants to medical work on all too much alive, microscopic human animal parasites in relation to malaria. After the war he returned to university teaching in Cambridge, among his students being C.F.A. Pantin, F.S. Russell, G.P. Wells and E.B. Worthington, all eminent later, and began complete reorganization of the Zoological Museum; he himself did much of the work of preparing skulls and providing carefully-written labels. Thus he became known as an enterprising and skilful museum superintendent and made his way from Cambridge to South Kensington. He was a likeable person who in his travels had got on well with a great diversity of people. Forster-Cooper's arrival at the Natural History Museum in 1938 was related as follows: 'He came to the Museum on the Wednesday and as he entered the gate he said to the porter [gate keeper], "I'm the new Director: how are you?" and shook hands. He repeated the same at the pound [reception desk] and created a wonderful impression.'

Meanwhile, the international situation worsened and brought the probability of a European war ever nearer. The Trustees of the Natural History Museum had already directed the Keepers of Departments to make recommendations as to specimens it would be desirable and practicable to remove from the Museum in the event of serious danger from air-raids and to consider precautions. Plans for the selection of type and other historic material to be evacuated to safe places and the removal, for example, of minerals to the basement, and other air-raid precautions, now became urgent and fortunately were well in hand by August 1938. The Munich agreement of September 1938, whereby Hitler engineered the dismemberment of Czechoslovakia with British and French acquiescence, was greeted with great public relief and much private scepticism as to its lasting nature. In January 1939 the Trustees decided to evacuate material to Tring, and air-raid precautions in the Museum, as elsewhere, went ahead. Classes of instruction in first-aid and anti-gas measures started. Rooms in the basement were reinforced to serve as air-raid shelters and telephones were installed at strategic places.

The cynical non-aggression pact of August 1939 between Germany and the Soviet Union now made war inevitable. The Museum closed to the public on 29 August; the air-raid precaution staff manned their posts. The German attack on Poland began on 1 September and so started the Second World War. Honouring their agreement with Poland, on 3 September Britain and France, together with Australia and New Zealand, declared war on Germany. The expected and awaited bombing assault on London, over which immediately floated uncountable barrage balloons, silvery and beautiful against the clear blue sky of those warm and anxious days, did not take place. In October, thirty lorry-loads of specimens went from the Museum to Tring; the Wallich Herbarium from the Royal Botanic Gardens, Kew and the Linnaean Herbarium from the Linnean Society were also evacuated there. The gemstones from the mineral gallery were moved to the Museum basement. Nevertheless, there remained in the Museum an enormous amount of valuable material impossible or difficult to evacuate then. Sand-bags had to be piled around especially vulnerable, bulky specimens, such as skeletons. The staff for such tasks rapidly diminished. By the end of October, forty-one members of the Museum staff had joined the armed forces and thirteen others had moved to other government departments; yet others were preparing to leave for service elsewhere. The demands of air-raid precautions day and night upon those remaining correspondingly grew; for their entertainment the Librarian, A.C. Townsend, (p.327) produced on 30 September 1939 the first issue of a typewritten, facetious bulletin called *Tin Hat*, which ultimately ran to sixteen numbers, ending on 16 August 1942 with contributions wisely anonymous or pseudonymous in view of their nature.

The lull in the war following the German and Russian partition of

Poland during September 1939 encouraged the Trustees to re-open for the public on 28 February 1940 the main and north halls, the reptile, fish and bird galleries and the whale hall, provided that visitors carried their gasmasks. Then on 29 May it had to be closed again. The Museum remained closed until 1 August 1942.

The German occupation of Holland, Belgium and northern France now provided the Luftwaffe with airfields close to England and in August 1940 the bombing of London began. By the end of August some twenty-eight bombs had fallen in the vicinity of the Museum; most did little damage, but they broke nevertheless many windows and rain poured in. On 9 September, two incendiary bombs and a large oil bomb, apparently jettisoned by a homeward-bound German plane, crashed at 4.30am through the roof of the east wing of the Museum housing the Department of Botany. The botanist J.E. Dandy was on duty as a fire-watcher. Prompt action brought the fire under control and ultimately extinguished it, though not before it had destroyed much of the roof and the internal woodwork and had badly damaged part of the herbarium. The water sprayed on to the fire inevitably soaked and damaged many other specimens. Drying them before removal out of London presented a major problem, as did renovation after the war. Many books were destroyed. Among the material immersed in water were some seeds of the pink siris or silk tree, *Albizia julibrissin* (Leguminosae), collected on the Macartney mission to China by Sir George Staunton in 1793. Surprised by this cold bath, after 147 years of dry storage, several of these seeds germinated.

Fortunately, the old-fashioned traditional herbarium cupboards had been made of wood, which is a poor conductor of heat, and the charring of the edges of many sheets of specimens was light, whereas had the cupboards been modern ones of metal, the heat transmitted through them would have caused much greater damage. Nevertheless, the place was in a sad state with fire-twisted roof girders over which an emergency roof of galvanised iron had to be quickly fixed to keep out rain and this remained until 1955. The old Department of Botany, in which so many British and foreign botanists had worked, was gone for ever. For years the upper east wing remained war-scarred, dark and dirty, its remaining contents in utter confusion. Consequently in June 1943 the upper mammal gallery, with its rodent extension, became 'temporarily' the home of the Department of Botany, which has possessed it ever since (p.306).

For fifty-seven nights, occasionally also in daytime, bombs dropped from an average of 200 German planes a day upon London and the Museum was fortunate indeed to survive at all amid so much hideous destruction. Thus on 10-11 September a high-explosive bomb came down in the east end colonnade, an oil bomb in a courtyard and a delayed action bomb in the forecourt. On 16 October incendiary bombs caused a fire in the shell gallery, the water used to extinguish it damaging part of the Diptera collection and a high-explosive bomb fell on a corridor housing hummingbirds. On 16 November two high-explosive bombs fell into a Museum courtyard. It had been evident for some time that too much valuable material still remained at risk in the Museum. Accordingly, as the owners of big country houses not yet requisitioned by the armed forces made accommodation available, more specimens and books were moved to them.

The 'Dig for Victory' campaign to increase food production by home vegetable growing, which was zealously and successfully promoted by the Royal Horticultural Society and the Ministry of Agriculture, had industrious converts among the Museum staff and on 14 March 1941 one of them dug the first allotment in the Museum grounds; all suitable space then became verdant with lettuces, cabbages, potatoes, etc. Meanwhile, the attacks on London slackened as the increasingly efficient British defences inflicted such heavy losses on the German airforce and so many German planes were needed for the coming invasion of Russia. Bombing virtually ceased. The danger to the Museum seemed to have passed, for the time being. Optimistically, the Trustees re-opened the Museum on 1 August 1942 and did not have to close it again until 6 July 1944; despite its war-time state, it attracted a remarkable number of visitors: 59,767 in 1942, 137,195 in 1943 and 51,017 in 1944. Nevertheless, this was a very trying time for the Director, as well as for his small continuously vigilant staff. Forster-Cooper lived in the Museum for long periods, sleeping in his office, cooking his own meals, subject to all the war-time restrictions and worries. Fortunately for him, and the Museum, he had at hand N.B. Kinnear, the Deputy Keeper of Zoology, to cope efficiently and coolly with each emergency.

Although the most important Museum collections had been removed and scattered and the German army and airforce were heavily engaged in Russia during 1942 and 1943, the danger to the Museum was by no means over. A phosphorus bomb penetrated the roof of a fossil gallery on 24 February 1944, starting fires which the Museum fire-fighting staff promptly extinguished. Later that year, from 15 June onwards, soon after the Allied landings in Normandy, flying bombs launched in north-western France began to fall on London, causing much destruction and loss of life. Two fell in Queen's Gate at the west side of the Museum, causing much damage, on 5 July. Another fell the same day in Cromwell Road, facing the Museum, from which fifteen people in the Museum were casualties, luckily sustaining nothing worse than severe shock, bruises and cuts from flying broken glass.

When peace came in May 1945, the Museum was in a sorry state; many windows had been shattered by the bombing, much of the roof had been destroyed and heavy rain came through the emergency covering; its neglected galleries were dirty, exhibits had been damaged or had deteriorated, some show cases had become unusable, the staff available was too small to cope with its problems. Nevertheless, despite war conditions and this war damage, which after all could be made good by determined effort, collectors still looked upon the Museum as the best repository for their precious material.

Gradually members, who had served in the armed forces and other government departments, returned and made preparation for the return to the Museum of the evacuated collections. The return of collections and staff continued in 1946, as did the receipt of new collections.

Clive Forster-Cooper had been knighted in 1946. It was his misfortune to have had the care of the Museum during a disastrous period and the strain of the war years had weighed heavily upon him; in May 1947, he arranged to retire on 30 September 1947. His health, however, deteriorated and he died on 23 August 1947. The Trustees, in anticipation, had appointed as Director Norman Boyd Kinnear, Keeper of Zoology, himself then about to retire, and he assumed his duties on 24 August 1947 on the understanding he would retire a year later. He stayed, however, until 30 April 1950 and thus saw and partly superintended much of the recovery of the Museum from its war-damaged state. His appointment was essentially a short-term or stop-gap one. In anticipation of Forster-Cooper's retirement on 30 September 1947, the Trustees had already made approaches to 'certain gentlemen' with regard to their becoming candidates for the director-ship, but apparently no-one satisfied with the post or satisfying the Principal Trustees was available when Forster-Cooper's death became imminent in August 1947. The Trustees accordingly appointed Kinnear in the hope of finding within the next year a successor able to give much longer service. He was a friendly, tactful, reliable person who made affairs run smoothly and, as he proved a capable administrator during the difficult post-war period, his tenure of office lasted much longer than intended.

Born in Edinburgh on 11 August 1882, Kinnear worked as a voluntary assistant in the Royal Scottish Museum there from 1905 to 1907, gaining experience and manifesting zeal and ability which led the museum's director, William Eagle Clarke, to recommend him in 1907 to the Bombay Natural History Society as Curator of their museum. This had been run until then by a few keen amateur naturalists in their spare time, but the increase of its important collections made a full-time, competent curator highly desirable, if not essential.

Kinnear took up his duties in India in November 1907. He set about re-arranging, labelling and cataloguing the exhibits and collections, organizing the Society's systematic survey of the mammals of India, Burma and Ceylon, and helping to edit its publications. He made a special study of Indian birds. Thus, although Kinnear was a good all-round naturalist, ornithology became his dominant interest. He possessed no academic background, but his experience qualified him for appointment as an assistant in the Department of Zoology at the Natural History Museum and he left India and joined the Museum staff in 1920, becoming an Assistant Keeper in 1928, Deputy Keeper in 1936 and Keeper of Zoology in 1945, when he had apparently only two more years of service in the Museum ahead of him. Meanwhile, he gained considerable repute as an ornithologist, publishing a number of papers, and was always ready to help fellow-workers, especially young ones, with advice, guidance and encouragement; his service on the

"Keep an eye on that woman. I happen to know she has been pestering every butcher for miles around for a few bones for stewing."

Fig. 21. Postwar shortage (cartoon from *Evening News*, 8 November 1946).

councils of the British Ornithologists' Union, the Zoological Society and the National Trust, made him widely known.

Even so, Kinnear would not have been appointed Director but for peculiar, after-war circumstances at the Museum which, undergoing so much repair and restoration, needed as its head for the time being someone of administrative ability, with an inside knowledge and experience of its pre-war state. The big problems confronting the staff were to find room for the returning, evacuated collections and the new acquisitions, and to provide material for the exhibition galleries so that they could be re-opened to the public when renovated. The Museum staff found the numerous halts and delays frustrating and demoralising when they were eager to tackle so many tasks and could not do so.

Many matters great and small called for attention and decision. Thus, much of the Museum ground had grown vegetables during the war; this use had now to stop in order that the Museum gardens could be re-opened to the public. The girders of the intended, but unfinished, Entomological Block continued to rust; and the collections remained crowded elsewhere. Despite urging, work was not resumed until 1950; there was so much to be done everywhere in bomb-devastated London, with so many people to house and with materials and skilled men hard to get; lack of reinforced glass, for example, had delayed roof repairs to the Museum and re-opening of galleries to the public.

Not everything languished and in October 1947 the Librarian, A.C. Townsend, submitted to the Trustees a memorandum of far-reaching importance, setting out in some detail a scheme for a Museum scientific periodical. Although the Museum had published many catalogues and monographs as independent works, as well as pamphlets and the *Natural History Magazine* (1927-1936) which was of a popular character, it lacked suitable institutional serials for the publication of research by Museum workers or based on Museum collections. In this it lagged far behind some important, comparable, foreign museums and even some private British ones. The Muséum National d'Histoire Naturelle in Paris had published from 1802 a series of periodicals comprising *Annales, Mémoires, Mémoires-Nouvelles Série* and *Bulletin*. The *Természatraji Füzetek* of the Hungarian National Museum had begun in 1877, the *Annalen des Natürhistorischen Museums*, Vienna in 1877. The *Publications of the Field Columbian Museum, Chicago* (1894 onwards, but title has been changed to *Fieldiana* since 1940) gave a precedent for the scheme envisaged by being divided from the start into separate series.

The Keepers of the departments discussed Townsend's proposals in December 1947 and strongly favoured the issue of a Museum scientific serial; in general they agreed with his scheme. It came before the Trustees in January 1948. They likewise agreed that such a serial would enhance the reputation of the Museum abroad, be a stimulus to the staff and provide valuable means of exchange of publications with other bodies. They proposed, as had been done at Chicago, that it should be issued at irregular intervals in five series corresponding to the Departments of the Museum, with the Librarian as general editor, but each Keeper responsible for contributions emanating from his own Department. It was considered important that the periodical should be royal octavo in size to coincide exactly with the *Proceedings* of the Royal Society. For convenience of citation, one-word titles for institutional periodicals were now becoming increasingly popular throughout the world; Townsend therefore proposed that the new periodical should be entitled *Sloanea*, convenient to cite and fittingly commemorating Sir Hans Sloane. The Trustees did not agree with this. They preferred something longer and less convenient, *Bulletin of the British Museum (Natural History)*, with the name of the Department appended for each series. The Treasury gave assent to the proposed periodical in May 1948.

Fig. 22. Postwar shortage (cartoon from *Daily Herald*, 19 May 1947).

The first part of the *Bulletin* to be published was in the Geology series and it appeared in 1949, while the Entomology, Mineralogy and Zoology series began in 1950, and Botany in 1951, with the Historical series originating in 1953. Mineralogy ceased in 1974 and henceforth became amalgamated with Geology. A supplement series to Entomology, Geology and Zoology was published from 1965 to 1976. The *Bulletin* serves primarily for the publication of papers based on the extensive material amassed over many years in the Museum collections. The existence of this medium for publication has, as the Trustees foresaw, undoubtedly stimulated the preparation of important and needed revisions of many groups of organisms.

The loan between institutions of specimens for study has long been recognized as an essential part of taxonomic research. Since the collections of one institution rarely, if ever, duplicate those of another, it follows that one may possess relevant material lacking in another; moreover the organisms of a given area may be much better represented in a local institution or in one with long historic associations, e.g. Paris with Madagascar, than elsewhere. The author of a thorough revision or monograph of a group, dealing with all its species, their variability and their distribution, can only get the information needed and form sound judgements by firsthand study of the material available in several institutions; he needs to put their specimens side by side in order to observe and evaluate their differences and resemblances. Obviously, the broader the material base of studies, the sounder and more useful should be the publication built on it. C.J. Humphries, for example, in his revision of the Macaronesian genus *Argyranthemum* in *Bulletin of the British Museum (Natural History)* Botany 5: 145-240 (1976), acknowledges the use of specimens in twenty-three scattered herbaria. Similarly, W.R. Dolling in his revision of African pod bugs of the tribe Clavigrallini in *Bulletin of the British Museum (Natural History)* Entomology 39: 1-84 (1979), lists twenty widely-scattered collections used. This system of international co-operation did not exist and could not have been envisaged when the Statutes of the British Museum were formulated in 1753. Lankester had found that, contrary to earlier supposition, the Museum could lend material for identification without infringing the Statutes. This proved of value to all concerned, to the author of the work citing the specimens, to other workers using his publication, to the Museum which consequently possessed material authentically annotated and thus increased in reliability for reference purposes. In January 1947 the Director informed the Trustees that legally the sending of specimens out of the Museum had been 'for the purpose of identification and classification, or of being mounted and prepared', but that in practice some departments had gone beyond this and not infrequently sent out fully elucidated material to assist other institutions or private specialists in their researches. He was reluctant to discontinue such loans, but their continuance required consideration from the legal standpoint. The Department of Botany had got round this difficulty by putting pencil question marks against the names on sheets so that they could be lent supposedly for proper identification! No-one, however, could pretend that a type specimen had not been properly identified. In March 1947 Lord Macmillan reported that, after studying the enactments governing the British Museum Trust, he was satisfied that the Trustees had no power to make loans of specimens for assisting other institutions or private specialists. The Trustees decided that they should obtain this power so far as natural history collections were concerned. For this a Government Bill would be necessary.

The Children's Centre, an important Museum innovation during Kinnear's directorship, owes its origin to the enterprise and forceful persuasiveness of an attractive, lively and unconventional young school teacher, Miss Jacqueline Grizel Georgiana Palmer (1918-1961). She was born in London, but spent much of her childhood on Alderney in the Channel Islands. She trained at the Froebel Educational Insti-

He. "WHERE DO ANIMALS GO WHEN THEY DIE?"
She. "ALL GOOD ANIMALS GO TO HEAVEN, BUT THE BAD ONES GO TO THE NATURAL HISTORY MUSEUM."

Fig. 23. A theological discussion (drawing by E.H. Shepard in *Punch*, 10 April 1929).

tute, Roehampton, gaining a first-class diploma in 1939, taught during the war at the Quaker school, Leighton Park, Reading, then went to Newnham College, Cambridge, and gained an honours degree in geography in 1948. One autumn day in 1948 she took two very young friends to the Museum and talked to them about the exhibits as they walked around. They found themselves joined by more and more children eagerly listening. No labels or push-button gadgets can compete for the entertainment and instruction of children with an enthusiastic, well-informed and understanding adult and Miss Palmer, soon to be affectionately known to young and old as Jacky, quickly realized the lack of special provision for the interests of children in the Museum and decided to do something constructive about it. She asked to see the Director. Kinnear was just the man to appreciate her zeal, ability and originality. Her proposal for a Children's Centre to capture the interest of children, who otherwise wandered aimlessly around the galleries, won his support. He placed a bay in the main hall at her disposal. On 23 October 1948 he informed the Trustees 'that arrangements had been made (on a part-time basis for the present) for a lady with teaching experience (Miss J.G.G. Palmer) to be available to help children visiting the Museum to understand and to show interest in the exhibits'.

Her Children's Centre immediately became popular with children during the Christmas holidays. In January 1949, the Trustees agreed to its continuance as an experiment until the end of March; they paid her £5 a week. From April 1949 onwards matters improved. An arrangement was made between the Museum and the London County Council for the latter to employ Jacky as a school teacher on secondment to the Museum for its Children's Centre, the Treasury reimbursing the Council for the teacher so employed. In this roundabout way she retained her educational status and superannuation, though working outside a school. She now received the material assistance needed. At the Centre she next founded the Junior Naturalists' Club to which children could graduate on completing a piece of original work. The popularity of her work led the London County Council to appoint another teacher, Miss MacIver, to help her.

During the next few years, as the reputation of the Centre grew among educationists and parents, it was realized that Jacky's methods could have a wider application. She left the Museum in 1956, with this important extension of the Museum's educational facilities firmly established and in good hands, and then became a London County Council visiting teacher for field studies, going from school to school and taking children to bombed areas, parks and public gardens for observation and study. The Junior Naturalists' Club was for children up to sixteen. Three years after founding that, she founded a senior group, the Field Observers' Club for young naturalists, which in 1958 became an independent body with international affiliations. The Chelsea Physic Garden, which had been established in 1673 for the teaching of young apothecaries, fittingly and generously gave her laboratory space for these clubs.

In 1960 Jacky rented Bourne Mill, Colchester, to serve as a field study centre, but to the great sorrow, not only of her friends in the Museum but also of so many who had come under her inspiring influence, Jacqueline Palmer died of cancer at Dereham, Norfolk, on 3 January 1961, aged forty-three.

Vacation studentships were an innovation of 1949. To encourage university students to work in the Museum for up to eight weeks during their vacation, on a task involving study of Museum material such as could not be undertaken in their own university, the Treasury permitted the Museum to accept ten (later more) students, to whom a weekly allowance covering lodging and travel expenses was payable. The scheme was envisaged as widening the experience of students by actual research under the supervision and encouragement of a Museum scientist, of helping the Department concerned by work relevant to its interest and of making contact with and trying out students who might be likely candidates for vacancies on the Museum staff. The science faculties of universities and university colleges welcomed the scheme and applications were received from 170 students. Financial restrictions permitted only three each for zoology, entomology, geology and botany and two for mineralogy. The scheme worked admirably; it afforded training to students and interested them in the work of the Museum and, although the Museum scientific officers necessarily gave up much time to them, they considered this time well spent. The success of this trial year of 1949 has led to the acceptance of vacation students ever since, except in some recent years when it has been precluded by financial stringencies.

Reconstruction of the exhibition galleries for birds and mammals stood high among the tasks requiring consideration in 1949. Since the collection of British birds with their nests had been damaged beyond renovation, it was decided to represent, in a bird pavilion at the end of the west wing on the ground floor, a series of habitats with several characteristic species in each; between forty and fifty British birds could thus be shown in their natural surroundings without overcrowding, as the Keeper of Zoology informed the Trustees. An artist, D. Lindsey Clegg, was engaged to execute full-scale paintings as backgrounds. Later Mrs Elizabeth Bird gave money towards the cost of the panorama in the new bird pavilion as a memorial to her son, Charles Godfrey Bird, who was killed during the war and who had devoted much of his life to ornithological work in the Museum.

Kinnear retired on 30 April 1950. His services to the Museum had been of special value during a difficult period, as the Trustees appreciated; he had seen the building repaired, the last of the evacuated collections returned, the exhibition staff increased to provide new exhibits in place of so much destroyed or needing renewal, most exhibition galleries renovated and re-opened, innovations such as the Children's Centre successfully made, important collections acquired and plans for new building and restoration put in hand with the minimum of friction. All this had been unexpectedly thrust upon him, for he had not sought the directorship; he had faithfully executed the wishes of the Trustees and he had lightened indeed the tasks for his successor. A knighthood in June 1950 was his reward. He had seven years of busy and happy retirement before his death on 11 August 1957, his seventy-fifth birthday.

The directorship of Kinnear had been a bridge between the long and largely unchanging period embracing the occupation of the Waterhouse building in 1881 up to the beginning of the Second World War, and the very different world into which the Museum was to emerge after the war.

Part IV

The Museum Departments

A Note on Staff Grades

The histories of the Scientific Departments and the Library are much concerned with the stories of the officers who staffed them. It is inevitable that over a period of about 230 years, the Museum's hierarchical structure has altered greatly; and it is helpful in tracing the progress of individuals' careers to have some indication of their working relationships with colleagues.

Throughout most of its history, the Museum's senior staff comprised Assistants, 1st and 2nd class; Assistant Keepers; and Keepers. These grades were retained until the assimilation of the staff into the Scientific Civil Service in 1947, and the existing grades were assigned to the appropriate level on a five-point scale ranging from Scientific Officer to Chief Scientific Officer.

The support staff were initially entitled Attendants, in three grades, who largely undertook menial duties with little, or no curatorial component. In 1917 they were restyled Museum Clerks, except for the retention of Boy Attendants until 1924. At the end of 1928, a further reorganization resulted in the introduction of Attendants and Technical Assistants, the more proficient of whom were encouraged to undertake curatorial duties. With the assimilation into the Scientific Civil Service in 1947, the Attendants were regraded as Assistants (Scientific) and the Technical Assistants into a four-point Experimental Officer grade.

The resulting three class system of Assistants, Experimental Officers and Scientific Officers was combined into a single eight-point Scientific Officer scale in 1971, as a result of the recommendation of the Fulton Committee.

12

Department of
Zoology

THE DEPARTMENT OF Zoology was first designated as such in
1856, but had existed as the Zoological Branch of the Department
of Natural History in the British Museum at Bloomsbury since 1837.
Zoology had indeed been within the scope of the British Museum at its
founding in 1756, because Sir Hans Sloane's collection contained so
much zoological material. The history of the Department is one of continuous growth in its collections necessitating staff increases, usually
belated, with more and more sub-division of its holdings and ever
narrower specialisation by its staff members leading, however, to
higher standards of work, greater public utility and more international
appreciation. In 1847 the Keeper of Zoology, J.E. Gray, had only four
Assistants, i.e. his brother G.R. Gray, A. White, W. Baird and E.
Doubleday, supported by eight Attendants, and he was acquainted
with the work of them all. Matters have changed greatly since then.
The distinction between the major groups of animals, and their
diversity of species now known and represented in the Museum's
collections, together with the specialized knowledge required for their
curation and study, now make it impossible for a Keeper of Zoology to
have expert knowledge of more than a small part of the organisms
under his care, and legally his responsibility. Thus section heads and
other senior staff, being authorities in their own fields, are free (and
indeed expected) to develop their own research programmes.

At present, the Department consists of the Sub-Department of Orni-
thology (located at Tring Museum) and sixteen sections: Mammals;
Amphibians and Reptiles; Fish; Echinoderms and Protochordates;
Crustacea; Arachnida and Myriapoda; Mollusca; Annelida-Clitellata;
Polychaeta and Porifera; parasitic worms; Nematoda; Bryozoa; Co-

161

elenterata; Protozoa; Experimental Taxonomy and Histology and Preservation. Staff in the sections number from two to eleven and the total complement of permanent staff is 102.

Unfortunately few of Sloane's zoological specimens can be found in the Natural History Museum today. During the eighteenth and nineteenth centuries, the chief preservatives for stuffed birds and mammals, namely arsenical soap and corrosive sublimate (mercuric chloride), probably did more harm to those applying them than they did to destructive moths, beetles and mites. These ate their way steadily through all parts inadequately poisoned, or not poisoned at all. Their continual increase could menace a whole collection. Many of the zoological specimens were therefore consigned to the bonfire (pp.17, 18). The difficulty of preserving birds especially is discussed by P.F. Farber in *Isis* 68: 550-566 (1977). Shells, like minerals, did not give the same trouble, but they tended to be discarded or exchanged, or even stolen. Guy L. Wilkins, however, when critically revising the shells in the Natural History Museum, was able to identify over 400 specimens as having come from Sloane's collection, some of them being associated with William Dampier, Martin Lister and William Courten, and thus

LESSER-KNOWN SIGHTS OF LONDON.
In the cellars of the Natural History Museum. Stuffing a giraffe.

Fig. 24. Stuffing a giraffe as imagined by a *Punch* artist (from *Punch*, 21 July 1926).

of great historical interest (cf. G.L. Wilkins in *Bulletin of the British Museum (Natural History)* Historical Series 1: 1-48, 1953).

The zoological collections and their Keepers played an extremely important part in the development of the British Museum at Bloomsbury and the creation of the Natural History Museum. They have always been much more in the public eye than those of other Museum departments, with, moreover, nine of the Directors of the Natural History Museum being zoologists as opposed to two mineralogists and no botanists, so that much of their history has been related in previous chapters.

Linnaeus's eminent student Daniel Carlsson Solander (1736-1882) (p.18), was an able zoologist, but having had to deal with the whole of natural history he left little mark on the collections. In 1799, however, the Museum received as part of the bequest of Clayton Mordaunt Cracherode (1730-1799) his collection of shells along with his minerals, coins, gems and superb library: this is described by Guy L. Wilkins in *Bulletin of the British Museum (Natural History)* Historical series 1: 121-184 (1957). Neither Edward Whitaker Gray (1748-1806), nor his successors George Shaw (1751-1813) and Charles Konig appear to have done much to increase the collections under their care.

In 1813 a young Edinburgh graduate in medicine, William Elford Leach (1790-1836), became Konig's assistant and took over the care of the zoological collections. He was a brilliant and lively young man, who gave most attention to insects and mollusca; he made natural history excursions even to the Orkney Islands and visited Cuvier in Paris, where at the great Muséum d'Histoire Naturelle he learned French methods of museum management. Young John Edward Gray (1800-1875) visiting the Museum at the age of sixteen found Leach a stimulating, inspiring companion and Leach took to him. In later life Gray remembered with gratitude his encouragement and help. From 1814 to 1817 Leach published *Zoological Miscellany* and in the *Dictionnaire des Sciences Naturelles*, but his health deteriorated; he had long periods of sick leave and ultimately in 1822 he resigned, going then to live in Italy. He brought to the Museum a freshness of outlook and began that appreciation of the work of Cuvier which later profoundly influenced two great and contrary Museum officials, J.E. Gray and Richard Owen.

Leach's place was taken by John George Children (1777-1851), then working as a librarian in the Department of Antiquities. Children's appointment, neither expected nor wanted by him, debarred a naturalist of repute, William Swainson (1781-1855), from the post which he ardently desired and for which he was better qualified than Children; his justified disappointment caused a friend, Thomas

Stewart Traill, to publish in the *Edinburgh Review* of May 1823 an anonymous and damaging attack on the Museum's bad management of its
natural history collections. This caused material from British government expeditions to be sent elsewhere. Children was, however, conscientious and diligent and, since the shell collection was now both
large and confused, he set out to learn about mollusca by translating
into English Lamarck's work on the genera of shells in his *Histoire
naturelle des Animaux sans Vertèbres*, vols 5-7 (1818-1822) and then arranging the Museum collection in accordance with this. He published a
much abbreviated translation, with etymological annotations, in
instalments in the *Quarterly Journal of Science*, vols 14-16 (1822-1823) and
then re-issued it as a single volume, in a limited edition, entitled
Lamarck's Genera of Shells, translated from the French (1823); his daughter,
Anna, drew the illustrations. Children later turned his attention to
entomology, made an extensive collection of insects and became first
President of the Entomological Society of which he was a founder. Not
the least of his contributions to zoology was his encouragement of two
remarkable men, the American ornithological artist John James
Audubon (1785-1851) and the British zoologist John Edward Gray
(1800-1875), his successor as Keeper of Zoology.

Gray belonged to a family which had included many naturalists. The
first recorded member, Samuel Gray III, was a seedsman in Pall Mall,
London, in 1680. One grandson, Samuel Gray V (1739-1771) and a
successor in the Pall Mall seed business, translated Linnaeus's *Philo-
sophia botanica* (1751) into English for James Lee's *An Introduction to
Botany* (1760); the other grandson, Edward Whitaker Gray, was
Keeper of the Natural History Department in the British Museum
from 1787 to 1806. Samuel Gray V had a son, Samuel Frederick Gray
(1766-1828), a pharmacist, who published in November 1821 *A Natural
Arrangement of British Plants* (2 vols). In preparing this book S.F. Gray
undoubtedly had help from both his sons, the elder Samuel Forfeit,
(1798-1872) and the younger John Edward Gray, who compiled the
bulky systematic part. The *Natural Arrangement*, a revolutionary work
both as regards classification and nomenclature, aroused the anger of
some conservative Fellows of the Linnean Society by rejecting
Linnaeus's admittedly artificial 'sexual system' of classification, critic-
izing his nomenclature and failing to mention James Edward Smith,
President of the Linnean Society, as the author of Sowerby's *English
Botany*.

It was thus very unfortunate that when some other Fellows proposed
J.E. Gray, then a medical student, for election to the Linnean Society
in February 1822, they included Richard Anthony Salisbury, who was
much disliked, but not Robert Brown, who was highly respected. At

the ballot for fellowship in April 1822 Gray was rejected by a large majority obviously due to lobbying beforehand by die-hard Linnaeans, J.E. Smith's over-sensitive friends. The Society never again repeated such a shabby business. Injustice or insult to an able and promising, ambitious but virtually unknown young man may rankle within him for years, but more likely inflame rather than suppress his latent powers; injured pride can be a very potent and dangerous force. It diverted Gray from botany, in which he had made so remarkable a start, but strengthened his determination to prove his opponents wrong. As Gray stated fifty years later (in *Journal of Botany (London)* 10: 375, 1872), 'it stirred up my spirit of resistance and I determined to leave the medical profession and devote myself to the study of natural science'. He turned his attention to zoology. His brother, Samuel Forfeit Gray, became a Fellow of the Linnean Society without difficulty in 1825. Embittered, J.E. Gray deliberately remained outside. After 1832, he would have been welcome at any time but the wound had gone too deep; not until 1857 when, as the Linnean Society's historian A.T. Gage has said, 'long after Smith and his touchy friends had passed away' and when Gray had been for many years President of the Botanical Society of London and Keeper of Zoology, did he condescend to join the Linnean Society.

Not long after Children had become Keeper, he met Gray in the Museum, soon recognized the young man's ability and knowledge and later, in 1824, was able to offer him a temporary post to prepare a catalogue of reptiles. Gray had already begun that ceaseless flow of publications which earned him both fame and notoriety. Children soon found him more and more useful, indeed almost indispensable, and he gave him every encouragement. He never ceased to commend Gray's activities to the Trustees. Shortly before his retirement in 1840, Children gratefully acknowledged 'the important assistance which, from first to last, he has daily and hourly received from the zealous operations of Mr Gray, without whose services the zoological department could hardly have been rescued from the confusion in which Mr Children found it.' He also referred to Gray's 'indefatigable industry', his 'general knowledge of species completely unrivalled', and his 'extensive acquaintance with internal structure', which had 'raised him to a level with the most eminent zoologist of this or any other country'. Such a report to the Trustees made Gray his obvious successor (p.24).

Gray's keepership of the Department of Zoology began on 25 March 1840. He was just forty. Now he could further his ambition of making the Museum's zoological collection the foremost in the world and of exhibiting it in the new galleries being opened in 1841. R. Bowdler

Sharpe, an assistant in the Department from 1872 to 1909, wrote in 1906 that Gray 'has never received full credit for his exertions, for he had to fight against much prejudice within the Museum walls, and when the grants for purchases had been expended, he would freely spend his own money in buying specimens which he deemed to be of importance to the collection . . . In the early days of the nineteenth century England occupied but a poor position from a zoological stand-point, and France was at the zenith of her fame as regards exploration and the encouragement of science. Paris, Berlin, Leyden, were all increasing their collections and England was put to the test to keep pace with the progress of continental museums. That this country held its own so well is undoubtedly due to the enthusiasm of John Edward Gray.' By 1874, when after much ill health he at last retired, though only two months before his death on 7 March 1875, he had achieved this ambition, had been honoured for it by a doctorate from the University of Munich, though ignored by British universities, and had seen the Department's affairs delivered into the capable hands of Albert Günther. Some account of the major happenings of those years will be found in Chapters 3 and 4.

An important innovation dating from 1837 and due to Gray was a register of accessions. It had been customary in museums when Gray became Keeper to put every zoological specimen on display. He later concluded (pp.36, 37) that it would be more instructive and pleasing for the public, and more useful for students and research workers to divide specimens into an exhibition series for the public galleries and have a study series elsewhere. The exhibition specimens filled tall cases along the walls of the galleries and table cases spaced along the centre of the floor. The study series was stored in the basement at Bloombsury under conditions far from congenial for the specimens and the workers upon them. For example, Gray formed an extensive collection of skulls and skeletons. According to Günther, this collection occupied a room in the basement, 65 feet × 35 feet (19.8m × 10.7m) fitted with wall- and table-cases. 'No ray of the sun penetrated into this locality, and a fire had to be kept in it all the year round to preserve the bones from damp and mould. No more unsuitable locality could be imagined for an osteological collection, yet it was the only room in the building available for the purpose.' Such conditions supplied a strong argument for the transfer of natural history specimens to a new building. As regards reptiles, batrachians and fishes, these were almost all preserved in bottles of alcohol packed as closely as possible on shelves in three rooms of the basement. 'The conditions of light and temperature,' observed Günther who spent years under them 'were most suitable for the preservation of the specimens, but less so for the comfort and health of the persons compelled to work in that locality.' At times of heavy rainfall, water from the springs of once rural Bloomsbury seeped over the stone-paved basement floors and the damp caused the bottles to lose their labels.

The Attendant in charge of the spirit collection and the galleries on Günther's arrival was Edward Gerrard (1811-1910). He joined the Museum staff as an attendant in 1841 and became the indispensable assistant, first of Gray and then of Günther. He published in 1867 the *Catalogue of the Bones of Mammalia* and was apparently responsible for much of Gray's *List of Osteological Specimens* (1847). The Department had so little working space that Gerrard wrote his work with a board across his knees to serve as a table. His period of service in the Museum extended to fifty-five years and, although he retired in 1896, he lived till 1910, dying within four months of his 100th birthday. He, or rather his family, ran a taxidermy business, Edward Gerrard and Sons, which did much work over many years for the Museum.

Gray's middle brother, George Robert Gray (1808-1872), had entered the service of the Museum in 1831 and later became Assistant Keeper. After J.E. Gray had suffered a stroke in May 1869 which paralysed his right side, but which he countered with characteristic determination by learning to write with his left hand, much of the administration of the Department rested on G.R. Gray and Günther. The death of G.R. Gray on 6 May 1872 made Günther the obvious choice as the next Keeper of Zoology. In 1874 he had a disagreement with Owen, whom he feared would now work against his appointment. Fortunately for both that did not happen, but the incident reveals the current view, expressed by Lyon Playfair, the distinguished chemist and politician, in 1875, of Owen as 'a bitter and relentless hater'.

Günther (1830-1914) became Keeper on 6 February 1875 at the age of forty-five and held office for twenty years. He was born on 3 October 1830 at Mohringen near Stuttgart, Württemberg, in southern Germany, where in the then unspoilt countryside teeming with birds, he acquired an abiding natural history interest. His father, a solicitor, died of typhoid in 1835. His education accordingly depended on grants and scholarships. In October 1847, aged seventeen, he entered the university of Tübingen as a student in the theological college, his maternal grandfather being a Lutheran pastor. Philosophy and theology proved little to his taste, but in the anatomy and physiology classes of the professor and physician, Wilhelm von Rapp (1794-1868), he found a living interest and in Rapp himself a considerate and generous teacher and friend. In September 1850 he began to study the collections in the royal natural history museum, the Königliches Naturalien-Kabinet, in Stuttgart. At the end of four years in Tübingen he completed his theological studies and received his Testimonia which would have qualified him to become a Lutheran clergyman, a vocation he no longer desired; henceforth he devoted himself to medicine and science. In 1853 he produced a thesis at Rapp's suggestion, *Die Neckar-Fische*, thus beginning the life-long systematic study of fish, which placed him among the greatest of ichthyologists. It was then customary for German students to go from university to university, attracted by the repute of particular professors. Günther accordingly travelled to Berlin in April 1853 to study medicine and zoology; here Johannes Peter von Müller (1801-1858), celebrated for his *Handbuch der Physiologie* but also eminent as an anatomist and zoologist, became his encouraging teacher. Like Owen, Müller had been influenced by Cuvier's concept of basic animal types reflecting a definite plan of creation and he in turn influenced Günther. After a year in Berlin, Günther moved to the university of Bonn and then back to Tübingen and qualified there as doctor of medicine in 1857. Meanwhile in 1854 his widowed mother, Eleonora Louise Günther, became desperate for money, emigrated to England and got employment as a teacher in Brighton. Here she came to know the sisters of Lord Macaulay, the historian, who was a Trustee of the British Museum, and thereby made a connection valuable later to her son, Albert. He joined her in Brighton in July 1857. The Misses Macaulay asked Lord Macaulay how Günther could get employment as a zoologist in the British Museum and he suggested writing to Gray. This introduction, together with a conversation between Macaulay and Owen, led to Günther's long association with the British Museum. He was taken into temporary employment in the Museum in November 1857 and was appointed to a permanent post in 1862.

His major works before becoming Keeper had been the *Catalogue of Colubrine Snakes in the Collection of the British Museum* (1858) and *Catalogue of the Fishes of the British Museum* (8 vols: 1859-1870), but he had also been the prime mover in founding the *Zoological Record* in 1865. For many years, unfortunately, he and Francis Day (1829-1889), a medical officer in India who had become an expert ichthyologist, were at odds and their rivalry hurt them both and reflected adversely on the Museum. They became reconciled and forgave each other their animosity (partly based on misunderstanding) in 1889, as Day was dying of cancer. An account of Day and his collection of Indian fishes has been published by P.J.P. Whitehead and P.K. Talwar in *Bulletin of the British Museum (Natural History)* Historical series 5: 1-189 (1976).

Gray's success in building the collections was not accompanied by equivalent increase of staff, but this had grown nevertheless. On Günther's appointment as Keeper in 1875 it consisted of Frederick Smith (1805-1879), who had joined in 1850 and had then become

38. Evelyn Cheesman (1881-1969), intrepid entomological collector and traveller, out in the wilds of Papua New Guinea in 1933.

39. *(Top)* New whale hall, built in
    1931, with life-size model of the
    Blue Whale *(Balaenoptera musculus)*,
    the world's largest mammal.

40. *(Bottom)* Skeleton of the Blue
    Whale being dismantled in the old
    whale hall, c.1933.

41. *(Bottom)* Skeleton of the Blue
    Whale being reassembled in the
    new whale hall, c.1934.

42. Presentation in July 1927 of group of Spanish Ibex *(Capra pyrenaica victoriae)* from Sierra de Gredos by King Alfonso of Spain in the presence of King George V.

43. Exhibit of fleas and bubonic plague in main hall in 1927.

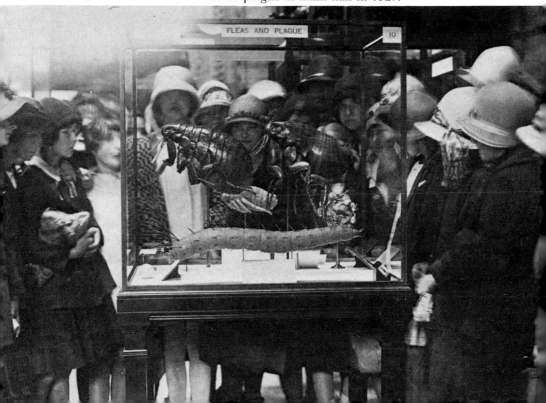

Assistant Keeper, three senior assistants, Arthur Gardiner Butler (1844-1925) appointed in 1863, Edgar Albert Smith (1847-1916) appointed in 1867 and Richard Bowdler Sharpe (1847-1909) appointed in 1872, two junior assistants, Charles Owen Waterhouse (1843-1917) appointed in 1866 and Edward John Miers (1851-1930) appointed in 1872, five 1st class Attendants and six 2nd class Attendants. By September 1878 he had gained three more 2nd class assistants, Michael Rogers Oldfield Thomas (1858-1929) appointed in 1876, Stuart Oliver Ridley (1853-1935) appointed in 1878 and Francis Jeffrey Bell (1855-1924) also appointed in 1878, a staff of twenty persons. Of these, Smith, Butler and Waterhouse were entomologists (p.210).

Throughout his keepership Günther continued to urge the need for more staff to curate and study the Department's ever growing collection. At his retirement in 1895, the staff consisted of an Assistant Keeper, A.G. Butler; seven 1st Class Assistants: E.A. Smith, R. Bowdler Sharpe, C.O. Waterhouse, Georges Albert Boulenger (1858-1937) appointed in 1881, M.R. Oldfield Thomas, F.J. Bell and William Robert Ogilvie Grant (1863-1924) appointed in 1882; seven 2nd Class Assistants: William Forsell Kirby (1844-1912) appointed in 1879, Reginald Innes Pocock (1863-1947) appointed in 1885, Charles Joseph Gahan (1862-1939) appointed in 1886, Randolph Kirkpatrick (1863-1950) appointed in 1886, Francis Arthur Heron (1864-1940) appointed in 1889, Ernest Edward Austen (1867-1837) appointed in 1895 and George Francis Hampson (1860-1936) appointed in 1895; and seven 1st Class Attendants, eight 2nd Class Attendants, two Boy Attendants, a taxidermist and an articulator, a staff in all of thirty-four persons. Of these, Butler, Smith, Waterhouse, Kirby, Gahan, Heron, Austen and Hampson were entomologists (see pp.210,211 ff).

Günther's major task on taking office was to prepare for the removal of the Department to the new museum planned at South Kensington. Building had begun in 1873 and it should have been finished in 1876, but many difficulties postponed completion until 1880 (p.55). That summer, the botanical, mineralogical and palaeontological collections were moved from Bloomsbury to South Kensington to be available for the official opening of the Museum on Easter Monday, 18 April 1881. Unfortunately, not until July 1882 were the zoological galleries ready to receive the Bloomsbury collections; most of these had to be carefully packed in special boxes and their transport took ninety-seven days; it was completed by October 1883 (p.61). The fish gallery, finished in 1885, was the last to be opened to the public.

A serious oversight in planning the new Museum was the complete lack of storage provision for the immense spirit collection of fishes, reptiles, etc., in the Bloomsbury basement, which occupied 52,635 bottles and was estimated to contain about 5,000 gallons (22,730 litres) of highly inflammable liquid. This constituted a major fire hazard. Günther accordingly proposed the erection of a special fire-proof building, separate from the main Museum. The Trustees approved but the Treasury, alarmed by the estimated cost of £20,552, did not sanction it until March 1879. Günther and the architect Waterhouse jointly worked out plans and the building, begun in 1881, was completed in 1883. It remained until 1953, but its contents were shifted between 1924 and 1938 into the New Spirit Building built between 1921 and 1930. The Old Spirit Building stood on the site now occupied by the lecture hall, general library, and mammal section.

Georges Albert Boulenger, who now had charge of the spirit collection on which Günther had worked so long and assiduously in the damp and dark Bloomsbury basement, was like him a foreigner and like him a research worker of high ability and amazing industry. He first came to England from Belgium in 1881. Günther noticed him in the zoological gallery, learned that he had worked on reptiles in the Brussels Musée Royal d'Histoire Naturelle, found him very well-informed and offered him the task of cataloguing the reptiles. Boulenger worked first in the Museum as an unpaid volunteer, as he had private wealth, but in 1883 was officially appointed to the staff as a 1st Class assistant. Owing to the lack of teaching of systematic zoology and of botany in English universities and colleges, a well-trained, competent zoologist such as Boulenger was a splendid acquisition.

Günther set Boulenger to work on new editions of catalogues which he or Gray had prepared earlier. The collections had much increased meanwhile and Boulenger had his own independent standpoint, so they became essentially new works. He began with the Batrachia and produced in 1882 a new catalogue of two volumes replacing Gray's work of 1850 on Batrachia Gradientia and Günther's of 1858 on Batrachia Salientia. Then between 1885 and 1887 came three volumes on the lizards replacing Gray's volume of 1845, followed in 1889 by one on the chelonians, rhynocephalians and crocodiles, in 1890 by an account of the Reptilia and Batrachia of India for *The Fauna of British India* and between 1893 and 1896 by three volumes on snakes. Such achievement merited recognition, but was unlikely to receive any without lobbying: Günther complained that his recommendation of Boulenger to the Royal Society was ignored, but Sir William Flower (Chapter 7), who was a man of influence, quickly obtained him election in 1894. The list of Boulenger's publications in *Annales de la Societé Royale Zoologique et Malacologique de Belgique* 52: 11-56 (1921) includes some 875 titles.

The German invasion in 1914 of his homeland, neutral Belgium, so angered, disillusioned and saddened Boulenger that he never read any German publication issued after 1914. In 1920 he retired from the Museum with the reputation as one of the world's leading herpetologists. His services to the Museum and to zoology had been immense. He then left England, returned to Belgium and worked thereafter at the Jardin Botanique de l'Etat in Brussels on the enormous rose herbarium of François Crépin; here he acquired a second reputation, that of a systematic botanist specializing in the difficult genus *Rosa*, a fact of which D.M.S. Watson was unaware when writing his obituary for the *Obituary Notices of Fellows of the Royal Society* 3: 13-17 (1940).

Boulenger, like Günther, worked at fish as well as reptiles and amphibians. Long before his retirement it had become impossible for any one individual to have an adequate knowledge of the Museum's collections of these groups, still less a world knowledge. Inevitably ichthyologists and herpetologists had to go their separate ways, forming separate though allied sections within the Museum by 1913. Charles Tate Regan (1878-1943) on his appointment as an assistant in 1901 was allocated to work on fishes under Boulenger and he devoted his life to their study thereafter, until his appointment as Director in 1927 (Chapter 10). He produced a succession of revisions and monographs of high quality and was more interested in problems of higher classification, geographical distribution and phylogeny than had been his predecessors, who had been disbelieving, sceptical, neutral or lukewarm about the theory of evolution. Among much else his work drew attention to the high endemism in the fish of the African lakes. He had an especial appreciation of the value of anatomical data.

Between Boulenger's retirement in 1920 and the appointment of Hampton Wildman Parker (1897-1968) in 1923 as Assistant Keeper in charge of the reptiles and amphibians, the collection was under the care of Joan Beauchamp Procter (1897-1931), a strong-minded young woman of high artistic and scientific ability whose short life was so marred by ill-health that from the age of twelve to her death from cancer at thirty-four she passed few days without physical pain. As a school girl at St. Paul's School for Girls, she became enthusiastically interested in reptiles and amphibians and so impressed Boulenger on a visit of enquiry that he encouraged her and, when because of her precarious health she could not proceed to a university, she worked as his assistant from 1917 to 1920. She published in 1922 a study of a remarkable tortoise *Testudo loveridgii* (now *Malacochersus tornieri*) in *Proceedings of Zoological Society of London* 1922: 483-526 (1922) which was considered to be her most important contribution to herpetology. She also impressed Chalmers Mitchell, the enterprising Secretary of the Zoological Society, by her technical ability and she moved to London

Zoo, helping Boulenger's son with the decoration of the new aquarium and later designing the new reptile house, when she had been put in charge of the reptiles and amphibians. A true naturalist, Joan Procter possessed a profound and sympathetic understanding of them as living creatures stemming from her childhood when she had kept them as pets; she even stayed in the reptile house all night listening to their varied calls, as they communicated with one another in the darkness. She paid such successful attention, founded on knowledge, to their well-being that an American university awarded her an honorary doctorate. Her skill in excising tumours and dressing sores was remarkable and an obituary in *The Times* of 21 September 1931 recorded that 'more than one distinguished surgeon has watched her with amazement and admiration operating on the mouth or the eye of a cobra or rattlesnake with apparatus of her own devising.' It required fourteen men to hold still a python, while she lanced and disinfected a sore. Although most at home with living reptiles, she described new species while working in the Museum.

Parker was Assistant Keeper in charge of the Amphibia and Reptilia section from 1923 to 1947 and Keeper of Zoology from 1947 to 1957. He was born in 1897 at Giggleswick, Yorkshire, where his father was a schoolmaster. Enlistment in the army during the 1914-1918 World War interrupted his education and he received a severe wound that made him lame afterwards, but did not hinder his athletic success later when, after demobilization in 1919, he returned to Cambridge, where he studied zoology, botany and chemistry. Appointed to the Museum he not only administered his section with high efficiency, but embarked on detailed taxonomic studies utilizing not only external characters, but less obvious though more fundamental skeletal and muscle characters. He published also a long series of descriptions of new species of reptiles and amphibians and faunistic lists in zoological journals. Many English universities up to about 1950 did not recognize taxonomic revisions as adequate tests of intellectual ability. But through the intervention of Professor L.D. Brongersma, Parker was enabled in November 1949 to submit his *The Snakes of Somaliland and the Sokotra Islands* (1949) as a thesis, together with subsidiary subjects (Stellningen), for public disputation at the University of Leiden, noted both for a more catholic attitude to biological studies and very high standards of scholarship. He stood his ground with convincing arguments and detailed knowledge and was duly awarded the prized Leiden doctorate.

Parker had outstanding ability for organisation and administration, an ability fully exercised during the period of postwar reconstruction and renewal of effort in the Museum which was hampered by shortage of funds. It has been said that 'Parker's staff may at times have complained bitterly when he refused some of their demands . . . nevertheless all were aware that he was controlled by limitations outside his authority and by his overriding desire to be absolutely impartial. . . He had a clear, logical and uncluttered mind and possessed the qualities of precision of thought and of expression, and a concentration on his research on the systematics of reptiles and amphibians, that put the mark of distinction on his numerous contributions to scientific journals. Many opportunities for pursuing his own research were, however, sacrificed in encouraging and assisting young scientists in this country and colleagues overseas.' He retired at the age of sixty and died of cancer in September 1968.

John Roxborough Norman (1898-1944) joined the staff in 1921, and worked with Tate Regan on the fish collections. He had served in the 1914-1918 World War and had been invalided out of the Army in 1918 with his health permanently affected. Ability and diligent work on the collections led to his becoming Deputy Keeper of Zoology, with charge of the collections at Tring between 1939 and 1944, the year in which he died. His major publications are *A History of Fishes* (1931; 3rd ed., by P.H. Greenwood, 1975) and *A Draft Synopsis of the Orders, Families and Genera of Recent Fishes* (1957), but he also published many papers in periodicals, including 'The South American Characid fishes of the subfamily "Serrasalmoninae" ' in *Proceedings of Zoological Society of London* 1928: 781-829 (1929). In many ways he followed the tradition of Günther rather than Regan. To ichthyology, Peter J.P. Whitehead writes, 'essentially Norman's contribution was that of the tidy housewife. He tidied up the collection, he tidied up the display gallery and, his most impressive though incomplete work, he tidied up the genera of fishes. Everywhere in his work "system" abounds, but this is not evolutionary or biological system; it is the system of intellectual tidiness. As a contribution it must not be decried, since it provided a physical basis for efficient curation as well as an important source for future retrieval of information.'

The interest of another Museum ichthyologist, Norman Bertram Marshall (b. 1915), who joined the Museum staff in 1947 and resigned in 1972 to become a professor at Queen Mary College, has been essentially in functional studies of marine fishes; relating structure to ways of life controlled by depth, pressure etc.; this work found expression in his *Aspects of Deep-Sea Biology* (1954), *Explorations in the Life of Fishes* (1976) and *Developments in Deep-Sea Biology* (1979). He was elected to the Royal Society in 1970. The concept of fish as living creatures, for the study of which Museum specimens in spirit are essential, but are expressive only of certain aspects, underlies modern work, which, as in other

Museum departments, aims at a broadly based taxonomy. Ethelwynn Trewavas (b. 1900), who became a member of the Museum staff in 1935, had, however, worked on fish since 1925 and her publications reflect this catholic attitude.

In many ways Peter Humphry Greenwood (b. 1927) has proved to be Regan's natural successor. Part of his research has concentrated on a detailed study of African cichlid fishes, in particular those of the Lake Victoria species flock and related flocks in other lakes. In parallel with this work, he has been much concerned with the higher classification of bony fishes, an interest which culminated in 1966 with a paper (co-authored with three American ichthyologists) which laid the foundation for a phylogenetic classification of teleosts.

While Boulenger was cataloguing reptiles, amphibians and fishes under Günther's supervision, another colleague, Richard Bowdler Sharpe (p.175) was engaged on an equally formidable task, the *Catalogue of the Birds in the British Museum* which ultimately ran to twenty-seven volumes published between 1874 and 1898. Although the Sloane collection is stated to have contained 1,172 ornithological specimens in 1753, and John Latham (1740-1837) in 1781 to 1785 described species from specimens in the British Museum, all these had perished before Bowdler Sharpe entered the service of the Museum in 1872. An even greater loss was the vast collection of British birds formed by George Montagu (1751-1815), a soldier and country gentleman who became the most perspicacious ornithologist of his time, the author of the classic *Ornithological Dictionary or Alphabetical Synopsis of British Birds* (2 vols, 1802) and *Testacea Britannica* (2 vols, 1803). Although the cirl bunting and Montagu's harrier had earlier been named on the Continent, Montagu first distinguished them in Britain and he first described the roseate tern (*Sterna dougallii* Montagu). The Museum bought his collection in 1816 on the recommendation of Leach and Banks for £1,200 — a large sum indeed. Unfortunately, according to Sharpe in *The History of the Collections* 2:79 (1906), 'not one of his specimens was properly prepared — apparently no preservative worthy of the name having been used. . . The bones of the neck and other bones of the body were left in the specimens, which were set up by no means badly. During the thirty years that they have been under my care, many have been attacked by small mites (in spite of the camphor-laden atmosphere of the cases) and have fallen to pieces . . . Owing to the specimens having no preservative, many of them, especially the fat and heavy ones, fell to pieces of their own weight in course of time. This was regrettably the case with the British-killed Great Bustard (*Otis tarda*) which collapsed a few years ago.' Despite the example set by Charles Waterton, British taxidermy made little progress until after the Great

Exhibition of 1851 in London when an outstanding exhibit from Stuttgart in particular showed what skilled foreign craftsmen could accomplish.

During the years that Gray was Keeper the collection of birds, as of mammals, increased enormously. Sharpe estimated that, when he took office in 1872, the ornithological collection numbered about 10,000 mounted birds and 20,000 specimens of skins and eggs. By 1906 it had grown to over 400,000 specimens, including close on 10,000 eggs. Most of these came from gifts and bequests, notably by Brian Hodgson, Allen O. Hume, Henry Seebohm, R.G. Wardlaw Ramsay (who presented the Marquess of Tweeddale's collection of specimens and books), F. Ducane Godman, Osbert Salvin, Philip Crowley, and Radcliffe Saunders. Behind such donations of vast private collections lay a confidence generated by Gray that the British Museum now provided the best repository for their care. Moreover the preparation of the *Catalogue of the Birds* persuaded private collectors that their collections would be critically studied and so contribute to ornithological knowledge. Such views were well founded. The Museum also purchased the collections of Alfred Russel Wallace, Philip Lutley Sclater and others, thereby coming to possess numerous type specimens. On G.R. Gray's death (p.167) Günther, with the birds as well as cold-blooded vertebrates now in his charge, conceived the plan of a catalogue of birds as detailed as his own *Catalogue of Fishes.*

Günther recommended and obtained the appointment of Bowdler Sharpe as an assistant to undertake the immense task of preparing the *Catalogue of Birds.* Sharpe was young and lacked private means, which meant that he could never be a rival to Günther, but he was enthusiastic and strongly motivated. The publication of his *A Monograph of the Alcedinidae or Family of Kingfishers* (1868-1871) had manifested his ability. He had worked as an assistant in Quaritch's bookshop and had then been librarian to the Zoological Society for seven years; he needed no introduction to ornithological literature. Günther, as an exacting and methodical taskmaster to himself as to his assistants, immediately put Sharpe to work on the proposed *Catalogue* and kept him at it; in his opinion 'this young and able assistant, who is only too ready to flit from one work to another for steady and methodical work', as Günther described Sharpe in 1874, had to be pinned down to the main task. Günther, however, had never been a shop assistant or a librarian subject to interruption so frequent that flitting from one task to another in response to continual varied demands became a way of life and a genial attitude towards it, an ingrained habit of mind.

The preparation of massive works by specialists within a museum, when widely known, always attracts an inflow of material and, as the gifts mentioned above indicate, the making of the *Catalogue* increased both the specimens and the labour upon them. Sharpe had to go out in 1885 to Simla to supervise the enormous collection donated by Allen Octavian Hume (1829-1912) which comprised 63,000 bird skins, 19,000 eggs and 371 mammals all from the Indian Empire, the result of well-organised collecting between 1862 and 1885; it includes 258 type specimens. Günther regarded the bird catalogue as the major achievement of his Keepership. The description of 11,548 species of birds was, however, too big a task for one man. Sharpe himself dealt with 5,181 of these, but, without the help of other specialists whom Günther enlisted, the work might not have been completed in the lifetime of either. It remains a monument to the industry of the one and the administration of the other. The first of the twenty-seven volumes appeared in 1874, the last in 1898.

Gray and Oldfield Thomas (p.185) managed to live comfortably on Museum salaries and had money to spare by marrying wealthy women and producing no children. Sharpe, however, had a wife and ten daughters to support and it was many years before three of them, Dora, Daisy and Sylvia, became skilled colourists of bird plates. He accordingly worked assiduously both day and night, sometimes until 2 a.m., in order to get on with the *Catalogue* and to ease his continual

Head and foot of *Aquila chrysaetus*.

Fig. 25. A typical engraving in R. Bowdler Sharpe, *Catalogue of the Birds,* vol. 1 (1874) portraying the golden eagle, *Aquila chrysaetus.*

financial worries by journalistic writing and editing, which as a full-time occupation would have paid him better than slaving in the Museum. Ultimately the Museum had to pay him for work on the *Catalogue* done at home, simply because otherwise there would have been little hope of its completion. By 1891 this one-time bookshop assistant had become internationally known as a leading taxonomic ornithologist and the University of Aberdeen conferred an honorary LL.D. upon him. Completion of the *Catalogue* in 1899 did not lessen Sharpe's labours in the Museum or at home. Already he had begun the compilation of a supplementary work, *A Hand-list of the Genera and Species of Birds* (5 vols, 1899-1912). Then Ray Lankester, as Director, set him to work on an historical account of the Museum's ornithological collections; this he did so thoroughly that it delayed the publication of *The History of the Collections* vol. 2 (1906), wherein it occupies pp. 79-515, more pages than all the other zoological contributions put together. Diverted though he often was from his main task by the many other demands upon his time, Sharpe stands out as one of the Museum's most industrious and prolific servants. He died in 1909 at the age of sixty-two.

The collection of eggs in the Natural History Museum was estimated by Sharpe in 1906 as nearly 100,000. After the completion of Sharpe's *Catalogue*, Eugene William Oates (1845-1911) began the compilation of a *Catalogue of the Collection of Birds' Eggs in the British Museum (Natural History)* (5 vols, 1901-1912). He had been an officer in the Public Works Department in Burma and had devoted his leisure to natural history. He had already published *A Handbook to the Birds of British Burmah* (1883), on which he had worked in the Museum in 1882 and 1883, and had edited a second edition of A.O. Hume's *The Nests and Eggs of Indian Birds* (1889-1890). Before illness forced him to relinquish his task, he produced four volumes of the British Museum catalogue of eggs.

Oates also wrote volumes 1 and 2 (1889-1890) on birds in W.T. Blanford's *The Fauna of British India*. He died at Edgbaston, Birmingham, on 16 November 1911. According to Sharpe, 'no more conscientious worker has ever lived'. There is, however, a curious mistake in the *Fauna*. The call-note of the streak-eyed pied wagtail, *Motacilla alba ocularis*, is described in S. Ali and S.D. Ripley, *Handbook of the Birds of India and Pakistan* 9: 290, 295 (1973) as 'a sharp *chi-cheep* usually uttered in flight'. That is not how it is described in *The Fauna of British India, Birds*. When writing this, Oates happened to leave his manuscript open on a table in the Bird Room and had gone for lunch when Sharpe and Ogilvie-Grant (see p.178) came by. Sharpe, who was a jovial extrovert character loving a joke, said to Ogilvie-Grant, 'Let us add something funny to Oates' description' and did so, feeling sure that

Oates would spot this little piece of mischief on his return. He did not and neither he nor Blanford noticed it in the proof. Accordingly in *Birds* 2: 290 (1890), the account of *Motacilla alba ocularis* ends with the apparently authoritative statement: 'The note of this species is a loud "Pooh".'

On Sharpe's death, the charge of the ornithological collections passed to William Robert Ogilvie-Grant, (p.105), who came from Edinburgh, where he had been educated at Fettes College. Ogilvie-Grant had a life-long interest in travel and he visited Madeira in 1890, Socotra in 1898 to 1899 and the Azores in 1909. Thereafter, with the help of the Museum's Assistant Secretary C.E. Fagan, he organized expeditions for other people, notably the Ruwenzori Expedition of 1905 to 1906 and the British Ornithologists' Union Expedition to Dutch New Guinea of 1909 to 1913. He thus did much more than study the Museum's collections. Like Sharpe and Flower, he took an active part in furthering the protection of birds and did much to enhance the repute of the Museum as an institution concerned with the preservation of the living world in all its diversity. Unfortunately he was stricken with paralysis in 1916 and retired in 1918. He died in 1924 at the age of sixty-one. Although credited with an overbearing temper and a sharp tongue, he seems to have been basically a kindly man without malice.

Ogilvie-Grant's illness and war conditions meant that little was done with the bird collection for some years. In November 1919 Percy Roycroft Lowe (1870-1948), who had joined the Museum's staff in 1919, took charge of the Bird Room and tackled the much needed reorganization of its collections. He was born at Stamford, Lincolnshire, and educated at Jesus College, Cambridge, and Guy's Hospital, London, for a medical career. In 1899 he went out to South Africa as a civil surgeon to serve in the Boer War; he found the birds so interesting and attractive that he took up ornithology as a hobby.

On his return to England he became private physician to Sir Frederic Johnstone and made six yachting voyages with him to the West Indies, during which he collected some 3,000 birds. He served as the medical officer on an ambulance ship on the Mediterranean during the 1914-1918 World War, then retired from medicine and devoted his life thereafter to the study and protection of birds. Unlike Sharpe and Ogilvie-Grant, Lowe had less interest in the description of new species and infraspecific variants of birds than in the classification, anatomy and osteology of major groups, possibly as a result of his training as a surgeon. He gave special attention to waders and some other not distant groups such as cranes, bustards, rails and gulls. Internal as well as more easily observed external characters, e.g. coloration, played a part in his classification. He became a leading authority on the skeletons of birds. Among the queries which came to him was the identification of bones of birds eaten by the Romans and excavated in quantity. Formerly supposed to be those of the pheasant, they proved to be bones of the domestic fowl, thus disproving them as evidence for the supposed introduction of the pheasant into Britain by the Romans. The status of wild fowl in Europe, particularly with regard to indiscriminate shooting and threats to their habitats, became a matter of special concern to him. In 1939 he succeeded in getting the close season lengthened in Britain for geese and ducks.

Lowe retired on 2 January 1935, his sixty-fifth birthday. Norman Boyd Kinnear (p.149), who had come to the Museum from Bombay in 1920 and whose reputation as an ornithologist primarily interested in Asiatic birds had steadily grown during the years 1920 to 1935 when he worked with Lowe, was now given full charge.

Unable to increase its permanent staff the Museum happily employed, at a fixed rate per hour, outside specialists and capable interested people on a temporary basis. These hard-working associates gave valuable service and brought honour to the Museum by the repute of their work. They make a long list and in this present history only a few can be mentioned. Among the ornithologists, David Armitage Bannerman (1886-1979) stands especially high. After education at Wellington College and Pembroke College, Cambridge, he joined the temporary staff of the Museum in 1910 to work on birds. He suffered from the ill health which paradoxically sometimes leads to longevity. He had adequate private means for travel and visited the West Indies, South America, North, South and West Africa and the Atlantic Islands, as well as Europe, for ornithological study. These journeys gave Bannerman first-hand geographical knowledge and field acquaintance with birds which provided an ideal background for his massive comprehensive works. Being graded as medically unfit for military service during the 1914-1918 World War, he nevertheless served first as an ambulance driver, then as a staff officer of the British Red Cross Society, and received both British and French War Medals including the Mons Star. After the Armistice, he rejoined the temporary staff of the Museum and worked there until the outbreak of the 1939-1945 World War. After the war he again returned to the Museum, was made an Honorary Associate in 1950 and then retired in 1952, but continued to write his ornithological books until shortly before his death.

Apart from reports on the birds of numerous Museum expeditions, and papers in *The Ibis*, Bannerman's major publications during his Museum period are *The Canary Islands, their History, Natural History and Scenery* (1922), *The Birds of Tropical West Africa* (8 vols, 1930-1951) and

The Birds of West and Equatorial Africa (2 vols, 1953). His later, superbly illustrated publications utilizing earlier experience include *The Birds of the British Isles* (12 vols, 1933-1963), wherein the ambition of the celebrated bird artist George Edward Lodge (1860-1953) to illustrate in print every native British bird was fulfilled, posthumously despite Lodge's longevity, and, in collaboration with Mary Bannerman, his wife, *Birds of the Atlantic Islands* (4 vols, 1963-1968). When I saw Bannerman, then aged ninety-one, at his home in Slindon, West Sussex in October 1978, he had become physically frail, but his memories of the Museum were still vivid and he maintained his interest and enthusiasm to the last. He died on 6 April 1979. With him and Riley (p.219), who died on 26 May 1979, perished the last living links with the Department of Zoology before the upheaval of the 1914-1918 World War.

In 1954 an Honorary Associate of the Museum, Richard Meinertzhagen (1878-1967) presented his ornithological collection of about 25,000 skins and 402 tongues of birds. These were in addition to his herbarium of over 5,000 specimens and his collection of Mallophaga (lice) estimated to contain 587,610 specimens mounted on slides and in spirit, together with 510 books and reprints on Mallophaga.

In earlier times the Trustees had had good reason for suspicion and distrust of Meinertzhagen's activities, and he had criticized the management of the 'Bird Room'. Now all was forgiven on both sides. The Trustees conferred the designation of Honorary Associate upon him and even provided a gallery for the reception of his birds, in which he could hang some trophies and pictures of birds, giving it a very personal atmosphere. No-one who knew Meinertzhagen even cursorily could ever forget him. Tall and erect, strongly-built, with a well-sculptured shortly-bearded face, often unconventionally dressed, he was a striking figure, even in old age, as he strode through the Museum to the 'Bird Room'. Of the many soldiers and sportsmen whose collections have enriched the Museum, there has probably been none more colourful, adventurous, cunning, unscrupulous, highly intelligent and entertaining than Meinertzhagen.

Through his discovery in Kenya of the giant forest hog *Hylochoerus meinertzhageni,* specimens of which he had sent to the Natural History Museum where Oldfield Thomas described this new beast. He then became interested in African big game, however, Meinertzhagen's primary interest was in birds and remained so. He gave most attention to those of Egypt, Arabia, Palestine and Syria. His major publications are *Nicoll's Birds of Egypt* (2 vols, 1930), *Birds of Arabia* (1954) and *Pirates and Predators* (1959), all filled with interesting first-hand observations —

together with papers in *The Ibis.* The material on which these were primarily based came to the Museum.

His own account of his extraordinary life can be read directly in his *Diary of a Black Sheep* (1964), *The Life of a Boy* (1947), *Kenya Diary 1902-6* (1957), *Middle East Diary 1917-56* (1960) and *Army Diary 1899-1926* (1964), or indirectly in John Lord's *Duty, Honour, Empire: the Life and Times of Colonel Richard Meinertzhagen* (1970) which, however, deals scantily indeed with his contributions to natural history. The old warrior died on 17 June 1967, aged eighty-nine. An account of and assessment of his achievements as a naturalist deserves to be written.

Sharpe worked during a period when an immense number of undescribed species of birds were coming into European collections and he spent much of his life classifying and naming them. That necessary pioneer stage has long since passed away. There followed several decades during which the main ornithological research of the Museum, with the exception of P.R. Lowe's anatomical studies, was devoted to working out the details of geographical distribution of birds, especially in the lesser known parts of the world, and describing their sub-specific variation. That phase too is now very largely complete. Present interests centre on the study of evolutionary trends, the co-evolutionary relationships of birds with other organisms, and the morphological and behavioural adaptions that fit them to their different ways of life. Examples of such studies are P.J.K. Burton's anatomical research on *Feeding and the Feeding Apparatus in Waders* (1974) and D.W. Snow's (b. 1924) synthesis of the results of field work on frugivorous birds in tropical forest, *The Web of Adaptation: Bird Studies in the American Tropics* (1976). A further Museum task has been the preparation of comprehensive surveys, exemplified by the Museum publications *Pigeons and Doves of the World* (1967) by Derek Goodwin, *An Atlas of Speciation in African Passerine Birds* (1970) by B.P. Hall and R.E. Moreau, and *An Atlas of Speciation in African non-Passerine Birds* (1978) edited by D.W. Snow. For these works of synthesis, the collections amassed in earlier times provided the indispensable basis. In 1971 the ornithological collections began to be moved from South Kensington to Tring Museum (p.138).

During Günther's Keepership, although the study of insects, fish, reptiles, amphibians and birds occupied most attention, other groups were not ignored. J.T. Quelch was appointed in 1882 to study Polyzoa, Hydrozoa and Anthozoa. Ridley studied sponges but better prospects as curator of the museum in Georgetown, British Guiana, led him to resign in 1886. However, Reginald Innes Pocock (1863-1947), appointed in 1885 and put in charge of Arachnida and Myriapoda in 1886, did not leave until 1904 when he became Superintendent of the

Zoological Gardens at Regent's Park. He had attended geological and biological courses at University College, Bristol, under two brilliant professors, Conwy Lloyd Morgan (1852-1936) and William Johnson Sollas (1849-1936) and entered the Museum by competitive examination. His first task, one for which Sharpe had no time to spare, was to arrange the British birds in the public gallery. Thereafter for the next eighteen years until 1904 he devoted himself wholeheartedly to the Arachnida, including spiders and scorpions, and Myriapoda, including centipedes and millipedes, producing so many papers and describing so many new species that his work attracted from 1889 onwards numerous gifts of specimens. These together with others obtained by exchange and purchase raised the Myriapoda to about 8,900 specimens and Arachnida to about 31,000; they represented 4,350 named species and numerous unnamed ones, thus making the Museum's holding the richest in the world. The credit for this enrichment of the Museum in material and its high repute belonged entirely to Pocock's enthusiasm and knowledge. Not all of this material was dead; some scorpions reached him alive! In her journal for 13 June 1896 Beatrix Potter recorded that she had taken certain things to the Museum for identification and was impressed, as she had evidently been earlier, by the slowness of the officials: 'They do not seem anything but kind, but they do not seem to be half sharp.' She added, however, 'from this contumelious disquisition I except Mr Pocock.'

By 1897 Pocock had become interested in mammals. He published that year a paper on the species and sub-species of Zebra, but his friend, Oldfield Thomas, had charge of the mammal section and no transfer was possible. At this time big changes in the Zoological Society and the management of its Zoological Gardens in Regent's park had become imminent. The death of the Zoo's remarkable Superintendent, Abraham Dee Bartlett (1812-1897), and the attacks on the Society's distinguished but autocratic Secretary, Philip Lutley Sclater (1829-1913), who held office for forty-three years, convinced the Society of the need for new men. Peter Chalmers Mitchell (1864-1945), lecturer in biology at the London Hospital, cleverly obtained his own appointment as Secretary in 1903, following Sclater's resignation in 1902, and ran the Zoo with enterprise and approval until 1935. One of his first acts was to get Pocock appointed as the Zoo's Superintendent. He resigned from the Natural History Museum in January 1904 and, although such a move from the study of dead spiders, millipedes, centipedes and scorpions to the care of living seals, monkeys, camels and snakes had no precedent, neither they nor he suffered from it. After his retirement in March 1923 at the age of sixty, he returned to the Museum, becoming a temporary scientific worker on mammals for the next twenty-four years; at the age of eighty-four, he journeyed almost every day to the Museum and was working there the day before he died suddenly on 8 August 1947. Among the achievements of this third period of Pocock's life were two volumes (1939-1941) on primates and carnivores in *The Fauna of British India* and a posthumous *Catalogue of the Genus Felis* published in an edition of 500 copies in April 1951.

William Flower (Chapter 7), on becoming Director of the Museum in 1884, soon found his activities therein severely restrained by the virtual independence of the Keepers who controlled the policy, arrangements, spending and exhibits of their four Departments and who made his position, as Richard Lydekker (p.184) said, 'of a somewhat peculiar and anomalous nature' comparable to that of Richard Owen as Superintendent. His territory within the Museum was limited to the main hall. This alone gave him the opportunity to transfer to the Museum the ideas on museum display he had formed and used during his many years as Conservator at the Royal College of Surgeons. An especially noteworthy and historic exhibit, which survived in the Museum until 1978, was one illustrating the comparative anatomy of a man and a horse by means of skeletons and half models (p. 185) carefully labelled, placed in juxtaposition, as Lydekker stated in 1906, 'in order to display the special adaptations for, on the one hand, the upright posture and great brain-capacity, and, on the other, the high degree of speed and endurance essential to an otherwise defenceless quadruped living, in a wild state, on open plains. In this exhibit, which forms the frontispiece to his well-known and deservedly popular little work on *The Horse* (1891), Sir William always took an especial pride; and it was one of the first objects to which he directed the attention of the many illustrious and distinguished visitors who sought his guidance in viewing the collections under his charge.'

For Flower, Günther's retirement as Keeper in 1895 was too good an opportunity to lose of putting himself as Director on a level with the Keepers. He thereupon became acting Keeper of Zoology as well as Director and thus gained control at last of the west wing of the Museum devoted to Zoology. Here he did away with the separation of skeletons in one gallery, the uppermost, from the mounted skins of the same animals in another gallery and put them as close as possible together. Whenever he could, he replaced badly mounted or inadequate ones by better examples and provided new descriptive labels. Gradually, the Zoological galleries became more informative and more pleasing, although it must be pointed out that the celebrated exhibits of British birds in their natural habitats (see p.55,56) were the creation of Sharpe and Günther, although Flower added to them.

Whales, dolphins and porpoises had long held an especial interest for Flower, certainly earlier than 1864, when he published his first three papers on them. In 1895 there was a skeleton of a sperm whale in the main hall, but other specimens of Cetacea, i.e. skeletons, skulls, whalebone and teeth, lay in a basement. He therefore urged upon the Trustees the need for a special annexe to display such bulky creatures, with the result that a temporary building of galvanised iron was erected at the back of the Museum. Flower placed here not only the skeletons, but half models in plaster constructed to indicate the size and shape of the living animal. This exhibition, certainly unique at the time, was opened to the public in 1897. It was the predecessor of the present Whale Hall (p.131).

Flower's chief collaborator in the Museum was Richard Lydekker (1849-1915), who later became his scientific biographer by contributing a volume, *Sir William Flower* (1906), to the *English Men of Science* series. Lydekker's family came originally from Holland but had been resident in England for several generations before his birth. After graduating from Trinity College, Cambridge, he entered the Geological Survey of India in 1872, explored the mountains of Kashmir and did much work on the Tertiary vertebrate fossils in the Indian Museum, which resulted in his *Indian Tertiary and Post-Tertiary Vertebrates* (1879-1887), before returning to England in 1882 after the death of his father, a barrister-at-law and a Hertfordshire magistrate, in 1881. He inherited the family home, Harpenden Lodge, Harpenden, Hertfordshire, and lived there for the rest of his life. He could not, however, abandon his palaeontological interests to become simply a country gentleman and county magistrate, although he was both, and he accordingly undertook the preparation of a *Catalogue of the fossil Mammalia in the British Museum (Natural History)* (5 vols, 1885-1887), to be followed by a *Catalogue of the Fossil Reptilia and Amphibia* (4 vols, 1888-1890) and a *Catalogue of the Fossil Birds* (1891). This work for the Department of Geology under Henry Woodward necessitated reference to the recent collections in the Department of Zoology under Günther and he came to know Flower. Their joint *Introduction to the Study of Mammals Living and Extinct* (1891) marked the beginning of a close friendship. In 1896, when Flower had got control of the Department of Zoology, he engaged Lydekker to re-arrange the mammals in the exhibition galleries, thus leaving Oldfield Thomas (p.185) free to devote himself to the mammal collections which were now reaching the Museum on an ever-increasing scale. That year Lydekker published his *A Geographical History of Mammals*. His relations with Edwin Ray Lankester, Flower's successor as Director, were equally harmonious.

Ray Lankester (Chapter 8) became both Director and Keeper of Zoology in 1898, after Flower's retirement. Lankester's relations with those above and below him were often not harmonious. Lydekker, an esteemed helper of the Museum with private means but not an offical servant of the Trustees, was on a different footing. Darwin had used the variation of domesticated animals through human selection as cogent evidence for evolution by means of natural selection and Flower had illustrated this in the Museum with exhibits of breeds of pigeons, so beloved by Darwin. Lankester, with an enterprise too often associated in him with lack of tact, decided to devote the north hall behind the main hall of the Museum entirely to an exhibit of domesticated animals. He made the project widely known among breeders and as a result the Museum received skins and skeletons to form a unique collection of breeds, hybrids and abnormalities. Lydekker collaborated wholeheartedly, his connection with *The Field* being an asset, and in 1912 produced *A Guide to the Domesticated Animals (other than Horses) Exhibited in the Central and North Halls of the British Museum (Natural History)*. The exhibit was dismantled in 1959, although the unique collection of dogs which formed part of it is now displayed at Tring.

Lydekker's association with the Museum lasted until his death. He produced a *Catalogue of the Heads of Indian Big Game bequeathed by A.O. Hume* (1913), but a much bigger allied undertaking was a *Catalogue of the Ungulate Mammals in the British Museum (Natural History)* (5 vols, 1913-1916). Few zoologists have worked with greater speed. Apparently he did not begin his *Catalogue of the Ungulate Mammals* until 1913, but had practically finished it by the time of his death on 16 April 1915, 'working on his sick bed at the proofs of the fourth and the MS of the fifth and last volume', which was published in July 1916.

During the second half of the nineteenth century, the wilds of India and Africa literally provided happy hunting grounds for well-armed Europeans, such as army officers and high-placed government officials and men of wealth seeking a little adventure, for whom the collecting of big-game trophies to display to visitors gave the romantic pleasure of life in the open and the atavistic sporting pleasure of skilful killing. Much of their collections has ultimately enriched the Museum with numerous heads, less often hides and skeletons, of such large mammals. Lydekker's later work is based on these. He thus lightened the task of the Museum's mammal curator Michael Rogers Oldfield Thomas (1858-1929), appointed to the Museum Secretary's office in 1876 and transferred to the Zoological Department in 1878. Gray published in 1843 a list of the mammal collection as it was then, enumerating 3,062 specimens assigned to 1,031 species; by 1904 it had risen to about 45,650. For the period 1850-1859, the average annual acquisition was 477 specimens (an average boosted, however, by the gift of the collection of the Indian Museum formed by the Hon. East India Company), for 1860 to 1869 it was 327. For 1870 to 1879, the annual average was 334; for 1880 to 1889 the annual average was 448. By this time Oldfield Thomas had become known as an active mammal expert, eager to investigate and publish; the mammal collections coming to the Museum increased as a consequence. For 1890 to 1899 the annual average was 1327 and for 1900 to 1906 it was 1976.

There were, in addition to big-game hunters, scientifically-minded collectors who gave much attention to rodents, bats etc. Trapping a rat in the jungle may be scientifically valuable, but does not provide such conspicuous evidence of prowess as shooting a driven tiger from the back of an elephant. Hence from about 1895 Oldfield Thomas, who had married the heiress to a small fortune in 1891, encouraged professional collectors of lesser mammals by privately employing them and presenting their specimens to the Museum which by 1904 had received 3,136 mammals from him. These efforts were necessarily confined to limited areas. The Museum possessed much Indian material derived from Thomas Hardwicke, Brian Hodgson, the Indian Museum of the Hon. East India Company and other sources, and there were in India keen and competent amateur naturalists belonging to the Bombay Natural History Society, founded in 1883, which from 1886 onwards had published a *Journal* with contributions of high quality, mostly relating to zoology. The Society by 1911 possessed 1,500 members. Encouraged by Thomas it initiated a survey of the mammals of India, Burma and Ceylon. The collections made were identified in the Museum, samples and type specimens retained and the remainder sent back to India. Oldfield Thomas described about 2,000 reputed new species and sub-species of mammals in all, from many parts of the world. As with the investigation of African plants during the same period, this was pioneer, descriptive work based on specimens inadequate for assessment of variability within populations, and undoubtedly Thomas distinguished more species than later workers with much more material have found acceptable.

Oldfield Thomas had John Guy Dollman as an Assistant 2nd Class from 1907 onwards and he too became a mammal specialist. Much of his time before his retirement was occupied with exhibition work for which Lydekker had earlier been responsible. He published a series of illustrated articles in the *Natural History Magazine* on interesting mammal specimens received by the Museum.

Another distinguished Museum worker on mammals, and in particular rodents, was Martin Alister Campbell Hinton (1883-1961), who joined the staff in August 1921, became Deputy Keeper of Zoology in

December 1927 and Keeper in December 1936 and retired in 1945. His career, like that of J.E. Gray, did not follow the now customary pattern of state-aided university education and early entry into the scientific staff of the Museum. His father, a legal shorthand writer in London, had died when he was ten and he had to leave school at twelve to work as a lawyer's clerk in the City. Self-educated in geology, palaeontology, zoology, languages, and English and French literature, he often spent his evenings working in the Geological Museum and in the famous Reading Room of the British Museum. He thus acquired early the spirit of independence and will to work necessary for a fatherless boy anxious to rise in a fiercely competitive world.

When only sixteen he read a paper in 1899 on Pleistocene deposits around Ilford and Wanstead, which the Geologists' Association published in its *Proceedings* 16: 271-281 (1900). Fortunately a lawyer, later a judge, John Cameron Brown, himself interested in natural history, invited young Hinton to work in his office. The hours of work were long but the tasks were not burdensome; Brown allowed him much time for private study and thereby gained Hinton's life-long gratitude. From 1905 onwards, he became a regular visitor to the Natural History Museum and worked as a volunteer on fossil rodents, meanwhile rising to senior clerk in the law office. Living rodents engaged his interest as much as their Pleistocene representatives and he published in 1913 and 1914 a study of the island voles of the Hebrides and the Orkney Islands. Although not a Museum staff member he wrote a Museum economic pamphlet, *Rats and Mice as Enemies of Man* (1918; 2nd ed., 1920; 3rd ed., 1931), which has been described as 'a minor classic . . . clear, concise, vivid, written with an easy style and tinged with wit, yet packed with accurate records and sound advice.' It deals comprehensively with the history, habits and zoology of these pests, as well as their control and their menace; it indicates the contribution of gamekeepers to the increase of rats, notably through their destruction of weasels, stoats and owls. For appointment in 1921 to the Museum staff, despite his age and lack of academic qualifications, Hinton needed no recommendation other than this Museum publication. At the Museum he devoted most of his time to taxonomic work on rodents, resulting above all in his *Monograph of the Voles and Lemmings*, vol. 1 (1926), but his most important service to the community was urging and planning the extermination of the muskrat (p.128) before, as on the Continent, it became ineradicable; failure to heed his warnings against the menace of the coypu has cost the nation dear. Hinton's biographer, R.J.C. Savage, in *Biographical Memoirs of Fellows of the Royal Society* 9: 155-170 (1963), has summarised his four major contributions to science:

'1.   He was the first to recognize the zonal value of Pleistocene Microtinae and apply this to the interpretation of the stratigraphy, with its extensions to correlation of different types of deposit, cave, crag and terrace. From this work the age and correlation of British Pleistocene deposits began to be understood. Nowadays the rodents are universally recognized as most powerful faunal elements in dating, not only in Pleistocene, but also further back in Tertiary strata.

2.   He laid the basis for systematic studies of the Microtinae, a sub-family of un-nerving complexity, through detailed investigation of all characters, taken in relation to their functional adaptations.

3.   He preached and had put into practice the biological control of murine pests, and his work in connexion with the eradication of the muskrat plague from Britain was a major public service, though the State never rewarded its piper.

4.   His work on the *Pseudorca* school is a major contribution to the population dynamics of Cetacea.'

Hinton was a gifted unorthodox character and his ways, as well as his thoughts, were certainly unusual. To quote R.J.C. Savage: 'In spite of the number of administrative jobs he undertook, he was never an organized man. He had the innate habits of a squirrel; literally everything was kept. He boasted of smoking an ounce of tobacco every day of his life since he was seventeen years old and never threw a tin away — they (or at least a few) came in useful to contain his rodents. After his death, his rooms yielded over 10,000 tobacco tins, cheque book stubs, receipts for groceries, rent, clothes, notices of meetings, catalogues, used envelopes and advertisements — over a ton of paper, leaving aside correspondence, manuscripts and the like; all was completely mixed up together, and some of it going back over sixty years.'

His mind had the same miscellaneous capacity. He was not only interested in chess, Shakespeare, Verdi and Beethoven; he read in the original French all seventy volumes of Voltaire's works and he left at his death some 300 paintings by himself in oils and watercolours. Men of such versatility are capable of unexpected acts. By 1912 his self-education had given him a remarkable knowledge of Pleistocene stratigraphy and Pleistocene mammals. He was a frequent visitor to the Departments of Geology and Zoology and was well acquainted with their collections and the working of their members. He was one of the few people with the requisite knowledge and facilities to have perpetrated the Piltdown hoax (p.245). His possible involvement has been publicly stated by L.B. Halstead in *Nature* 277: 596 (1979) and privately suspected earlier by others. If so, his motive for committing it could have been simply to test and unmask the fallibility of accepted authority, which was only too well proved. Initially his reason for not revealing it may have been the possibility of future employment in the Museum. Later it would have caused acute embarrassment. Suspicion here is not proof, but it is certainly a tribute to Hinton's ability and knowledge. Hinton in a letter to *The Times* on 22 December 1953 stated, however, that he had not seen the Piltdown material until the reading of the paper by Dawson and Woodward in 1912. If he had been involved earlier, he was then deliberately lying. That I myself find difficult indeed to believe.

Subsequent work in the Mammal Section included the preparation of *The Families and Genera of living Rodents* by John Reeves Ellerman (1909-1973), of which vol. 1 was published in 1940, vol. 2 in 1941 and vol. 3 in 1949. This was followed by a *Checklist of Palaearctic and Indian Mammals 1758 to 1946* (Nov. 1951; 2nd ed., 1966), compiled by J.R. Ellerman and Terence C.S. Morrison-Scott (later to become Director, p.340) and *Southern African Mammals, 1758 to 1951, a Reclassification* (1953) by J.R. Ellerman, T.C.S. Morrison-Scott and Robert William Hayman (b. 1907), who joined the Department in 1921 as a Boy Attendant and retired in 1967 as a Chief Experimental Officer. John Ellerman, described in 1957 as 'Britain's richest, shyest, most elusive millionaire', inherited at the age of twenty-three from his father, Sir Johann Herman Ellerman (d. 1933), shipowner of Kingston-on-Hull, not only a baronetcy, but £40,000,000 which death duties reduced to £18,000,000; this, by judicious management of investments in shipping, land, breweries, property, newspapers (including *The Daily Mirror*) and investment trusts, had increased at the time of his death to above his father's fortune. As a boy he was much interested in small mammals and their critical study became an absorbing, serious hobby, as fleas had become earlier with Charles Rothschild. Small rodents are shy animals, keeping out of view as much as possible; they and Ellerman had that at least in common. His dislike of publicity was obsessive. He happily spent many hours studying the rodent specimens in the obscurity of the Museum basement and during the 1939-1945 World War the rodent collection was evacuated to his mansion at Bagshot. He paid for the printing of these rather grandly produced Museum publications and contributed to the cost of Jacqueline Palmer's Children's Centre in the Museum. Several months of every year he spent in South Africa, where he learned Afrikaans and also braille so as to spend time with blind, handicapped and maimed ex-service men and others, to whom he was both a deeply sympathetic and secretly generous friend. He was such a recluse that only a few workers at the Museum knew of his existence, or connected this shy, tall, lean, middle-aged student of rodents with the fabulously wealthy director of the Ellerman Shipping Line.

For a long period, however much Directors and Keepers might feel themselves shining in international esteem, two lesser men represented the Museum to the British public and were much better known, J.H. Leonard (p.136) the guide lecturer by his tours of exhibits and William Plane Pycraft (1868-1942) by his popular articles and books, most of which, though based on Museum information, had little to do with his official duties as an osteologist.

Skeletons, which were stored and exhibited apart from stuffed skins, came for a time under Pycraft's care. He was born in Yarmouth, but he moved to Oxford, where from 1892 to 1898 he was the assistant to the Linacre Professor of Comparative Anatomy, Edwin Ray Lankester, who much esteemed him. Apparently when Lankester became Director of the Museum in 1898 he brought Pycraft with him as his private helper and in 1907 he obtained Pycraft's appointment to the Museum staff to take charge of osteology. Pycraft had already manifested his wide-ranging curiosity in natural history and his zest for publishing works and articles about it. His *The Story of Bird-Life* appeared in 1900 and was followed by *The Story of Fish-Life* (1901) and *The Story of Reptile Life* (1905), *The British Museum of Natural History* (1910), *A History of Birds* (1910), *The Infancy of Animals* (1912), *The Courtship of Animals* (1913), *Birds in Flight* (1922), *Camouflage in Nature* (1925) and *Birds of Great Britain and their Natural History* (1934), as well as more technical publications on the anatomy of penguins etc.

Pycraft wrote weekly very good articles for the *Illustrated London News* and, reading them as a schoolboy, I used to think that Pycraft must be one of the world's greatest naturalists. He republished selections of these articles as *Random Gleanings from Nature's Fields* (1928) and *More Gleanings from Nature's Fields* (1929). Unfortunately, he was partially crippled and incapable of much active exercise and this physical disability, while saving him from service in the 1914-1918 World War, handicapped him in field work, so that he had to rely considerably on museum work and the observations of others.

Following Pycraft's retirement, charge of the mammalian osteological material passed to Francis Charles Fraser (1903-1978) appointed in January 1933. Born in Dingwall, Ross and Cromarty, in 1903, Fraser received his zoological training under Graham Kerr at Glasgow University, and, after a year there as demonstrator in the Department of Geology, was appointed zoologist to the *Discovery* investigations. During the period 1925-33, he served in the Antarctic both at sea (aboard the research vessels *Discovery*, *William Scoresby* and *Discovery II*), and in South Georgia. His researches at this time were concerned mainly with krill (Crustacea: *Euphausia superba*), the food of the large baleen whales. At the Museum, besides continuing and expanding the programme for maintaining records of cetaceans stranded on British coasts initiated by Harmer in 1913 (p. 120) and directing work on the Whale Hall (p. 190), he researched extensively on the biology and taxonomy of cetaceans, and in collaboration with Peter Ernest Purves (b. 1915) made outstanding contributions to knowledge of the functional anatomy of cetaceans, particularly the structure of their auditory mechanisms. In 1957 Fraser succeeded H.W. Parker as Keeper, but relinquished office in 1964 in order to devote more time to research. He was elected to the Royal Society in 1966. After his retirement in 1969, he regularly visited the Museum to continue studies and cherished the little room that was allotted to him — it was near his beloved Whale Hall. He died on 21 October 1978.

Mammals, birds and insects naturally catch public attention more strongly than worms, sea-urchins, spiders, mites, crabs, sponges, corals, molluscs and amoebae, but these come equally within the Department's field of activity. The groups they exemplify are all

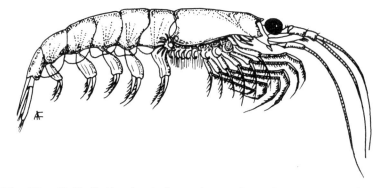

Fig. 26. Krill, *Euphausia superba,* an Antarctic marine crustacean about 5-6 cm in length and belonging to the Euphausiacea, is renowned for its swarming behaviour, especially in the Weddell Sea. Densities of 60,000 per cubic metre are not uncommon. It forms the main diet of baleen whales, 2-3 tons of krill being filtered out from the seawater at a single feeding. Krill is a major component of many short food chains in the Southern Ocean, being eaten not only by whales but also by crab-eating seals, fish and squid. High in protein (up to 50-60 per cent dry weight) harvested krill could provide a valuable source of protein for direct human consumption or indirectly as animal feed. If it is to be harvested in a rational way then it is essential that an effective catch quota system is implemented. Not belatedly, and ineffectively, as was the case with whales.   Text and drawing by A.A. Fincham.

represented in the Museum's zoological collections. The history of the study of each one within the Museum deserves more attention than can be given in the present work

Crustacea were classified by Linnaeus in 1758 as wingless insects, as were scorpions, spiders, woodlice and centipedes. Adam White (1817-1879; see p.206), who was primarily an entomologist, had charge of the Crustacea and dutifully produced in 1847 a *List of Specimens of Crustacea* 140 pages long. As in other sections of the Museum, the efforts of a talented and dedicated worker gave the Department a high reputation as a place of research on Crustacea. He was Edward John Miers (1851-1930), who joined the Museum staff in 1872, worked from then until 1886 on Crustacea and produced some fifty papers before ill-health followed by a complete breakdown forced him first to resign from the Museum in November 1885 and then to abandon scientific work. He belonged to a distinguished family. His grandfather John Miers (1789-1879) was a distinguished botanist whose herbarium came to the Department of Botany. His father, Francis Charles Miers, was a distinguished civil engineer who worked in South America, as his own father had done, and Edward John Miers was born in Rio de Janeiro, Brazil. Having studied for a year in Lausanne he had acquired a good knowledge of French, as also of Latin and Greek, together with some German, and thus possessed the most essential and indeed the most useful qualifications then for Museum entry. His brother, Henry Alexander Miers (1858-1942), the mineralogist and university administrator, also had a period of service in the Museum (p.267). E.J. Miers worked on the *Challenger* Crustacea. It is evident that through his early retirement, the Museum lost a capable and industrious worker after an all too short, productive period.

The period of service of dapper Francis Jeffrey Bell (1855-1924) was much longer and less distinguished. It was said of him that the time he could spare from the neglect of his duties, he devoted to the adornment of his person. He became an Assistant in the Museum in 1878, but was also from 1879 to 1896 Professor of Comparative Anatomy at King's College, London and published in 1885 a *Manual of Comparative Anatomy and Physiology*. From the short historical account which he contributed to the *History of the Collections* 3: 731-740 (1966) it is evident that the collection of Crustacea increased slowly up to 1874, when the Department received 989 specimens, then in 1876 from Lake Baikal and elsewhere 1,181 specimens, rising to the maximum accession of 580,245 specimens in 1903 presented by the Trustees of the Indian Museum.

The charge of the Crustacea passed in 1904 to William Thomas Calman (1871-1952), who became Keeper of Zoology in 1927, having revolutionized the study of Crustacea within the Museum. Calman was born in Dundee, where his father, blind from birth, taught music, but he died when the boy was only six years old. His mother Agnes (née Maclean) managed by running a small millinery business in Dundee to give him and his sister an adequate education and he was then apprenticed as a clerk to the Caledonian Insurance Company for four years, at the end of which the company suggested that, on account of his stammer, he should find employment elsewhere. The gift of a toy microscope had enabled him to study pond life and to discover a number of rotifers in the sludge which came through Dundee taps as drinking water. Very fortunately he became acquainted with that remarkable biologist and scholar D'Arcy Wentworth Thompson (1860-1948), who had been Professor of Biology at the University College of Dundee since 1884. Thompson, quick to perceive the promise of young men, made him his laboratory assistant, so that he could study for a science degree at St. Andrew's University, with which the Dundee University College was affiliated. He then became Thompson's assistant lecturer and demonstrator and gained a doctorate from St. Andrew's in 1903. Meanwhile, his illuminating publications on Crustacea had caught the attention of Ray Lankester, Keeper of Zoology as well as Director of the Museum. He invited Calman in September 1901 to write a volume on Crustacea for the *Treatise on Zoology* he was editing and, with characteristic impatience, wanted to have it ready for the press by the end of 1902. It was published in 1909 and became a classic work. Lankester gave Calman a temporary post in the Museum, which led to his receiving a permanent appointment in 1904 to take charge of Crustacea, Pocock having resigned late in 1903.

Calman's work gave a new direction to work on Crustacea in the Museum and added to its repute, but he took part in activities outside the Museum, being Zoological Secretary of the Linnean Society from 1923 to 1928 and President from 1934 to 1937; one of his presidential addresses was 'The meaning of biological classification' (cf. *Proceedings of the Linnean Society* sess. 127 (1934-35): 1936). He retired in 1936 and died suddenly in 1952 at the age of eighty-one. Perhaps in gratitude for all he owed to his widowed mother, he was largely instrumental in getting women admitted to the scientific staff of the Museum, but this was more likely to have been simply the exercise of common sense.

Calman introduced an element of functional morphology to crustacean research and this was continued by Isabella Gordon (b. 1901), who made valuable contributions through her studies of the reproductive appendages of crabs. She also researched on the Pycnogonida (sea spiders) which although now regarded as Chelicerata (and therefore allied to the Arachnida) are still attached to the Crustacea Section. She retired in November 1966.

John Phillip Harding (b. 1911) joined the Department of Zoology in October 1937 as an Assistant Keeper in charge of the 'lower Crustaceans' (Entomostraca). His early studies were concerned with lacustrine entomostracans, particularly those from Lake Titicaca in Bolivia and Peru, but they later extended to embrace copepods and ostracods from all parts of the world. He also digressed into biometrics and chromosome studies and his interests in engineering and microscopy led him to design a micro-dissecting apparatus. He became Keeper of Zoology in December 1964 and retired in November 1971.

Although not a member of staff, Sidnie Manton (Mrs J.P. Harding) (1902-1979) was closely associated with the Crustacea Section for over thirty years, having been elected Honorary Associate in May 1948. One of the most distinguished invertebrate zoologists of the century, Sidnie Manton graduated at Cambridge in 1925, and then began a series of investigations embracing a wide range of arthropods, studying especially their embryology and functional morphology. Her early studies of the embryology of Crustacea and Onychophora have been unsurpassed, and in 1948 she was elected a Fellow of the Royal Society, one of the first women to achieve this honour. The first part of her classic series of papers on arthropod locomotary mechanisms was published in the *Journal of the Linnean Society* (Zoology) in 1950 and the final paper (the eleventh) appeared in 1973. Her work culminated in the *Arthropoda* (1978), a monument not only to her scholarship but to her courage, for in her last years she had to cope with grave physical handicaps. She died on 2 January 1979.

The molluscan collection was first seriously studied by Children and J.E. Gray, who estimated it in 1836 as containing 4,025 specimens. It included shells from the Sloane Museum and the specimens of eminent collectors such as Leach and Lister, as well as the collection of Sir Joseph Banks containing material from the Cook voyages. From 1841 to 1871 William Baird (1803-1872) had charge. His few publications on the group include *Nomenclature of Molluscous Animals and Shells in the British Museum* (1850), but his major contribution was in curation by arranging, mounting, registering and labelling, thus making the collection available for scientific study. Among the acquisitions of this period were the important shell collections of Alcide Dessalines d'Orbigny (1802-1857) and Hugh Cuming (1791-1865). The Trustees purchased the Cuming Collection in 1866, a special grant for its acquisition being made by Parliament. This collection was unequalled for its wealth of type and figured specimens, for although Cuming himself had described no new taxa, his collection had been made available for study to all leading conchologists of his day, many of whom were unstinting in their praise of his generosity. Although deprecatory remarks have been made about this collection, its value must not be under-estimated.

Edgar Albert Smith (1847-1916) wrote in the *History of the Collections* 2: 710-711 (1906): 'When acquired by the Museum at the moderate price of £6,000, it consisted of 82,992 specimens. It is famous on account of the beauty of most of specimens and the enormous number of types it contains. The actual number of species and types was never estimated, but when we regard the twenty volumes of Reeve's "Conchologia Iconica," the five volumes of Sowerby's "Thesaurus Conchyliorum," and the numerous papers by Pfeiffer, Broderip, H. and A. Adams, Deshayes and others, all descriptive of this collection, we get some idea of the historic interest attaching to this. This collection of shells was the main object of Mr Cuming's life. He not only devoted several years of personal collecting to its formation, but he purchased largely, and obtained very many species by exchange with foreign museums and private collectors in all parts of the world.'

Whereas for Gray the Mollusca were but one among the many groups of animals which received his eager attention, for E.A. Smith they became an absorbing life-study to which he devoted all his time and care. He was the third and youngest son of Frederick Smith (1805-1879), the engraver who became a distinguished Museum ento-mologist on the Museum Staff (p.206), and he inherited his father's meticulous and patient attention to detail. He joined the Museum staff in 1867 as an Assistant, became an Assistant Keeper in 1895 and retired in 1913, having been President of the Conchological Society for 1889 and 1890 and of the Malacological Society for 1901 to 1903. This was a period of expansion, with collections from many regions of the world being donated. Aware that their collections would be competently investigated collectors tended more and more to put them in Smith's hands. Notable acquisitions included material from the *Challenger* voyage, the Museum Normanianum of Alfred Merle Norman (1831-1918), the immense collection of land and freshwater snails from the Atlantic Islands made by Richard Thomas Lowe (1802-1874) and material from the Indian sub-continent collected by Henry Haversham Godwin-Austen (1834-1923), immortalized as the surveyor of Mount Godwin-Austen (K2), the world's second highest mountain. Godwin-Austen's material is of particular interest, since he paid attention to the 'soft-parts' and it therefore includes many spirit-preserved anatomical specimens. These and other collections made the Museum collection the finest of its kind in the world, and, thanks, to Smith's care and growing reputation, it so remained. Between 1871 and 1916 the collection provided Smith with material for more than 300 papers, including revisions of thirteen genera and he described some 2,000 new species of shells. Most of his work was of a faunistic character, listing specimens collected from various regions, one of the most important being an account of the Lamellibranchia in *Report Challenger Expedition Zoology* 35: 1-341 (1885).

There followed a period of further consolidation, building on the foundations laid by Smith, and important additions have included the collections of Ronald Winkworth (1864-1950) in 1951, Ernest Ruthven Sykes (1867-1954) in 1954 and those of the Reverend Herbert Edwin James Biggs (1895-1973) purchased in 1973. It is estimated that the mollusc collections now comprise more than six million specimens.

The early collections and hence the work based upon them concentrated on the empty shells. Nevertheless, interest in the 'soft parts' gradually increased. Certainly Guy Coburn Robson (1888-1945) did not regard the Mollusca as inanimate objects or as animals important primarily for their inanimate covering. He began his academic career as a classical scholar at New College, Oxford, later studied at the marine biological station of Naples and entered the service of the Museum as a zoologist in June 1911. He fought in World War I and suffered from shell-shock thereafter, but became an Assistant Keeper 1st Class in 1926, and Deputy Keeper from 1931 to 1936, when he retired. Robson's papers on the anatomy of *Potamopyrgus jenkinsi* (*Paludestrina jenkinsi*) in 1920, on the anatomy and affinities of *Hydrobia ventrosa* (*Paludestrina ventrosa*) in 1922 and on parthogenesis and genetical behaviour in *Potampyrgus jenkinsi* in 1923 and 1926 testify to a widened view of research within the Museum. He published in 1926 *The Species Problem* and in 1936, together with O.W. Richards, *The Variation of Animals*. The latter is an intriguing work for one of its themes was that, while accepting the major tenets of Darwinism, it was impossible to ascribe a selective advantage to the variation exhibited by many forms or to many of the features used in discriminating species. Robson's major contribution was, however, *A Monograph of Recent Cephalopoda* (1931-1936), a work which attempted to fuse taxonomic studies with investigations of functional morphology. Interest in cephalopods was maintained by William James Rees (1913-1967) who was appointed in July 1946. Before taking charge of the Coelenterata section in 1955, where he researched principally on hydroids, he worked on molluscs, and his collaborative study with William Adam on the genus *Sepia* brought order to the group and consolidated the earlier studies of Robson. Rees died suddenly on 12 October 1967.

Recent studies of molluscs have attempted to link field work with collection-orientated studies, for example the work on the diversity of marine species of predatory molluscs living on coral reefs has extended our knowledge of their remarkable devices for finding, attacking, catching and eating living prey. Investigation of their surprising armoury of gastronomic weapons has been much aided by the use of the scanning electron microscope as can be seen from illustrations in *Report on the British Museum (Natural History)* 1975-1977: 32-33 (1978). From Darwin's work on the Galapagos Islands fauna onwards, the animals and plants of islands have provided valuable evidence on the course of evolution but, being extremely vulnerable to human interference, are more and more in danger of extinction; many species have already disappeared. Investigation of the distribution of and evolution of the snails on islands, in particular those of Melanesia and Polynesia, provide further opportunities for combining field and museum studies. Indeed, this has formed the basis of the research programme undertaken by John Fordyce Peake (b. 1933), former head of the Mollusca Section and now Deputy Keeper of Zoology.

The mere curation and traditional study of the Mollusca collection could suffice to occupy the attention of the Museum's staff, but modern techniques and modern needs have opened yet further lines of enquiry. Thus, various freshwater snails serve as hosts at an early stage in the life-cycle of the minute flatworms of the genus *Schistosoma*, which, when they have later infected the blood vessels of man, cause the disease bilharziasis or schistosomiasis, but these parasites are fastidious in the snails they use. Indeed, some strains of schistosomes will only develop successfully in certain populations of a particular host species, and there is a need for methods capable of detecting differences in both the snails and the parasites at levels where morphological characters are of no help. Christopher Amyas Wright (b. 1928) and his collaborators in the Experimental Taxonomy Unit have developed biochemical, cytological and immunological techniques to supplement the more traditional morphological investigations of both the parasites and their snail hosts. Integration of the results of detailed laboratory studies and field investigations in Africa have made fruitful contributions to knowledge of the taxonomy of both groups of animals. While the detection of biochemical differences in the bodies of the snails and parasites is far removed from the examination of shells by Children, Gray and Smith, it constitutes a logical modern development at an institution as dynamic as the Natural History Museum.

Pocock's activity up to 1904 brought the Arachnida Section into prominence (p.182). He said, however, that he did not like to study creatures less than ½ inch long, thus the Acari (mites and ticks), a group which includes many thousands of species less than 1mm in length, escaped his attention! The Acari are the most heterogeneous sub-class of the Arachnida and include many species of great economic importance. Thus, some are serious pests of farm and garden crops and many are important in human and veterinary medicine, either as a direct cause of skin disorders (for example *Sarcoptes scabiei*) or as vectors (carriers) of disease-causing organisms. The causal organism of scrub typhus, for example, is transmitted by the larva of a chigger mite (*Leptotrombidium* species), and a very wide range of pathogens (including viruses, rickettsias and bacteria) are transmitted by ticks. Up to 1906 the Museum collection of Acari consisted mainly of unstudied specimens — a notable exception being a collection of slide preparations presented in 1879 and 1888 by Albert Davidson Michael, a London solicitor, who made valuable contributions to the study of beetle mites (Cryplosrigmata) and forage mites (Astigmata).

Arthur Stanley Hirst (1883-1930) initiated a period of work which was instrumental in changing the Museum's acarine collection from one of meagre importance to one of the richest in the world, critically studièd and replete with type specimens, and he himself became a world authority. He was educated at Merchant Taylors' School and University College, London, where he studied zoology. He joined the Museum staff as an Assistant in October 1905 and worked for a short while on mammals, before taking charge of the Arachnida and Myriapoda. Hirst entered upon his new duties with enthusiasm and sedulity. He began in 1907 with descriptions of new scorpions, spiders and millipedes and continued to describe further new species of these (as well as new species belonging to other macro-arachnid groups, such as sun spiders and harvestmen) for some years, until the Acari came gradually to monopolize his time. Publications from 1910 onwards (about fifty in all) included papers on new species of phytophagous mites and many on new species parasitizing mammals and birds. He also produced two important economic handbooks: *Species of Arachnida and Myriopoda injurious to Man* (1917; 2nd ed., 1920) and *Mites injurious to Domestic Animals* (1922).

Hirst's work increased public understanding of the economic importance of the Acari and led to many specimens and enquiries reaching the Museum, quite as much as he could deal with. His health had long been far from good and its deterioration caused him to resign in 1927 and emigrate to Australia in the hope of benefiting from a drier climate; he continued to work at Acari there, but died at sea on a return voyage on 4 May 1930. According to W.T. Calman in *Nature* 125: 899 (1930) Hirst's papers were marked by great accuracy of description and laborious investigation of detail. 'Many of them contain facts and suggestions which will one day be found to have contributed much to a scientific knowledge of the group. Especially noteworthy were his identification of one of the familiar and troublesome harvest bugs; his demonstration of a tracheal system in the group of mites named from the supposed absence of the system the Astigmata; and his description of the fossil arachnids from the Rhynie chert, the oldest known air-breathing animals.' To follow Hirst, the Museum appointed Susan Finnegan (b. 1903) (later Mrs W. Campbell Smith) in 1927 and she worked mainly on Acari until her resignation in 1936. She was followed by Richard James Whittick (b. 1912), appointed in October 1936, who worked in the section up to 1940, mainly on ticks. Gwilym Owen Evans (b. 1924), appointed in March 1951, published between then and his appointment to a professorship in 1967 some sixty papers concerned with Acari. His contributions to acarine systematics were outstanding. As well as producing a series of important taxonomic revisions concerned mainly with the Mesostigmata-Gamasina, his detailed comparative morphological studies led to the development of the system of naming the setae which has now been universally adopted for this group of mites.

John Gordon Sheals (b. 1923), appointed in April 1958, became a pioneer within the Museum by applying computer techniques to acarine taxonomy (*Proceedings of the Linnean Society of London* 176: 11-21, 1965; *Acarologia* 11: 376-396, 1969) and together with D.A. Griffiths and D. MacFarlane, used the scanning electron microscope for their study (*Annales de Zoologie — Ecologie Animale* 3: 49-55, 1971). He left the section in December 1971, on appointment as Keeper of Zoology. Thus, there has been a continuing expansion of the acarine work iniated by Hirst. No small part of the credit for the upkeep of the Arachnida collections irrespective of changing higher personnel must be awarded to Ernest Browning (b. 1896), who joined the Museum staff in September 1911 as a Boy Attendant at £33 18s 2d (£33.91) a year and retired in 1958 as a Senior Experimental Officer, having supported Hirst, Finnegan, Whittick and Evans as a loyal and able assistant and having contributed for many years to the section on Arachnida for the *Zoological Record.*

The curation and study of the Vermes (worms) together with echinoderms, corals, sponges, and foraminifera and molluscs were in 1867 the responsibility of E.A. Smith (p. 195). The term Vermes, one of the six classes of Linnaeus' system (*Systema Naturae*, 10th ed., 1758), long survived in the Museum (albeit with increasing restriction) as a category of administrative convenience for many worm-like animals, such as Platyhelminthes, Nematoda, Nemertinea, Annelida, etc., classified in a number of different phyla.

In 1878 Smith's impossible task was lightened by relieving him of the foraminifera and sponges which were put under S.O. Ridley, and of the Vermes and echinoderms which were put under F. Jeffery Bell, who also had charge of Crustacea. In 1904 responsibility for the Crustacea passed to Calman, and in 1913 Harry Arnold Baylis (1889-1972) was appointed to take charge of the Vermes and echinoderms — instead of birds as he had hoped!

Baylis at first worked on African earthworms, then gave his whole attention to parasitic worms. He paid special attention to nematodes, a group hitherto neglected in the Museum, and published *A Synopsis of the Families and Genera of Nematodes*, as well as numerous papers in such journals as *Annals and Magazine of Natural History, Parasitology* and *Annals of Tropical Medicine.* Baylis' work established the Museum as one of the leading centres in the world for research into the systematics of helminths, a position that it seems to have maintained. He retired in 1949 and was succeeded by Stephen Prudhoe (b. 1911). Subsequently a succession of organizational changes were made. Currently responsibility for the Platyhelminthes and parasitic nematodes is with a 'Parasitic Worms' section, and a separate section has been established to cater for 'free-living' nematodes and certain other 'free-living' aschelminth groups. Research in the 'free-living' section is now concerned mainly with marine nematodes.

Darwin's *Formation of Vegetable Mould through the Action of Worms* (1881) was probably the first work to direct popular attention to the importance of earthworms in the economy of nature, but their diversity in form, size and manner of life and their large number of species remain virtually unknown, except to a small number of specialists. The earthworms belong to the class Oligochaeta (which also includes many aquatic species as well as the semi-aquatic potworms), and with the bristle worms (class Polychaeta), which are mainly marine, and the leeches (class Hirundinea) are classified in the phylum Annelida.

A Catalogue of British Non-parasitical Worms, prepared by George Johnston, who was not a member of the Museum staff, was published in 1865, but in the Museum significant studies of annelids were long delayed, although an awareness of their importance led to the purchase in 1904 of the huge collection of earthworms assembled during the previous twenty years by Frank Evans Beddard (1858-1925), the author of *A Monograph of the Order of Oligochaeta* (1895) and of the section on earthworms and leeches in *The Cambridge Natural History*, vol. 2 (1896).

The appointment of Charles Carmichael Arthur Monro (1894-1942) in 1922 as an Assistant Keeper in charge of the Annelida and Echinodermata collections brought new energy into the study of 'free-living' worms and relieved Baylis of all responsibility for them. His Scottish ancestors included three who almost made the Edinburgh professorship of anatomy the heritage of an Alexander Monro, i.e. primus

44. Specimen of African Elephant *(Loxodonta africana)* being removed
in 1927 for renovation by Messrs Rowland Ward.

45. Bottle-nosed Whale *(Hyperoodon ampullatus)*, 25 feet (7·6m) long, stranded
at Scunthorpe, Lincolnshire, being unloaded at the Museum.

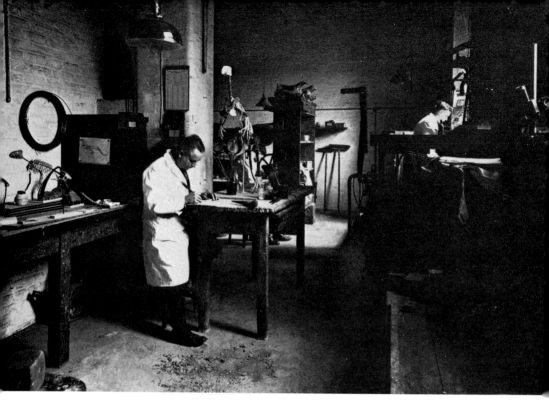

46. Preparator's workshop in Department of Geology (now
Palaeontology) in 1934.

47. Laboratory in Department of Palaeontology in 1980.

48. Jars of fish in preservative fluid in Department of Zoology's
New Spirit Building.

49. Herbarium of Department of Botany open to the sky after damage by incendiary and oil bombs on 9 September 1940.

50. G. W. F. Claxton *(left)* and J. E. Yateman *(right)* in bomb-damaged Department of Botany in 1940.

(1697-1767), secundus (1733-1817) and tertius (1773-1859), occupying the professorial chair from 1720 to 1846, and his father, director of public instruction in the Central Provinces, India, was likewise an Alexander Monro as was his elder brother. His early interests were, however, in classics, but the outbreak of the 1914-1918 World War interrupted his classical studies at Oxford and he never returned to them, although they provided a background to his later zoological work. In the war he was both wounded and shell-shocked. Back at Oxford in 1920 he turned to zoology and in November 1922 he joined the Museum staff. Monro concentrated his attention particularly on the polychaete worms and published thirty-seven papers relating to them between 1924 and 1939. It now became widely known that the Museum possessed a specialist able to deal with the collections made on marine expeditions. He was not, however, a narrow specialist; he produced the Museum's 1931 *General Guide to the Exhibition Galleries*, edited the *Museums Journal* from 1925 to 1927 and was esteemed as a man of charm, learning and culture, interested in theology, philosophy and poetry, as well as polychaete worms. In 1939 the outbreak of war again interrupted his studies. He was transferred to the Ministry of Food, but his health had not been good for several years and he died on 21 June 1942. Though Monro's gifts were thus prematurely lost to the Museum, since the war the study of Annelida has remained within the Museum's field of research.

Monro could give little attention to the Echinodermata, the phylum which includes the sea-urchins, starfish, brittle-stars, feather-stars and sea-cucumbers. David Dilwyn John (b. 1901) was accordingly appointed in 1935 to take charge of them, having been engaged as a zoologist on *Discovery* investigations in Antarctic waters from 1925 to 1935. He resigned in 1948 to become Director of the National Museum of Wales.

The polychaete worms were relatively neglected in the Museum from Monro's death until the appointment in August 1950 of Norman Tebble (b. 1924). He worked chiefly on planktonic polychaetes, and made significant contributions towards understanding the movement and composition of marine plankton. In 1961 Tebble was moved to take charge of Mollusca. Since that time the classification of the oligochaete worms has been studied using numerical taxonomic methods.

The collection of Foraminifera in the Department consisted up to 1884 of specimens on about 200 slides and tablets, according to Randolph Kirkpatrick in *The History of the Collections* 2: 767 (1906). This was a very small representation indeed of an order of Protozoa now estimated to include about 20,000 known species. Their geological history goes back to the late Devonian period, thus there were also fossil specimens in the Department of Geology. Thomas Rupert Jones published a catalogue of these in 1881. The shells or tests secreted by these minute animals are of marvellous diversity and make fascinating objects of study for microscopists. The first major addition to the Department's collection was in 1888 with the arrival of the bulk of the *Challenger* collection mounted on 612 slides and determined by Henry Bowman Brady, who had written the account in the *Challenger* zoological reports, vol. 9, (1884). An even more important acquisition came by the purchase in 1894 of a collection of about 50,000 specimens mounted on 2,265 slides which had been formed by William Kitchen Parker and catalogued by T.R. Jones. By 1904 the Department collection had increased to about 5,130 slides. Thereafter there were continual additions, but nothing to equal those of 1894 and 1925.

In 1925 the Museum received the gift of 90,000 slides bearing some 25,000,000 specimens of Foraminifera and 720 volumes mostly relating to Foraminifera from Edward Heron-Allen (1861-1943), who served the Museum as honorary curator of the Foraminifera from then until his death. He was a man of astonishing versatility. The son of a London solicitor, he worked in the family firm for some years, then, possibly bored by the law, spent the years 1886 to 1889 in the United States earning his livelihood as a lecturer, writer, actor and circus rider in a manner uncertain or perilous enough to cause his return to the family firm in London; from this he retired in 1911 the better to devote himself to the study of Foraminifera and his other interests. He mastered both the art and craft of making violins and the Persian language as well as the intricacies of the Foraminifera, his work on these even leading to fellowship of the Royal Society, where his other activities such as palmistry might have been suspect. He also wrote novels and verse. The titles of some of his publications will indicate Heron-Allen's range of interests: *Codex Chiromanticae* (1883-1886), *Violin-making as it was and is* (1884), *A Manual of Cheirosophy* (1885), *The Princess Daphne* (1885), *Kisses of Fate* (1888), *The Love-letters of a Vagabond* (1889), *A Fatal Fiddle* (1890), *De Fidiculis Bibliographia, being an Attempt towards a Bibliography of the Violin* (1890-1894), *The Ballades of a Blasé Man* (1891), *The Ruba'iyat of Omar Khayyàm, translated* (1898), *The Lament of Bàbà Tàkir; the Persian Text translated and annotated* (1902), with Arthur Earland *The Recent and Fossil Foraminifera of the Shore-sands at Selsey Bill, Sussex* (1908-1911), *Selsey Bill, historic and prehistoric* (1911), *Alcide d'Orbigny; his Life and his Work* (1917), *Barnacles in Nature and in Myth* (1928), *The Gods of the Fourth World* (1931) and *The Parish Church of St Peter on Selsey Bill, Sussex* (1935), as well as studies of Irish, Portuguese, East African, Corsican and Antarctic Foraminifera. Within the Museum only Gavin de Beer (p. 337) has come near to like versatility.

After the death of Heron-Allen there followed a period of neglect for the protozoan collections. This was rectified by the appointments of Ronald Henderson Hedley (b. 1928) in September 1955 and Charles Geoffrey Adams (b. 1926) in November 1956. R.H. Hedley (Head of the Protozoa Section 1955-71) joined the Museum to work on the biology and shell structure of Recent Foraminifera, while C.G. Adams's interests lay in fossil forms (p.252). It was during the tenure of a New Zealand Research Fellowship at the Oceanographic Institute, Wellington, that Hedley first became interested in the fine structure of Protozoa, and on his return he was responsible for the establishment of an Electron Microscope Unit within the Department in 1964.

While searching for freshwater representatives of the Foraminifera, Hedley became interested in testate amoebae and particularly in their shell structure. This led to a series of papers on their general biology and fine structure. In 1968 the section was divided, Adams moving to the Department of Palaeontology as Deputy Keeper and as head of a new Protozoa Section with responsibilities for recent and fossil Foraminifera, Radiolaria and Heliozoa. On the appointment of Hedley as Deputy Director in June 1971 charge of the Protozoa Section in the Zoology Department passed to Colin Robert Curds (b. 1937) who changed the main course of research towards ciliated protozoans.

British sponges (Porifera) were among the many groups to which J.E. Gray turned his attention and in 1848 he published a *List of the Specimens of British Animals in the British Museum, part 2, Sponges.* A notable addition came in 1877 with the purchase of the collection of 1,932 specimens and preparations formed by James Scott Bowerbank (1797-1877), the author of *Monograph of British Spongiadae* (4 vols, 1864-1882). Stuart Oliver Ridley, who joined the staff in July 1878, had charge of these, and, for a time, the Polyzoa, but he resigned in 1886 to take holy orders. The *Challenger* expedition made as usual an important addition to the Department's collection, in all 829 specimens and 1,151 preparations between 1884 and 1889. The collection by 1904 consisted of 8,800 specimens, of which 2,500 were unnamed. These were under the care of Randolph Kirkpatrick (1863-1950) from his appointment as a 2nd Class Assistant in September 1886 until his retirement in 1927 — he continued to work at the Museum until a few days before his death at the age of eighty-seven. His major interest lay in the African sponge fauna. Maurice Burton (b. 1898), who joined the Museum in January 1926, took over from Kirkpatrick. He had been a student of Arthur Dendy (1865-1925), who had worked on the sponges of the *Challenger* expedition in the 1880s, and the classification of the sponges as a whole was a matter to which Burton gave much attention for thirty-one years. He published a volume on the calcareous sponges and some technical papers, and wrote extensively on natural history matters of popular interest. He became Deputy Keeper of the Department in 1948, and retired in 1958.

During the 144 years of its existence, the contribution of the Department of Zoology to systematic zoology has been substantial and enduring. Significant additions have been made to our knowledge of nearly all the major animal groups, and few other institutions have approached its record of achievement. Probably the most useful contributions have been the long series of revisionary studies which, in addition to contributing to an understanding of evolutionary history, have provided a firm basis for a great deal of work in other fields. As for the future, the attitudes and achievements of the younger members of staff reflect credit on the Department; its reputation appears safe in their hands, and they can be expected to enhance it.

13

Department of
Entomology

THE DEPARTMENT OF Entomology came into existence as an independent unit within the Museum in April 1913; the entomological
collections and staff, formerly known as the 'Insect Room', were then
formally separated from the Department of Zoology, of which they had
hitherto been almost the largest section. The Department's newly-
appointed Keeper was Charles Joseph Gahan (1862-1939), a specialist
on beetles, who had joined the Museum staff in 1886. Although not as
an autonomous department under its own Keeper, its history goes back
far beyond 1913, back indeed to the founding of the British Museum in
1753. However, until 1913, its history is entwined with that of the other
zoological collections. The designation 'Insect Room', long used at
South Kensington, originated at Bloomsbury where the entomological
collection of the British Museum, according to Albert Günther, 'was
kept in a large room — the Insect Room — a well-lighted apartment
fifty feet by thirty feet, in which the cabinets were arranged along the
walls or in rows intersecting the room, so as to divide it into several
partitions, the twenty-drawer cabinets, of which eight or ten were
supplied each year, being piled on the top of the old ones almost to the
ceiling'. By 1861, the collection of which Günther wrote had certainly
outgrown the working power of the two entomological Assistants.
Sloane's collection acquired at the British Museum's foundation in
1753 was stated to contain 5,394 insects, although Arachnida and
Myriapoda were at that time included in the Insecta. In 1833 a report
by J.G. Children proclaimed 'the melancholy fact' that of Sloane's
thousands of insects 'literally not a vestige remains'.

The early history of the study and curation of the entomological collection is obscure because the meagre natural history staff had to deal

with such a wide range of organisms. Apparently from 1813 to 1835, William Elford Leach (1790-1836), notorious for his 'periodical bonfires of Sloanian specimens', John George Children (1777-1852) and George Samouelle (d. 1846) looked after the collection, the last-named very inefficiently. Samouelle was appointed as an Assistant in 1821, but was sacked in 1841, because he had taken to drink, neglected his duties, addressed his superiors with insulting language, and spited his fellow worker Adam White (1817-1879) by deliberately removing the registration numbers affixed to the specimens, thereby creating utter confusion! He had begun well by publishing in 1819 an *Entomologist's Useful Compendium*, followed in 1826 by *General Directions for Collecting and Preserving Exotic Insects and Crustacea* and in 1832 and 1833 by *The Entomological Cabinet*, and Konig had appointed him in preference to J.E. Gray. Evidently conditions in the Museum had proved too much for him.

Adam White was an industrious Scot who came to London from Edinburgh at the age of eighteen and found employment in the Museum in 1835. He displayed remarkable ability as an entomologist and from 1835 to 1841 was responsible for almost all the work done on the entomological collection. The appointment of Edward Doubleday (1810-1849) in 1842 to take charge of the Lepidoptera lightened the burden upon White, who henceforth was able to give most of his attention to arranging and cataloguing the Coleoptera, although he also had charge of Crustacea (p. 192).

In 1840 John Edward Gray (1800-1875) became Keeper of Zoology. Gray assigned the cataloguing of the Coleoptera and the Crustacea to White. Between 1847 and 1855 White published a *List of the Specimens of Crustacea* (1847) and six parts of *Nomenclature of Coleopterous Insects* (1847-1855). He also published fifty-eight papers between 1839 and 1861. Unfortunately a mental breakdown caused his retirement in 1863 and he spent his last years in a Scottish asylum.

In 1850 Frederick Smith (1805-1879) joined the zoological staff as a replacement for the lately-deceased Edward Doubleday. He was a steel engraver by trade, having served an apprenticeship under W.B. Cooke, a celebrated engraver of landscapes, for whom he engraved pictures by Turner, Constable and others. As a young man he had become an ardent collector of bees and ants and observer of their habits. He thus became well enough known for the Entomological Society of London to appoint him as curator of the Society's collections and library. Gray's staff of two entomological Assistants, White and Doubleday, could not cope with both the preparation of catalogues and the curation of specimens which came in quantity, for example the collection, mostly from Nepal, bequeathed by Thomas Hardwicke in

1835; 1,749 insects, mostly Lepidoptera and Coleoptera, purchased from G. Milne in 1839; 8,286 insects purchased from J.G. Children in 1840; and 6,735 insects presented by the Entomological Club in 1844. Gray accordingly engaged Smith as an outside worker to arrange the Museum Collection of Hymenoptera. Doubleday, who published from 1844 to 1848 the Museum's first entomological catalogue, *A List of Lepidopterous Insects in the British Museum*, died in December 1849. Gray thereupon offered Smith a permanent position as an Assistant. Although it was said that Smith 'suffered from want of a general and special education', he possessed an unrivalled knowledge of the British Hymenoptera which formed a sound basis for wider study. After Smith's death, J.W. Dunning wrote in *The Entomologist* 12: 91(1879) that 'regular and methodical in his habits, patient and persevering, laborious and industrious — like his favourite ants and bees — he plodded on, piling fact upon fact, and adding to his ever-increasing store of knowledge'. He had learned as an engraver to give meticulous attention to detail. His *Catalogue of Hymenopterous Insects* (7 parts, 1853-1859), dealing with bees and ants, had for the time a high scientific value, enhanced by the clear and precise little illustrations which he drew and engraved for it. He also produced parts 5 (1851) and 6 (1852) of the *Nomenclature of Coleopterous Insects*. In 1875, when Albert Günther became Keeper, Smith was promoted to Assistant Keeper of Zoology.

White and Smith were careful and competent workers, whose catalogues upheld the repute of the Museum. Gray was less fortunate in employing Francis Walker (1809-1874), whose catalogues impress the uninitiated by their volume and appal the initiated by their content. He was the tenth child of John Walker who owned Arno's Grove, Southgate, Middlesex and thus grew up in pleasant rural surroundings, as M.W.R. de V. Graham's account of his life in *Entomologist's Gazette* 30: 7-20 (1979) makes evident: the abounding insect life entranced him and he became a sharp-eyed field entomologist who discovered and described numerous species of aphids mainly from Britain. According to Doncaster, he added nearly 50 species to the 200 aphids then known in Europe, certainly a remarkable achievement. Unfortunately, he was a bad, but extremely industrious, museum taxonomist, who described the same species more than once under different specific names and put it in different genera too often for the good of his reputation and the utility of his work. Thus of forty species of Coleoptera described by Walker from Vancouver Island, four are now accepted. He produced for the Museum, between 1844 and 1873, catalogue upon catalogue comprising some sixty-eight little volumes, replete with descriptions of supposed new species. Although Walker

possessed inherited private wealth which enabled him to travel, this did
not suffice for the rearing of a family, and the Museum payment of £1
for the description of a new genus, and a shilling for a new species,
helpfully raised his income at the expense of science, working on the
scale and at the pace which he did. Fortunately most of his types are
extant in the Museum. Neither Walker nor the Museum escaped
severe criticism in consequence of his numerous, hastily-described
species. 'Walker's name has come to be a by-word among insect-
taxonomists for inaccuracy and superficiality. There is no doubt that,
at one time, the reputation of the Museum suffered considerably from
his poor systematic work.' Thus wrote W.E. China in introducing
John P. Doncaster's *Francis Walker's Aphids* (1961), which provides
detailed descriptions based on Walker's types, for luckily he preserved
some 1,300 specimens of aphids in balsam mounts. Walker's earlier
work published in the *Annals and Magazine of Natural History* between
1848 and 1850 was evidently better than his later work in the Museum
catalogues; thus, according to Doncaster, of thirty new species of
aphids published by him in 1852, only seven can be accepted as valid:
'in all, Walker's contributions to aphidology posed more problems
than they solved'.

Riley in his preface to C. Betten's and M.E. Moseley's *The Francis
Walker Types of Trichoptera* (1940), has judiciously commented on the
situation: 'It is estimated that in the sixty-eight little 12mo volumes by
Francis Walker, published by the British Museum between the years
1844 and 1873, some 50,000 species of insects were listed. Many of
these were described as new, and all the principal Orders of insects
were thus catalogued by Walker wholly or in part, except the
Coleoptera. Similar catalogues by other authors were also published
simultaneously. These volumes mark a period in the entomological
history of the British Museum of which, however, there is little cause to
be proud, yet it would be unfair to judge them by modern standards or
to ignore the circumstances of their publication. Had they remained
but simple stock-taking lists, they would have served equally well their
original purpose and avoided the just criticism of students. As it is,
though their influence upon the care of the collections has undoubtedly
been beneficial, the same cannot always be said of their influence on
entomology; they are an example of the unwisdom of allowing the
curatorial needs of Museum work to outweigh its scientific standards.
Nevertheless, there is no disputing that the publication of these lists
created a nucleus of described species, and a catalogue of named
specimens around which many of the collections have been built. In the
Trichoptera, or Caddis Flies, Francis Walker certainly laid the foundations for all subsequent work on the American species, of which, in

his time, very few had been named. It is unfortunate that in those early days, nearly one hundred years ago, neuropterists had not realized, as students of some other orders had, that colour and wing pattern unsupported by any but the grosser structural characters, were quite inadequate guides to specific recognition in the Trichoptera. As a consequence it has become increasingly difficult, with the lapse of time, to associate certainly the old, faded, and often fragmentary specimens, which are the types of Walker's descriptions, with the species now established upon morphological characters of which Walker was unaware. In consequence much confusion in nomenclature has arisen, especially among the North American species, which could only be dispelled by a critical re-examination of Walker's types, preferably by someone thoroughly acquainted with those species.'

Meanwhile the entomological collections grew and grew. In 1855 the Museum received a collection 4,000 Coleoptera from Madeira and the Salvages, collected and arranged by Thomas Vernon Wollaston (1822-1878), the author of *Insecta Maderenses* (1854). Wollaston later published *Catalogue of the Coleopterous Insects of Madeira in the Collection of the British Museum* (1857) and *Coleoptera Atlantidum* (1865). The other collections included the first from Alfred Russel Wallace made in the Malay Archipelago and the Moluccas. In 1856 came a collection of European Lepidoptera, 1,000 named German Coleoptera, and 1,004 European Curculionidae; in 1857 at least 10,858 European Coleoptera and 1,196 European Coccinellidae; in 1858 the remainder (5,631 specimens) of Wollaston's Madeiran insects and 5,628 insects from the Entomological Society. Thus, year by year, the Museum acquired entomological material on a large scale from North America, New Zealand, Australia, India, Ceylon, the Malay Peninsula, the Canary Islands, the Cape Verde Islands, the Azores and elsewhere, including numerous type specimens.

Two valuable gifts of 1863 were the insect collection formed by Joseph Banks, containing numerous types of species named by Fabricius, and the Coleoptera collection of John Charles Bowring (1821-1893) amounting to 230,000 specimens. The Bowring collection was the largest yet acquired by the Museum, since it included not only the specimens collected by Bowring himself, but also many others from Wallace, Bates, Mouhout and other collectors. The accessions, shortly before the move from Bloomsbury to South Kensington, were 34,347 in 1879, 15,359 in 1880, and 27,599 in 1881. The Museum entomologists in 1882 were Arthur Gardiner Butler, Charles Owen Waterhouse and William Forsell Kirby. It seems incredible that they were able to attend to the curation of these enormous collections and also do scientific research on certain groups; to cover all insects was impossible. Their achievement is impressive and their careers merit notice.

Arthur Gardiner Butler (1844-1925) joined the 'Insect Room' staff at Bloomsbury in 1863, having evidently impressed the Keeper of Zoology, J.E. Gray. The collection of Lepidoptera in the Museum was then of such a size that he was barely able to re-organise it all in two years. He published in 1868 *A Catalogue of Satyridae in the British Museum* and in 1869 *A Catalogue of the Fabrician Types of Lepidoptera Rhopalocera*. During his thirty-eight years of service in the Museum he raised the collection of Lepidoptera from minor importance to being one of the world's largest. He retired in 1901 on account of ill health, but lived, however, for another twenty-four years. He described some thousand species as new, unaware like his contemporaries of seasonal variation within a single species. On the death of Frederick Smith in 1879, Butler became Assistant Keeper.

The association of Charles Owen Waterhouse (1843-1917) with the Museum began at a very early age, since his father George Robert Waterhouse (1810-1880) entered the service of the Museum in 1843 and was Keeper of Mineralogy and Geology from 1851 to 1857, then Keeper of Mineralogy from 1857 to 1880. His godfathers were Charles Darwin and Richard Owen. C.O. Waterhouse entered the Museum service in 1866 as a Junior Assistant, became a 1st Class Assistant in 1899 and Assistant Keeper in 1905; he retired in 1910. He specialised in Coleoptera and contributed an account of some Central American species to Godman and Salvin's *Biologia Centrali-Americana*, but he also published a more general work, an *Aid to the Identification of Insects* (2 vols, 1880-1890).

Waterhouse devoted much time to preparing models and diagrams for exhibition purposes, but this work has now been superseded by the new Insect Gallery.

William Forsell Kirby (1844-1912) became an Assistant in the Museum in 1879 after Frederick Smith's death, having been from 1867 to 1879 a curator in the Museum of the Royal Dublin Society. He was born on 14 January 1844 in Leicester, where his father was a banker. Educated privately, he became very interested at an early age in butterflies and moths, and published in 1862 a small *Manual of European Butterflies*. He produced, while in Dublin, a *Synonymic Catalogue of Diurnal Lepidoptera* (1871; Supplement 1877). This established his reputation as an entomologist. At the Museum he published a succession of catalogues esteemed for their reliability, as well as *Rhopalocera Exotica* (1887-1897) with fine plates, an *Elementary Text-Book of Entomology*, and much else. He was a quiet, retiring man of prodigious industry with wide interests; he knew many languages and even translated the Finnish epic, the *Kalevala*, into English. He retired in 1909.

Charles Joseph Gahan (1862-1939), Keeper of the Department of Entomology from 1913 to 1927, began as an Assistant in September 1886. His father was a schoolmaster at Roscrea, Tipperary, Ireland, and he received his education at his father's school and Queen's College, Galway. He next studied science at the Royal School of Mines in London, where T.H. Huxley was a professor, and then moved to the Natural History Museum. He specialised on Coleoptera, especially longicorn beetles, but his interests were much wider and included mimicry and phylogeny. The Trustees did well to appoint this mild and capable man as Keeper of the new Department, rather than the irritable, hot-tempered and self-centred, though extremely industrious Sir George Hampson, who apparently expected the post, being senior to Gahan. Gahan was Keeper during a period of great expansion and interest in entomology, both as a pure science and as a subject of agricultural and medical importance. In 1912 the Departmental collections numbered 2,250,000 specimens. By 1927 the number exceeded 5,000,000.

George Francis Hampson (1860-1936) joined the staff in March 1895. He had been educated at Charterhouse School and Exeter College, Oxford, then went out to India to become a tea-planter in the Nilgiri Hills of Madras, Southern India. The wealth of butterflies and moths attracted his interest, and on returning to England he became a voluntary worker in the Museum, preparing his *The Lepidoptera of the Nilgiri District* (1891) and *The Lepidoptera Heterocera of Ceylon* (1893) as parts 8 and 9 of *Illustrations of Typical Specimens of Lepidoptera Heterocera of the British Museum*. At the suggestion of H.J. Elwes, he undertook *The Fauna of British India, Moths* (4 vols 1892-1896), a stupendous achievement running to 2,276 pages and including hundreds of new species. Much impressed by such industry, Günther offered him a post in the Museum and he entered officially as an Assistant in March 1895; on inheriting a title in 1896, he became even more eligible for promotion on account of his social status. In 1901 he was made acting Assistant Keeper. Thereafter he concentrated his attention on a *Catalogue of the Lepidoptera Phalaenae in the British Museum* (15 vols, 1898-1920) which, despite its extent, covered less than half of the order. The task was too great even for him. In 1906 Hampson published statistics indicating the state of the collection in 1904, some of which are as follows: Diptera, 46,900 specimens (15,000 unidentified), Lepidoptera, 355,767 specimens (22,629 unidentified), Coleoptera, 398,000 specimens (130,000 unidentified), Hymenoptera, 132,000 specimens (34,000 unidentified); Neuroptera, 9,056 specimens (1,200 unidentified); Orthoptera, 18,000 specimens (3,200 unidentified). The entomological staff consisted of A.G. Butler, C.O. Waterhouse, W.F. Kirby,

C.J. Gahan, F.A. Heron, E.E. Austen, G.F. Hampson and G.J. Arrow, i.e. half of the total zoological staff of the Museum, but still not enough to deal with the immense number of organisms concerned and of specimens representing them. By now, the economic importance of insects as pests in agriculture and as transmitters of disease had come to be recognised and with it the need to be able to identify them with precision. The recommendation was accordingly made to the Trustees in 1906 that a separate Entomological Department should be created out of the Zoological Department, but nothing came of this until 1913. In 1909 an independent organisation, the Entomology Research Committee (Tropical Africa) renamed Imperial Bureau of Entomology in 1913, with Sir G.A.K. Marshall as its first director (now the Commonwealth Institute of Entomology) was set up by the Colonial Office and located in the Museum. Its entomologists have continued to work there ever since, providing services largely to Commonwealth countries.

Meanwhile, the collections had continued to grow. In 1901 Henry John Elwes (1846-1922), equally as well known as a sportsman, arboriculturist and gardener, as an entomologist, offered the Museum all the specimens of Lepidoptera from his collection needed to supplement the Department's collection and he undertook to rearrange this. In all, during the succeeding years, he gave 11,369 specimens. He was a big, robust and domineering man, with a booming voice which carried well across the fields of his Gloucestershire estate, but was very disconcerting elsewhere. 'Is that a man or a foghorn?' someone remarked at a Royal Horticultural Society flower show. According to Riley, the Assistant in charge, Francis Arthur Heron (1864-1940), 'a kindly, shy and retiring personality must have found Elwes' methods very disturbing'. Heron was invalided in 1910 due to mental trouble from which he never recovered.

In 1910 the Museum received the Lord Walsingham's collection of Microlepidoptera amounting to about 260,000 specimens, thousands of them collected by himself on his travels in the western United States and the Mediterranean region. From 1876 onwards Walsingham had been a Trustee of the British Museum, but even so there was difficulty over the acceptance when he transferred his superb collection to the Museum by deed of gift in 1901. The terms of this transfer did not satisfy Lankester, the Director, who advised against acceptance primarily on the grounds that the value of the collection had been over-rated and the annual expenditure on its upkeep would be too high!

The staff of the Department of Entomology at its formation in 1913 consisted of the Keeper, C.J. Gahan, three 1st Class Assistants, Ernest Edward Austen (1867-1938) appointed in 1889, George Francis

Hampson (1860-1936) now a baronet, appointed in 1895, and John Hartley Durrant (1863-1928) transferred in 1910 from Walsingham's private employment to the Museum with the transfer of the Walsingham collection of Microlepidoptera, five 2nd Class Assistants, Geoffrey Meade-Waldo (1884-1916) appointed in February 1909, in charge of Hymenoptera who died suddenly of pneumonia in March 1916, Kenneth Gloyne Blair (1882-1952) appointed in November 1910 who, after being employed in the Paymaster General's office, was put in charge of Coleoptera, Frederick Wallace Edwards (1888-1940) appointed in November 1910, Norman Denbigh Riley (1890-1979) appointed in November 1911, and Bruce Frederic Cummings (1889-1919) appointed in January 1912, nine Attendants and two Boy Attendants.

Cummings' ambitions were frustrated by ill-health, eventually diagnosed as disseminated sclerosis, which caused him to resign in 1917. Becoming more and more paralysed and facing death, he compiled extracts from his diaries, published as *The Journal of a Disappointed Man* under the pseudonym W.N.P. Barbellion in March 1919.

In Riley's booklet *The Department of Entomology of the British Museum (Natural History) 1904-1964. A Brief Historical Sketch* (1964) he referred to the Insect Room as it was when he joined the Museum in 1911.

'In these early days conditions were very different from those now prevailing. The only heating in the Insect Room was from open fires which were locked behind screens at 4 p.m., artificial lighting was by naked gas jets and oil lamps which were so few and so unsafe that the staff was generally sent home in foggy weather or as soon as it got dark. The public galleries were devoid of lighting and heating. There was internal communication between the Keeper of the Department and the Assistant Keeper by means of a speaking tube; but if either wished to call on the other he would don his silk hat before leaving his study, even if it only meant crossing the corridor. However, by 1906 electric light had been installed in the studies and internal telephones between the departments. A year later the telephones were connected with the outer world, and two years later central heating and ventilation were installed. The latter, an extractor system, caused enormous quantities of soot to build up on the window screens (London was very dirty in those days) only to be precipitated on one's table in concentrated doses whenever a gale blew up. Hours of work were 10 a.m. to 5 p.m. daily, including Saturdays, and the evening patrol, which set out at 5 p.m., insisted gently but firmly that one ceased work and departed at 5 o'clock no matter what one was doing. Important letters and reports of which copies needed to be kept were written in copying ink and the copy made by pressing the letter on to a damp flimsy in the letter book. These conditions still prevailed in 1911 when the compiler of these notes was appointed an Assistant, 2nd class, in the Department of Zoology. Assistants were largely autonomous and each had one Attendant. There was little sense of the team spirit and, indeed, it was quite difficult to get to know one's colleagues at all well; one was curious to know, for example, whether Sir George Hampson, who worked in the next room, really was aware of one's existence... However, things were "looking up" in the entomological world... by 1912 the writer had been provided with a binocular microscope; a second telephone (in a public call box!) had been installed in the Department and by 1913, C.J. Gahan, now Keeper of the Department, had even obtained a typewriter, though this had only been supplied after Treasury sanction had been granted. The first shorthand-typist was not engaged until 1926. The outbreak of war in 1914 signalled the end of this age, though the end was slow in coming. A characteristic parting shot was an order issued to F.W. Edwards in 1915 that he wear a hat when coming to or leaving the Museum!'

Although the Department in 1913 had nine scientific members, the number of entomologists working in the Museum, though not part of its official established staff, was much greater than this. They included specialists of high repute, who studied the collections, arranged the specimens systematically and published works based upon them. Some with adequate private means worked in a purely voluntary capacity, giving their services unpaid and enjoying the satisfaction of research without administrative duties, as Hampson had on his return from India. Other volunteers were remunerated to some extent by small payments made on an hourly basis. Without such helpers the output of the Department over the years would have been much lower, because they were free of the administrative and curatorial duties and attention to demands of the general public and other government departments which necessarily occupied so much of the permanent staff's time. These expert supernumeraries often outnumbered the official members and were most welcome. Economic entomology came within the Museum's scope at the very end of the nineteenth century. The research of Ronald Ross (1858-1932) above all had conclusively demonstrated by 1902, when he received the Nobel Prize, that certain mosquitoes transmitted malaria, but he had experienced much difficulty when in India with the identification of mosquitoes which needed special taxonomic study. Ray Lankester, as Director of the

Museum and at the same time Keeper of Zoology, sought the assistance of the Colonial Office, the Foreign Office and the India Office. As a result, Joseph Chamberlain, then Secretary of State for the Colonies, distributed a circular to persons administering Britain's overseas territories, asking for collections to be made of their mosquitoes. Many specimens accordingly came to the Museum. These were studied by Frederick Vincent Theobald (1868-1930), who worked in the Museum but was never a staff member. After leaving the University of Cambridge he published Vol. 1 (the only volume) of *An Account of British Flies*. Unlike Kirby, who was a superb linguist, completely at home in almost all European entomological literature, Theobald was handicapped in this work by his inadequate familiarity with French and German. His entomological knowledge led, however, to his being invited in 1899 by the Trustees of the British Museum to prepare a world monograph on the Culicidae, the connection of mosquitoes with the spread of disease being now known. His *Monograph of the Culicidae or Mosquitoes of the World* (5 vols, 1901-1911) has received much criticism, but it was an important pioneer work; until the appointment of F.W. Edwards in 1910, the Department had no specialist for such an undertaking. For many years from 1905, Theobald was Professor of Economic Zoology at the South-Eastern Agricultural College, Wye, Kent.

Ernest Edward Austen (1867-1938) had likewise a strong interest in medical entomology. He was educated at Rugby School and the University of Heidelberg, and on joining the Museum zoological staff in 1889 was put in charge of Diptera. A collecting expedition to Brazil in 1895 and 1896 acquainted him with tropical conditions and in 1899 he accompanied Ronald Ross to Sierra Leone to collect mosquitoes. He also became interested in the blood-sucking tsetse-flies, of which twenty-two species are now known in the genus *Glossina*. These flies are vectors of trypanosomiasis, including the important sleeping sickness of man. Austen himself was bitten by this fly, but fortunately did not contract the disease. From Sierra Leone, he went off to South Africa to join the British Army in the Boer War. Back at the Museum he produced *Illustrations of British Blood-Sucking Flies, with Notes* (1906), *Illustrations of African Blood-Sucking Flies other than of the Tsetse-flies* (1909), *A Handbook of the Tsetse-flies* (1911) and *A Monograph of the Tsetse-flies* (1913). These, together with Theobald's work on mosquitoes, established the Department as a major centre for the taxonomic study of disease-carrying insects.

Austen became a member of the Sleeping Sickness and Tropical Diseases Committees set up by the Colonial Office. A man of initiative and drive, as well as courage, he realised clearly the need to spread essential information about noxious insects and to control them widely and effectively. He induced the Museum to publish authoritative and concise *Economic Leaflets* produced cheaply and on a large scale. He himself produced the first of these in 1913, on the housefly *(Musca domestica)*. It had a very popular reception, sold in vast quantities at one penny a copy and its success encouraged the Museum to produce others, to meet wartime and post-war requirements.

On the outbreak of World War I in 1914 Austen, who had maintained his military training, immediately became a company commander in the Artists Rifles, but was later transferred from France to Egypt as a medical entomologist. He had the rank of major and received the Distinguished Service Order. Gahan retired in 1927 and Austen was then appointed Keeper, himself retiring in 1932 and ensuring the appointment of Riley, who had become a captain during the War, rather than Edwards, who had been a conscientious objector and farm worker.

As Riley wrote in 1964, Austen and Edwards were two strongly contrasting characters. 'Austen, a figure of Victorian solidarity, was concerned with precision of detail. He arranged the collections with meticulous care, and his elaborate notes can still be seen, written in a miniature copperplate, and sparing no refinement of title or punctuation ... Austen was most reluctant to generalise, and left behind no synoptic works that would summarise his views on any of his favourite groups. He published mainly on Tabanidae and Bombyliidae, but with many small papers on other flies, mainly of medical interest. His attitude to entomology was that of a professional, but he was also a distinguished soldier.' After retirement he continued to work in the Museum writing his *Bombyliidae of Palestine* (1937), based mostly on specimens collected when on active service in 1917 and 1918; among these were forty-three new species.

Frederick Wallace Edwards (1888-1940) joined the Museum staff in 1910, a year ahead of Riley, who was nearly two years younger. He was the elder brother of Wilfred Norman Edwards, from 1938 to 1955 Keeper of Geology, and, like him was educated at the Cambridge County School. At the Museum he soon became absorbed in the study of Diptera, paying special attention to mosquitoes. He found that the scale characters used by Theobald had less taxonomic value than supposed. Later he studied the Mycetophilidae, Chironomidae and Tipulidae, while retaining his position as an internationally recognised authority on the Culicidae. As Riley has said, Edwards contrasted in every way with soldier Austen. 'He was a Quaker and a pacifist. Though a trained biologist and a professional dipterist, he had much of the amateur's outlook, and was equally at home at an international congress and in the field with his amateur friends. His output was prodigious. Any problem to do with flies aroused his immediate interest. Each new problem was rapidly filleted and its bones laid out in a quick paper. His judgements were largely intuitive, but his eye and memory were good, and he did not often make bad mistakes. He was, however, sometimes inaccurate in details. He wrote with apparently complete self-confidence, and his footnotes in other people's papers (e.g. *Diptera of Patagonia* series) often contradict what the wretched author is trying to say. Much of his actual writing and most of his correspondence were dealt with in the train on his journeys to and from work. Edwards' two major works are his volume on Culicidae in the *Genera Insectorum* (1932), and the third volume of the *Mosquitoes of the Ethiopian Region* (1941), posthumously). Yet among his 406 other papers, there are few without some comment or criticism, often illuminating. His attitude of the scientific naturalist was immensely stimulating to all who knew him personally.' Edwards adhered to his strongly-held pacifist views whatever the detriment to himself, and his promotion within the Museum was accordingly blocked for some years after the War. There seems little doubt that he was one of the most brilliant entomologists in the Museum's service and certainly one of the most industrious; he described some 2,000 new species of Diptera in a working period of about twenty-five years. Fellow entomologists expressed their appreciation of his labours by dedicating to him, for example, the genera *Edwardsina*, *Edwardsomyia* and *Edwardsellum* (now a subgenus of *Simulium*), species of the last named, transmitting the parasitic worm a filaria, causing human onchocerciasis. The Royal Society elected him to fellowship in 1938 at the age of fifty, 'a timely recognition of taxonomy', as was said in *Entomologist's Monthly Magazine*, but only just in time for he died of cancer in 1940.

The outbreak of the 1914-1918 World War in August 1914 drastically and rapidly reduced the staff of the Department. Eight, including Austen, left to join the Armed Forces in August, followed by four others in September. Ultimately the staff remaining consisted of men too old for service, such as Gahan and Durrant, or medically unfit, such as Cummings.

The war brought unpleasantly to notice a number of creatures which were the special concern of the Department. In March 1915 the Cambridge zoologist Arthur Everett Shipley published a very appropriately titled little book, *The Minor Horrors of War*, since it dealt with the louse, the bed-bug, the flea, the flour-moth, the house-fly, the bluebottle and mites. He followed it in 1916 with *More Minor Horrors of War* dealing with the cockroach, the bot- and warble-fly, mosquitoes, the biscuit-weevil, the fig-moth, the stable-fly, rats and mice. The depleted

Department staff had to deal with many enquiries related to these and, following the initiative of Austen, they produced the Economic Pamphlets. It must have been embarrassing for the Government, when the closing of the Museum was intended and the study of Microlepidoptera dismissed as an irrelevant activity, to learn of the enormous quantities of army rations destroyed or made uneatable by maggots of the flour-moth and of the preventive measures to which Durrant, the Microlepidoptera specialist in the Department, had contributed (p.108). The numerous enquiries reaching the Museum about insects of medical and economic importance caused a staff member, Frederick Laing, to be specially appointed to deal with them. He retired in 1950. Alfred W. McKenny Hughes came to the Museum in 1931 also to deal with economic enquiries, especially from the public and from public health authorities. He was involved in early work on the house-fly and the bed-bug. Meanwhile, other government departments were now becoming able to undertake research on aspects of this vast field, which it was beyond the Museum's resources to cover adequately, and when McKenny Hughes retired in 1955, the Museum ceased to have a special economic entomologist.

Wartime experience had emphasised the importance of economic entomology then, but damage to crops was just as important after the war as during it. This caused the Empire Marketing Board to become zealous on the Department's behalf. Even before the creation of the Department, lack of space for the continuously increasing collections of insects had become a major problem. This was temporarily eased by taking over basement rooms made free by removal of their contents into the New Spirit Building. By 1927 congestion had become as frustrating as it had ever been. The Empire Marketing Board accordingly made £30,000 available in December 1927 for an extension to the New Spirit Building to be used temporarily by the Department. This was ready in 1930 and provided much better storage and working conditions pending the erection of a special Entomology Block. Work on this began in 1934 and the first half of it was completed in 1936, but the Department gained no extra space by moving in, especially as the lower three floors were occupied by the collection of birds skins to the dismay of the entomologists. Further space could only result from completion of the whole block on which work began in 1938. Then came the 1939-1945 World War which halted work and, as stated by Riley, 'left it standing as a rusting maze of steel girders from early 1940 till 1950 when work was resumed'.

Conditions were made worse between the two World Wars by the very repute of the Departments which led to the gift and bequest of big private collections particularly of Lepidoptera; Joicey's collection of nearly 500,000 specimens merits special mention, if only for the eccentricities of its owner who, like Lord Rothschild, set up his own Museum, the Hill Museum at Witley, Surrey. In 1932 George Talbot (1882-1952), who had been Joicey's curator, came to work at the Museum on a part-time basis. Moreover the Museum bought collections, such as the bulk of the one formed by the printer Charles Oberthür (1845-1924) brought from Rennes, France in 1926 and 1927; this comprised about 750,000 specimens of butterflies and moths. Between the years 1929 and 1934, the intrepid Miss Lucy Evelyn Cheesman (1881-1969) presented over 50,000 insects collected by herself on expeditions into the wild interior of Papua and the New Hebrides. In 1932 David Sharp (1840-1922) presented his collection of 118,000 Coleoptera, whilst Richard S. Bagnall (1889-1962) gave his collection of thrips containing 17,000 specimens.

In 1937 Lord Rothschild bequeathed his private zoological museum at Tring (p.138) and this included his immense collection of Lepidoptera, estimated at about 2,500,000 specimens, almost equalling in size the entire general collection of Lepidoptera already in the Museum. It remained, however, at Tring and so did not add to the congestion at South Kensington, until in 1972, with the erection of purpose-built building at Tring, the bird collection was moved from South Kensington to Tring and the Rothschild Lepidoptera and fleas transferred to London.

Probably the most remarkable accession was the bequest of 100,000 specimens of Lepidoptera, mostly Microlepidoptera, by Edward Meyrick (1854-1938), who was himself a remarkable man. Many of the great British collectors of Lepidoptera have been men of great wealth and under no necessity to earn a living. Meyrick, an Oxford classical scholar, earned his as a schoolmaster, teaching Latin and Greek, from 1887 to 1914 at his old school, Marlborough College. His interest in entomology had begun, however, when he was a Marlborough schoolboy and lasted until his death at the age of eighty-four. As an amateur entomologist he made a profound study of the Lepidoptera, leading to fundamental reclassification, and during sixty-six years of spare-time work, he described some 20,000 new species as well as several new genera in about 420 books and papers in learned journals.

When Austen retired in 1932, Norman Denbigh Riley (1890-1979) became Keeper in his place. Austen's support of Riley, as opposed to Edwards', whatever the motive, was fully justified by events. Riley proved better fitted for administration than Edwards would have been and Edwards better for fruitful research. His Irish family name had already been made known in entomology by Charles Valentine Riley (1843-1895) but 'NDR', as he was often called was not related to him.

He was born in Tooting, London, in 1890, and, when a boy, had Richard South (1846-1932), editor of *The Entomologist* and author of *The Butterflies of the British Isles* and *The Moths of the British Isles*, for his next-door neighbour. Thus began his life-long interest in Lepidoptera. After schooling from 1904 to 1909 at Dulwich College, Riley studied entomology for a short time at the Imperial College of Science under Maxwell Lefroy, for whom he became demonstrator in 1911 and thus had occasion to visit the Insect section of the Natural History Museum on his behalf. He wished to name a collection of Indian Heterocera and went to Hampson, the authority, for help. 'Hampson took one glance at them, then with a wave of the hand indicating the entire BM collection, said "You will find them over there", picked up his pen and went on writing. It is small wonder that visitors complained, but Hampson did get on with his work'. In November 1911 Riley became Hampson's colleague in the Museum, hardly to know him but certainly to observe how he accomplished so much. 'This he achieved by a ruthless methodical routine with which nothing was allowed to interfere, standing day long at the high desk which was his only work bench and on which the only tools, pen, pencil, dividers, benzene and a hand lens were arranged.'

Riley joined the Army on the outbreak of war in 1914 and served until 1919, and was mentioned in dispatches. Back in the Museum he resumed work on his beloved butterflies, described new exotic species and subspecies in about sixty short papers, and became involved in administration for which he had a special talent. His knowledge became more and more detailed, but he never had time or maybe the inclination, for such synoptic work as that in which Edwards excelled. Nevertheless, as R.I. Vane-Wright wrote in *Antenna* 3: 134 (1979), 'the monographs he never wrote were written for him, by those around him, those hundreds and thousands of entomologists across the world who benefitted from his presence, his humour and his judgment'. From 1932 until his retirement as Keeper in 1955, he worked hard to increase the collections, as well as the staff and available space. The 1939-1945 World War frustrated much of his efforts, but he organised efficiently the evacuation and dispersal of the collections to Tring, Turville Court, Rodborough Fort, Wray Court, How Caple Court and Liscombe Park, although some of the Lepidoptera had to remain at South Kensington. The Museum was badly damaged by bombs, but the losses to the study collections as a whole, despite some injury by dampness and insect attack to those stored in the country, were negligible. Their return and incorporation was completed in 1946. The problem of space remained and was not solved until the completion of the new Entomological Block in 1952 and the removal of the ornithological specimens to Tring in 1972.

One of the notable events of Riley's keepership was the formation of the Rothschild-Cockayne-Kettlewell collection of British Lepidoptera, particularly valuable for its fine representation of local races and aberrations. This is the finest collection of Macrolepidoptera of any single country. It includes important material used by Kettlewell in his studies on industrial melanism. In 1958 Cockayne's executors gave the Museum £10,765 for the extension of the R.C.K. collection.

Riley retired in 1955, but remained active for some twenty years afterwards. In 1964, on the occasion of the 12th International Congress of Entomology, he produced *The Department of Entomology of the British Museum (Natural History) 1904-1964: a brief historical sketch*, well-written, packed with first-hand information and indispensable; those who need further information about the history of the Department must refer to this excellent detailed account. After his retirement, Riley produced two independent books, *A Field Guide to the Butterflies of the West Indies* (1975) and, in collaboration with L.G. Higgins, *A Field Guide to the Butterflies of Britain and Europe* (1970).

During his Keepership, the collections of all groups increased from about eight million to fifteen million. They have continued to increase since then, and a careful census in 1976 led to an estimate of 22,500,000 insect specimens as the Museum's holding, representing about 445,000 named species out of an estimated world total of about 827,000 described species. Beetles (Coleoptera) are by far the most numerous group of animals in the world, indeed they comprise at least a quarter of the known animal kingdom, and with an estimated total of more than 300,000 species outnumber the estimated total (about 236,000 species) of flowering plants. In 1905 the beetle collection contained about 67,800 named species. By 1976 this had risen to about 170,000 species. The entomological staff at the Department's founding in 1913 numbered twenty; it has now risen to over ninety, to which must be added about twenty from the Commonwealth Institute of Entomology and the Centre for Overseas Pest Research, who also work in the Department. Although sixteen persons work on Coleoptera, this means theoretically that each one has a curatorial responsibility for about 350,000 specimens and a taxonomic responsibility for about 19,000 species.

William Edward China (1895-1979), who joined the Museum staff in June 1921 and retired in 1960, followed Riley as Keeper in 1955. China was educated at Trinity Hall, Cambridge, and having taken a Diploma in Agriculture, as well as a Natural Sciences Tripos, brought a much more modern flavour when appointed to the Museum in 1921. His speciality was the Hemiptera and unlike many present-day spec-

ialists, he had a wide knowledge of the whole order, publishing over 200
scientific papers that dealt authoritatively with various aspects of this
important group of insects. He was widely recognized as a leading
international authority on their taxonomy, taking a Sc.D. in 1947.
After his retirement, he continued to work on Hemiptera, but also held
from 1962-1971 two positions dealing with Zoological Nomenclature;
Scientific Controller of the International Trust, and Secretary to the
International Commission. China's Keepership is probably best
remembered as a time when the whole emphasis was beginning to
change from mere descriptive taxonomy to a more synoptic or analytical approach which was to receive a greater impetus in the next two
decades.

John Priestman Doncaster (b. 1907), who joined the staff in October
1937 and retired in 1969, was also educated at Cambridge. He joined
the Museum as Exhibition Officer, but was seconded during the War to
the Agricultural Research Council to continue his work on the
transmission of potato viruses by aphids. He returned to the Museum
in 1945 and was responsible for the rehabilitation of some of the war-
damaged galleries, especially the Bird Gallery. In 1951 he transferred
to the Department of Entomology with responsibility for aphids and
thrips, thus sharing with China that agriculturally important group of
insects, the Hemiptera. Doncaster succeeded China as Keeper in 1960
and the gradual modernisation of the Department continued. During
his Keepership, the Trustees allowed a special grant of money for the
purchase of several dozen new microscopes to replace the outmoded
and inefficient existing instruments. This improvement in research
facilities, together with the appointment of new senior staff with
overseas agricultural research experience made the Department as
much a research institute as a storehouse.

A notable event during Doncaster's Keepership was the provision of
a new Insect Gallery. Early in the century Waterhouse had spent much
time making and maintaining exhibits in the Insect Gallery as well as
dealing with departmental matters. According to Riley, 'his lean
sparse figure, always clad in a frock coat, was constantly in motion
between these two objectives'. His gallery escaped damage during the
war, but was by then so out of date that it was closed and handed over as
an annexe to the Zoological Library. The Shell Gallery had, however,
suffered badly during the bombing and this gallery, when restored by
the Ministry of Public Buildings and Works and now completely
empty, was partly handed over in 1965 to the Department of
Entomology and the Exhibition Section, to provide a new Insect
Gallery. In many respects, the displays in the new Gallery, which were
largely designed by Paul Freeman under the direction of Doncaster,

departed from the old Museum tradition. The aim was to give the ordinary intelligent adult, with no knowledge of entomology, a general impression of the special features of insects. Some displays showed the major insect groups, others touched on topics of particular interest, such as migration, coloration, habitats and the influence of insects on human activities from medical, veterinary and agricultural stand-points. The Gallery was opened to the public on 1 October 1968 and has proved one of the most pleasing, attractive and instructive galleries in the whole Museum.

Paul Freeman (b. 1916) succeeded Doncaster as Keeper in 1968. The most notable feature of Freeman's Keepership has been an increase in the purposeful management of scientific policies as well as the controlled growth of the collections.

Early taxonomic work in entomology necessarily needed to be des-criptive. This was because the collections contained vast numbers of undescribed species. Nowadays, however, the description of new species without revision of the groups to which they belong is not regarded as an adequate activity. Research projects are therefore selected with care and purpose, to summarise all available knowledge on each particular aspect, with special reference to general biological problems, such as evolution, zoogeography, host specificity, or to economic importance in medical and agricultural fields.

The study of insects of medical importance received an impetus during the Second World War by the publication of *A Handbook for the Identification of Insects of Medical Importance* by John Smart, a book of great value to colonial entomologists and others, both during and after the War. This was revised and expanded, mainly by the staff of the Department, and re-issued in 1973 under the editorship of Kenneth G.V. Smith. After the War, Peter Frederick Mattingly (b. 1914) continued mosquito studies until his retirement in 1979, and Harold Oldroyd wrote three masterly volumes on African horse-flies. Freeman, who looked after most of the Nematocera, published exten-sively on Chironomidae, Mycetophilidae and Simuliidae, and Roger W. Crosskey (b. 1930) is continuing the work on African Simuliidae.

There has also been a recent marked expansion of work on insects of agricultural importance, particularly those which are vectors of plant viruses — aphids, psyllids, coccids, white-fly and leaf-hoppers — following the appointment of entomologists with overseas experience. In particular, mention should be made of Victor F. Eastop (b. 1924) (aphids) and Laurence A. Mound (b. 1934), (thrips and whitefly). Fundamental studies are being made of the chromosomes of aphids in an attempt to unravel differences between species and between different races of the same species, including those that show varying susceptibility to insecticides. In contrast, the huge butterfly collection, which includes over 90% of the known species, contains a wealth of biological information now being tapped in studies of polymorphism, species evolution and sexual selection. Other major projects in recent years include the work on insect fossils transferred from the Palaeontology Department to Entomology; the production of authoritative catalogues to the 30,000 names of Lepidoptera genera, together with their type-species, four volumes of which are now in print. Also, the outstanding curatorial effort in which the hundreds of thousands of insects accumulated in unsorted accessions by previous generations have now been sorted into family, genus or even species.

The increase in size of the collections to the present total of 22,500,000 specimens has been brought about in a variety of ways including the mounting of expeditions. The expedition to Patagonia and Southern Chile, organized by F.W. Edwards in 1929 to compare the fauna of Australia and New Zealand with that of South America, resulted in more than 20,000 specimens being brought back to the Museum and the publication of seven volumes of scientific reports. The South-west African expedition of 1972, undertaken by five staff members using a purpose-built mobile laboratory, collected several hundred thousand insects from all types of habitat, including forest and desert. Wherever possible, staff from the Department are attached to other expeditions, such as the Royal Geographical Society's expeditions to the Matto Grosso (Brazil) and Gunong Mulu (Borneo). Additionally, staff have gone abroad for lengthy periods at other institutes' expense, for example L.A. Mound, who was attached to the Commonwealth Scientific and International Research Organization Canberra for a year and V.F. Eastop, who was appointed visiting professor for periods of several months in both Brazil and Iran.

The necessity for a large expert entomological staff arises from the remarkable success of insects, not only in adapting themselves to every available land and freshwater habitat throughout the world, but also in feeding on almost every animal and plant, including man himself, his crops and his domestic animals. There are also, of course, a vast number of animals from ant-eaters down to microscopic worms which feed on or within insects. As pollinators of crops, as pests of crops and foodstuffs, as carriers of diseases, as destroyers of furniture, clothes and other artefacts, insects seriously affect human activities. Correct identification of the insects concerned, supplemented by knowledge of their habits, is vital to their control, but often far from simple, and what has been generally considered to be one species sometimes proves on critical investigation to be a complex of several. Such species may be almost indistinguishable, except for subtle difference in structure, but they may have different patterns of behaviour and preferences for different habitats. For example, some species of grasshoppers and crickets are kept from interbreeding because the males produce different sounds, often called 'songs', to attract their respective females. The Department accordingly installed an acoustic laboratory in 1973 under David R. Ragge (b. 1930) for recording such sounds. It is now equipped with tape recorders for field and laboratory use and an oscilloscope and oscillograph for analysis of the sounds recorded.

Other modern techniques include electrophoresis and cytological studies, as well as the routine use of computer-based morphometrics in the analysis of variation. These new methods are valuable aids to investigation, but they can never replace the traditional methods of comparative study of the numerous morphological details, to evaluate which a large collection of specimens is essential. Current research projects are frequently based on the study of many thousands of specimens, in order to understand the variation within and between species.

The last two decades have seen big changes in the Department. New style cabinets, making more effective use of space, have been available in larger numbers than ever before; the whole of the Entomology Building is now occupied by the Entomology Department, following the removal of the Bird Skin Collection to Tring; and many more sophisticated modern microscopes and other equipment have been purchased. New equipment and new techniques have made it possible to apply up-to-date methods to problems that earlier generations found difficult to solve, but those areas of scholarship in which the Department has always excelled, based on the unrivalled library and collections, are not neglected and continue to be developed.

This is merely a brief outline of the history of the most comprehensive insect collection, and largest scientific department in the world devoted entirely to taxonomic entomology. Certainly no more than one half, and some estimates suggest as little as one fifth, of existing species have so far been described. The challenge for successive generations is to determine the correct approach to this daunting prospect.

14

Department of
Palaeontology
(formerly Geology)

THE TERM 'GEOLOGY' referring to the science of the earth; its composition, structure, processes and history has in recent years lost its primacy and has been swallowed up by the enveloping term 'earth sciences'. Nevertheless, stratigraphy, palaeontology, mineralogy and petrology are cognate branches of the science of geology. Paradoxically, the Department of Palaeontology (formerly Geology) is concerned with the first two; and the Department of Mineralogy with the second two. Stratigraphy is the study of strata, their succession, composition, history and fossil content; while palaeontology is specifically the study of those selfsame fossil remains. The term 'fossil' (from Latin *fossilis*, dug up), like geology, had formerly a wider application than now. It was used for anything that was dug out of the earth, accidentally or by excavation, such as minerals, flint implements and the remains, usually petrified, of animals and plants, to which it is now restricted. Sir Hans Sloane's collections, from which the Museum originated in 1753, included many fossils as well as minerals.

In 1765 Gustavus Brander (1720-1787), a prosperous London merchant of Swedish parentage, with a country residence at Christchurch, Hampshire, gave the Museum a collection of fossils, mostly molluscs, from the Hampshire cliffs. Daniel Solander (1733-1782) (p.19) described them in his *Fossilia Hantoniensia collecta et in Musaeo Britannico deposita a Gustavo Brander* (1776).

Only part of this material now survives. The presence of an important collection in a museum often stimulates the gift or bequest of others. In 1791 Lord Cremorne gave a pair of antlers of the giant long-extinct Irish deer *Cervus giganteus*. In 1799 the Rev. Clayton Mordaunt Cracherode (1730-1799) bequeathed to the Museum his collection of books and 'rarities of art and nature', including 100 animal fossils and 6 plant fossils. Such accessions were, however, relatively few during the Museum's first half century.

It acquired by purchase, between 1816 and 1818, William Smith's very important collection of British fossils, numbering about 2000, which formed the basis of his pioneer work, *Strata Identified By Organized Fossils* (1816-1819). This collection illustrates the foundation study of stratigraphical geology, as now understood. William Smith (1769-1839) is a father figure in the history of modern geology and palaeontology, but he came into their study almost by accident. When he was eighteen a surveyor, Edward Webb, came to the village of Churchill, Oxfordshire, where Smith lived, in order to survey the common land for enclosure and he wanted a bright boy to hold the chain and make notes. Smith's intelligence impressed Webb, who took him into his employ and taught him surveying. Later he became a surveyor in his own right, noted for his skill in land drainage and canal planning of which there was much to be done in England at the end of the eighteenth century. During the cutting of canals, Smith noticed that different layers of rock and earth could be recognized by the different fossils they contained and that there was a regular succession of such layers. As Loren Eisely has said in his *Darwin's Century* (1958), 'in attempting to arrange sedimentary rocks which he would have been unable to classify on the basis of physical properties, he had selected and brought to attention the one thing on this planet which had consistently and identifiably altered itself through the long eras of the past, namely, life itself'. Thus with a purely practical intent Smith had by 1800 unwittingly laid the foundation on which future work in stratigraphy and palaeontology within the Museum and elsewhere was to develop during the nineteenth century. His collection was then unique. Unfortunately, he ran badly into debt and was consequently forced to sell his collection to the Museum for £600, much below what he had expected.

Thereafter the Museum's palaeontological and mineralogical collection grew continuously, partly through the general interest of amateurs and professionals, partly through the special interest of Charles Konig (1774-1851) (p.21). He was a native of Germany from Brunswick, who had been educated at the University of Göttingen, joined the Museum staff in 1807 as an Assistant Keeper, and became Keeper of the Department of Natural History in 1813. Although he had earned good repute as a botanist and was joint editor with John Sims of the *Annals of Botany* from 1804 to 1806, Konig was also much interested in fossils and minerals and was requested on his appointment to give them special attention. He later published *Icones Fossilium Sectiles*

(1825). In 1819 he received from Sir Everard Home part of the vertebral column of an *Ichthyosaurus* from Lyme Regis, Dorset, a locality already known to coach passengers on the Dorchester-Exeter road as one where pebbles, shells and ammonities could be bought, and this specimen probably came from Richard Anning's (d. 1810) shop, or from his daughter, Mary Anning (1799-1847), 'the female fossilist'.

It was Mary Anning who made Lyme Regis famous for its remarkable fossils. In 1811 she found in the cliffs an *Ichthyosaurus* skeleton and in 1824 an almost complete skeleton of a *Plesiosaurus*. During her lifetime as a collector and seller of fossils, interest in collecting and studying them became a serious hobby of well-to-do amateurs, notably Sir Philip Egerton and Lord Enniskillen, who recalled in his old age how he had clambered over the cliffs with Mary Anning. Indeed, many celebrated palaeontologists were indebted to her for specimens. The collections of these enthusiasts in time enriched the Museum, the ultimate repository of much material privately assembled. They provided more and more evidence that the world in the distant past was strangely different from that of the present, evidence of dramatic change which from the seventeenth century onwards had puzzled and disquieted the enquiring minds of such men as Ray, Hooke, Burnet, Woodward, Steno, Buffon, J.G. Lehmann, Lamarck and Cuvier.

In the middle of the nineteenth century the explanation of organic change given by Darwin and Wallace became a storm centre of controversy in which Richard Owen was deeply involved.

Major changes in the Museum were foreshadowed by the formation of a Botanical Branch in 1835 under the care of Robert Brown. It diminished Konig's responsibility and, much as he respected Brown, certainly disquieted and annoyed him. In 1837 came a further division of the Natural History Department. The zoological collections were put under J.C. Children to form a Zoological Branch. Konig, although he retained a vague supervisory power over what had been his whole department, was limited to charge of the Mineralogical and Geological Branch. This division of the Department of Natural History into three independent branches, following a decision of the Trustees in January 1837, naturally angered Konig, who felt himself degraded in status. Nevertheless the increase of all the collections had made the change inevitable. There still remained more than enough to occupy Konig's attention as the long list of accessions of fossils between 1834 and 1851 makes clear. These included, among much else, in 1834 a collection of Liassic ichthyosaurs and plesiosaurs illustrated by Thomas Hawkins in his *Memoirs of Ichthyosauri and Plesiosauri* (1834) and *The Book of the Great Sea-Dragons* (1840), of which it was said by Gideon Mantell, 'They had been obtained with so much labour and expense, and were as admirably put together, and chiselled out with so much skill, that the sum awarded for them was scarcely sufficient'. The important collection of Cretaceous fossils from the south of England, made by Mantell, was purchased in 1839, also, sad to say, involving him too in a considerable loss. In the following year the balance of Hawkins's marine reptile collection was purchased and an extensive collection of Tertiary mammals from the Siwalik Hills, India, was presented by Sir Proby Cautley. In 1844 a series of remains of *Mammut* [*Mastodon*] *americanus* from Missouri were purchased from a Mr. Koch who had exhibited them as a side-show, and a number of these were subsequently reassembled to construct a single skeleton which was given pride of place at the entrance to the Fossil Mammal Gallery. Important purchases in 1845 were a major collection of Pleistocene mammals including the giant ground sloth *Megatherium*, from Argentina, and bones of Dinorthidae, a family of giant birds from New Zealand. The latter were further supplemented by purchases of dinornithid bones from W.D.B. Mantell, the eldest son of Gideon Mantell who had emigrated to New Zealand in 1848; though the major acquisition from him was made in 1856, comprising a large collection of bones gathered from old Maori midden-heaps. The important collection of Cretaceous and Eocene fossils made by Frederick Dixon (1799-1849) and described by him in his *Geology and Fossils of Sussex* [1852] was purchased in 1850.

On Konig's sudden death in 1851, his assistant Robert George Waterhouse (1810-1888) became Keeper of Mineralogy and Geology. He was trained as an architect, but evidently preferred beetles to bricks, and in 1836 he became curator of the Zoological Society's museum. His repute led Darwin to entrust him with the study of his South American mammals and beetles for the zoological account of the voyage of the *Beagle*. When, however, he became an Assistant in the British Museum in 1843, he was allocated not to entomology, which was and remained his primary interest, but to mineralogy and geology, of which he then knew virtually nothing. This was not the last example of arbitrary though successful allocation of staff in the Museum. Waterhouse then devoted himself conscientiously to these new subjects, assisted Konig during the next seven years, obviously with competence and growing interest, and so became his successor.

Waterhouse's fellow Assistant, G.F. Richardson, who had been appointed in 1838, died in 1848 and the ensuing vacancy was filled by the first of the succession of Woodwards to join the Department, although since they were not related they cannot be called a dynasty. This was Samuel P. Woodward (1821-1865) who was first employed on a temporary basis in the Library of the British Museum in 1838, though he left in the following year to become Sub-curator of the Geological

Society. In 1845 he was appointed Professor of Botany and Geology in the Royal Agricultural College at Cirencester, but he relinquished this seemingly prestigious post for the humbler capacity of Assistant in the Department of Geology and Mineralogy in 1848. S.P. Woodward worked principally on Mollusca, and his major contribution was the determination of the affinities of the aberrant bivalve group, the rudists. He also compiled a widely used textbook, *A Manual of Recent and Fossil Shells* (1851-56). A chronic asthma sufferer, the last twenty years of Woodward's life were clouded with ill health which severely restricted his output of publications.

By 1856, in which year Richard Owen was made Superintendent of the Natural History Departments, the collections under Waterhouse had become so extensive that in 1857 they were divided in two separate Departments. This separation had indeed been advocated by J.E. Gray in 1840 when he stated to a Royal Commission, on the basis of his experience of comparing fossil and Recent Shells as well as his interest in osteology, that everything palaeontological should be removed from the Mineral Department. Geology had Waterhouse as Keeper; while M.N. Story-Maskelyne, an Oxford professor, became Keeper of Mineralogy. Waterhouse's period of service extended to 1880 and during this time the palaeontological collections increased enormously through gifts, bequests and purchases; the aim was to make the Museum's holding as comprehensive and complete as possible, with material from all over the world and also representative of all geological periods and epochs.

Stratigraphers had by then reached general agreement as to the classification and nomenclature of the systems (i.e. Cambrian etc.), certainly as far as Europe was concerned, and thereby facilitated the arrangement of the Museum's material. Among the many specimens acquired at Waterhouse's instigation and with Owen's support was a slab of lithographic stone quarried at Solenhofen, Bavaria, on which were embedded the remains of an astonishing reptilian bird which Hermann von Meyer had named *Archaeopteryx lithographica* in 1861. Karl Häberlein was a medical practitioner to whom, in return for pro-fessional services to them and their families, the quarrymen gave the fossils which came to light as they worked. Thus he acquired a remark-able collection consisting of the *Archaeopteryx* specimen together with 1703 other fossils, among them 23 reptiles, 294 fishes, 1119 invertebrates and 145 plants. Waterhouse travelled to see his specimens at Pappenheim, Bavaria, in 1862 and was able to negotiate their purchase by the British Museum in two instalments in 1862 and 1863 for £700. This provided a dowry for Häberlein's daughter. Owen described *Archaeopteryx* at length in the *Philosophical Transactions of the*

Royal Society 153: 33-47 (1853) under the name *Archaeopteryx macrurus*; de Beer investigated it anew on becoming Director of the Natural History Museum and produced a comprehensive monograph *Archaeopteryx lithographica, a Study based upon the British Museum Specimen* (1954).

Other notable acquisitions of Waterhouse's period included the first major purchase of type specimens of British invertebrates in 1860, namely, the Sowerby collection illustrated in *Mineral Conchology of Great Britain*, and the Gray collection of Silurian fossils from the Wenlock Limestone of Dudley in instalments in 1861 and 1869. Another important acquisition of fossil invertebrates was made in 1865, when a large selection of British Mesozoic and Tertiary fossils, including much figured material, was purchased from the wealthy London distiller and noted amateur geologist J.S. Bowerbank. The collection of another distinguished amateur N.T. Wetherill, a medical practitioner, mainly from the London Clay and including many type and figured specimens was purchased in 1871; and the extensive collections of F.E. Edwards, largely comprising British Tertiary molluscs were purchased in 1872-3 and 1875. Fossil plants were not neglected, a notable collection of Tertiary plants from Austria including many type and figured specimens was purchased from Baron Constantin von Ettingshausen in instalments between 1878-82, the Baron — a noted professor of botany at Graz — coming to the Museum to arrange and work further on his collections. The last year of Waterhouse's Keepership, 1880, was notable for a major acquisition from the Museum of Practical Geology in London (later the Geological Museum) of some 50,000 non-British specimens, which served to emphasize the Natural History Museum's international interests.

The appointment in May 1856 of Richard Owen as Superintendent of the Natural History Departments of the British Museum had far-reaching consequences both as regards the Museum as a whole and the Department of Geology in particular.

When Owen arrived in the Museum, he had made a name for himself as a palaeontologist and, excluded from much of the Museum's affairs, he devoted most of his time profitably to the study and increase of the Museum's rich collection of fossils. Waterhouse, being himself primarily an entomologist, and temperamentally unlike J.E. Gray, probably welcomed rather than resented Owen's continuing research on the material of his Department. Waterhouse retired in 1880 and died on 21 January 1888. The burden of transporting the palaeontological specimens from Bloomsbury to South Kensington and re-arranging them there in 1880 thus fell upon Waterhouse's successor as Keeper, Henry Woodward (1832-1921) and his staff, which consisted of an Assistant Keeper Robert Etheridge, two 1st Class Assistants, one

2nd Class Assistant and six Attendants.

Henry Woodward was born in Norwich on the 24th November 1832, and left school aged fourteen. He became a bank clerk at the age of seventeen in Norwich but devoted his leisure time during the next seven years while employed in the bank to studying fossils and natural history so successfully that Owen appointed him as Assistant in the Department of Geology under Waterhouse in 1858. When Keeper he initiated a series of popular guides to the exhibits, as well as the 'Catalogues' of the collections, which were comprehensive monographs rather than mere lists, and remain major sources of taxonomic information.

In 1864 he became editor of the *Geological Magazine* and continued to edit it with customary diligence and exactness until 1920. His 300 publications, largely based on material in the Museum, are wide-ranging in subject, embracing invertebrates and vertebrates, from the Cambrian to the Pleistocene.

According to Civil Service Rules Woodward's time of service expired in 1898, but on the recommendation of the Trustees, the Treasury sanctioned his continuation in office. He retired as Keeper in 1901 but was employed by the Museum for another three years. He thus served the Museum for 46 years. Well-earned honours came to him, among them Fellowship of the Royal Society, an honorary LL.D. from St. Andrews University, and the premier award of the Geological Society, the Wollaston Medal; and he also served as President of a number of learned societies. Concerning his work, an obituary in *The Times* of 8 September 1921 stated that: 'His aptitude was towards sane and patient labour, for ranging known facts, cutting out errors, and filling in gaps. He recognised and encouraged all sound work, pricked the bombastic with gentle irony, stimulated the slothful and restrained the vagaries of the erratic. In all his personal relations he was sympathetic and loyal, and few scientific men have gained the affection and esteem of so large a body of friends'. Woodward was certainly not the least of Owen's contributions to the prestige of the Museum.

Throughout Woodward's period of office the accessions had continued to come in on a large scale, and they were always more than the staff of the Department of Geology could study. Woodward's longest-serving colleague was William Davies (1814-1891) who, when he joined the Museum as an Attendant in 1843, had studied botany and not geology. However, put to work under Konig he first devoted himself to the mineral collections and became in the process a very competent general mineralogist. He was then diverted to work on the fossil vertebrate collections, and in conjunction with Sir Antonio Brady formed a fine collection of Pleistocene mammals from the Thames

51. General Library, c.1909, with Mrs A. E. Wilson *(left)*,
C. Hadrill *(at back)* and B. B. Woodward *(at front)*.

52. Reading room of General Library in 1980.

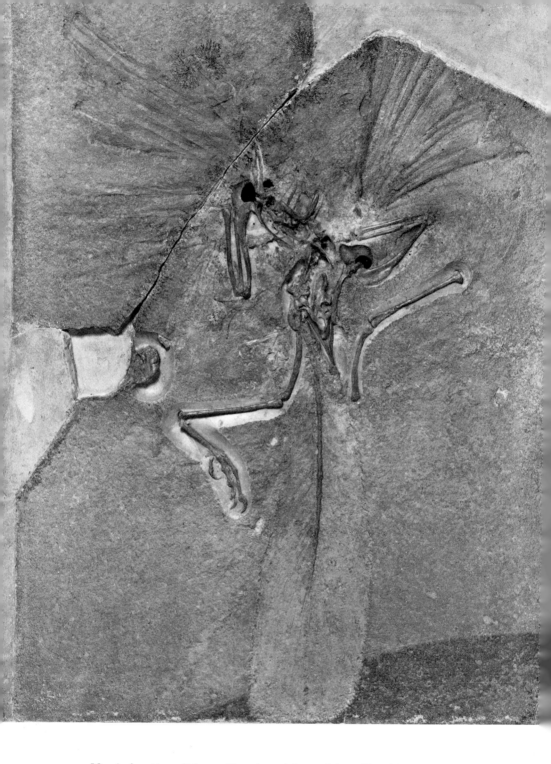

53. *Archaeopteryx lithographica,* the celebrated 'reptilian bird' of the late Jurassic period, about 140 million years ago, from Solnhofen, Germany.

54. *(Above)* 'The Piltdown Men'
in 1915: *Left to right,*
Frank O. Barlow *(back)*,
G. Elliot Smith, Arthur
Keith measuring the
Piltdown skull, Charles
Dawson *(back)*, W. P. Pycraft
(front), A. Smith Woodward,
E. Ray Lankester; portrait of
Darwin on wall (painting by
John Cooke at Geological
Society of London).

55. *(Right)* The Piltdown skull as
reconstructed by
F. O. Barlow, plaster-cast
maker at the Museum, with
the original fragments
represented in black.

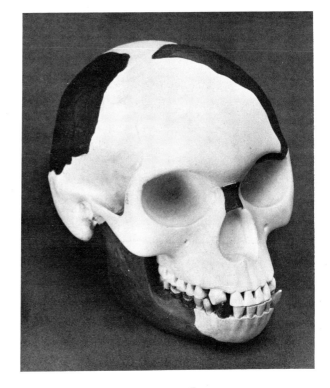

56. Taxidermist making the 'form' on which to mount the skin
of a Lion *(Panthera leo)*, retaining the skull but replacing the
other bones by metal rods covered with wood-wool, 1980.

57. Taxidermist putting finishing touches to mouth of mounted
specimen of a Wolf *(Canis lupus)*, late 1920s.

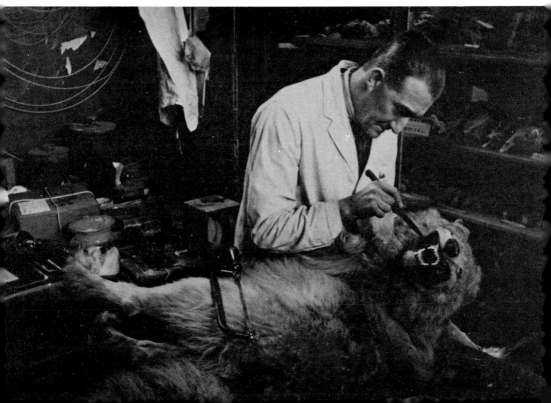

Valley Brickearth which he later described and figured. He was also noted as an able collector and preparator and was responsible for the excavation and preservation of the skull of the Ilford elephant.

Brought into the ambit of such distinguished contemporaries as Owen, Mantell, Falconer, Agassiz and Egerton, Davies gave freely of his experience, but as was tactfully recorded by Smith Woodward, 'Wanting in the literary training which it was difficult for any but the rich to obtain. In his early years, he usually avoided the laborious task of writing an account of his work in a suitable form for publication. His discoveries and conclusions were always at the service of those who could make best use of them.'

Despite this reticence, his worth was widely appreciated and Davies was awarded the first Murchison Medal by the Geological Society in 1873. Two years later he was made Assistant, and in 1880 was promoted to Assistant 1st. Class in recognition of his valuable services. These were much in evidence in the following year, when he was very actively involved in the transfer of the collections to South Kensington. He retired in 1887 having completed 44 years of devoted service.

Davies had outserved a number of fellow Assistants, most of whom had only brief careers with the Museum, when in 1878 he was joined by Robert Etheridge Jnr. (1847-1920). The able son of a famous father who was to join him in the service of the Museum three years later, R. Etheridge Jnr. worked in the 1860's as a field geologist in Australia; but when the survey was disbanded because of a political crisis, he returned to become Palaeontologist to the Geological Survey in Scotland. With the prospect of the move from Bloomsbury to South Kensington in view, he was transferred to the Museum staff to pack the collections and help with the transport. His interest centred on the invertebrates and his principal contribution was the *Catalogue of Blastoidea* (1886) in collaboration with P.H. Carpenter, but he also worked on molluscs, worms, Archaeocyatha and Foraminifera. However, Australia still called and he returned there in 1887 to become Palaeontologist to the Geological Survey of New South Wales and in 1895 Director of the Australian Museum in Sydney.

His father, Robert Etheridge Snr. (1819-1903), had already had a long and distinguished career before, like the son, being transferred from the Geological Survey to the Museum in 1881, in order to assist with moving of the collections. His career had begun as Curator to the Museum of the Philosophical Society in Bristol between 1850-57. During most of this time he also acted as Lecturer in Botany and Geology at the Bristol Medical School. He was introduced by a mutual acquaintance to Sir Roderick Murchison who contrived his appointment as Assistant Palaeontologist under J.W. Salter, in the

Museum of Practical Geology. He wrote numerous palaeontological reports and accounts, embracing everything from vertebrates and invertebrates to plants, from localities throughout the world. He had been elected a Fellow of the Royal Society in 1871 and at the time of his transfer to the Museum was President of the Geological Society, in which capacity he served between 1880 and 1882, having been awarded the Society's Murchison Medal in 1880. His noteworthy contribution to the Museum was the preparation of an exhibit on British stratigraphy and palaeontology, and although he retired in 1891, he was re-employed for a further two years after which the Treasury vetoed further continuation.

Another stalwart recruited to assist with the transfer to South Kensington was Richard Bullen Newton (1854-1925). He was temporary assistant to Professor Huxley, prior to his joining the Museum in 1880. Although his special interest was Tertiary Mollusca, and he had charge of very large mollusc collections on which he completed some 120 papers, he was also responsible for the fossil plants. A kindly and helpful man, his service, too, was retained beyond the date of his compulsory retirement in 1920, and he continued to occupy his room in the Department until the time of his death in 1925.

Despite these additions to the staff of the Department of Geology, the accessions of specimens far outstripped their ability to cope and Woodward, like his successors, was always happy to enlist the help of outside workers.

Thus, the Austrian palaeobotanist Constantin von Ettingshausen (1826-1897), today possibly best known for his beautifully illustrated works on leaf-venation, worked at the Museum between 1878 and 1882 studying and arranging material. Another important worker was Albert Charles Seward (1863-1941) from Cambridge. He began his association with the Museum about 1887 and he worked as a palaeobotanist primarily on Mesozoic plants. His major publication on them is his *Catalogue of the Mesozoic Plants in the Department of Geology* parts 1-4 (1894-1904); parts 5-6 (1913-1916) were by Marie Stopes. Seward became professor of botany at Cambridge in 1906 and, on retiring in 1936, came to London so that he could work at the Museum. Even to students not particularly interested in palaeontology, Seward's lectures gave another dimension to their biological thinking, that of change over long periods of time.

Henry Woodward was succeeded as Keeper in 1901, by Arthur Smith Woodward (1864-1944), in no way related, who had joined the Department's staff in 1882, shortly after its transfer to South Kensington. He was born at Macclesfield, Cheshire, on 23 May 1864 and went from the local grammar school to Owen's College, Manchester, where he came under the influence of William Boyd Dawkins; this probably led him to apply for the Museum post before graduating but he continued his scientific education in London by attending evening classes on comparative anatomy and general biology. The Keeper put him to work under Davies, then engaged in preparing fossil vertebrate exhibits for the new Museum galleries, and an illuminating account of his first day in the Museum can be found in the letter he wrote to his mother, which has been published in the *Journal of the Society for the Bibliography of Natural History* 4: 78-83 (1962). The Museum purchased in 1882 the entire palaeontological collection of Sir Philip Malpas de Grey Egerton (1806-1882), and in 1882 and 1883 that of his friend William Willoughby, 3rd Earl of Enniskillen (1807-1886). About 1830, Louis Agassiz at Neuchatel aroused their interest in fossil fishes; he described some new species from their collections in his *Recherches sur les Poissons fossiles* (1838-1844) and they became life-long collectors of these fossils. Their superb collections came into the Museum soon after Smith Woodward's appointment and the Keeper directed him to catalogue the entire Museum collection of fossil fishes. This resulted in his *Catalogue of the Fossil Fishes in the British Museum (Natural History)* in five volumes (1889-1901), which has been described by W.D. Lang (p.240) as standing out among his 600 or more publications, mostly papers in scientific journals, 'not only as a monument of meticulous accuracy, of intense research, but also as the source of many other ichthyological publications'. He became Assistant Keeper in 1892. His time, apart from administration, was spent not only on fossil fishes, for which he was the world expert, but also on other vertebrates, about which he knew much less. Thereby he was led sadly astray. His greatest apparent triumph came in 1912 when on 5 December *Nature* reported that 'remains of a human skull and mandible, considered to belong to the early Pleistocene period, have been discovered by Mr Charles Dawson in a gravel-deposit in the basin of the River Ouse, north of Lewes, Sussex'. By the following week *Nature* had received more detailed information. It described the fossil skull and mandible as 'the most important discovery of its kind hitherto made in England', stated that they had come from a gravel deposited by the River Ouse near Piltdown Common, Fletching, Sussex, and were associated with remains of a Pliocene elephant, a mastodon, hippopotamus, beaver, horse, red deer and early Palaeolithic implements, and then gave particulars of the human remains which represented a very low type of man with a high forehead. On 18 December 1912 Charles Dawson, (1864-1916), a lawyer, amateur geologist and antiquarian, and Arthur Smith Woodward, presented Piltdown Man which he named *Eanthropus dawsoni* to the academic public at a meeting of the Geological

Society. The Museum technician, F.O. Barlow, had provided a plaster reconstruction of the skull. It was a crowded meeting, the scientific excitement only equalled by that generated in 1953 by the proof that the whole occasion had been based upon a forgery. The minutes of the Standing Committee of the Trustees for 22 February 1913 record: 'Read a report by Dr Woodward, 20 February, of the present from Mr George M Maryon-Wilson of a remarkable human skull and mandible, associated with mammalian fragments and flint implements, discovered by Mr Charles Dawson in an early Pleistocene gravel near Piltdown Common, Sussex; stating that these remains, which were of the highest scientific interest, formed one of the most important gifts ever received by the Department of Geology, and recommending that the specimens be temporarily exhibited in the Central Hall, and that a special guide be prepared to explain the collection, at a cost estimated not to exceed £50 for 2,000 copies. The Trustees approved, and directed that their special thanks be sent to Mr Maryon-Wilson for his gift, and an expression of their appreciation to Mr Dawson in recognition of his important discovery; and they further agreed to Dr Woodward's suggestion that the specimens should not be registered until after they had been exhibited at the two soirees of the Royal Society in the summer.'

Woodward spent an inordinate amount of time on Piltdown Man, both before and after his retirement in 1924; it diverted him from other work for which he was better qualified; and in the end it proved a scientific disaster for him, as may indeed have been intended. He died on 2 September 1944, having dictated in his blindness a little book about it, *The Earliest Englishman* (1948), only a few years before a member of his former department, K.P. Oakley, helped to reveal how completely he had been deceived.

Nevertheless, Woodward's outstanding contribution in the field of palaeoichthyology is attested by the many distinguished awards that he received both in Britain and overseas and by the high offices that he held in several learned societies. Thus, he was awarded a Royal Medal by the Royal Society to which he had been elected in 1901; the Lyell and Wollaston Medals of the Geological Society over which he presided; the Linnean Medal of the Linnean Society of which he was also President; as well as awards from other societies in Britain, U.S.A., France and Australia. He also received honorary doctorates from the Universities of St. Andrews, Glasgow, Athens and Tartu; and he was knighted on his retirement from the Keepership in 1924. 'A man of imposing presence and iron constitution . . . he had only a half-day's sick leave in forty-two year's service, and that to have a broken arm set . . . Sir Arthur enjoyed the friendship of a wide circle of distinguished colleagues, whom he and his wife delighted to entertain.' It was their custom to invite their guests to autograph a treasured tablecloth, the signatures then being finely embroidered by Lady Woodward. Thanks to the generosity of colleagues at the American Museum of Natural History, this tablecloth is now in the Department of Palaeontology.

Both the Woodwards had good colleagues. One of the most brilliant of these was Charles William Andrews (1866-1924), who began his career as a schoolmaster but entered the Department of Geology as an Assistant in 1892. He specialised in studying fossil birds and described in his first paper the remains of a giant Madagascan bird, *Aepyornis titan,* as tall as the big New Zealand moa, *Dinornis maximus.* Later he studied other fossil vertebrates, possibly his most important contribution being *A Descriptive Catalogue of the Marine Reptiles of the London Clay* (1910-1913) published by the Museum. Andrews is best known for his discovery of mammals in the lower Tertiary deposits of Egypt, where he had gone to recuperate from illness in the winter of 1900, which culminated in his *A Descriptive Catalogue of the Tertiary Vertebrata of the Fayum* (1966), 'one of the classics of vertebrate palaeontology', produced in the sumptuous format then characteristic of the Museum's palaeontological publications. The value of his researches was acknowledged in his being elected Fellow of the Royal Society in 1906, and by the award of the Geological Society's Lyell Medal in 1916. Unfortunately Andrews suffered from continuous ill-health after 1900, and endured many operations bravely before he died on 25 May 1924.

Another colleague of both the Woodwards was George Charles Crick (1856-1917), a quiet, unassuming and kindly man who had distinguished himself at the Royal School of Mines with a succession of 1st class passes in Geology, Biology, Physics, and Mathematics. He began as a voluntary worker in the Department of Geology in 1881, and was made temporary assistant in the following year, finally achieving permanency as Assistant 2nd class in 1886. Crick's field of research was cephalopods and his major contribution was *A Catalogue of Fossil Cephalopoda* (1888-97) prepared in collaboration with A.H. Foord. In the year following Crick's permanent appointment he was joined by two fellow Assistants who were destined to achieve greater distinction, Francis Arthur Bather (1863-1934), and John Walter Gregory (1864-1932). Gregory, who had the shorter career with the Museum, was one of the most able and versatile geologists ever to serve it. Shortly after his appointment in 1887 he travelled widely in Europe, North America and the West Indies, an experience which whetted his appetite for exploration. In 1892-93 he undertook an expedition to East Africa and became fascinated by the Great Rift Valley, upon which he subsequently became a great authority and in 1896 he accompanied Lord Conway on a crossing of Spitsbergen. Gregory found time in the midst of his travels for palaeontological research, as evidenced by his *Catalogue of Fossil Bryozoa* (1896-1908) and *Jurassic Corals of the Cutch* (1900). He resigned from the Trustees' service to fill the Chair of Geology in the University of Melbourne in 1901, and he quickly established himself as an authority on water supply and artesian water sources. Gregory returned to fill the newly-founded Chair of Geology at Glasgow in 1904, and he actively pursued his diverse interests embracing palaeontology, stratigraphy, glacial geology, petrology, ore deposits, and sociology until he was drowned at the age of 68 while taking part in an expedition in Peru.

An equally colourful character in his own way, F.A. Bather was educated at Winchester School and New College Oxford, from which he graduated in 1886; he entered the Museum in 1887 as an assistant to replace William Davies in the Department of Geology and became Assistant Keeper in 1902, and Keeper in succession to Smith Woodward in 1924. Three publications alone would serve to indicate his diverse interests, *Puns of Shakespeare* (1887), *The Genera and Species of Blastoidea* (1899) and 'Biological classification past and future' in *Quarterly Journal of Geological Society of London* 83: Proc. lxii-iv(1927). He gave much thought to museum management, joining the Museums Association at its founding in 1889, and held that the major functions of a museum were 'Inspiration, Instruction and Investigation', the last justifying the assembling of collections. He had a schoolmasterly mind and when he became Assistant Keeper his assistants in charge of invertebrate fossils soon began to experience both his wisdom and his tiresomeness. His own studies were primarily on echinoderms and in particular the crinoids and his 'Caradocian Cystidea from Girvan', *Transactions of the Royal Society of Edinburgh* 49: 359-529(1913) has been praised as an exemplar of what such works should be. His fussiness, which doubtlessly seemed excessive when directed to the precisely right ways of making tea or cooking an omelette, was salutary when concentrated on preparing manuscripts for publication. 'Well grounded in classical and English literature, trained to clear thinking, and naturally gifted with a ready pen, he was inevitably dissatisfied with the lack of method and general carelessness of presentation apparent in much of the published work on systematic palaeontology', according to his obituarist and one-time assistant W.D. Lang, he did all he could to raise standards by precept and example. Unfortunately when he became Keeper he lost some of his former zest and had only four years of office in contrast to Smith Woodward's twenty-four years. Apparently there had been some tension between him and Smith

Woodward on the way the Department should be run. Nevertheless like his predecessors, Bather's scientific contribution and scholarship was acknowledged by learned societies in Britain as well as overseas who conferred on him Corresponding Membership, and in the case of the National Academy of Sciences, Washington, the Mary Clark Thompson gold medal. He was awarded the Lyell Medal by the Geological Society, which he also served as President, and he was elected to the Royal Society in 1909. He also served as President of the Museums Association in 1903; subsequently becoming a world authority in the newly emerged field of museology. He retired in 1928 and died in 1934, having made a greater impress on museum management, on nomenclature and the philosophy of science than is obviously apparent, apart from his specialised technical publications on echinoderms etc.

Although accessions to the collections continued to increase during the early part of the century, any increase in the size of the departmental staff to cope then lagged well behind. A further consequence of the large accessions of material was the problem of finding storage space in an already congested Department. This was noted in a report made by Smith Woodward in 1909, in which he also commented on the inadequacies of the existing accommodation for staff and visitors. He further stated (sounding a familiar note in view of the current preoccupation with Health and Safety at Work) that 'the painters continually complain that their workshop is not sufficiently ventilated to prevent injury to their health by the lead used in the paint', and recommended that they should be moved to more airy premises as soon as possible.

When Bather became Keeper in 1924, the permanent full-time scientific staff of the Department of Geology comprised F.A. Bather (echinoderms), C.W. Andrews (reptiles and mammals), W.D. Lang (coelenterates and sponges), W.N. Edwards (plants), L.R. Cox (bivalves and gastropods) and E.I. White (fishes); in addition L.F. Spath (cephalopods) and Miss H.M. Muir-Wood (brachiopods) were part-time workers. But 1924 saw not only the change of Keepership, but the recruitment of two more staff to take over responsibility for the groups curated by Andrews who died in that year, namely, A.T. Hopwood (mammals) and W.E. Swinton (reptiles).

In 1925, after four years of negotiations with the Treasury, initiated by Smith Woodward and completed by Bather, their Lordships graciously sanctioned that Thomas Henry Withers (1883-1953) should be translated from Clerk to Assistant, though they less graciously ordained that he should enter his new grade at his existing salary. Withers, a jaunty cockney character, had entered into the service of the

Trustees as a fifteen-year old Boy Attendant in 1898. He continued his education by attending evening classes at the Regent Street Polytechnic Institute, and his ability and enthusiasm prompted Bather to encourage Withers to study the almost wholly neglected group of fossil barnacles. Through his native acumen and by dint of solid application over the next fifty years, he became the world authority, leaving ample testimonial to that fact in numerous papers and his three volume *Catalogue of Fossil Cirripedia* (1928-53), as well as contributions on decapods. He retired in 1944.

A senior colleague as different from Withers in character and background as could be imagined was William Dickson Lang (1878-1966) who followed Bather as Keeper in 1928, having received from Bather what he described as 'a painful, but wholesome, training in Museum method.' Lang was born in Kurnal in the Punjab on 29 December 1878, his father being a civil engineer in India, and was educated at Christ's Hospital, Harrow School and Cambridge, where he took zoology as a first subject and geology and mineralogy as additions, under Adam Sedgwick, Graham Kerr, Stanley Gardiner, Sidney Harmer, Hans Gadow and A.E. Shipley — a very remarkable assemblage of zoologists. He graduated in 1902 and entered the Department of Geology as an assistant. Smith Woodward put him in charge of Protozoa, Coelenterates, Sponges and Polyzoa (Bryozoa) under Bather and for many years, according to his own account, much if not most of his time was spent on registering and labelling specimens and writing and sticking register labels on them, tasks that had formed no part of the university education fitting him for a Museum appointment. As Keeper, many of his staff felt that he personified the Victorian qualities of authority and respectability, perhaps over-much so in a changing age. His special interest was in the Lower Lias cliffs of Charmouth, Dorset, but in the first place it was a young lady there and not the cliffs which caused him to visit Charmouth for ten years and, the opposition of her parents at last overcome, to marry her. Seemingly fragile health enabled him to live to the age of eighty-eight and when he retired from the Museum at the age of sixty, glad to be free of uncongenial administration and never to enter it again, he settled in Charmouth and devoted his time to study of its natural history. Being unfit for military service during the 1914-1918 World War he was directed to medical entomology and ultimately produced a *Handbook of British Mosquitoes* (1920) for the Museum. Lang carefully husbanded his physical resources and adopted an unusual regime, rising exceptionally early and retiring equally early; a life-style which precluded his full participation in the activities of the learned societies, and certainly from service as an officer. However, he was elected to the Royal Society in

1929, and he was awarded the Lyell Medal of the Geological Society in 1928.

The careers of Wilfred Edwards (1890-1956), Keeper of Geology from 1938 to 1955, and his brother Frederick Wallace Edwards (1888-1940), Deputy Keeper of Entomology from 1937 to 1940, both born in Peterborough, were decisively influenced towards science by their education at the Cambridge and County School for Boys. Whereas W.W. Edwards was most influenced at Cambridge by A.E. Shipley and became an entomologist, W.N. Edwards was most influenced by A.C. Seward and became a palaeobotanist. He graduated in 1912 and joined the Department of Geology in March 1913, the first palaeobotanist appointed to the Museum staff. A member of the Society of Friends, he served in the Royal Army Medical Corps from 1914 to 1918. When he returned to the Museum in 1919, he was faced with the formidable task of rearranging what was certainly one of the world's largest and most important collections of fossil plant remains. This proved so time-consuming that he published relatively little, whereas his entomologist brother described some 2,000 new species of Diptera. He produced however, in 1931, *A Guide to an Exhibition illustrating the early History of Palaeontology* which revised and reissued has now become *The Early History of Palaeontology* (1967, reprinted 1976).

Although his own publications were relatively few and not commensurate with his ability, Edwards, like his predecessor fifty years earlier Henry Woodward, possessed a fine command of English (linked to an acerbic wit, and a lively pen) and he was an excellent editor. He also played a major role in the inception and design of the *Bulletin* series of the Museum which have, in turn, been the model for other successful scientific publications. He saw to the publication from his Department of a number of important works by others, all meticulously edited and finely produced, notably *The London Clay Flora* (1933) by Eleanor M. Reid and Marjorie E.J. Chandler, long-serving associates of the Museum; *The Miocene Hominoidea of East Africa* (1951) by W.E. Le Gros Clark and L.S.B. Leakey, being part 1 of the *Fossil Mammals of Africa,* and *The British Rhaetic Flora* (1938) by T.M. Harris.

Edwards was unfortunate in that the collections had become excessively over-crowded in the thirties before new accommodation could be provided and that he had to contend with the care and evacuation of specimens during the Second World War and with their post-war return to the war-damaged Museum building, there being no prospect of further accommodation during that difficult time. The Trustees sympathised with the Department's need for more room but could do nothing immediately. Most fossils are not like fleas and diatoms of which an immense number can be stored in a single cabinet. They include many bulky and heavy specimens. In 1954 Edwards pointed out to the Trustees the worsening problem of storage, at the same time suggesting the creation of an independent Anthropological Department. He retired in 1955, bequeathing these problems to his successor. Unfortunately he did not long enjoy his retirement for he died of cancer the year after, as his brother had done in 1940. Despite his Keepership having coincided with the war (when he also served as Secretary of the Geological Society) and its long-protracted aftermath, Edwards greatly relished his period as Keeper and, unlike his immediate predecessor, thoroughly enjoyed his administrative duties — even to the extent of being reluctant to relinquish them.

By the time of Edwards' retirement in 1955, most of his colleagues had been long established in their careers. Leslie Reginald Cox (1897-1965), who had joined the Department in 1922, was an acknowledged world authority on bivalves and gastropods and had contributed some 160 papers, including a major contribution to the Mollusca volumes of the *Treatise of Invertebrate Paleontology*. Cox was also an authority on William Smith (p.227) and had a more than passing resemblance to the bust of the 'father of English Geology' which he kept in his study. Cox was elected to the Royal Society in 1950, and in the following year was awarded a special merit promotion to Senior Principal Scientific Officer, that is, to the level of Keeper or Deputy Keeper but without the burden of administrative duties, in which he had shown little interest. Thus, his acceptance of the Deputy Keepership in 1961, two years before his retirement, invoked astonishment in his colleagues. Cox, a survivor of the Zeebrugge raid in the First World War, was extremely hardy; he cycled daily to the Museum from his home in Hendon whatever the weather, and he had virtually no sick-leave throughout his 41 years of service. Many honours came his way, including the Lyell Medal of the Geological Society in 1956, and he also received the O.B.E.

Cox's predecessor as Deputy Keeper in 1955 was Helen Marguerite Muir-Wood (1895-1968) who had begun work in the Department as a part-time worker in 1919 and was made more formally a part-time assistant in 1920, but was not appointed to the permanent staff until 1936. Miss Muir-Wood undertook pioneer work on the classification of Mesozoic brachiopoda on the basis of their internal structure; she made a major contribution to the advancement of fossil brachiopod studies, in recognition of which she was awarded the Geological Society's Lyell Medal in 1958. Though she formally retired in 1961, she continued to work on in the Museum until 1965.

Another distinguished palaeontologist whose name is irrevocably linked with the Department of Geology is Leonard Frank Spath (1882-1957), although he was never a member of the permanent staff. He was born in Munich, but his family emigrated to England when he was still very young. Spath was largely self-educated and his successive degrees obtained from the University of London, B.Sc. First Class Honours (1912), M.Sc. (1920), D.Sc. (1921), were all taken externally. He was first given temporary employment in the Department in 1912, assisting with the curation of the brachiopod collection; but ammonites were already his main interest and encouraged by W.D. Lang, and by his transfer to the ammonite collections, the seeds of his life-time career were sown.

Spath served with the Middlesex Regiment from 1916-19 and on his demobilization was offered an established post by the Museum, which he declined since he considered the terms to be unacceptable. This, as it happened, unfortunate decision determined the pattern of the rest of his working life, for resuming part-time employment in the Museum, the miserable pittance he received necessitated his seeking other sources of income. Thus, for the next forty years his mornings were spent working in the Museum, his afternoons at home writing up his research or occasionally determining ammonites for the Geological Survey, and two or three evenings each week teaching at Birkbeck College (as a temporary lecturer). It is astonishing that on this precarious basis Spath was able to build an outstanding international reputation and to publish over 100 papers. In recognition of his contribution he was awarded the Geological Society's Lyell Medal in 1945 and was elected to the Royal Society in 1940 and to the Royal Danish Academy of Sciences and Letters in 1951. In his later years, Spath's health and sight began to fail, finally forcing him to end his long association with the Museum in 1954.

When Arthur Tindell Hopwood (1897-1969) joined the Department of Geology in 1924 having graduated at the University of Manchester, his heart lay in the field of fossil molluscs, especially the genus *Conus* on which he became an authority, and in which he never lost his interest. However, Cox was already in post and and so Hopwood was set to work on mammals instead. He developed a particular interest in fossil elephants and primates, and was a pioneer worker with Reck and Leakey at Olduvai, Kenya; it was he who jokingly named *Proconsul* after the then famous performing chimpanzee named Consul. After his retirement from the Museum in 1957, Hopwood became Professor at the Lycée Français where he taught Zoology.

Another recruit destined to make his name in the field of fossil vertebrates, and who like Hopwood joined the staff in 1924, was William Elgin Swinton (b.1900). He had graduated with the equivalent of First Class Honours in 1922 at the University of Glasgow, where he participated in a Scottish expedition to Spitsbergen. After two years of post-graduate research he was appointed in 1924 to be responsible for the fossil amphibians, reptiles and birds. A natural communicator and consummate lecturer, Swinton was the author of numerous popular books, and as an authority on the ever-popular dinosaurs became one of the Museum's best-known public figures. He did much to further the interests of the Museums' Association, which he served as President; and of the British Association for the Advancement of Science, of which he was Secretary. He resigned from Museum in 1961 to become successively Head of the Division of Life Sciences, and Director of the Royal Ontario Museum and subsequently Professor at Massey College, University of Toronto.

To redress this balance of vertebrate workers H.D. Thomas and L. Bairstow were recruited in 1928 and 1931 respectively. Henry Dighton Thomas (1900-1966) a Cambridge graduate, worked principally on corals and Bryozoa, though he also had at various times responsibility for sponges, graptolites, Protozoa and Problematica. Lameness resulting from a fall in early childhood restricted his ability to undertake fieldwork, particularly in later life. Thomas served as Deputy Keeper from 1963 until his retirement in 1965. Leslie Bairstow (b.1907) joined the Museum staff in 1931 after a distinguished academic career at Cambridge and assumed responsibility for the echinoderms and dibranchiate cephalopods. He also had a great interest in the stratigraphy and palaeontology of the Lias, especially of Robin Hood's Bay in Yorkshire. He retired from the Museum in 1965.

A further recruit to the field of invertebrate palaeontology was Kenneth Page Oakley (b.1911) who joined the Museum in 1935. He had graduated with First Class Honours in 1933 at University College, London, subsequently gaining a Ph.D. in 1938 and a D.Sc. in 1955. Oakley was first employed as geologist with the Geological Survey (now the Institute of Geological Sciences), to which he returned on secondment from the Museum during the war, to investigate sources of phosphate for use as a fertilizer. At this time he chanced upon some neglected mineralogical work which was to lead to his subsequent utilization of fluoride in the relative dating of fossil bone and to the exposure of the Piltdown hoax. However, Oakley was initially made responsible for the Department's residue of invertebrate groups, including Palaeozoic Bryozoa, Palaeozoic Mollusca, sponges and worms. Nevertheless arising from his initial work for the Geological Survey on the geology of the London area he had developed a consuming interest in the vertebrate faunas from its terrace deposits, and especially in fossil man. Encouraged by Edwards to develop this interest, he was made responsible for the Anthropological Sections of the Departments of Geology and Zoology in 1954, and these were consolidated into the Sub-Department of Anthropology attached to the Department of Palaeontology in 1959, with Oakley as Deputy Keeper in charge.

He had long been interested in the enigma posed by the Piltdown remains; and since the much-publicized announcement in 1912 (p.235) of the discovery of the Piltdown remains many more fossil hominids had been discovered, all of which made the Piltdown association more puzzling and questionable. Thus at the meeting of the British Association for the Advancement of Science in 1947, Oakley suggested that the fluorine dating technique might provide a means of resolving the enigma. The technique is based on the naturally-occurring phenomenon whereby the fluorine content of bones increases with the length of time they are buried. Thus the higher the fluorine content the greater the age of the specimen is likely to be. Oakley accordingly developed criteria for dating fossils by comparing the fluorine content of modern, subfossil and fossil material of reasonably known age. Applied in 1949 to the skull discovered by Alvan T. Marston at Swanscombe, Kent in 1936, Oakley's fluorine test confirmed that this belonged to the Middle Pleistocene period. Oakley had already, before 1943, contemplated application of the same test to the Piltdown remains and, after a request by Marston, he did so in 1949 with the co-operation of C.R. Hoskins. The results were disconcerting; the beaver, red deer and horse remains had a high fluorine content indicative of Lower Pleistocene age, but the Piltdown skull remains showed little fluorine and this evidence thus suggested, to quote Oakley, 'that Piltdown, far from being an early primitive type, may have been a late specialized hominid which evolved in comparative isolation'. No-one then suspected trickery. The teeth of the jawbone were, however, peculiar and the idea occurred to J.S. Weiner, Reader in Physical Anthropology at Oxford, that they had been deliberately ground down. A paper by Weiner, Oakley and W.E. Le Gros Clark in *Bulletin of the British Museum (National History)* Geology 2: 139-146 (1953) entitled 'The Solution of the Piltdown Problem' stated that 'the mandible and canine are actually those of a modern ape (chimpanzee or orang) which have been deliberately faked to simulate fossil specimens'.

The co-operation of twelve more experts, including three (G.F. Claringbull, M.H. Hey and A. Foster) at the Museum, using a range of refined chemical and physical tests, proved beyond doubt that the Piltdown cranium and jaw had had different origins, as stated in their remarkable joint publication entitled 'Further Contributions to the Solution of the Piltdown Problem' in the *Bulletin of the British*

Museum (Natural History) Geology 2: 225-287 (1955). It was now indisputable that these remains had been deliberately stained to give them an appearance of great and equal antiquity; associated with them were the remains of likely animals from at least three different sources. None could have found its way naturally into the gravel of the Sussex Ouse at Piltdown. They had been deliberately planted there by a strongly motivated person with a detailed knowledge of comparative osteology, of palaeontology and of archaeology, having access to a range of expendable material from which relevant specimens could be taken, and also knowing precisely about Dawson's collecting area and habits.

J.S. Weiner in his fascinating firsthand work, *The Piltdown Forgery* (1955), puts suspicion for complicity strongly upon Dawson himself. Ronald Millar, *The Piltdown Men* (1972), exonerates Dawson but implicates Grafton Elliot Smith (1871-1937), professor of anatomy at Manchester from 1909 to 1919. Oakley in a paper 'The Piltdown Problem Reconsidered' in *Antiquity* 50: 9-13 (1976) leaves the question open. Beverly Halstead in *Nature* 276: 11-13 (Nov. 1978) has plausibly claimed William Johnson Sollas (1849-1936), professor of geology at Oxford from 1897 to 1936, as the mysterious figure behind it all, 'a figure of omnipotence not to be despised by Mephistopheles himself', basing this identification on a statement by James Archibald Douglas (1884-1978), professor of geology at Oxford from 1937 to 1950. Sollas, the author of *Ancient Hunters and their Modern Representatives* (1911; 3rd ed., 1924) was distinguished in geology, chemistry, palaeontology and anthropology and the relations between him and Woodward were at times unfriendly. According to Halstead, this elaborate Piltdown fraud was intended to discredit Woodward; certainly it engaged him in futile endeavour over many years. If so, it misfired by deceiving so many other eminent men as well and, thanks to its complexity, saved Woodward from seeming to be a gullible incompetent. Another suspect is Martin Hinton (p.188) who might have intended it simply as an elaborate joke. Millar had remarked on 'the extraordinary waste of time, the absorption of brilliant minds that was the result of the Piltdown hoax'. It certainly occupied much of the time of talented Museum staff. From the Museum standpoint the ultimate investig-ation and results were, however, beneficial not only for removing a palaeontological anomaly but also for demonstrating the availability and utility of a range of techniques for critical investigation. It also convinced, one hopes, the public that even a scientific group so eminent as that portrayed by John Cooke with the Piltdown skull before them, namely W.P. Pycraft, Arthur Keith F.R.S., A.S. Underwood, Ray Lankester F.R.S., F.O. Barlow, G. Elliot Smith F.R.S. and A. Smith

Woodward F.R.S., could be astutely duped. One can indeed be grateful to the hoaxer for occasioning such a group portrait including four Museum stalwarts, Pycraft, Lankester, Barlow and Woodward. The experience of art dealers leads them to expect faking: non-commercial scientists do not. That is why the real nature of the Piltdown material in the Museum stayed so long unsuspected and therefore undetected.

In addition to his contribution to the exposure of the Piltdown hoax, Oakley has published over 100 scientific papers, notably the three volume *Catalogue of Fossil Hominids* (1967-77) compiled in collaboration with B.G. Campbell and Miss T.I. Molleson. His book *Frameworks for Dating Fossil Man* (1969) is an authoritative reference work; while his popular Museum handbook *Man the Toolmaker* (1949, 6th ed. 1974) has also had world-wide distribution and has been translated into several languages.

Oakley was promoted to Senior Principal Scientific Officer for special merit in 1955; and he was elected to Fellowships of the British Academy in 1957 and of University College, London in 1958. He received the Geological Society's Prestwich Medal in 1963. Despite his later years being clouded by ill-health which forced him to retire from the Museum in 1969, he has continued to pursue his research interests.

A colleague of Oakley whose career was cut tragically short by ill-health was William Noble Croft (1915-53). A Cambridge graduate, Croft had subsequently studied palaeontology under Prof. W.H. Lang at Manchester before joining the Museum in 1939 to work on its fossil plant collection. Shortly after his appointment he accompanied E.I. White in 1939 as a member of the British-Norwegian-Swedish expedition to Spitsbergen, from which they were forced to make a hurried return, arriving back in Britain the day after war had broken out. Croft joined the Royal Engineers with whom he served in the Middle East, India and throughout the Italian campaign. In 1945 he was seconded to the Falkland Islands Dependencies Survey as geologist and palaeontologist and spent a year mapping and collecting in the Antarctic Peninsula. He returned to the Museum in 1947 to write up the results of his Antarctic research and to resume his palaeobotanical studies.

Besides being a most competent and meticulous scientist, Croft was ingenious in devising equipment and techniques to further his palaeobotanical researches, which required high-magnification microscopy. One device which arose from sheer desperation was a shock-proof mount for his microscope. Croft's study was situated in the colonnade at the rear of the Museum, immediately above the site on which piles were being driven for the (then) new General Library and Lecture

Theatre. By means of an ingenious system of suspension and damping, Croft was able to continue his microscopy throughout the months of shock and vibration. He also devised a machine for serial-sectioning specimens to very fine limits which went into commercial production as the 'Croft Serial Grinder'.

Not least of his attributes, Croft was a fine field geologist and he had long been occupied in mapping the Old Red Sandstone of the Brecon Beacons and Black Mountains in South Wales. Unhappily, owing to his tragically early death from cancer the results of this outstanding contribution were never published.

Croft's death in 1953 meant that the most recent recruit to the scientific staff of the Department of Geology, Oakley, had been appointed as long ago as 1935. However, within the next few years, during the Keepership of E. I. White, the staffing situation was destined to improve both in terms of scientific and support personnel to a degree that his predecessors would have considered incredible.

Errol Ivor White (b.1901), who became Keeper of Geology in 1955 on the retirement of Edwards, was a follower of Smith Woodward in the study of fossil fishes. However, on going up to King's College, London, in 1919, he had intended to read Chemistry, and while seeking a fourth subject in addition to first year Chemistry, Physics and Mathematics, was recommended by a fellow student to consider Geology as 'an easy option'. In the event, the fascinations of the 'easy option' outstripped those of his main subject, and he transferred to the Honours School of Geology from which he graduated in 1921. At the end of that year a vacancy in the Department of Geology was advertised, with the intention of recruiting a permanent ammonite specialist in lieu of L.F. Spath who had rejected the opportunity of filling the post. However, Smith Woodward decided that he would retire on his 60th birthday and that he would use the vacancy to recruit and train his successor; this was the first time in the history of the Department that such an overlap had been arranged. A chance meeting with Smith Woodward on a geological field meeting in Belgium in 1921 prompted White to apply for the vacant post to which, after completing the statutory and lengthy preliminaries, plus an examination in Arithmetic, English and Précis and a competitive interview, he was appointed late in 1922. By the time of Smith Woodwards's retirement in 1924, he was already preparing a number of papers. Over the next fifty-five years these swelled to some 120 contributions covering all groups of fishes throughout the whole of their geological range, and from every continent; plus important works on the stratigraphy of the Old Red Sandstone.

The chance submission of some specimens from the Lower Old Red Sandstone of Herefordshire in the early 1930s set White on a course which was to occupy, in conjunction with his long-time colleague H.A. Toombs, much of his working life, and on which he was to make many outstanding contributions, especially his paper 'The Ostracoderm *Pteraspis* Kner and the Relationships of the Agnathous Vertebrates' published in the *Philosophical Transactions of the Royal Society* (B) 225: 381-457 (1935). Subsequently, White in addition to describing the intractable and fragmentary remains succeeded in establishing a general sequence which enabled, for the first time, the correlation of the beds in which they occurred in the northern hemisphere.

Another chance submission of specimens in 1939, this time from Australia, introduced White to a remarkably preserved Devonian fish fauna. However, the intervention of other pressing events, including secondment for 1940-44 to the Ministry of Health with responsibility for dealing with aftermath of the air-raids in southern England, prevented him from pursuing this new research direction until nearly twenty-five years later. By this time thanks to two very successful collecting trips undertaken by Toombs in 1955 and 1963, the original five specimens had swelled to well over five hundred. Moreover, the acid preparation technique had been devised and perfected by Toombs and A.E. Rixon, Head of the Departmental Laboratory, which enabled the fish to be removed from the enclosing matrix in an hitherto unequalled degree of perfection.

White had himself participated in successful collecting expeditions, the first in 1929 when he participated in an Anglo-Franco-American expedition to Madagascar. In addition to making a valuable collection of Pleistocene birds, reptiles and mammals, he had 'hit the jack-pot' at the proverbial eleventh hour with an outstanding collection of Triassic fishes from the north of the island. He was also a participant in another notably successful collecting expedition, this time from the Old Red Sandstone of Spitsbergen in collaboration with W.N. Croft and colleagues from the Museum of Oslo and Stockholm in the summer of 1939, the year in which he was appointed Deputy Keeper. The value of White's scientific contribution is evidenced by his election to the Royal Society in 1956 and the award of the Murchison Medal of the Geological Society in 1962 and the Linnean Medal of the Linnean Society, which he also served as President in 1964-1967. He was also appointed C.B.E. in 1960. The Department's long association with scholarly studies on fossil fish has been continued through to the present day by Colin Patterson (b.1933), awarded merit promotion to Senior Principal Scientific Officer in 1974.

In 1956, the Trustees changed the designation of the Department from Geology to Palaeontology, presumably to emphasize its pre-occupation with fossil studies and to distinguish it from the several other Geological Institutions and Departments then resident in South Kensington. Nevertheless the change was not wholly appropriate since the Department was, and still is, much concerned with stratigraphical research.

By the time that White became Keeper, the post-war burgeoning of science was under way. One manifestation of this was the diversific-ation and expansion of the geological sciences; both the size of the Department's staff and the range of its work were to change dramatic-ally. Hitherto the Department of Geology had largely been concerned with taxonomic and evolutionary studies, and stratigraphic palaeon-tology and palaeoclimatology. Moreover, stratigraphic studies became more refined, demanding much fuller, detailed and precise records of the nature of occurrence and locality than had been customary hitherto. Thus, large parts of the collections were no longer a source of material for primary research, though because of the excellence of the individual specimens they still formed an invaluable resource in a support capacity. A further problem was the necessity of collecting sufficient material to permit valid statistical analysis. All of these factors served to further exacerbate the perennial problem of the chronic lack of space, not only for specimens but also for the rapidly increasing staff.

On arrival at South Kensington from Bloomsbury in 1881, the staff of the Department of Geology numbered 11, comprising the Keeper (Henry Woodward) an Assistant Keeper, three Scientific Assistants and six Attendants. Thirty years later, Henry Woodward's successor, Sir Arthur Smith Woodward was impelled to remind the Trustees that his Department had had 'no permanent addition to the scientific staff since 1886, which was so small in proportion to the increasing collection of fossils that the greater part of official time is occupied with the incorporating of acquisitions and attending to scientific visitors, that there is little time for making progress with the catalogues of publications. An additional assistantship assigned to the Department in 1887 was "temporarily" (*sic*) transferred to the Department of Zoology in 1901 and has not been returned'. Consequently, in an attempt to fill the gaps much use had been made of temporary workers, including one specially noted by Sir Arthur — 'Marie Stopes D.Sc. (not a member of staff) has prepared a Catalogue of Cretaceous Plants and has already delivered the first volume'.

Despite this plea, growth in the number of staff was slow as can be seen in the sequence of decades from 1900 when it numbered 18; 1910, 18; 1920, 21; 1930, 21; 1940, 30; 1950, 35; 1960, 52; 1970, 62; 1980, 70. It has been noted that at the beginning of this century much use was made of temporary workers, including many distinguished scientists, and this expedient continued into the early 1960's. At a lower level of expertise, the experiment of employing students during their long vacation introduced in 1949, was very successful – as it has continued to be, several of the students having achieved eminence in later years.

In the wake of the political changes which took place in the post-war years, and which resulted in the independence of many former colonial territories, a concomitant change occurred in the structuring and relationship of their geological surveys. The Department had long provided assistance in the determination of fossils and the dating of strata on an informal basis. This relationship became more positive in 1956 when White negotiated an agreement through the Commonwealth Geological Survey Scheme, by which in return for funds which enabled extra staff to be employed in specific fields, overseas surveys could call upon the services of the whole Department. From the provision of three extra staff in 1956, this figure had risen to fifteen in 1958. Since that time, other major changes have occurred, especially the incorporation of the Overseas Geological Surveys with the Geological Survey of Great Britain to form the Institute of Geological Sciences; but the service provided by the Department still continues, though at a reduced level, six staff being supported by O.G.S. funds.

The Department staff has altered not simply in numbers but in composition. In 1881 not one had been university educated, not even the Keeper, Henry Woodward, though this does not mean that the members of the Department did not possess high ability; Woodward's honorary doctorate from St Andrews and his fellowship of the Royal Society testify to that. In 1910 the scientific staff of six comprised three graduates: the Keeper, Arthur Smith Woodward, although not a graduate had a well-deserved honorary doctorate and was also a Fellow of the Royal Society, as were two members of his staff. It is of interest to note that when the total Museum scientific staff consisted of thirty-three men, eight had been elected to the Royal Society. The general tendency in the Department, corresponding with more widespread and increased State-aided facilities for university education, has been for non-graduates to be replaced by non specialist graduates and these by specialist graduates with a Ph.D. or D.Phil. degree. Thus, at the time of White's retirement in 1966 the scientific staff (in a pre-Fulton sense) of the Department comprised twenty-one individuals, all graduates and eighteen with doctorates. Gone were the days when six talented individuals, as in 1900, were expected to be able to deal with the whole range of palaeontological material. The bulk of material now available and the extensive literature to be used in dealing with it have made specialization essential.

It has already been recorded that as long ago as 1909 Smith Woodward was drawing the inadequacies of the Department's accommodation to the attention of the Trustees. Year by year the problems of finding room within the Museum for palaeontological material, so much more bulky than that of botany and entomology, became more and more difficult. White complained to the Trustees in 1956 about this chronic problem of overcrowding, pointing out that unlike some other departments his own had received no additional space for 25 years: one gallery had had to be closed to the public in order to get storage room and another might have to follow.

At this time the collections and staff were scattered through the building, posing difficulties for both curation and research. The Department of Mineralogy was also sorely pressed for space and the respective Keepers, White and Claringbull, decided that the most practical solution would be for the Department of Palaeontology to be transferred to new accommodation, and for the Department of Mineralogy to move into the space then vacated in the main building. This would also permit the return to the Departments of Zoology and Botany of studies and storerooms loaned to Geology to provide temporary relief.

In response to White's irrefutable submission, the Department of the Environment architects in 1960 prepared a pilot scheme for a new building. From this was developed a proposal to erect a large block to the north-east of the Waterhouse building, which in addition to accommodating the Department of Palaeontology, would provide space for administration, exhibition, photography and expansion for the General Library. However, because of the building's size and occupation density this proposal failed to achieve planning approval and instead it was agreed that a smaller north-east tower block would be constructed, and that Palaeontology would be housed in a new wing to be constructed on the south-east of the site. Having, so to speak, laid the foundations White had, perforce, to leave the planning of the new building to his successor, on his own retirement in 1966.

Harold William Ball (b.1926) took over the keepership of the Department of Palaeontology in July 1966, and William Thornton Dean (b.1926) was appointed Deputy Keeper. The ensuing administrative pressures within the Department necessitated the appointment of a second Deputy Keepership and Charles Geoffrey Adams (b.1926) was transferred from the Department of Zoology in 1968 (p.370) to fill this position and to take charge of the reinstated Protozoa Section. Graham Francis Elliott (b.1916) was appointed Deputy Keeper in 1971 following the resignation of Dean and he also assumed responsibility for the Palaeobotanical Section. Ball's tenure of office has also seen major changes, resulting from increase of staff, the advent of new techniques, and latterly more accommodation both for specimens and workers as well as more attention to public exhibits. He has summarised the history of the Department as being two hundred years of relative stability and twenty years of profound change, in his résumé of the history of the Department of Palaeontology 'The Evolution of a National Collection' in *Special Papers in Palaeontology* 22: 149-156 (1979). Ball's first years as Keeper were pre-occupied with the planning, construction and furnishing of the new Palaeontology building, in congenial and fruitful collaboration with John Pinckheard, the nominated architect, and Adams. The outline plans for the building were approved in 1966, construction began in 1970, and the finished wing was officially opened in May 1977 by Mrs Shirley Williams, Secretary of State for Education and Science.

The building is designed on an 'open plan' basis to provide 10,000 square metres of floor area in seven floors, including a basement and sub-basement. Studies are located around the periphery of each floor, allowing ready access to the collections stored in the 'core' area. Each study is supplied with a full range of services comprising electricity, gas, compressed air, vacuum, hot and cold water. In addition each floor is furnished with a small laboratory. There are also a number of specialist laboratories and a large Departmental Laboratory. The atmosphere in the building is filtered and controlled to maintain a temperature of 68°F (20°C) and a relative humidity of 50% providing a mean between the different requirements of pyritized material and specimens in clay matrices, skeletal collections, and the Departmental Library.

The building has been fitted with specially designed storage units providing the maximum degree of flexibility in the utilization of drawers of different heights, shelves, and pallets on rollers. There is in addition a large cold store accommodating the Sub-Department of Anthropology's serological collections. The provision of this excellent accommodation has enabled a major re-organization of the collections, improving their distribution and accessibility. Not least, it has greatly improved the working conditions of the seventy members of staff and visiting scientists alike. It is also gratifying to note that the building has met with praise from the architectural press.

The scientific staff of the Department of Palaeontology including the Sub-Department of Anthropology now comprises sixty-six Officers. Of these twenty-nine work on invertebrates, the major groups being arthropods with graptolites, brachiopods, bryozola, corals, echinoderms and protochordates, molluscs, ostracods, and protozoa; twelve on vertebrates, namely, fish; amphibia, reptiles, and birds; and mammals; seven on plants and palynology; and seven in the Departmental Laboratory who are responsible for conservation, casting and preparation. The Sub-Department of Anthropology has eleven staff, of whom five are concerned with palaeoanthropology, five with biological anthropology (including serology) and one with casting and preparation.

In common with the other scientific departments, the Department of Palaeontology is primarily concerned with taxonomic studies, which also form the foundations on which its other research activities are based, and it is presently much preoccupied with evaluating the nature and application of criteria utilized in the classification of organisms and with the principles and philosophy of systematics and evolution. In addition to taxonomic research, the Departmental staff are engaged in a wide diversity of investigations in the fields of stratigraphy, palaeoecology, taphonomy, palaeogeography and palaeoclimatology on a world-wide basis, literally on every continent and from the Arctic to the Antarctic. Many of these are collaborative projects with research institutes and universities in the respective countries, and in common with the rest of the Museum there is much emphasis on such joint undertakings in the Department's research strategy.

Research projects range from those to compensate of direct economic application and importance, to those that are at present only of philosophical interest. Thus research is being undertaken on the utilization of fossil foraminifera in the erection of a stratigraphical zonation scheme in both the Tertiary Deposits of south-east Asia which is of direct application in the search for oil; and in Cretaceous and Tertiary strata of Ecuador – a collaborative undertaking with the Overseas Geological Survey Division of the Institute of Geological Sciences (I.G.S.) and the Geological Survey of Ecuador for the compilation of a geological map of that country. Researches on fossil calcareous algae have also been of value to the oil industry, and there are several collaborative ventures in train with the I.G.S. relating to molluscs, trilobites, ostracods and plants. Research is also in hand in such diverse fields as the structure of coral reefs; the composition and mode of occurrence of ancient floras; the utilization of brachiopods in elucidating the history of the proto-Atlantic; the displacement of the continents through time; fossilization under Arctic conditions; the role of the Arabian peninsula as a migratory route between Europe, Asia and Africa for mammals during the Tertiary; a comparison between European and North American Carboniferous amphibians; the interrelationships of fishes; and the origin of the chordates.

Much of this work has been facilitated by the availability of the scanning electron microscope, and of techniques devised and perfected in the Departmental Laboratory for the preparation of fossil material. This is particularly true of acid preparation techniques which enable specimens to be extracted from the enclosing matrix in an hitherto unprecedented state of perfection. The Laboratory has also played an important part in the field of conservation of fossil materials. Contrary to popular belief the concept of "Rock of Ages" does not apply to a significant part of the fossil collections, which are subject to attack by the atmosphere. Thus, specimens in clay matrices, sub-fossil bones and ivory, crack and disintegrate if the atmosphere is dry; while specimens containing or preserved in pyrite (iron sulphide) decompose if it is damp. In an appropriately British compromise, the Palaeontology Wing is air-conditioned to maintain a relative humidity of 50% and a temperature of 68°F (20°C), which meets the needs of both the collections and the Library. Nevertheless the safety of the collections demands constant vigilance, and the Laboratory is engaged in research on the conditions which influence, and the physical and chemical processes which occur during decomposition and disintegration. The Laboratory is also responsible for the provision of finely-detailed casts (commonly in plastics and fibre-glass) of unique specimens for research and display in museums throughout the world.

The Sub-Department of Anthropology (see p.245) is concerned essentially with physical anthropology, and with the evolution of the primates and man. In addition to investigating fossil forms the Sub-Department has collaborated with a wide variety of organisations, and in particular with the Department of the Environment, in the evaluation of the physical characteristics and pathology of exhumed historical populations, and it is also active in the investigation of genetic and physical variation in modern man. Consequently in addition to the vast numbers of fossils that comprise its collections, the Department of Palaeontology houses skeletal material of Recent man, and even the National collection of blood sera. The Sub-Department of Anthropology is also concerned with the relative dating of fossil skeletal material, as well as with the palaeontology and taphonomy of fossil man. In this context, the whole Department is collaborating in major excavations in the Gower Caves, and at Westbury sub Mendip where the earliest artifacts hitherto recorded in Britain have been found.

The aim so confidently manifested a century ago of making the collections truly comprehensive (p.230) is now known to be both over-optimistic and unrealistic. Quite apart from any other considerations the far from unlimited accommodation available to house the collections makes the accomplishment of such an aim impracticable. Thus the present working objectives of the Department have been framed to meet the realities of the modern world but still to honour its national and international obligations. They are: To enhance the major collections of national or international importance, which are of continuing research interest; to augment the collections that are the subject of current research by Museum staff; and to collect material to initiate new research areas; to accept the donation of type and figured specimens and material of exceptional or historical importance; and in consultation with appropriate bodies, to collect from and record important geological sections threatened with destruction, and from temporary exposures in areas of especial geological interest.

Fig. 27. Skeleton of the giant sloth, *Megatherium* and an inebriate visitor to the Palaeontological Gallery (from *Punch,* 4 April 1891).

15

Department of Mineralogy

FROM TIME IMMEMORIAL, metals and stones of various kinds have been used by man for decorative and practical purposes. The earliest writers to describe them as natural objects, and not solely in terms of their usefulness, were the Greek philosophers Aristotle (c.384-322 BC), in his *Meteorologica*, and his contemporary Theophrastus (c. 371-287 BC), in the rather more detailed work *Peri Lithōn*. The most complete account of the mineralogical knowledge of the classical period was given by the Roman encyclopaedist Pliny the Elder (c. 23-79 AD), in books 33-37 of his *Historia Naturalis*. Many later authors wrote on minerals, usually in works on gems, alchemy, metallurgy, and materia medica, but the modern era of the study and classification of minerals is generally considered to have begun with the writings of the German mine physician Georg Bauer, who latinized his name as Agricola (1494-1555).

Probably these authors, along with monarchs, noblemen and mine owners, had collections of natural curiosities, but, with the exception of jewellery and other worked objects, none of their specimens has survived. Collecting objects, both natural and man-made, seems to have become fashionable among the wealthier classes in the fifteenth century and more widespread by the sixteenth century. No British collections of mineral substances, however, are known from periods before the late seventeenth century according to W. Campbell Smith, 'Early Mineralogy in Great Britain and Ireland', *Bulletin of the British Museum (Natural History)* Historical series 6, 49-74 (1978). Until the early years of the nineteenth century, the term 'fossil' (from Latin *fossilis*) denoted any natural body that had been dug out of the earth: fossils, in the modern sense, were termed 'extraneous' or 'adventitious' fossils, whereas   minerals were 'native' or 'natural' fossils. Although the nomenclature had been superseded, the association of rocks and minerals with fossils at the British Museum lasted for a hundred years, and from 1837 to 1857 they were covered by a single department, the Mineralogical and Geological Branch.

The catalogue of the mineral collection of Sir Hans Sloane (1660-1753), the original foundation of the British Museum's material, contained 8,649 entries. These were grouped under such headings as 'Pretious Stones, Agates, Jaspers, &c.', 'Chrystals, Sparrs, &c.' and 'Metals, Mineral-Ores, &c.'. A more complete listing of categories, and the present whereabouts or probable fate of Sloane's mineral specimens are discussed by Jessie M. Sweet in *Natural History Magazine* 5: 97-116, 145-164 (1935). For many years after Sloane's death and the founding of the British Museum the mineral collection received little attention, attracting scant interest and few gifts. There were, however, a few minor presentations such as a polished slab of brown and yellow jasper from the Earl of Exeter in 1765 and two polished slabs of labradorite from the Rev. B. La Trobe in 1772. No rock or mineral specimens appear to have survived from the Royal Society's collections, given to the Museum in 1771, with the possible exception of the type columbite analysed by Hatchett (v. infra).

External characteristics such as those on which Sloane's crude arrangement was based became less important for the classification of minerals towards the end of the eighteenth century and the beginning of the nineteenth. At that time work on the chemical composition and the crystalline form of minerals by H.M. Klaproth, J.B.L. Romé de l'Isle, R-J Haüy and their followers made evident more fundamental characteristics.

The real foundation of the present mineralogical collections was the purchase in 1799 of the extensive collection of minerals belonging to Charles Hatchett (1765-1847). A wealthy man who devoted much of his time to chemical analysis and his money to the acquisition of minerals, he had assembled through his travels in Britain and on the Continent and through correspondence some 7,000 specimens which the Trustees bought for £700. A committee consisting of C. F. Greville, Philip Rashleigh, and Joseph Banks was requested by the Trustees to inspect Hatchett's collection and 'to examine into the propriety of its being purchased for the use of the Collection'. To this end they viewed the Museum's Collection and found 'that the greater part of the specimens of which it consists have been collected by Sir Hans Sloane, at a period when the science of mineralogy was in its earliest infancy, and that most of these have either been chosen by persons of little skill, or have been intended for the elucidation of some system now obsolete, many of them are therefore now wholly useless and of no value whatever. . .' They also examined a collection given to the Museum by Gustavus Brander in 1766, of which 'the greater part are of little value, even as duplicates', and recommended that a very small collection from the Northwest coast of America, made by Menzies on Vancouver's voyage and acquired by the Museum in 1796, ought to be kept separate 'as it supplies a kind of Mineralogical History of an extensive coast very little known'. These mineral specimens have not survived. The committee also looked in vain through the whole, 'for anything resembling a regular collection of minerals of England, and indeed we saw very few specimens at all good, from Derbyshire, Cornwall, or the Lead Hills, all of which are constantly enquired after by Foreigners, who naturally expect in a British National Collection to meet with excellent specimens of all kinds of British Minerals. . . we cannot hesitate in giving it as our opinion that a systematic collection of minerals is much wanted in the British Museum. . . .' The Trustees also received in 1799, by bequest, the collection of a lately deceased Trustee, the Rev. Clayton Mordaunt Cracherode (1730-1799) including gems, minerals, and fossils. This was much smaller than Hatchett's but contained very fine, well-chosen specimens, in all 868; together, these two collections formed the nucleus of a good British representation.

At this time the Museum staff included no-one with a special interest in and knowledge of minerals. Edward Whitaker Gray (1748-1806) had been Keeper of the Natural History Department since 1787, and following the committee's report he had the part-time help of Hatchett and of the French emigré mineralogist Jacques Louis, Comte de Bournon (1751-1825). Gray had already started to discard specimens and Bournon, in the preface to his printed catalogue (1813: lxxxii), described how he saw bruised and broken specimens being collected in a basket for burial in the Museum garden. Auction sales were held in 1803 and 1806, at which the Trustees sold 3,700 mineral specimens, many of which must once have belonged to Sloane. An attempt was made in 1933 to trace specimens at Bloomsbury and South Kensington that could definitely be identified with Sloane catalogue entries, but only 161 were found. Those which survive, not having been displaced by better specimens, are nearly all hand-worked objects such as bowls of mocha-stone, agate, nephrite, and carnelian, preserved more for aesthetic than scientific reasons. A number of these are illustrated in Jessie Sweet's paper (1935). Hatchett had indicated to the Trustees his willingness to help arrange the collections and to advise on the retention or rejection of existing specimens, and he obtained permission to remove fragments for chemical analysis; in a specimen from the Sloane collection, probably originally from the Royal Society's collection, he discovered the chemical element columbium (now niobium) (see J.M. Sweet: 116, 1935). Bournon, a friend of Romé de l'Isle, was one of the most able crystallographers of the time; he had hoped to gain permanent employment at the Museum, but there was evidently mutual ill-feeling between him and Banks. E.T. Svedenstierna (1765-1825), a Swedish metallurgist, visited the British Museum in the winter of 1802/3 and noted that whereas Hatchett had arranged the displays according to Werner's system, Bournon had recently rearranged them according to his own system (See *Svedenstierna's Tour [of] Great Britain 1802-3*, translated by E.L. Dellow, 14, 18, 1973). In February 1807 a German naturalist, Carl Dietrich Eberhard König (1774-1851) who quickly anglicised his name to Charles Konig (see p.21) was appointed as assistant to the new Keeper, George Shaw (1751-1813), and given the task of cataloguing the minerals. His previous work had been botanical, but he soon became interested and competent as he examined, listed, and arranged the Sloane and Hatchett specimens.

Konig's experience with these became important in 1810 when the Trustees bought the mineralogical collection of Charles Francis Greville (1749-1809), son of the Earl of Warwick. Greville had been collecting minerals for over 30 years, had purchased important collections abroad including that of Ignaz von Born, and had come to possess 'the finest collection of minerals which had been seen in England': Parliament specially voted the sum of £13,727 for its acquisition. Bournon, who had spent twelve years to 1806 in cataloguing and managing the collection for Greville, was not allowed to help with its transfer to the Museum. There seems little doubt that the conflict of personalities between Bournon, Banks and Konig is responsible for so little of the Greville collection being identifiable at the present day; no catalogue survives. In 1815 numerous minerals came to the Museum with the library and natural history collections of Baron K. E. von Moll (1760-1838); the collection of Baron F.C. von Beroldingen (1740-1798) purchased in 1816 added another 14,000 specimens. Less numerous but of great interest were specimens of berzelianite, yttrocerite and other recently discovered Swedish minerals presented by the celebrated Swedish chemist J.J. Berzelius (1779-1848). Two minerals came from their eponyms, wavellite from William Wavell (d. 1829) in 1817 and hatchettite from Charles Hatchett in 1821. Over many years Teodoro Monticelli (1759-1846), first a professor of ethics at Naples, then, after six years in prison for political reasons, professor of chemistry at Naples, gave much attention to the products of Mount Vesuvius, which resulted in Monticelli and

N. Covelli's *Prodromo della Mineralogia Vesuviana* (1825); the purchase in 1823 of his collection of some 2,000 Vesuvian specimens greatly enriched the Museum. King George IV presented a suite of choice pyrargyrite and other specimens from the Harz Mountains in 1828.

By 1811 the mineral collections were in the upper Saloon of Montagu House, which the Trustees in 1801 had designated as a 'proper place' for their display, after the floor had been strengthened to bear the extra weight. Whereas almost all exhibits had formerly been in cabinets, glass-covered table-cases were now provided, twenty-four in all, in which Konig arranged specimens according to his own modification of Abraham Gottlob Werner's widely accepted system.

In 1813 Konig became Keeper (Under-Librarian) of the whole Department of Natural History, which covered botany and zoology as well as geology and mineralogy. He had only one assistant, William Elford Leach (1780-1836), who dealt with zoology. Konig remained the only Museum official directly concerned with the mineralogical collection until 1843 when Robert George Waterhouse (1810-1888), then primarily an entomologist, became his assistant. A change of location in 1829, to the 'Long Room' of the eastern wing, consequent on the rebuilding of the British Museum (p.41) enabled Konig to rearrange the minerals between 1830 and 1832 according to the later, chemically-based system of Berzelius. The number of table-cases had risen to 64. Konig himself wrote the labels, a task still occupying him in 1834. The specimens filled more than 12,000 trays. Another move took place in 1837 on the completion of the northern part of the new building, when the minerals were transferred to the floor above the Printed Books, where they remained until removed to South Kensington in 1880. All this placed a heavy burden upon Konig. He should therefore have regarded as a relief the removal from his care of the botanical and zoological collections and the limitation of his special duties to the mineralogical and geological collections which came in 1837 with the formation of the Mineralogical and Geological Branch but in fact he resented it as a lowering of his status. A very important innovation of that year was the registration in bound foolscap volumes of all new acquisitions. As Campbell Smith has made clear in his 'A history of the first hundred years of the mineral collection in the British Museum with particular reference to the work of Charles Konig' in *Bulletin of the British Museum (Natural History)* Historical Series 3: 235-259 (1969) the Museum owes much to the care which this kindly and conscientious (if sometimes difficult) man devoted to the mineral collection. He felt he had received little encouragement; he said in 1849 that 'not a word of approbation has been bestowed upon me'. However, his forty-three years in the Museum were well spent and his mineral exhibits were much admired by the public. He also laid the foundations for the later development of the meteorite collection. During the first few years of the nineteenth century, it was somewhat embarrassing for a large museum to possess meteorites since it was 'known' that stones could not fall from the sky and iron meteorite 'finds' were considered to be native metal of terrestrial origin. Luckily, in 1802 and 1803, specimens of three stony meteorites were presented by Sir Joseph Banks and a fourth by Professor J.B. Biot in 1804; presentations from such eminent persons could not easily be dismissed. Subsequently, various other meteorites were obtained either by gift or by purchase as parts of the Greville and other mineral collections, and it was in Konig's time that falls of meteoritic stone and iron became accepted scientific fact. He was therefore able to pursue the acquisition of meteorites with the same vigour which he applied to enlarging the mineral collection; at the time of his death seventy meteorite falls were represented in the Museum.

Konig died on 1 January 1851, aged seventy-five, and Waterhouse became Keeper of the Mineralogical and Geological Branch. When this was divided in 1857 into two departments, he retained charge of the Department of Geology for his interests were palaeontological rather than mineralogical. Indeed, between 1851 and 1857, the Museum had no permanent staff member qualified for the care and study of its now large mineralogical collections, which continued to grow, albeit. In 1852-3 the Trustees allocated £300 for the part-time employment of James Tennant (1808-1881), who was paid £2 a day to arrange and catalogue the minerals. Tennant was a mineral dealer, taught mineralogy and geology at King's College in the Strand, and was Mineralogist to Queen Victoria; in 1852, he supervised the re-cutting of the Koh-i-nur diamond for the Crown Jewels.

The new Department of Mineralogy was put in charge of Mervyn Herbert Nevil Story-Maskelyne as Keeper of Minerals, a newly created post. He was born at Basset Down House, near Wroughton, Wiltshire, on 3 September 1823, and there he died on 20 May 1911. During those eighty-seven years he was a professor at Oxford, a Keeper in the British Museum, a Member of Parliament and an active country gentleman and agriculturalist. After graduating in mathematics at Oxford in 1845, he studied law but abandoned this for science and was invited to lecture in Oxford on mineralogy in 1850. Analytical chemistry had become an essential part of mineralogy, but had never been taught in a practical manner in Oxford. Story-Maskelyne insisted on being given a laboratory and in 1856 he was appointed professor of mineralogy. Next year he was invited to become Keeper of Minerals and, although he then resided in London, he retained his Oxford professorship until 1895.

The publication by Gustav Rose (1798-1873) of his *Das krystallo-chemische Mineralsystem* (1852) was a notable event in the development of nineteenth-century mineralogy since it provided a synthesis of chemical and crystallographic properties for the classification of minerals; it is the basis of the classification used in the systematic mineral displays at the Museum today. On his arrival at the Museum in August 1857 Story-Maskelyne set about rearranging its specimens in accordance with Rose's system, which must have directed his attention to deficiencies in the collection. He then did everything within his power to make it the finest in existence, giving special attention to meteorites of which the number represented in the collection trebled in his first six years of office. At first he had no help at all but in February 1858 the Trustees gave him an attendant, Thomas Davies (1837-1892), who had had little education and no experience of mineralogy but he proved nevertheless very intelligent, diligent and quick to learn and remember the minute details of specimens. In 1862 Davies was promoted to the scientific grade of Museum assistant, the reward for his usefulness and ability. He became a valued colleague both of Story-Maskelyne and his successor, Lazarus Fletcher, and was put in charge of the extensive collection of rocks. These were in a poor state, having been moved to the basement in 1824 where many labels were destroyed by dampness; and it is probable that rocks collected by Sir John Ross on his Arctic expedition of 1818 were lost at this time. Story-Maskelyne's research interests lay in minerals and meteorites rather than terrestrial rocks, and Davies had little opportunity to do more than restore some order to the rock collections. Also in 1862, Viktor von Lang joined the staff and for a busy two years before returning to Austria he helped Story-Maskelyne in his crystallographic work and in the design of a new goniometer and a polarising microscope. The progress following Story-Maskelyne's advent was described by Fletcher in 1904:

> 'Before 1857 little importance had been assigned to the statement of localities of specimens [which was true for other parts of the Museum], and there were scarcely any locality labels with the exhibited portion of the Collection; there were no labels at all with the unexhibited specimens, many thousands in number. The latter were preserved in drawers in the Gallery and Basement of the Museum and were entirely unarranged. In the course of a few years Mr Maskelyne, aided solely by Mr Davies, was able to furnish locality labels from the documents preserved in the archives of the department; further, he examined, sorted

and arranged into species all the unexhibited specimens, at the same time setting aside the duplicates for future disposal. The ends of many of the cabinets were altered, glazed and fitted, thus making it possible to exhibit those mineral specimens which are too large to be placed in the table-tops. During the Keepership of Mr Maskelyne, the Mineral Collection was completely re-arranged. In addition to two large private collections, the Allan-Greg [about 9,000 specimens bought in 1860] and Koksharov [about 3,250 specimens bought in 1865], numerous isolated specimens were acquired by purchase, presentation or exchange, and incorporated with the systematic collection; special attention being given to the improvement of the series of Meteorites, which was separated by Mr Maskelyne from the systematic mineral collection itself in 1863-64, and arranged into special wall-cases. In 1857 the Museum was in no way equipped for the making of scientific research on minerals, so necessary for their accurate discrimination; there was virtually no physical apparatus, and there was no chemical laboratory at all; further, the necessity of avoiding any risk of the destruction of the Museum by fire made it impossible to allow the use of gas and to fit up laboratories, or even use a blowpipe, within the building.'

Story-Maskelyne continued to press for a chemical laboratory, and in 1867 the Trustees agreed to rent a room near the Museum, at no. 46 Great Russell Street, which was renovated and converted into a laboratory for the sum of £25. Walter Flight (1841-1885) was appointed to the staff as an analyst in the same year, and for the next eighteen years published many analyses of minerals and meteorites. However, because of the inconvenient separation of the laboratory from the Museum accommodation, Flight and Story-Maskelyne had to rely on written messages for much of their communication William James Lewis, one of Story-Maskelyne's students at Oxford, worked on the staff as an outside worker in 1872 and was a full-time staff member from 1875-1877; he retired owing to ill-health, but later became Professor of Mineralogy at Cambridge. Fortunately, Story-Maskelyne was able to leave much of the routine accessioning work to Thomas Davies and so found time for research; but the poor lighting available for microscopy and crystallographic measurements caused permanent damage to his eyesight, which may have contributed to his decision to retire from the Keepership in 1880 and become Member of Parliament for Cricklade. His father's death the previous year had left him the additional work of managing the family estate of Basset Down.

The collections had flourished under Story-Maskelyne. In Konig's

58. Main hall with dinosaur exhibit opened in 1979.

59. Lionel Walter Rothschild (1868-1937), 2nd Baron Rothschild, a Trustee 1899-1937, with a team which includes three zebras (*Equus burchelli*) which he drove \ through London.

60. Zoological Museum at Tring, Hertfordshire, founded by
Lionel Walter Rothschild to house his private zoological
collections, opened to the public in 1892 and
bequeathed to the British Museum in 1937.

61. Ornithological sub-department at Tring Zoological Museum built
to house bird collections from South Kensington, opened in 1972.

62. Exhibit of Gannets *(Sula bassano)* and other birds of the rocky coast, in the British Bird Pavilion.

63. Skeletons of male and female Giant Deer *(Megaceros giganteus)*, the so-called 'Irish Elk', long extinct but formerly widespread in northern Europe, in the Fossil Mammal Gallery.

last years some 200 specimens were added each year. In Story-Maskelyne's first year they rose to 723, and at his retirement the annual purchase grant for minerals was £850; the total number of specimens acquired under Story-Maskelyne was about 43,000. The prospect of moving the Natural History collections to a new site at South Kensington prompted a new surge of activity in putting them in order, and Davies devoted much time to the registration of specimens acquired before 1837 although the bulk of this task was carried out after the move, in 1883. The register entries contained less information than Story-Maskelyne considered necessary for a true catalogue, and in 1875 he started a new project, a 'Scientific Catalogue of the whole Collection, with crystallographic descriptions and chemical analyses of those specimens the composition of which it is desirable more accurately to determine.' This catalogue has not yet been completed, nor has any part of it been published, but in the preparation of the material for it successive assistants have found abundant subjects for original research, and the most important results of this work have been published in the *Mineralogical Magazine* from time to time.' *(Mineralogical Magazine* 29: 257, 1950). The study of mineralogy in the British Isles was at a low ebb, despite the efforts of Miller at Cambridge and of Story-Maskelyne at Oxford; so much so that the latter wrote despairingly (in 1875) 'I find the greatest difficulty in getting hold of men competent to undertake the most ordinary crystallographic calculations.' It must have been a considerable joy to him to find a competent man at Oxford in Lazarus Fletcher (1854-1921), who joined the Museum staff in 1878. Confident of Fletcher's ability, Story-Maskelyne retired and Fletcher succeeded him as Keeper in June 1880. Fletcher's rise from poverty to directorship of the Natural History Museum and a knighthood is outlined elsewhere (Chapter 9). A month after his appointment he was called upon to remove the mineral collection from Bloomsbury to the new Natural History Museum, the building of which Story-Maskelyne had opposed in 1863 on the ground that the British Museum should remain an undivided repository of all knowledge. The removal was finally completed in April 1881, the month of the Museum's opening (p.59).

Always careful about his health, Fletcher found the new Museum too bleak for his comfort. He accordingly wrote to John T. Taylor, Assistant Secretary at Bloomsbury, on 22 January 1881: 'I cannot discover that the "rooms" have been as yet supplied with thermometers. Is it possible to lend two or three thermometers for my room to investigate the temperature simultaneously at various parts of it? Near my desk, although there has been a large fire all morning, the temperature is 13°F above freezing point and it is absolutely necessary for the state of one's health to keep on a hat and overcoat while using the room. An anemometer to determine the strength of the current of cold air from window to fire would also be of use. Unless some improvement can be introduced the room will be uninhabited another winter. I remain, Yours very truly Laz. Fletcher.' On 27 January 1881 he had occasion again to write to Taylor: 'I beg to inform you that water is falling rapidly into the Mineral Gallery and also into the corridor between the Gallery and my room. The recess next to the one in which the large meteorite is placed is in a deplorable state and I need scarcely mention that as the tarpaulin has not yet arrived the specimen is in a precarious state.' There were other deficiencies to report to Taylor. Thus on 14 January 1881: 'The drawers of the wall cases in the corridor are immovable and thus useless for the ordinary purpose for which drawers are expected to serve. Will the Office of Works take the matter in hand.' Then, 'It would be very convenient if a mantelpiece clock were provided for my room and also a wall-clock for the room of Mr Davies in the basement.' Also 'I am informed that the enclosed knife was supplied by the authorities for the purpose of testing the hardness of specimens. If such are still supplied I shall be glad if you will supply *three* according to requisition.' On 9 February 1881 he pointed out that 'owing to the small number of our attendants, namely two, the loss of one of them who has been for years in this service is a much more serious matter in this department than it would have been to that of Zoology which claims eleven attendants or to that of Geology which claims six or even to that of Botany claiming five: in fact after another fortnight we may have only a single attendant left with any experience of the departmental work.' Poor Cinderella Mineralogy! On 4 March 1881 Fletcher, in trying to get adequate equipment, pointed out that 'hitherto we have used and thanks to the kind offer of the late Keeper, are still using apparatus which is the private property of Prof. Story-Maskelyne. With regard to item No 1 it has up to this been impossible to do accurate work on ordinary specimens in the Museum itself, owing to the nature of the light; all work requiring exactitude has been done out of the Museum with an excellent goniometer costing probably £60 to £70 which is Prof. Maskelyne's private property. I need scarcely add that such work could not be done upon specimens belonging to the Trustees. I may add that we are still using the late Keeper's "chemical balance".' Such representations did not fall upon deaf ears, although they may have been hard of hearing. By 1904 he was able to report that, despite the demands made upon the staff by the selection, registration, incorporation, labelling and arrangement of specimens and the formation and cataloguing of the departmental library, they had never-theless found time 'for research on the specimens. For this purpose the

Department has been gradually equipped with an excellent set of the most modern apparatus necessary for the physical and goniometrical investigation of the minerals, and good illumination has been provided for use with the instruments; the chemical laboratory is no longer isolated from the Museum, but has been fitted up in the building itself.'

His staff in 1880 consisted of two 1st Class Assistants, Walter Flight and Thomas Davies, one 2nd Class Assistant, Henry Maurice Platnauer, and two Attendants. Platnauer, who had joined the Department in 1880, left in 1883 to become Curator of the York Museum.

Fletcher continued the study of meteorites initiated by Story-Maskelyne and, in addition to scientific papers on them, published an *Introduction to the Study of Meteorites, with a List of the Meteorites represented in the Collections* (1881). He followed this with an *Introduction to the Study of Minerals, with a Guide to the Mineral Gallery* (1884) and an *Introduction to the Study of Rocks* (1894).

In 1882, shortly after the removal of the collections from Bloomsbury, Henry Alexander Miers (1858-1942), who had simultaneously studied classics, mathematics, crystallography and mineralogy at Oxford and then crystallography at Strasbourg under Paul Groth, joined the Department. An adventurous soul, he obtained permission from the Museum in August 1888 to fly from London to Austria by balloon. Owing to an unsuitable wind, the balloon was blown to pieces, his companion was killed, and he was picked up unconscious; however, after six weeks' absence from the Museum he seemed none the worse for this mishap. His duties at the Museum were mostly concerned with the routine tasks of arranging the mineral collection but these involved crystallographic research. In 1895 he left the Museum to become Waynflete Professor of Mineralogy in succession to Story-Maskelyne, whose only student he had been in 1881. His work in the Museum under Fletcher prepared him for his subsequent even more fruitful research in Oxford, which brought him Fellowship of the Royal Society in 1896 and a knighthood in 1912; in addition he was a Trustee of the British Museum from 1911 to 1920. He died in 1942 at the age of eighty-four, the holder of innumerable honours, among them six honorary doctorates.

Fletcher's tenure of the keepership extended from June 1880 to May 1909. The Trustees wished to appoint him Director of the Natural History Museum in 1898 (see p.79) but outside pressure, based ostensibly on the contention that a mineralogist was not a fit person to direct such an institution but really intended to instal Ray Lankester, a zoologist, delayed his appointment as Director until 1909, when his health was failing. George Thurland Prior (1862-1936), who had joined the Department in 1887, then became Keeper and remained in office until 1927. His two 1st Class Assistants were Leonard James Spencer (1870-1959), who was Keeper from 1927 to 1935, and George Frederick Herbert Smith (1872-1953), who was Keeper from 1935 to 1937, having been Museum Assistant Secretary from 1921 to 1930 and Secretary from 1930 to 1935; the Director obtained his appointment as Keeper, so it is said, to get him out of the Museum office! The other members of his staff were four Attendants and two Boy Attendants. Although the work of the Department had increased, the scientific staff was smaller in 1909 than it had been in 1880.

George Thurland Prior was born on 6 December 1862 in Oxford where his father, George Thomas Prior, kept a small chemist's shop. In 1881 he gained a scholarship to Magdalen College, Oxford, and graduated with first class honours in chemistry in 1885 and in physics in 1886. He then went to Germany to study chemistry under A. Classen at Aachen. The standards set for the examination of candidates for a 2nd Class Assistantship in the Department, which included inorganic chemistry, crystallography both theoretical and practical, advanced mathematics, crystallographic and general optics, French and German, were exacting. In consequence its scientific officers, though few, were well-trained men of high intellectual powers who attained distinction in mineralogy. Prior thus came to the Museum in 1887 well qualified for a mineralogical post and Fletcher put him in charge of the chemical laboratory and subsequently, on the death of Thomas Davies in 1892, also in charge of the rock collection. An unusually skilled chemical analyst, he took especial care that his analyses were based on the very same material that had been determined by physical investigation with goniometer or polarising microscope and he thereby avoided the kind of mistake which had been made in the past by analyses based on associated material. He turned to the study of meteorites on Fletcher's elevation to the directorship in 1909 and produced a new classification of these based upon the ratio of nickel to iron in the metallic portion and the ratio of ferrous oxide to magnesia in the silicate. From 1910 onwards nearly all of his published work was concerned with meteorites. Based on the exceptional quality of his chemical analyses, in 1916 he formulated two rules concerning the relationship of nickel to oxidised and metallic iron. Prior's rules, although not without their critics, are an accepted part of meteoritics today. Part of Prior's analytical technique was the magnetic separation of metallic nickel-iron from the silicate portion of stony meteorites. For this he devised weakly magnetic combs, which are still used today. He published in 1923 a *Catalogue of Meteorites with special Reference to those represented in the Collection of the British Museum (Natural History)* with an

Appendix to the Catalogue in 1927, and in 1926 *A Guide to the Collection of Meteorites*. His publications number ninety-six in all. He retired as Keeper under the age limit in 1927 and died at Hatch End near London on 8 March 1936, aged seventy-three. He was elected to the Royal Society in 1912. Prior excelled above all in fine chemical analysis and, through his association with the discovery of eleven new minerals, one of which, priorite from Swaziland, South Africa, was named after him. Thus he maintained the high repute which the Department had earned under Lazarus Fletcher.

Leonard James Spencer (1870-1959), who followed Prior as Keeper in December 1927, was eight years his junior and entered the Department in 1894, seven years after him, filling the vacancy created by the death of Thomas Davies. The Department then consisted of three Oxford graduates, Fletcher, Miers and Prior, with four attendants. Spencer was thus a Cambridge intrusion but a welcome one. Never before had a small museum department been staffed by men of such high intellectual calibre, each making outstanding contributions to the study of mineralogy.

Spencer was born at Worcester on 7 July 1870, the son of a schoolmaster, who gave him a geologist's hammer at the age of seven and by thus encouraging him in the collection of minerals, rocks and fossils may have determined his subsequent career. He became a student at Sidney Sussex College, Cambridge, and graduated in 1893 just before a vacancy in the Department of Mineralogy became available. On Fletcher's recommendation he went to study crystal-lography at Munich under Paul Groth, as Miers had previously done at Strasbourg, before taking up his appointment. Paul Groth (1843-1927), founder of the *Zeitschrift für Kristallographie*, seems to have had the same influential attraction for British students of crystall-ography that Sachs had for British botanical students. By now the Museum's laboratory had become well equipped in response presumably to Fletcher's insistent demands. Spencer's duties included the arrangement and labelling of specimens in exhibition cases and cabinets, as well as preparation of a descriptive catalogue which, although never completed, necessitated research. He worked with Miers until the latter left for Oxford. Between November 1909, after Prior had become Keeper, and July 1935, when he himself retired, he was responsible for over 20,000 entries in the current registers of accessions, but nevertheless he managed to produce important original papers which included the description of new minerals. In 1924 he made a long journey to Canada and the United States, which resulted in him shipping back to the Museum 12 cwt. (610kg) of minerals, including twelve species new to the collection. In 1929 a second long journey took him to South Africa, visiting mines, and resulted in seventeen cases of minerals being shipped back to the Museum. It is noteworthy that in 1933 Spencer, and M.H. Hey (see below), coined the term 'explosion crater' for the effects of high-energy meteorite impact. They were able to demonstrate in two cases that large iron meteorites had mostly been vaporised by the heat released when they hit the Earth's surface. Desert sands had thus become contaminated by nickel-iron from the explosion. This work foreshadowed the studies of cratering which preceded and accompanied lunar exploration, and which are now an established part of the earth sciences. Despite the administrative and routine demands of his department and his own research, Spencer nevertheless edited the *Mineralogical Magazine* from 1901 to 1955 with meticulous care, started and edited *Mineralogical Abstracts* from 1920 to 1955, was President of the Mineralogical Society from 1936 to 1939 and its Foreign Secretary from 1949 to 1959. He was elected a Fellow of the Royal Society in 1925.

Spencer retired in July 1935 and died on 14 April 1959, aged eighty-nine. W. Campbell Smith, for many years a colleague of Spencer, wrote in an obituary: 'No one who worked with him could fail to appreciate the depth of his knowledge, his limitless energy and power of concentration, and, beneath a somewhat brusque manner, a saving sense of humour and a truly kind heart.'

On Spencer's retirement, George Frederick Herbert Smith (1872-1959), who had left the Department in 1921 to become the Museum's Assistant Secretary, now returned to it as Keeper of Minerals. He entered the Department in 1897 at the age of twenty-five, having studied mathematics and physics at New College, Oxford, and then spent a year studying crystallography at Munich under the celebrated Paul Groth. Soon after joining the Museum staff he devised a three-circle goniometer for working on his crystallographic problems. He became interested in gemstones and scientific methods for identifying faceted stones, which led him to devise in 1906 a refractometer for measuring their refractive indices which was so convenient in use that jewellers everywhere adopted the Herbert Smith instrument for gem testing. Out of this work he produced, as well as original papers, a standard book *Gem-stones and their distinctive Characters* (1912), of which a 13th edition appeared in 1958 and a 14th edition revised by F.C. Phillips in 1972. Herbert Smith's relations with Spencer had long been uneasy, and in 1921 he moved out of the department to become Assistant Secretary of the Museum in succession to Charles E. Fagan (see page 116). As an administrator he played an important part in persuading the Empire Marketing Board to grant money for the Department of Entomology's accommodation. Among his innovations was the preparation and sale of postcards illustrating specimens in the Museum, including, of course, minerals and he edited for its entire existence the Museum's *Natural History Magazine* (1927-1936). He gained the reputation of being severe, reserved, obstinate and auto- cratic, according to W. Campbell Smith, and usually succeeded in getting done those things he wanted done and in the manner he wanted them done. During his two years as Keeper he spent much time on arranging new exhibits of precious and semi-precious stones in specially illuminated cases, which had however to be dismantled in 1939 for the storage of their contents under safer conditions. He died on 20 April 1953, having devoted much of the fifteen years of his retire- ment to groups for the preservation of wild life.

Herbert Smith was followed as Keeper by Walter Campbell Smith (b.1887) who had charge of the Department from 1937 to 1952, which included the anxious years of World War II. Educated at Solihull School and Cambridge, he became an Assistant in the Department of Mineralogy in 1910, filling the vacancy left when Fletcher became Director and Prior succeeded him as Keeper. He served with dis- tinction in the Artists' Rifles from 1910 to 1935 and then from 1939 to 1942, being twice mentioned in despatches and gaining the Military Cross on the Western Front in the 1914-1918 World War; he was made a Lieut.-Colonel in 1918. His work in the Museum began with a brief spell on silicate minerals, as part of the continuing project of scientific cataloguing, but Prior's increased involvement with the meteorite collections left the rock collection untended. Despite his preference for mineralogical research, Campbell Smith had studied petrology at Cambridge under Alfred Harker and was well qualified to take charge of the rock collections. The scientific study of rocks began in 1847, when Henry Clifton Sorby at Sheffield devised the method of grinding slices sufficiently thin to be studied under the microscope. Story- Maskelyne had pioneered the study of meteorites in thin section, but the method had been little used on the rock collections until Prior took them over from Davies. Almost immediately, the Department was inundated by the transfer of the extensive collections of the Geological Society of London in 1911 and Campbell Smith was fully occupied in sorting and cataloguing over 10,000 foreign rocks; specimens lacking labels or documentation were thrown away. British rocks from the same collections were transferred to the Museum of Practical Geology at the same time. Shortage of staff in the earlier years of the Department had resulted in concentration of effort on the mineral and meteorite collections, and the rock collections only began to be catalogued seriously under Prior; thus Campbell Smith became involved at an early stage, and the present state of the rock collections rests solidly on his efforts. In 1928 he produced the first of several printed catalogues of the Museum's rocks *(Catalogue of the Rock Collections in the Mineral Department of the British Museum (Natural History) arranged geographically. Part I Africa.)*, and the Introduction contains a list of the more important historical collections and suites of rocks. These include the lavas of Monte Somma, Vesuvius—lavas given by Sir William Hamilton between 1767 and 1779; specimens collected on Flinders' voyage in 1801-3, probably the earliest extant collection of Australian rocks; Italian volcanic rocks collected by T. Monticelli, bought in 1823; many suites from European localities, given or bought between 1870 and 1880 and forming the foundation of a systematic rock collection; a large collection of Indian rocks, transferred from the India Museum in 1879; collections made by the *Challenger* expedition of 1873-6, by many Arctic and by most of the Antarctic Expeditions up to the last voyages of Scott in the *Terra Nova* and of Shackleton in the *Quest*. Campbell Smith's scientific work was notable for his studies of rocks collected by Antarctic expeditions and of alkaline igneous rocks from Africa. In particular, he was among the first to recognise that certain African rocks rich in calcium carbonate were carbonatites of igneous origin rather than blocks of limestone caught up in igneous complexes.

Herbert Smith's departure to the Director's Office left a vacancy which was filled by Edgar Donald Mountain in 1922, after he had taken first class honours in both parts of the Cambridge Tripos. Mountain was at the Museum for only four years, in which he published several papers and contributed to the silicate section of the mineral catalogue, before he developed pneumonia and moved on medical advice to Rhodes University, South Africa, where he became Professor of Geology in 1928. Prior had taken notice of the newly developing science of X-ray crystallography and its application to the study of minerals, and in 1927 Frederick Allan Bannister (1901-1970) was appointed to fill the place left by Mountain. Bannister was a Cambridge physicist who had worked for a short time in the research laboratory of the Western Electric Company, and after joining the Museum staff took a course in X-ray crystallography under Sir William Bragg before setting up X-ray apparatus in the Mineral Department. Prior's own retirement in 1927 left a vacancy in the department for an analytical chemist, and in 1928 Max Hutchinson Hey (b.1904) joined the staff. Hey had taken first class honours in chemistry at Oxford and studied crystallography under T.V. Barker, and had worked at the Patent Office for two years before the Museum post fell vacant. He and Bannister formed a perfect team, complementing each others skills, and were pioneers in the joint application of chemical, optical, and X-ray methods to the characterisation of minerals. Both of them worked on the scientific cataloguing of the mineral collections, and Hey's classic papers on minerals of the zeolite group were a breakthrough in the understanding of these complex species.

The mineral collection had continued to grow in the early years of the twentieth century, largely under Spencer's devoted attention, and important gifts became more frequent from private collections. In 1893 John Charles Williams (1861-1939) of Caerhays Castle, Cornwall, presented a selection of 550 choice Cornish specimens, the largest gift for many years, but the new century saw many more: Miss Caroline Birley's bequest, rich in fine zeolites, in 1907; specimens from the Morro Velho mine in Brazil, from Frederick Tendron, 1910; Sir Arthur Church's cut gemstones, in 1915: Swiss minerals from the Rev. J.M. Gordon, 1922; Dr C.O. Trechmann's finely crystallised specimens, 1926; the Australian collections of Prof. A. Liversidge, 1927; and several suites of European and American minerals, Irish zeolites, and superbly catalogued Swiss minerals from Frederick Noel Ashcroft (formerly Fleischmann) (1878-1949) in the years from 1901 to 1937. The largest gift in the history of the mineral collection, however, came in 1964 with the bequest of the celebrated British collection of Sir Arthur Russell (1878-1964). A close friend of Campbell Smith, Spencer, and the Department for many decades, Russell had collected British minerals for over seventy-five years and his 13,000 specimens, with the Ashcroft Irish and Swiss collections, are the only regional collections kept separate and unincorporated from the systematic mineral collection. More recently A.C.D. Pain (1901-1971) bequeathed to the Museum his collection of 128 Burmese gemstones, some of which are now displayed in the mineral gallery.

For over a century, from the time of Konig to that of Spencer, curation of the meteorite collection had generally been the direct reponsibility of the Keeper who also carried out research in this area. Campbell Smith continued the tradition when he became Keeper in 1937, but gradually passed the curation to Hey who was interested in the chemical but not the petrographic side of the work. Hey took his curatorial duties seriously, and has been jokingly credited with formulating the two basic rules of curation; 'get it, and keep it' (*American Mineralogist* 52: 574, 1967). In 1940 he published an Appendix to Prior's *Catalogue of Meteorites* (1923) of which he also produced new editions in 1953 and 1966; the latter remains the standard reference work. The high point of his acquisition of specimens came in 1959 with the successful negotiation of the purchase of half of the Nininger collection of meteorites, for which the Nuffield Trust generously supplied the price of £50,000. A completely new meteorite exhibit was built in the pavilion at the east end of the mineral gallery and opened to the public in 1970.

In 1935 John Dugdale Holt Wiseman (b. 1907) and Gordon Frank Claringbull (b. 1911) joined the staff. The extensive collections of Sir John Murray, which included specimens collected by the H.M.S. *Challenger* expedition in 1872-76 and were originally housed in the Villa Medusa, Edinburgh, were given to the Museum by Murray's widow and son in 1922. The Trustees decided, in 1935, to separate the sediments, manganese nodules, and rocks from the much larger zoological part and to transfer them to the Department of Mineralogy. The 9,746 sounding samples, on which Murray had based his deep-sea deposits map of the world, became the nucleus of the Museum's collection of ocean-bottom deposits. Rock samples in the Murray Collection came from volcanic islands visited by H.M.S. *Challenger*, including St Paul Rocks; others were dredged from the Mid-Atlantic Ridge and parts of the Pacific. The Museum already possessed other collections of oceanic rocks and Wiseman was recruited to curate and study the newly amalgamated ocean-bottom collections. He had gained his doctorate in petrology at Cambridge, his first work at the Museum was to describe the Carlsberg Ridge basalts, accurately characterising ocean-floor tholeiite some thirty years before it became recognised as a very widespread rock type. Wiseman continued his petrological work, and developed a partnership with C.D. Ovey of the Department of Zoology in palaeoclimatic studies based on foraminiferal shells and coccoliths. He was seconded to the Admiralty during the Second World War, as a result of which he developed close links with the Hydrographer of the Royal Navy. This led to survey ships taking grab and other samples which have contributed largely to the more recent additions to the collection. After the war, Wiseman became involved in the establishment of the National Institute of Oceanography, now the Institute of Oceanographic Sciences, and from 1956-1963 was a member of the National Oceanographical Council. He was Deputy Keeper of the Department from 1968 until his retirement in 1972.

When Campbell Smith became Keeper in 1937, he was helped in his work on the rock collections by S.E. Ellis (see below), Claringbull, and Philip Malcolm Game (b. 1911), who filled the vacancy left by Herbert Smith's retirement. Stanley Ernest Ellis (b. 1904) was first appointed as a Boy Attendant in 1927 and later obtained a first class honours degree from the University of London by part-time study, a considerable achievement in the days before day release and financial assistance. Much of his work was on systematic igneous petrology, and he retired in 1968. Game specialised in the accurate optical determination of the feldspars and finally retired from the Museum in 1972.

In 1939, when war was imminent, specimens that were considered particularly valuable and irreplaceable were carefully packed in crates and transported to Sir Arthur Russell's home at Swallowfield Park, near Reading, for the duration. A second category of specimens was also packed in crates, and stored in the Museum's basement. The third category, deemed least likely to suffer serious damage or to cause irreparable loss to the collections if destroyed, remained in the cabinets in the Mineral Gallery, carefully protected by sand-bags. All members of the departmental staff helped in this formidable task, and in the preparation of detailed lists of the contents of the various packing boxes. These precautions proved their worth, for although the Mineral Gallery was not directly damaged by bombing, it suffered considerable water damage following the destruction by fire of the Cryptogamic Herbarium immediately above. Miss Jessie May Sweet (1901-1979) had joined the department as a temporary assistant in 1927 to work with Spencer on the mineral collections when he became Keeper, and soon became an established staff member. By cataloguing the collections and registering accessions, she acquired a superb knowledge of their content. During the war she was one of the small band who remained at the Museum, carrying out her duties as well as fire-watching, and she spent some of this time with the indexes planning in collaboration with Hey the systematic arrangement of the collection, in preparation for the restoration of the specimens to the Gallery, after the war.

The years of the 'cold war' following the end of the World War delayed restoration of the displays. In the early 1950s British minerals were displayed in cases on the balcony outside the gallery, and there was a small display of selected specimens open to the public just inside the gallery. Miss Sweet laid out the whole of the systematic displays between 1949 and 1958; when she had finished she was the only person to have handled personally every specimen in the collection. She was awarded the M.B.E. in recognition of her services and retired in 1961.

An outcome of the war years was Hey's *An Index of Mineral Species and varieties arranged chemically*, more widely known as the *Chemical Index of Minerals*; the first edition was published in 1950, the second in 1955 with separate appendices in 1963 and 1974. This internationally acclaimed reference work began with a request, in 1942, for a listing of all the known silicates of magnesium; no such list existed, and its preparation led Hey to complete the work for the remainder of the mineral kingdom. He retired in 1969.

Campbell Smith retired in 1952 at a time of considerable economic restraint in the Museum, and was briefly succeeded as Keeper of Minerals by Bannister who shortly after appointment suffered a serious illness and had to retire. Hey became acting Keeper for a few months, until Claringbull was appointed to the post in 1953. Claringbull had been seconded for special duties during the war, and after his return joined Bannister in the X-ray section to work on minerals instead of rocks. He was interested in exhibition techniques, and in addition to preparing displays on crystal structures he designed the present layout of the mineral collection, which had previously shown each specimen in its own wooden tray all tightly packed together in the table cases. Alfred Allinson Moss transferred to the Department in 1953 as an analytical chemist from the British Museum's research laboratory; he became Keeper in 1968 when Claringbull became Director, and he retired at the end of 1974. Moss, like Prior and Hey before him, set himself and all who worked for him in the chemical laboratory very high standards of accuracy and industry. The laboratory added to its range of equipment, and the techniques of atomic absorption spectroscopy, X-ray fluorescence analysis, and infra-red absorption spectroscopy were introduced. In more recent years research work has also expanded into the field of geochemistry.

In the 1950's, methods began to be developed for the rapid analysis of rocks and minerals and the Department quickly introduced the new techniques. These rapid methods are nearly all based on comparison between the unknown and some standard or series of standards in which the concentration of particular elements has been determined, usually by traditional gravimetric methods. Most of them suffered from the disadvantage, so far as minerals are concerned, that comparatively large amounts of material were required, usually far more than could be spared, say, in the determination of a rare species. However, in the late 1950's Claringbull saw the possibilities of the newly developed electron probe microanalyser as a non-destructive analytical tool enabling quantitative analysis to be made of mineral grains only a few micrometres across and in polished thin sections that can be examined microscopically. A pre-production model of the Geoscan electron microprobe was delivered in 1964 and, fitted now with an energy dispersive analytical system, still gives excellent results. In the 1970's computers came to be used not only to perform calculations rapidly, but also to control machine function, so that the Microscan 9 electron microprobe, installed in 1979, produces an analysis within 11 minutes. Several new minerals, which occur in grains too small previously to have been analysed chemically, have been discovered in this way.

Following the retirement of Bannister and Claringbull's appointment as Keeper, Richard John Davies (1926-1977) took charge of X-ray crystallography and besides undertaking research on specific minerals, continued to develop the Department's unrivalled reference collection of catalogued powder diffraction photographs of minerals which are essential for identification purposes. In 1969 the Department began the study of opaque minerals and a computer-controlled, reflected light microscope now enables mineralogical constants of such minerals to be calculated from reflectance and quantitative colour data.

The study of meteorites begun by Story-Maskelyne was continued by Prior and Hey, both in association with their other duties. The landings on the moon provided great impetus to extra-terrestrial studies, including meteoritics. After the retirement of Ellis, Arthur Clive Bishop (b. 1930) took charge of the rock collections and was appointed Keeper of the Department in 1975.

Wiseman retired in 1972 and David Ronald Charles Kempe (b. 1927) took charge of the collection of ocean-bottom deposits and since then research has concentrated on the sediments and submarine igneous rocks. The collection itself was housed after the war in a wartime, bomb-proof building to the east of the Museum. In 1964 this building, which is constructed partly below ground level, flooded to a depth of several feet and, though the specimens themselves suffered no harm in their glass jars, some labels were damaged or lost. The 'War Room' was later incorporated into the East Wing. In 1969 the collection was moved, together with staff, to an outstation at North Acton. The staff returned to South Kensington in 1977 and the collections were moved to new accommodation in 1980 at South Ruislip.

Since its transfer from Bloomsbury to South Kensington in 1880, the Department of Mineralogy has occupied rooms at the east end of the south-east basement, but owing to the expansion of staff, collections, and techniques, additional space had to be found wherever and whenever it became available and by the 1960's the Department was widely dispersed through the eastern part of the Museum. In 1979, however, the Department was able to move into the basement, which needed extensive renovation, occupied up to 1977 by the Department of Palaeontology. Most of the Department is now housed in a single connected area designed to meet its present and foreseeable future needs.

Unlike the other scientific departments, the Department of Mineralogy is almost wholly concerned with inorganic material. Minerals, meteorites and rocks, however, are an integral part of natural history and they have been represented among the Museum's collections from its earliest days. The present scope, quality and international standing of the Departmental collections reflect the care they have received from staff and Keepers. The work of the Department is concerned with the nature and origin of the Earth and its constituent materials, and with the processes that occur within it. Since man is, in large measure, dependent on raw materials obtained from the Earth, the need for a more thorough understanding of minerals is unlikely to diminish as far as can be seen into the future.

16

Department of
Botany

TWO MAJOR COLLECTIONS, those of Sir Hans Sloane (1660-1753) and Sir Joseph Banks (1743-1820), both long-serving Presidents of the Royal Society, form the historic basis of the Department of Botany. Sloane evidently began to collect plants in the fields and gardens around London, which had not yet encroached on the villages of Kensington, Fulham, Chelsea and like rural areas, between his arrival from Ireland in 1677 and his journey to Paris in 1683. He gathered more specimens in France, notably in the fields and gardens around Paris and Montpellier, in 1683. Over the years he added to it the specimens collected during his stay in Jamaica from 1687 to 1689. These formed the basis of Sloane's *Catalogus Plantarum quae in Insula Jamaica sponte proveniunt vel vulgo coluntur* (1696) and his massive two-volume *Voyage to the Islands Madera, Barbados, Nieves, S. Christophers and Jamaica* (vol. 1, 1707; vol. 2, 1725).

It is also through Sloane that the Museum can claim an historical association with the Chelsea Physic Garden. The Worshipful Society of Apothecaries founded the Garden in 1673 to enable apprentices to become familiar with medicinal plants. It formed part of the Manor of Chelsea which Sloane owned from 1712 until his death in 1753. An agreement between Sloane and the Society stipulated that fifty dried specimens of different species of plants should be presented to the Royal Society annually. By this simple provision, Sloane ensured an active policy of plant introductions and the maintenance of a good stock of plants. The specimens, some 3,750 in all, were transferred to the Museum with the Royal Society collections and they continue to provide valuable data on plants introduced at that time and named by Philip Miller, William Hudson and William Curtis. In recent years, the Department has forged strong new links with the Garden, which is now the home of the Cytology Section, and provides general facilities for the growth and study of living plants.

The second major acquisition was the Herbarium of Sir Joseph Banks (1743-1820). Banks's career has been outlined in numerous publications, most notably in H.C. Cameron, *Sir Joseph Banks, K.B. PRS, the Autocrat of the Philosophers* (1952), Warren R. Dawson's calendar of his manuscript correspondence *The Banks Letters* (1958) and J.C. Beaglehole, *The Endeavour Journal of Joseph Banks* (2 vols, 1962). In 1766 Banks made an expedition to Newfoundland and Labrador aboard a fishery protection vessel, H.M.S. *Niger*. His journal remained unpublished until 1971 when, edited and annotated with painstaking scholarship by Averil Lysaght and embellished with plates from contemporary drawings by G.D. Ehret of plants and by Peter Paillou and Sydney Parkinson of birds, it appeared as a handsome volume of 512 pages entitled *Joseph Banks in Newfoundland and Labrador, 1766.*

Belated publication has deprived Banks's Canadian work of the scientific importance it would have had if issued in the eighteenth century; at least one hundred of the specimens of flowering plants collected by Banks represented species then nameless and a few new species were much later described by other authors from his material. This voyage proved nevertheless important for his career. It gave Banks first-hand experience of seafaring and of natural history collecting in biologically unknown territory. It prepared him for the greatest adventure of his life, the voyage round the world with Captain Cook in the *Endeavour* (p. 19).

Although the botanical material of the *Endeavour* voyage, the specimens, drawings and descriptions remained Banks's private property until his death in 1820, all had been freely accessible to the many botanists who visited his herbarium at Soho Square. Joseph Gaertner from southern Germany, Charles l'Héritier de Brutelle from France, Olaf Swartz from Sweden and A.P. de Candolle from Switzerland were but a few of those who came to London to consult the specimens and the books which continuously increased within Banks's London residence. They described new species from his collections. Among these were not only those of the *Endeavour* voyage but many gathered by other travellers, notably by Francis Masson (1741-1806) who was sent by Banks to the Cape of Good Hope, the Azores, the Canary Islands, Madeira, the West Indies, Spain, Portugal, Tangier, Morocco and eastern North America. Thus over the years the Banksian herbarium became one of the most extensive, and possibly the most extensive in the world, being very rich in type specimens. Cook's other two voyages also enriched the herbarium. Further information regarding the botanical results of these three voyages will be found in E.D. Merrill *The Botany of Cook's Voyages* (1954) and in *Endeavour* 27: 3-10 (1968), *Notes and Records of the Royal Society* 24: 64-90 (1969), *Records of the Australian Academy of Science* 2, iv: 7-24 (1974) and *Pacific Studies* 1: 147-162 (1978). Banks also acquired by purchase other collections, among the most important being the herbaria of George Clifford (1685-1760) typifying Linnaeus's *Hortus Cliffortianus* (1738), P. Hermann (1640-1695) typifying Linnaeus's *Flora Zeylanica* (1747), and J.F. Gronovius typifying his *Flora Virginica* (1739-1743). Banks's influential association with the royal botanic garden at Kew also enriched eventually the British Museum's Department of Botany.

A botanic garden was laid out in the grounds of Kew Palace by William Aiton (1731-1793) in 1760 for Princess Augusta, the Princess Dowager of Wales, with the Earl of Bute and John Hill as her botanical advisers. She died in 1772 and her son King George III then moved from Richmond to Kew. Banks had sailed round the world with Cook under the King's auspices, as it were, and on his return, being higher in the social scale than Cook, he received from the newspapers and society much of the adulation and renown which should more justly have been Cook's. He was accordingly presented to the King at Windsor, together with Solander (p. 18). Banks gave an account of their travels and thus began an association and friendship lasting almost forty years, based on their common interest in navigation, gardens and sheep. Bute had now fallen from royal favour. Banks gradually assumed control of the Royal Garden at Kew and used his wealth and enterprise to enrich its stock of plants not only by obtaining them from other gardens but by sending out collectors to get new plants from the wilds of South Africa and elsewhere. The specimens they gathered went into his herbarium at Soho Square. The plants raised at Kew from their seed needed identification, which could only be done by a botanist such as Solander with both Banks's herbarium and rich library at hand. Thus specimens grown at Kew likewise came into the Banksian herbarium. During the summer of 1781 Banks, Solander and Linnaeus's son Carl von Linné (1741-1783) spent four days a week studying cultivated plants for the preparation of a catalogue of those at Kew. After Solander's death another Swedish botanist Jonas Dryander (1748-1810) took over the preparation of this work which appeared in 1789 as William Aiton's *Hortus Kewensis* with a second edition in 1810 to 1813 having the name of his son William Townsend Aiton on the title-page. Thus Solander and Dryander, according to J.B.C. Ker Gawler (1764-1842), were robbed of the reward of their erudition 'to give immortality and renown to vulgar ignorance, the names of native dunces being suffered to usurp the place belonging to those of the genius and talent of another land'

(*Botanical Register* 9: t.729; 1823). Many new species were named in this work, which must be attributed to 'Aiton' or 'Aiton fil', although Solander and Dryander coined the names and drafted the Latin diagnosis. The types of the *Hortus Kewensis* are not at Kew, as is often expected, but in the Department of Botany at the Natural History Museum, having come with the Banksian herbarium.

Banks employed the celebrated botanical artist Georg Dionysius Ehret (1708-1770) to portray the plants brought back from his visit to Newfoundland and Labrador, and later Sydney Parkinson (c. 1745-1771) as his artist on Cook's first global voyage. In 1790 he employed Austrian-born Franz Andreas Bauer (1758-1840) as his resident artist at Kew and here Bauer lived for the rest of his life, portraying its plants with a grace and meticulous accuracy equalled only in the work of his brother Ferdinand Lucas Bauer (1760-1826). The original drawings of these two unrivalled botanical artists are now among the treasures of the Botany Library.

Banks bequeathed to Robert Brown (1773-1858), his botanist librarian, a life-interest in the Banksian collections. On Brown's death they were to pass to the British Museum. Brown had the option of transferring them to the Museum during his lifetime if he wished, which he did after prolonged negotiation with the Trustees during which he stated that, if these collections formed a separate botanical department within the Museum, he would be willing to take charge of it, a reasonable offer in view of his eminence, with the status of an Under-Librarian, i.e. Keeper.

Brown was born at Montrose, Scotland, on 21 December 1773, the son of an Episcopalian clergyman. After completing his medical studies at Edinburgh, he joined the Fifeshire Regiment of Fencibles in 1795 as an ensign, with the duties of a surgeon's mate, and went to Ireland with the regiment. Here he devoted his time to his medical duties and rigorous self-education in botany and the German language. He came to London in 1798, apparently on a recruiting mission, was introduced to Banks and evidently impressed the great man, now highly influential at the Admiralty, by his ability and knowledge. When in 1800 plans were being made for a surveying voyage of the coast of Australia, then called New Holland, under Matthew Flinders, Banks offered Brown the post of naturalist aboard Flinders's ship the *Investigator.* Ferdinand Bauer, who had earlier travelled as Sibthorp's artist in Greece and Asia Minor, was appointed as natural history draughtsman. Brown was now twenty-seven. The *Investigator* sailed on 18 June 1801 and returned in October 1805 without Flinders, then unfortunately interned by the French on the island of Mauritius. During Flinders's circumnavigation of Australia, which he proved to be one large land mass and not two or more vast islands, Brown made extensive collections on its southern, eastern and northern coasts; he also spent nine months in Tasmania (Van Diemen's Island). In all he collected nearly 3,900 species, the greater part of them new to science. They all came to the Museum after the death in 1876 of his assistant and successor John Joseph Bennett (1801-1876). One of Brown's tasks back in England was to condense his detailed descriptions made on the voyage into concise diagnoses. He published in April 1810 the first and only volume of his *Prodromus Florae Novae Hollandiae* which included about 2,000 species. This has long been esteemed as a botanical classic. Brown himself paid for its printing in an edition of 250 copies, but it sold only 26 copies and, thus disappointed, Brown withdrew it from sale and never published the intended second volume, much to the loss of systematic botany. Brown's specimens and descriptions are in the Department of Botany, together with the superb finished drawings by Ferdinand Bauer of the living plants. The Basilisk Press publication, *The Australian Flower Paintings of Ferdinand Bauer* (1976), with reproductions of some of Bauer's illustrations and transcripts of Brown's text, makes evident the high quality of both.

After the voyage Brown never returned to the army. He became 'Clerk Librarian and Housekeeper' of the Linnean Society of London in 1806, a post he retained until 1822, and also in 1810, on the death of Dryander, Banks's librarian and curator at Soho Square.

Brown possessed one of the most penetrating intellects that have ever probed botanical problems, together with insatiable curiosity and acute powers of observation, but his most creative endeavour belongs to the period 1806 to 1820 when he was so closely associated with Banks. However in 1831 he called attention to the existence in plant cells of an opaque body he called 'the areola or nucleus'. He noticed when examining pollen grains of *Clarkia pulchella* that particles suspended in a fluid within the grain were evidently moving; he extended his observations to other pollen grains and then to finely powered coal, glass etc. and found that such movement occurred in all these when reduced to a powder fine enough to be suspended in water. He recorded these observations on what is now called the 'Brownian movement' in a privately printed pamphlet, *A Brief Account of Microscopical Observations* (1828). Brownian movement is now known to be due to the constant vibration of molecules in the liquid state. By such work Brown established a reputation as one of the most astute, knowledgeable and thorough botanists of his period, a reputation in no way diminished by the passing of time. His life and contributions to science are summarized in the *Dictionary of Scientific Biography* 2: 516-522 (1970). One of his most influential achievements was undoubtedly the establishment of a botanical department in the Museum.

Thus in 1827 Brown agreed to the transfer of the Banks herbarium and library to Bloomsbury and he was officially appointed Under-Librarian with the designation of Keeper of the Sir Joseph Banks Botanical Collection (the Banksian Collection).

He stated later that Banks bequeathed both his books and his specimens with an anxious desire for their being kept together as mutually illustrative of each other; unfortunately this wish of the Museum's great and wise benefactor was intentionally disregarded in 1880 when the specimens were moved to South Kensington, but most of the Banksian library was retained at Bloomsbury to the dismay of the scientific staff. Brown believed that by this transfer during his life-time 'I had secured the permanency of a Botanical Department, obviously wanting in the Museum'. It was open to visitors only two days a week and then between 11am and 4pm provided the visitor had an introduction from a Trustee, an officer of the Museum or a botanist of repute; in practice Brown allowed foreign botanists to work in the Department five days a week. Brown's assistant was John Joseph Bennett (1801-1876) formerly a surgeon and apothecary. They had to do everything in the Department, 'even the merest manual drudgery' without any outside assistance for the next eight years.

The collections which continued to come to the Banksian Herbarium during the latter years of Sir Joseph Banks's life and during Brown's tenure were relatively small. Nevertheless the great accumulation of unclassified material would have fully occupied the time of Brown and Bennett even if they had possessed the dynamic energy of their forceful botanical contemporary John Lindley (1799-1865) and their equally forceful zoological colleague J.E. Gray (1800-1875).

The largest and in some respects the most important collection which came into their hands was that made by Thomas Horsfield (1773-1859) in Java between 1802 and 1818, which included over 2,000 specimens, mostly representing new species, for Horsfield went high into the mountains where no collector had ever been and explored province after province. He was an American doctor, born at Bethelehem, Pennsylvania, who entered the service of the Dutch East India Company in Java in 1801 and was commissioned by the colonial government to investigate the medicinal plants used by natives. In consequence of the annexation of the Netherlands by France in 1806, the British Hon. East India Company's governor Lord Minto despatched an expedition to take over Java in 1810 and Stamford Raffles (1781-1826) became lieutenant governor in 1811. Raffles's many interests included natural history. He persuaded Horsfield to enter British service and encouraged him to investigate antiquities and minerals as well as plants. At Raffles's instigation Horsfield communicated with Banks and sent him a collection of 237 plants from Java in 1814. Other botanical consignments followed. He retired to England in 1819 and became the first Keeper of the Hon. East India Company's Museum, Leadenhall Street, London. His zoological collections he studied himself and based on them his *Zoological Researches in Java and the neighbouring Islands* (1824) and other works. He passed his botanical collections to Robert Brown in the expectation that Brown would prepare within a few years a detailed illustrated enumeration of them. He was sadly disappointd, for in spite of many entreaties the first part of the *Plantae Javanicae Rariores* did not appear until 1838. The fourth and last part was issued in 1852. Even then as John Lindley wrote in a review in the *Gardeners' Chronicle* of 26 June 1852 (p.406) the work only included 'an account of just 50 species of plants out of the 2,196, which Dr Horsfield had placed in the editor's hands'. He further added that 'another consequence has been that the honour to which Dr Horsfield had a most unquestionable claim, has passed away into the hands of Dutch and other continental botanists, and that he now stands before the world as the poor collector, in Java, of about fifty plants (several of which had been known before) during the long period which elapsed between 1800 when he first visited Batavia, and 1819, when he quitted the island. A greater wrong could not have been done him than the wrong thus inflicted.'

Nevertheless, despite its limited scope the *Plantae Javanicae Rariores* remains a classic of Indonesian botany and has been described by a modern authority, J.C.G.G. van Steenis, as one of the best books on Javan plants. The material on which it is based, together with Horsfield's ignored specimens, is in the Department of Botany.

From 1827 to 1834 no money was allowed for the purchase of botanical specimens. Subsequently £80 a year was made available from 1834 onwards, later raised to £100. Thus when the immensely important Russian herbarium of John D. Prescott (d. 1837), containing about 25,000 specimens, was offered to the Trustees for £1,000, the Treasury would not authorize its purchase and it was bought by a private individual, Henry Borron Fielding (1805-1851), who bequeathed it to the University of Oxford (cf. H.N. Clokie, *An Account of the Herbaria of the Department of Botany in the University of Oxford*: 43-44, 103-106, 164; 1966). Lack of money later also prevented the Museum obtaining intact the even more important and extensive herbarium of Aylmer Bourke Lambert (1761-1842). This was accordingly dispersed by auction in 1842. The Museum purchased the American plants of Ruiz and Pavon, the Russian plants of Pallas, the Younger Forster's herbarium, Buchanan Hamilton's Nepal herbarium and Martin's French Guiana herbarium at the Lambert sale.

In a memorandum to the Trustees of the British Museum in 1834 Robert Brown stated: 'The Banksian general herbarium, contained in cabinets consisting of sixty-seven cubes having eight drawers each, is arranged according to the Linnaean system, and by means of alphabetical and systematic indexes it may be consulted without difficulty. The number of species in this arranged herbarium is 23,400, of which 20,856 are phanerogamous and 2,544 cryptogamous plants; the specimens of many, however, being more or less complete. Connected with the general herbarium there is a collection of fruit and seeds, systematically arranged and contained in sixty-four drawers. There is also a collection of flowers and fruits, chiefly of the more rare or succulent plants, preserved in spirits, and contained in 326 bottles. One of the presses contains sixty-seven large specimens chiefly parts of fructification, fronds, and sections of trunks of palms.' Brown also mentioned collections kept separate from the general herbarium particularly Clifford's herbarium, 'the principal authority for the plants described in one of Linnaeus's earliest and most celebrated works', Clayton's Virginian herbarium used by Gronovius, Hermann's Ceylon herbarium, many specimens collected in the Near East by Tournefort and others collected by Loureiro. The unarranged specimens and duplicates consisted of 1,700 parcels, presenting an enormous task of incorporation and comparison not only for Brown but for his successors.

Until 1853 the British Museum herbarium was the only public herbarium in the London area but access to it was restricted. The leading botanists of the first half of the nineteenth century found it necessary for their research to amass large private herbaria. John Lindley (1799-1865), for example, living at Turnham Green some seven miles (11 km) from the British Museum had a rich private herbarium, now divided between the Royal Botanic Gardens, Kew and the Botany School, Cambridge. There was no herbarium at Kew when William Jackson Hooker (1785-1865) arrived there in 1841 to be Director of the newly emergent Royal Botanic Gardens. He brought from Glasgow his rich private herbarium and library, for the Gardens possessed only living plants, no specimens or books. During Banks's time his botanist-librarians and the Banksian herbarium and library at Soho Square, London had satisfied all Kew's scientific needs.

Kew acquired its first official herbarium in 1853 when Miss E. Bromfield presented the herbarium and library of her brother William Arnold Bromfield (1801-1853), a much-travelled doctor resident in the Isle of Wight who devoted many years to compiling his posthumously published *Flora Vectensis* (1856). His library included some 600 volumes, with many costly illustrated works among them. In 1854 George Bentham (1800-1884) presented his herbarium consisting of about 103,000 sheets of specimens representing between 50,000 and 60,000 species. It needed four railway trucks to bring it from Pontrilas, Herefordshire, to Kew. His library, likewise presented, comprised some 1,200 volumes. In 1858 seven wagon-loads of specimens came to Kew from India House. Many other collections flowed into Kew, and the increasing richness of the Kew collections and the facilities for study there attracted more and more botanists intent on research. All this contrasted with the static conditions prevailing at the British Museum's Botanical Department.

Robert Brown died on 10 June 1858, whereupon the care of the Department of Botany then rested entirely upon J.J. Bennett, who became Keeper. The immediate consequence of Brown's death, undoubtedly anticipated, was a letter of 14 June 1858 sent with unseemly haste to the Lords Commissioners of the Treasury by the Principal Librarian of the British Museum, Antonio Panizzi, stating that the Trustees had been 'induced [a word indicating pressure upon them] to institute an examination into the question whether it may be expedient or otherwise to remove the botanical collection from the Museum as it presents a case in some degree peculiar'. They wished to be supplied with information of the views of the Government as early as possible. The sub-committee appointed to take evidence on the question of moving the Botanical Department from the British Museum met on 16 June 1858 and heard the views of William Hooker, his son J.D. Hooker, and Lindley followed by those of Bennett and Owen and then, on a later occasion, 21 June 1858, those of George Bentham, Arthur Henfrey and Hugh Falconer. The unwonted speed with which all this was put in hand only a few days after Brown's death clearly indicates it had all been well prepared in expectation.

William Hooker was of the opinion that the removal of the botanical collection from Bloomsbury would be expedient for the safety of the collection in as much as it would be removal to a purer atmosphere. Since 1853 great efforts had been made to build up the Kew herbarium and it was by now much more extensive than that of the British Museum; the Museum collections were to a great extent duplicates of those at Kew but contained many of great historic interest; there was scarcely a day when a botanical visitor was not busy consulting the collections which included those of Bentham and Bromfield; his own private herbarium was four to five times more extensive than the public one. J.D. Hooker stated that the herbarium and library at Kew being now so extensive and essential for the garden, 'it is one sense immaterial to us what becomes of the British Museum herbarium'; moreover, 'botanists coming to this country for the purpose of study invariably reside at Kew for the sake of being near the herbarium there; and find it an inconvenience to go into town to consult that of the British Museum'. Bennett stated Brown's 'strong desire that they should remain at the Museum; recently and to the very last'. Lindley considered the transfer to Kew would be of great advantage; the value of the Banksian herbarium was that it contained much authentic material needed for comparison with material in the Kew Herbarium: union of the collections would make comparison easy and save much time. Owen, now Superintendent of the Natural History Departments at the Museum, but himself a zoologist and palaeontologist, was 'of opinion that the botanical collections might be removed to Kew without any material disadvantage to the other great natural history collections now in the Museum. The only disadvantage would arise from the loss of certain specimens of recent botany to illustrate fossil plants'.

George Bentham was then 'of opinion that the removal of the whole of the botanical collection to Kew would not be advantageous to science'. He added, however, that 'supposing Government to carry out as contemplated the plan of providing a suitable building at Kew for the national herbarium, and adding to the present herbarium, Sir W. Hooker's Herbarium and providing a proper staff for the use of that herbarium and library, I think the Banksian Herbarium would be more useful at Kew than at the British Museum'. Questioned about his motive in presenting his valuable herbarium and library to Kew, Bentham said, 'I thought at that time there was no herbarium and library in London sufficiently open for the use of botanists, and I presented them on condition that they should form the nucleus of a national herbarium and botanical library, to be kept up at the expense of Government and open to the free use of botanists'. This implicit criticism of the state of affairs at the British Museum was later stated by William Carruthers to have been based on an erroneous suppostion as contemporary records of the Department as well as the testimony of botanists visiting it showed the collections were fully and freely accessible to botanists and largely used by them. Bentham concluded that 'it appears to me of great consequence that so long as natural history is exhibited to the public in the British Museum a botanical collection should be included in that exhibition'.

Hugh Falconer then gave a long and lucid account of the functions of botanic gardens and herbaria and their relations to one another, based on his experience in India from 1831 to 1855. His views, which were essentially to maintain matters as they were, prevailed. In addition to the botanical establishment at Kew, he said, 'I believe that a separate public herbarium and library in the centre of London, and easily accessible, are so useful and necessary, that it would be in the highest degree inexpedient to do away with them, whatever might be the excellence and richness of the collection at Kew. I would be for having a good public herbarium at both places. For strangers, Kew may be the most convenient, and that most resorted to; but for people living in London, and having business engagements, it is inconveniently distant.'

The Museum Trustees' Sub-Committee on Natural History concluded that it was not desirable to recommend the transfer of the botanical collections from the British Museum to Kew, which could not then provide suitable conditions for their reception: 'The herbaria at Kew, and the library there, are, by far the greatest part of them, private property, and only accessible to the public under certain conditions, there are no buildings belonging to the gardens in which the united collections could be deposited, and no staff sufficient for its care and the arrangement of necessary accessions.'

Lindley, however, was not to be deterred. He organised a memorial addressed on 18 November 1858 to the Chancellor of the Exchequer on 'the arrangement by which the national collections can be best adapted to the twofold object of the advancement of science and its general diffusion among the public'. These included the proposal that the whole of the Kew herbaria became the property of the state, that a permanent building be provided for their accommodation and the British Museum botanical collections be transferred to it. The memorial was signed by Huxley, Bentham, W.H. Harvey, Henfrey, J.S. Henslow, Lindley, G. Busk, W.B. Carpenter and Darwin, all Fellows of the Royal Society except Bentham. Lindley gave it publicity by printing it in the *Gardeners' Chronicle* which he edited.

This and other notices which continued in the *Gardeners' Chronicle* up to December 1859 helped to bring into existence a Parliamentary enquiry in 1860 to which Bennett submitted a long and well-reasoned document of objections to the removal of the botanical collections from the British Museum to Kew. Panizzi and Owen, so often at variance from their scientific colleagues in the Museum, favoured their transfer.

In 1871 the matter came before the Royal Commission on Scientific Instruction and the Advancement of Science more conveniently known as the Devonshire Commission from its chairman William Cavendish (1808-1891), seventh Earl of Devonshire. This Commission on account of its searching review of scientific and technical education in Britain and its practical recommendations, particularly as regards the universities of Oxford and Cambridge, was one of the most influential of the nineteenth century. Bennett had now retired and

William Carruthers (1830-1922), an assistant in the Department since 1859, had been appointed as Keeper only two months before giving evidence to the Commission, which addressed a great range of pertinent questions to its witnesses. These included J.D. Hooker, Bentham, John Ball, Thomas Thomson and Carruthers. They were orally examined in 1871 and submitted detailed supplementary memoranda in 1872 and 1873.

George Bentham, certainly one of the greatest systematic botanists of all time, had had a legal training in his youth — he had been called to the Bar in 1832 and had earlier published an *Outline of the new System of Logic* (1827) — and his statements to the Commission were characteristically judicious, even if not always well-informed, as Carruthers took pains to emphasize. They contain an account of the requisites of a herbarium as valid now as it was then. Among much else he thought it 'very important that there should be two botanical establishments, one in London and the other in Kew, working in harmony together, but for different purposes', 'with unity of plan, both in general arrangements and in matters of detail'. Ball's evidence was very much biased against the British Museum, which he visited only once in twenty-five years, and was later searchingly criticized by Carruthers. Thomson, part-author with J.D. Hooker of the *Flora Indica* (1855), did not consider desirable the maintenance of two collections.

The defence of the autonomy of the Department of Botany rested upon its new Keeper, William Carruthers. He was a tough but kindly lowland Scot from Moffat with an impressive presence, described by a colleague as 'a good fighter' who 'when he had made up his mind that his cause was a just one was very tenacious in maintaining his ground'. He had originally intended to become a Presbyterian clergyman but, when studying at Edinburgh, abandoned an ecclesiastical career for a scientific one, becoming especially interested in geology and palaeontology. He lectured in botany at the New Veterinary College in Edinburgh, then in 1859, on the recommendation of John Hutton Balfour, entered the Department of Botany at the British Museum as Bennett's assistant. He became an experienced palaeontologist. Accordingly, when giving evidence to the Commission, he dealt at length with the necessity of having a good collection of recent plants in association with fossil material: he regarded the limitation of botany to plants now living as 'a grave defect'. In a long, well-argued document, Carruthers concluded that 'in the event, then, of its being resolved to maintain only one great national collection, I would submit that it should not be cut off from the allied biological collections, but should be placed with them in the same building in London. And that, for this end, the collections presented by Mr Bentham to the public, and all that have been added to them by purchase or presentation be removed to London and incorporated with the National Herbarium; and further that the extensive botanical library formed at the national expense at Kew be made, with the Banksian library, the foundation of that National natural history library which will be required for the National Museum of Natural History.' In short, instead of the British Museum collections being transferred to Kew, the Kew collections should be transferred to the British Museum. Personally, Carruthers himself favoured the separate maintenance of the two herbaria and presented reasons which the Devonshire Commission found conclusive when it issued its report in 1874.

Pending the Commission's report, the threat of abolition or crippling hung over the Department of Botany. Owen, who in 1858 would happily have seen the Museum's botanical collections transferred to Kew, now saw the unity of his proposed great national museum of natural history at South Kensington menaced by Kewensian imperialism. He was a venerable and formidable figure in British science, with much influence among non-scientists and his views on Darwinism were more acceptable to the general public, who preferred to have Adam and Eve as their ancestors instead of apes, than were those of J.D. Hooker at Kew and his friends in the Royal Society. The unhappy relations at Kew between the First Commissioner of Works and the Director, J.D. Hooker, provided Owen with the opportunity for an unexpected counter-attack. The Commissioners of Works were responsible to Parliament for the management of the Royal Botanic Gardens, Kew. The First Commisioner of Works from 1869 to 1873 was a solicitor with no scientific knowledge or interest, Acton Smee Ayrton (1816-1886), appointed by Gladstone, Owen's friend. During his tenure of office he made life uncomfortable indeed for Hooker by continual meddling, for the sake of economy, with the running of the gardens. Hooker never knew where Ayrton would next interfere. In 1872, by which time Hooker confessed that his life 'had become utterly detestable', and asked 'what can be more humiliating than two years of wrangling with such a creature'. Ayrton requested Owen to favour him with views on the management of Kew. A leading question was 'whether the sum now spent on the collections, library, and establishment for botany at Kew, might be expended on completing and improving the establishment at Kensington, or be saved'. Owen's report of 16 May 1872 was a clever well-documented attack on Hooker and on the justification for maintaining a herbarium at Kew; coming from Owen it could not be other than astute. His report, which suited Ayrton, went to the House of Commons on 23 July 1872. Hooker, now placed in a difficult and worrying position, replied on 6 August 1872 that he was 'unequivocally opposed' to the transfer of the British Museum collections to Kew. Owen had thus achieved what he had cunningly set out to do.

In its fourth report (1874) the Devonshire Commission recommended 'that the collections at the British Museum be maintained and arranged with special reference to the geographical distribution of plants and to palaeontology; and that the collections at Kew be maintained and arranged with special reference to systematic botany.' The Commission further recommended 'that all collections of recent plants made by Government expeditions be, in the first instance, sent to Kew, to be there worked out and distributed, a set being reserved for the British Museum, and that all collections of fossil plants made by Government expeditions be sent to the British Museum.' Taken as a whole these proposals were later found to be impracticable apart from maintaining the two institutions as separate entities, and were ignored.

This episode had been an embittering experience for the botanists most concerned; the hostility created lasted for many years. It soon became evident in opposing attitudes over the will of Friedrich Martin Joseph Welwitsch (1806-1872), who was born at Maria-Saal near Klagenfurt, Austria. He entered the faculty of medicine of the University of Vienna in 1824, studied botany under Joseph Franz von Jacquin, Nicolaus Thomas Host and Leopold Trattinick, all celebrated botanists, and qualified as a doctor of medicine in 1836. In 1839 he went to Portugal to collect plants for the Unio Itineraria, of Württemberg, founded by Hochstetter and Steudel; the following year he became director of the botanic garden at Ajuba near Lisbon and made numerous collections in Portugal over the next twelve years. A government decree authorizing the despatch of a naturalist to the Portuguese colonies for investigation of their natural products led to the choice of Welwitsch for such a mission. He landed at S. Paulo de Luanda, the capital of Angola, in September 1853. Between then and December 1860, when he began his return voyage to Portugal, his collections far exceeded in number, quality and documentation any hitherto made in tropical Africa. They resulted from numerous arduous and hazardous journeys in biologically virgin territory and included about 3,000 species of plants, most of them then new to science.

Welwitsch found it impossible to identify his plants satisfactorily in Lisbon and decided he must do this elsewhere. He chose London on account of the numerous specimens for comparison and the relevant literature readily available in the British Museum and at Kew, where moreover there were botanists able to help him in his enormous task. He arrived with his material in October 1863, the Portuguese government having arranged to pay his salary. He felt after a time that his specimens did not receive at Kew the special attention that in his opinion they merited — in fact the limited Kew staff could not tackle his material without seriously neglecting other work — and he moved to the British Museum. Despite ill-health he worked incessantly at the collections, but his relations with the Portuguese government worsened and from February 1866 his salary was suspended. In 1870 he prepared to take his material back to Portugal but found he had not enough money for the journey. A long illness ended with his death on 20 October 1872.

Only a few days before this Welwitsch had made a will directing that the first complete set, his study set, of specimens should be offered to the British Museum for purchase, the next three sets should be given to Portugal, other sets should be distributed to Berlin, Geneva, Vienna, Copenhagen, Rio de Janeiro, Carinthia and Kew. He bequeathed to Portugal the whole of his general herbarium, books, instruments and zoological specimens. Evidently towards the end of his life Welwitsch regarded his specimens as his own property. They had, however, all been gathered when he was a paid servant of the Portuguese government, which accordingly held a legal claim to them. On 31 October 1872 the Portuguese government demanded the return to Portugal of all Welwitsch's collections. Welwitsch's executors were William Carruthers, the bookseller Frederick Justen, Georg Schweinfurth in Berlin and W.P. Hiern at Kew. Upon Carruthers and Justen fell the duty, at great pecuniary risk to themselves, of defending Welwitsch's intentions in a lawsuit filed in the name of King Luiz I of Portugal on 31 January 1875. The executors suggested a compromise solution which the Portuguese rejected. The case came before Vice-Chancellor Hall on 22 March 1873. Since Welwitsch's will benefited the British Museum, the Kew authorities supported the Portuguese claim for the return of all his material. The judge suggested that its disposal was a case for compromise and adjourned the matter so that an arrangement could be made. It came before the Court of Chancery on 7 July, 1875, and again the judge suggested a compromise. Carruthers and Justen then proposed that the study set should go to the King of Portugal, that the British Museum should receive the first set of duplicates together with copies of Welwitsch's detailed field notes, the King of Portugal the second set of duplicates and the institutions named by Welwitsch the remaining duplicates, and £1,195 should be paid to the defendants, being a quarter of the salary withheld from Welwitsch. The King's counsel lacked authority to accept this offer. Accordingly decision was further delayed. Agreement had, however, been reached when the case finally came before the Court of Chancery on 17

November 1875. The Vice-Chancellor then decided that the King of Portugal was entitled to all the Welwitsch botanical collections, but it was agreed that the study set and the best set next were to be separated from the rest of the collections and Welwitsch's field notes be copied; then the study set was to go to the King of Portugal, the next best set to the British Museum, and all the others to the King of Portugal; the King was to pay the executors £600. Basically this was the compromise offered originally but it took three years and much expense to reach such a solution. It further embittered the relations between the British Museum's Department of Botany and Kew, which received in the end a poor set of duplicates; others went to Berlin, Geneva and elsewhere.

Paradoxically, out of this unhappy affair came the mutually beneficial co-operation which has existed since then between the Department of Botany and Portuguese institutions concerned with the study of African plants. The division of the Welwitsch collections was entrusted to a competent amateur botanist with adequate private means on the staff neither of Kew, nor the British Museum, William Philip Hiern (1839-1925). He carefully separated the specimens and transcribed the notes, which were in Latin, and began to prepare an annotated catalogue. Then he had to return to Devon to manage his family estate and work on the catalogue lapsed for fifteen years. Ultimately the Trustees of the British Museum persuaded Hiern to return to London and resume work on the catalogue. He finished the account of the dicotyledons; other workers, notably A.B. Rendle, dealt with the monocotyledons, gymnosperms and cryptogams. Volume 1 of the *Catalogue of the African plants collected by Dr Friedrich Welwitsch* was published by the Trustees in four parts between December 1896 and August 1900, volume 2 in two parts between May 1899 and May 1901. It led indirectly to the later *Conspectus Florae Angolensis* (1937 onwards).

Year by year the collections at the British Museum accumulated. The year 1876 is an especially important one in that J.J. Bennett died on 29 February 1876 and bequeathed to the Museum the Australian herbarium of Robert Brown; that year the second set of Welwitsch's African plants became legally Museum property. Next year the Museum purchased the private herbarium of Robert James Shuttleworth (1810-1874). This included more than 170,000 specimens from all parts of the world and enormously enriched the Museum with type specimens. Shuttleworth came of a wealthy Lancashire family but was born in Devon; his mother died a few weeks after his birth and on his father's remarriage he was taken to Switzerland where he spent most of his life. He was educated in Geneva and after studying medicine in Edinburgh, lived from 1834 to 1866 in Bern, Switzerland, where he amassed, by continual purchases of collections and the financial support of collectors, his enormous herbarium; he moved in 1866 on account of ill-health to Hyères, southern France, and he died there in 1874. He subsidized the German collector Friedrich Rugel (1806-1879), who made large collections in Florida, and he acquired the herbarium of Johann Jakob Roemer (1763-1819), but, although he had so many specimens at his disposal and often annotated them critically, his only publication of note is conchological not botanical, *Notitiae Malacologicae* (1856). In 1879 the Museum received by bequest the herbarium of John Miers (1789-1879), an engineer who worked and travelled in South America from 1819 to 1838, at the same time collecting and studying plants, to which he devoted all his available time after returning to England. He was primarily interested in morphology and had a somewhat mechanical outlook as regards taxonomy; this led him to describe a large number of taxa based on minor characters and it is fortunate that his specimens are available for their interpretation.

The promotion of Carruthers to keepership of the Department created a vacancy filled by the appointment in 1871 of James Britten (1846-1924) as an assistant. Britten was born in Chelsea on 3 May 1846, lived for a time in High Wycombe and then in 1869 joined the Kew herbarium staff as an assistant, where he prepared an account of the *Crassulaceae* for Oliver's *Flora of Tropical Africa* 2: 385-401 (1871). He had always a grateful memory of Oliver's kindness during his Kew period but never regretted moving to the Museum under Carruthers, in whose Department a 'happy family feeling' prevailed. 'Coming from Kew where the casual enquirer was officially discouraged', he wrote after Carruther's death, 'I was struck by Carruther's almost excessive readiness to supply information or to answer questions of the most trivial nature'. Through his long service, 1871-1909, and his editorship of the *Journal of Botany* from 1880 to 1924, Britten became its best known staff member. Although according to his colleague for many years, A.B. Rendle, he rarely used a lens and still less a microscope and rarely dissected a flower, he had a good eye and a retentive memory for plants and thus proved a competent herbarium assistant. He was especially interested in the historic side of his work and in nomenclature and continually brought to notice the significance of the older collections in the Museum, giving special attention to those of Banks and Sloane. Thus he produced between 1900 and 1905 three volumes of *Illustrations of the Botany of Captain Cook's Voyages round the World in HMS 'Endeavour' in 1768-71* which made known the drawings by Sydney Parkinson and the descriptions by Daniel Solander which had lain so long ignored in the British Museum. He recorded over many years the collections represented in the 334 volumes of Sloane's *hortus siccus* and, although he never completed his annotated list, it forms the basis of *The Sloane Herbarium* (1958), revised and edited by J.E. Dandy. A cognate activity in association with George Simonds Boulger (1853-1922) was the compilation of their *Biographical Index of deceased British and Irish Botanists* (1893) with supplements in 1899, 1905 and 1908. He and Robert Holland compiled an invaluable *Dictionary of English Plant Names* (1878-1886). His greatest contribution to botany in Britain was however his editorship of the *Journal of Botany* which became so closely associated with the department as to serve in place of an official Museum botanical periodical.

The years 1880 to 1900 were characterized by steady growth, particularly in the acquisition of European, including British, and North American specimens in which Kew, with its Imperial commitments predominant, had officially little interest. Thus in 1880 the Department acquired 2,482 British plants collected by Alfred French (1839-1879), an Oxfordshire baker who became an attendant in the Department from 1874 to 1879. The Director of Kew transferred to the Museum the British herbaria of James Forbes Young (1796-1860), Thomas Moore (1821-1887) and Thomas Knowlton (1691-1781). There were also marked increases in cryptogamic material for which Kew had little or no interest. Thus the Department purchased 1,464 European lichens, together with microscope preparations, from William Joshua (1828-1898) and 300 European algae from A. Le Jolis in 1880, a collection of 1,155 preparations of diatoms made by Eugene O'Meara (c.1815-1880) in 1882, 40,000 British and foreign fungi bequeathed by Christopher Edmund Broome (1812-1886) in 1886, 650 slides of diatoms prepared by Hamilton L. Smith in 1881, 2,383 lichens, presented by Horatio Piggott (1821-1913) and 4,429 microscope preparations made by Anton de Bary (1831-1888) in 1889. The holdings of the Department and Kew continued to diverge both in systematic groups and the geographical areas covered, with comparatively little duplication of material and work; the unhappy relations between Carruthers and Britten on the one hand and Sir William Turner Thiselton-Dyer (1843-1928), the Director of the Royal Botanic Gardens (1885-1905), on the other hand fortunately did not mar the friendly inter-relations and co-operation between their respective staffs.

Carruthers retired as Keeper in 1895 and was succeeded by George Robert Milne Murray (1858-1911), a lowland Scot like Carruthers. He was born and educated in Arbroath, then in 1875 studied cryptogamic botany for a year under the great cryptogamist Anton de Bary (1831-1888) at the refounded German university of Strasbourg. On his return to Britain he became an assistant in the Department of Botany,

64. Excavation of fossil bones by a Museum team in 1964 from clay at Aveley, Essex, which revealed remains of Mammoth *(Mammuthus primigenius)*, Straight-tusked Elephant *(Palaeoloxodon antiquus)* and other Quaternary mammals.

65. Exhibit of bones from Aveley in their original positions embedded in or lying on the clay as excavated.

66. Use of a plankton net from a rubber dinghy to collect larval
    stages of the Ditch Shrimp *(Palaemonetes varians)* at Adur
    estuary near Shoreham, Sussex, in 1979.

67. Taking of sand-cores from the sea-bed, for study of kinds and
    distribution of animals inhabiting sand, off Blacksod Point,
    County Mayo, Eire in July 1980.

68. Excavation in 1979 of Pleistocene cave deposits at Westbury-sub-Mendip, Somerset, which have provided the earliest evidence of man in Britain.

69. Caroline Whitefoord, botanist, and Christopher Lyal, entomologist, in May 1979 at their camp in tropical forest of Toledo district, southern Belize.

70. Collection of insects at night, using a light-sheet, on a Department of Entomology expedition to south-western Africa in 1972.

where he remained until his retirement owing to ill-health in 1905. He was primarily interested in diatoms and other algae, but was associated as a naturalist with several expeditions to the West Indies. In all he published about forty papers on cryptogams and oceanography, most in the *Journal of Botany*.

The thorny question of the relationship between the Department of Botany and Kew was resurrected in 1900 when the Lords Commissioners of H.M. Treasury, apparently believing the existence of two separate botanical institutions in the London area was an unnecessary drain upon the public purse, appointed a committee known as the Committee on Botanical Work 'to consider the present arrangements under which botanical work is done and collections maintained by the British Museum, and under the First Commissioner of Works at Kew respectively; and to report what changes (if any) in those arrangements are necessary or desirable in order to avoid duplication of work and collections at the two Institutions'. Sir Michael Foster (1836-1907), the distinguished Cambridge physiologist, a keen gardener, was appointed chairman and Benjamin Daydon Jackson (1846-1927), the compiler of *Index Kewensis*, secretary. The committee consisted of Lord Avebury and Frederick DuCane Godman, both Trustees of the British Museum, Stephen Edward Spring Rice, Horace Alfred Damer Seymour, Isaac Bayley Balfour, Queen's Botanist for Scotland, Francis Darwin and Sir John Kirk, the East African administrator, who was also a keen naturalist. They met on fourteen occasions, examined eighteen witnesses, considered several documents submitted and produced in March 1901 a detailed quarto report of twenty-four pages with minutes of evidence occupying 108 double-column closely printed pages. This provides a valuable account of the collections, work and financial support of both institutions as they were in 1900; it also indicates, unintentionally, much about the characters and attitudes of the witnesses.

Carruthers, though retired, was called as a witness, but Murray as Keeper officially represented the Department. He stated that its collection consisted of:

A General Herbarium composed as follows:

Flowering plants	975,000 specimens
Cryptogams	513,000 specimens

In all, therefore, about one million and a half

A British Herbarium composed as follows:

Flowering plants	50,000 specimens
Cryptogams	135,000 specimens

The Sloane and other pre-Linnean Herbaria,
   numbering about 90,000 specimens

Fruits in boxes, 11,650 specimens in the general collection;
   12,532 in the Sloane Herbarium;   12,220 wood specimens

1,900 specimens in preservative fluids

52,000 microscope slides

1,853,293 Grand Total

The botanical staff had now risen to two senior or 1st Class Assistants, three junior or 2nd Class Assistants and one temporary assistant.

The main drift of the committee's questioning was to bring out the essential and divergent features of both institutions and to ascertain opinions on the desirability and feasibility of transferring all or part of the Department's material to Kew. The palaeobotanical material at the Natural History Museum was very extensive, at Kew almost non-existent, and the palaeontologists Albert Charles Seward and Henry Woodward looked with grave misgiving upon the possible removal of all the recent plants needed for comparison with their fossil ones. William Botting Hemsley (1843-1924), originally a Kew gardener, who had become Keeper of the Herbarium and Library at Kew in 1899 and had always been on cordial terms with the Natural History Museum botanists, was questioned especially on the consequences of amalgamating the two collections at Kew and how this could be effected. He pointed out that incorporation at the present time was impossible; the herbarium sheets at the British Museum were larger than those at Kew and it would be a pity to cut down the historical British Museum specimens to the Kew size. They would have to be kept in separate cabinets with possibly a new building provided for them at Kew. He considered equally impracticable the suggestion that all the Kew specimens should be remounted on sheets of the British Museum size. Attention was also called to the overcrowding at Kew and the urgent need for additional room and that the herbarium building at Kew was not fire-proof; hence it had no fires and no lighting. The difference in size of the herbarium sheets was a historical accident. Linnaeus, being a poor man when he began his herbarium, used small separate sheets, $12\frac{3}{8}$ in x $8\frac{1}{8}$ in (31.4cm x 20.6cm), for each specimen which enabled him to re-arrange his specimens and to compare them for scientific purposes. Joseph Banks, being a rich man, could afford to buy larger sheets, 17 ½ in x 11 ¼ in (44.5cm x 28.6cm), and the Banksian herbarium thus established the standard size in the British Museum. William Hooker when a young man had a small herbarium cabinet, with compartments for sheets 16 ½ in x 10 ½ in (41.9cm x 26.7cm), made for him in Norwich and this determined the size for the Hookerian herbarium as it grew and hence for the Kew herbarium and the herbaria throughout the British Commonwealth modelled on Kew.

The 1901 report dealt with the history of the British Museum and Kew collections, their relative value, duplication of specimens, the previous enquiries into the advantage or possibility of union from 1850 onwards, notably the Devonshire Commission of which the recommendations had not been carried into effect, the arguments for and against union, the relative convenience of Kew and the Natural History Museum to enquirers and other matters. The majority report recommended that statutory powers should be obtained for the transference of the general herbarium of the British Museum, including the Sloane herbarium and the botanical library, to Kew and that the united herbaria should be subject to an advisory board; it made no recommendation regarding fossil plants. Lord Avebury and Horace Seymour dissented from their six colleagues as to the advisability of creating a new advisory board since there already existed a body well fitted for this function, the Trustees of the British Museum. Avebury regretted that he could not agree with his colleagues in their recommendation that the herbarium then in the British Museum should be transferred to Kew. He stated: 'The British Museum is the greatest museum in the world and is justly the pride of the nation. To dismember it, by depriving it of so integral a part as the Botanical Department would be destructive of its unique character as a fully representative museum, and especially of a natural history museum: would be vehemently opposed by many, if not most British botanists, and as it seems to me, would be a great injury to science.' His fellow Trustees took the same view. They declined to promote any legislation for dismembering the Museum. Thus the only result of all that discussion and giving of evidence was an informative Government publication of 248 pages, to which nobody paid any effective attention.

Thereafter the Department of Botany and Kew continued essentially as they had done before, with little overlap of activity, until 1961 when at the instigation of the Treasury an agreement was reached formally defining their respective areas geographically and taxonomically (p.309).

After Murray's retirement in 1905, Alfred Barton Rendle (1865-1938) became Keeper of Botany in 1906 and remained in office

until 1930. He had studied natural sciences at Cambridge and joined
the Department of Botany as an Assistant in 1888, taking the place of
Ridley. His herbarium duties were mostly the care of the
monocotyledons but his interests embraced the phanerogams as a
whole and led to the publication of his standard work *The Classification
of Flowering Plants* with volume 1 on the gymnosperms and
monocotyledons published in 1904, but volume 2 on the dicotyledons
not published until 1925. While Director of Public Gardens and
Plantations in Jamaica from 1886 to 1908, William Fawcett gave much
attention to promoting the botanical exploration of that floristically rich
island, especially the collecting of its orchids, and on one of his return
visits to the Natural History Museum he and Rendle agreed to
collaborate in a monograph of the Jamaican orchids. The work
proceeded slowly until 1908 when Fawcett, having retired from
Jamaica, gave it his full attention at the Museum. He and Rendle then
decided to make their orchid work the first volume of a complete *Flora of
Jamaica*. This was published in December 1910. It is the only Flora
which starts with the most highly evolved family of petaloid
monocotyledons, the *Orchidaceae.* Volume 3 appeared in 1914, volume 4
in 1920, and volume 5 in 1926. Fawcett died in 1926, but Spencer Le
Marchant Moore (1851-1931) took over the account of *Rubiaceae* and
Compositae and Volume 7, which contained these, appeared in 1936,
leaving volumes 2 and 6 yet to be prepared. At the time of its inception
this work, much influenced by Urban's *Symbolae Antillanae,* was the
most scholarly of British Colonial Floras.

'The Kew tradition as to nomenclature has always been lax' Britten
wrote in the *Journal of Botany* in 1893, and so continued until in the 1920s
it aroused the interest of one of the most able and scholarly of Kew
botanists, Thomas Archibald Sprague (1877-1958). On the other hand
it deeply interested Britten as a bibliophile and 'botanical antiquarian',
together with his colleagues, notably Rendle whose work had made him
well known by 1904 as a distinguished taxonomist. The Trustees
accordingly sent Rendle as their representative to the International
Botanical Congress at Vienna in 1905 to put forward amendments to
the Paris code of botanical nomenclature, a matter from which Kew
under Thiselton-Dyer held itself aloof. He was made a Vice-President
of the Nomenclature Committee and with J. Briquet, Ch. Flahault and
H. Harms was responsible for editing the very important *International
Rules of Botanical Nomenclature* (1906) adopted by the Congress.

Rendle was a steady dependable hard-working botanist under whose
direction the Department grew and its activities widened. The removal
by the Trustees of the threat of incorporation with Kew under
Thiselton-Dyer and his retirement in 1905 cleared away the main cause

of friction between the Department and Kew. Thiselton-Dyer was followed as Director by the much-liked David Prain (1857-1944), a Scot whose rise from poverty to botanical eminence and in 1912 a Knighthood, by way of the Indian Medical Service and the Royal Botanic Garden, Calcutta, would have gratified Samuel Smiles (1812-1904), the author of *Self-Help*. Thereafter, relations between the two institutions passed from hostility to harmonious co-operation. Rendle's staff in 1911 consisted of two 1st Class Assistants: Antony Gepp (1862-1955), an algologist who had joined the Department in 1886, and Edmund Gilbert Baker (1864-1941), who had joined in 1887 and specialized in Malvaceae and Leguminosae, later bequeathing the Baker Fund to the Department. There were three 2nd Class Assistants: Herbert Fuller Wernham (1879-1941), who had joined in 1909, John Ramsbottom (1885-1974), a mycologist who had joined in 1910, and Alfred James Wilmott (1888-1950), who joined in 1911 and had charge of European plants. All of these gave loyal service to the Department and distinguished service to botany.

Britten retired officially in 1909 but he continued to frequent the Department and edit the *Journal of Botany* until the day before his death on 8 October 1924 at the age of seventy-eight. The Principal Trustees appointed Herbert Fuller Wernham (1879-1941) to succeed him in December 1909. Wernham's career is one of botanical triumph and personal tragedy. He had a creative period of little more than ten years; his services as an assistant in the Department lasted from November 1909 to December 1921. During those years he became internationally known as a specialist on tropical Rubiaceae, revised eight genera, described 13 new genera and 467 new species, and produced a major general work, *Floral Evolution, with particular Reference to the sympetalous Dicotyledons* (1913) reprinted from the *New Phytologist* vols 10 (1911) and 11 (1912). From 1903 to 1909 he worked in the General Post Office, London but gained the degree of BSc from the University of London in 1908, obviously through intense evening study. He overworked himself in the Department and had a nervous breakdown in 1913, joined the Army early in 1915 but was discharged on medical grounds in May 1916; personal deterioration associated with alcoholism caused his compulsory resignation from the Museum in 1921. He lived until 20 September 1941 but never did any more botany. The quality as well as the quantity of Wernham's publications from 1910 to 1921 manifest both high taxonomic ability and astonishing industry and it is sad that his span of useful activity which brought so much credit to the Department was cut short so drastically.

In May 1911 Alfred James Wilmott (1888-1950) came to the Department from Cambridge, where he had been associated with Charles

Edward Moss (1870-1930) in work on the new *Cambridge British Flora.*
Rendle had decided to keep Continental European and British vascular
plants in two special herbaria for convenient reference separate from
the main herbarium and the whole of Wilmott's career, as stated by
Iolo A. Williams in *Proceedings of the Linnean Society* 162 (1949-50):
234-236 (1951), was devoted to the building up and organisation of
these British and Continental herbaria. Wilmott was a botanical
philosopher abounding in ideas for complicated, labour-intensive
methods for doing everything and he became so devoted to the
elaboration of method as to achieve little else; hence his relatively few
publications mostly in the *Journal of Botany* do little justice to his fine
logical intellect, his outstanding knowledge of the European flora and
his industry in the herbarium and nothing, of course, to his prowess as a
table tennis player. The last explains how he came to possess such a
quantity of table tennis balls that the Museum bought them from him
to construct models of molecular structure.

Wilmott made a useful contribution to biological nomenclatural
methodology by coining the now internationally used term
'protologue' to cover all the printed matter (i.e. diagnosis, description,
comments, illustration etc.) accompanying the original publication of a
name or epithet but slipped it so unobtrusively into a paper on British
Sorbi in *Journal of Botany* 77: 206 (July 1939) that it escaped notice until
adopted in my *Introduction to the Species Plantarum* 126 (1957). His close
friendship over many years with Charles Carmichael Lacaita
(1853-1933) resulted in the latter's herbarium, especially rich in Italian
and Spanish plants, coming to the Museum. Both Wilmott and Lacaita
were robust characters with volatile temperaments and contemporary
accounts testify as to the vigour of their exchanges on botanical matters.
It may be no coincidence that both of them met sudden ends through
cardiac arrests.

Over the years many unidentified specimens had accumulated in the
Department. For example, Henry Ogg Forbes (1851-1932), the author
of *Naturalist's Wanderings in the Eastern Archipelago* (1885), had made
extensive collections in 1878 to 1883 in the Dutch East Indies, mostly
Java and Sumatra, and in 1885 and 1886 in New Guinea, in all about
4,650 specimens, which the British Museum bought in 1879 to 1889.
When Rendle became Keeper, they mostly awaited classification and
naming; indeed, they waited until 1924 to 1926 for their enumeration
as a supplement to the *Journal of Botany* vols 62 to 64. Rendle set himself
and his staff the task of dealing with these arrears. They came mostly
from areas where botany was still in a pioneer stage and contained
many species new to science, but the Department then lacked the
experienced specialists to identify and describe them quickly.

The plants collected by Welwitsch in Angola had given the Department an interest in the plants of tropical Africa which for a long period had been almost a Kew monopoly. Rendle collaborated with J.G. Baker in the account of *Convolvulaceae* for the *Flora of Tropical Africa* 4. ii: 62-206 (1905-1906) produced at Kew. From 1890 onwards Richard Frank Rand (1856-1937), medical officer to the British South Africa Company which colonized Mashonaland and Rhodesia under Rhodes's direction, made large collections there which he presented between 1898 and 1902 to the Department. Later Percy Amaury Talbot (1877-1945), a district officer in Nigeria, together with his wife Dorothy (1871-1916), gave the Department a large collection of plants they had gathered in the Oban district of Southern Nigeria between 1909 and 1912. Over the years the Department had acquired by gift and purchase much African material, but these later collections, unrepresented at Kew and from botanically little known areas, provided a special stimulus to research.

Rendle and his assistants, Edmund Gilbert Baker (1864-1949), H.F. Wernham, Antony Gepp (1862-1955) and John Ramsbottom (1885-1974), together with voluntary helpers, notably Spencer Moore (1851-1931) and Annie Lorrain Smith (1854-1937), immediately began work on the Talbot collection. It contained a remarkable number of apparently undescribed species which were published in Rendle and others, *Catalogue of the Plants collected by Mr & Mrs P.A. Talbot in the Oban District, South Nigeria* (April 1913). Thus the Department came to play a significant part in the investigation of the African flora. The outbreak of World War I interrupted such work. Edmund Baker retired in 1924 having had charge of the earlier families (1-66) in the Bentham and Hooker classification, according to which the herbaria both at Kew and the Department were arranged. Arthur Wallis Exell (b. 1901) was appointed to succeed him.

Exell had worked on mycological problems in Cambridge with Frederick Tom Brooks (1881-1952). He had no experience whatever then about the taxonomy of tropical African flowering plants. However, from 1903 onwards, the Department had been receiving excellent well-annotated specimens collected in Angola by John Gossweiler (1873-1952), a Swiss horticulturist in the employ of the Portuguese government as his predecessor Welwitsch had been; Rendle accordingly set Exell to work on a systematic list of the Polypetalae in the Gossweiler collection. Another set of Gossweiler's specimens had gone to Coimbra, but there too they had remained virtually unworked. The first part of Exell's enumeration was published as a supplement to the *Journal of Botany* vol. 64 (1926). Publication of further parts continued until its completion in vol. 74

(1936), with George Taylor, Ronald D. Good, Spencer Moore and Cecil Norman elaborating various families. Exell made his first direct acquaintance with tropical African vegetation in 1932 on an expedition with the entomologist W.H.T. Tams to the islands of Sao Tomé and Principe in the Gulf of Guinea. On the way there, they visited Coimbra and became acquainted with Luiz Wittnich Carisso, the professor of botany, who had led a botanical mission to Angola in 1927. Carisso had planned an enumeration of the plants of Angola. As Welwitsch had found, this could not be done wholly in Portugal; outside the country the Natural History Museum, where so much work had recently been done on the Gossweiler collections by Exell and others, offered the best facilities. John Ramsbottom, who was Keeper from 1930 to 1951, cordially welcomed Carisso's plan, offered the assistance of his staff and was rewarded with an honorary doctorate from Coimbra in 1938. Accordingly, Exell visited Coimbra in 1934 and acquainted himself with the work already done. The Anglo-Portuguese botanical collaboration resulted in the publication in 1937 of the first part of the *Conspectus Florae Angolensis*. Exell's work was justly recognized in 1962 by an honorary doctorate from Coimbra.

Ramsbottom had a keen scholarly interest in the history of botany, particularly mycology, his own special field, and held the presidency of the Society for the Bibliography of Natural History from 1944 to 1972. His most important publications are a *Handbook of Larger British Fungi* (1923) and *Mushrooms and Toadstools* (1953). Ramsbottom is also remembered for his presidential addresses to the British Mycological Society, the Essex Field Club and the Linnean Society of London. Notable events of his keepership include Anglo-Portuguese botanical co-operation, the association with the Department of Frank Ludlow (1885-1972) and George Sherriff (1898-1967), who enriched it with their immense collections from south-eastern Tibet and Bhutan, the avoidable and much regretted cessation of the *Journal of Botany*, World War II (p.306) and the beginning of post-war reconstruction.

Frank Ludlow, after graduating at Cambridge, went out to India and became Vice-Principal of the Sind College at Karachi, then Inspector of European Schools, a post which led to his being invited to Gyantse, Tibet, in 1923 to open a school. His hobbies for many years were ornithology and shooting; he became expert with a catapult for collecting birds where shooting was forbidden. When on an expedition to Chinese Turkistan in 1929 he met George Sherriff, an army officer, at Kashgar and there began a close friendship and collaboration which lasted up to Sherriff's death in 1967. They made their first plant-collecting expedition in 1933 when they visited central Bhutan. This was so successful that they planned a series of expeditions to survey botanically and ornithologically Bhutan and south-eastern Tibet. These were in 1934, 1936, 1937, 1938, 1942, 1943, 1944, 1945, 1946, 1948, 1949 and 1950, of which details will be found in H.R. Fletcher's *A Quest for Flowers* (1975) and *Bulletin of the British Museum (Natural History)* Botany 5: 243-268 (1976). George Taylor from the Department of Botany joined them on their 1938 expedition. From their travels, largely financed by Sherriff, the Department received over 21,000 gatherings made in areas hitherto virtually unknown. These included many new species and provided valuable information about the Sino-Himalayan flora between Sikkim and Yunnan.

The pre- and immediate post-war period was also notable for the association of the Department with Frank Kingdon-Ward (1885-1958), the well-known explorer and plant collector. Kingdon-Ward, who devoted his life to the botanical exploration of the eastern Himalaya and South-Eastern Tibet, published numerous books in which he described his travels in these little known regions. He introduced many important new plants to British gardens and, with the exception of a few very early collections which are at the Botany School, Cambridge, and the Royal Botanic Garden, Edinburgh, his specimens, including vouchers for his introductions, are preserved in the Department.

In 1927, through the good offices of Sir Clive Wigram and at the instigation of Thomas Hay who wanted new plants for the Royal Gardens and George Taylor who wanted herbarium material for the Natural History Museum, the Nepal government commissioned an officer, Lall Dhwoj, in the Nepal Army to collect seeds and dried specimens. These specimens, presented by the Maharajah of Nepal to King George V, were sent to the Natural History Museum on permanent loan. They supplemented the old but important collection made in Nepal by Francis Buchanan (later Hamilton) in 1802 and 1803. Nepal, apart from the valley of Kathmandu and its eastern and western border regions, had hitherto been almost unknown botanically European access being prohibited for political reasons, and this material was thus most welcome at the Museum. Such a land of varied topography extending some 500 miles (800 km) along the Great Himalayan Range could not be other than rich in a great diversity of species, now estimated as about 6,500 species of flowering plants. These collections by Dhwoj and Khadanad Sharma of 1927 to 1933 initiated the modern period of botanical exploration in Nepal by revealing a little of its floristic richness and thereby providing the stimulus for a succession of expeditions from 1949 onwards under the auspices of the Natural History Museum.

From March to October 1952 an expedition to central Nepal was mounted jointly by the Museum and the Royal Horticultural Society, under the leadership of L.H. John Williams of the Department of Botany with Oleg Polunin and William Sykes. They collected between 15,000 ft (4,570m) and 20,000 ft (610m) in an area previously unvisited by Europeans and gathered 5,300 herbarium specimens which came to the Museum in December 1952. The expedition cost £3,700. Such expeditions and others, notably those under the auspices of the University of Tokyo, have now changed Nepal from being botanically the least known Himalayan region into one of the best known. They have resulted, surprisingly but successfully, in a joint Anglo-Japanese botanical project, *An Enumeration of the Flowering Plants of Nepal* (1978 onwards) by Hara, Stearn, Williams, and Chater, with the assistance of numerous specialists, published by the Museum.

The Department of Botany from its arrival in 1880 onwards occupied the second floor of the east wing of the Museum. The first part of the gallery contained the public exhibition galleries with exhibits almost unchanged since installed by Carruthers in 1880; then came the general herbarium, its wooden cases crowded with specimens; and at the far end (now occupied by the mineralogical library) was the botanical library. The west wing displayed rows of bleached mammalian skeletons. Two incendiary bombs and an oil bomb shattering the roof and setting the Department ablaze on the night of 9 September 1940 changed all this for ever. Many important specimens and costly books had been evacuated in 1939 but a good working herbarium contains much besides type specimens and can indeed serve botany without any. The damage inflicted, though it would have been much greater but for the fire fighters, was grievous; some parts were totally burned, others charred and many damaged inevitably by the water jetted against the flames (p.147). Everything remaining was then evacuated to Tring, where the process of drying out material took a long time; an emergency often leaking roof of galvanized iron was put over the derelict gallery; derelict, gloomy and dirty it remained until 1955. The west wing then became temporarily and in the end permanently the home of the Department. This damage placed a heavy burden upon Ramsbottom, who had also many calls upon him for his expert knowledge of dry rot and moulds, notably *Penicillium*, and upon his limited staff.

In 1945 members of the staff on war service began to return and almost all were back by June 1946, but not until the end of 1948 were all the needed cabinets, some 200 to replace those destroyed or damaged beyond repair, installed in the west wing henceforth to house the general herbarium. Meanwhile valuable collections such as the herbarium of the apothecary John Blackstone (1712-1753) and those of Patrick Martin Hall (1894-1941) and Thomas Petch (1870-1948), and the Ludlow-Sherriff material, came into the Department's possession. Edmund Gilbert Baker, who had been an assistant in the Department from 1887 to 1924, died on 17 December 1949. He was the only son of the Kew botanist John Gilbert Baker (1834-1920); he never married and had no close relatives. He bequeathed to the Museum the sum of £5,000, the income from which the Keeper of Botany was to use for staff visits to continental herbaria or for botanical collecting expeditions. This Baker Fund has proved a valuable asset to the work of the Department.

Wilmott died suddenly on 27 January 1950, creating a vacancy later filled by the appointment of Alexsandr Melderis, a Latvian botanist who, as a war refugee, was then working in Sweden. Exell, who had been transferred to the Foreign Office during the war, was recalled to the Museum in March 1950. Ramsbottom, having reached the age of sixty-five, retired in October; George Taylor then became Keeper and Exell Deputy Keeper. The appointment of the one led to a special interest for the Department in the Himalayan flora, by supporting and organizing expeditions (p.305), and of the other to renewed interest in the tropical African flora, leading in 1954 to plans for a *Flora Zambesiaca*, to cover Zimbabwe, Zambia, Malawi, Mozambique and Botswana.

Meanwhile, returned herbarium material and later acquisitions had been dumped in boxes in the east wing, which still had a leaking emergency roof and was still very grimy, pending their incorporation in the main herbarium. They were found, however, to be infested with herbarium beetle. The disinfestation of some 5,000 boxes containing 250,000 specimens before they could be transferred to the west wing presented a major problem, solved by the economic entomologist Alfred McKenny-Hughes (p.218) and L.H. John Williams from the Department. McKenny-Hughes recommended dipping every specimen in a solution of 3.25 lauryl penta chlor phenate in 50.50 xylol and white spirit; Williams devised a practical method of doing this. Thus it was possible by 1955 to clear the old east wing herbarium in preparation for its rebuilding. The Trustees had decided in January 1954 that all accommodation on the second floor west of the east tower should go to the Department of Botany. A survey of the east wing led Taylor to suggest in June 1954 the insertion of a mezzanine floor, thanks to the solid construction of Waterhouse's building, which would almost double the space available and permit an exhibition gallery and laboratory to be placed above a cryptogamic herbarium. Plans for the reconstruction, making use of this excellent proposal, received approval in January 1955, the work itself to begin in August 1955 and to be completed in two years, a special grant of £10,000 for the exhibits to be spread over three years being provided. The building was completed in June 1958 and by then much work had been done in planning the exhibits for the new gallery.

The planning of the gallery was entrusted to John Francis Michael Cannon (b. 1930), who joined the Department staff in 1952. When studying at the University of Durham he had worked in the Department as a vacation student, an act of enterprise which had made evident his capabilities and potentialities for appointment; he became Keeper in 1977. As Cannon stated in an article in *Curator* 5: 26-35 (1962) 'the old gallery was a monument of botanical erudition, but its austere and academic approach would not have made much appeal to the museum visitor of today. In addition its restricted scope and age left many subjects of great interest and importance untouched'. There had accordingly to be a new approach untrammeled by any past exhibits, its subject matter extending across the whole field of botany but giving special attention to aspects of particular current interest, e.g., ecology, palynology and cytology, at a level of information within the grasp of a six-form pupil at a British secondary school. Models, drawings and backgrounds had to be not only scientifically accurate which meant that almost all had to be based directly on first-hand information, i.e., the objects themselves or photographs, but also aesthetically pleasing. The design and preparation of the exhibits were undertaken by H.R. Allen and his staff of Preview, a small firm specialising in modelling work for architects and museums under the close supervision of Cannon with the co-operation of other members of the Department. The gallery, although not large, was the first within the Museum to be planned as a whole since the war, with definite principles and aims governing its detail. Her Majesty Elizabeth the Queen Mother, herself a keen botanist and horticulturist, opened the gallery on 31 October 1962.

Taylor, whose managerial dynamism had contributed so effectively to the post-war reconstruction of the Department, left before its completion to become Director of the Royal Botanic Gardens, Kew, on 1 October 1956. He was succeeded as Keeper by James Edgar Dandy (1903-1976) who had come to the Department from Kew in 1925. At Kew he had been assistant to John Hutchinson (1884-1972), then elaborating his new system of classification for the families of flowering plants and his assignment of the families Magnoliaceae, Saxifragaceae and Loasaceae to Dandy provided him with life-long interest, to which, as subjects for special study, the pondweeds and other aquatic plants, petaloid monocotyledons, Watsonian vice-counties, the Sloane Herbarium, plants of the Sudan, West Indies and the British Isles, early generic names and, above all, botanical nomenclature were later added. Few botanists of modern times have possessed such a wide and profound taxonomic knowledge of vascular plants, and have placed it so generously at the disposal of all who wanted it, so that the Department became a kind of nomenclatural court of appeal. Unfortunately, with his own standards so high and his criticism of unscholarly, illogical or inadequate work so cutting and sarcastic, despite his basic geniality and kindness, Dandy became almost morbidly reluctant to publish his own continually revised manuscripts. He edited the Botany series of the Museum's own *Bulletin* with meticulous care and he early became involved, unobtrusively and effectively, with looking over manuscript accounts of genera for the *Flora Europaea* and purging them of nomenclatural errors. The *Flora Europaea* (1964-1980), through Dandy's keen interest, which continued after his retirement in 1966, was closely associated with the Department. For this project the rich European herbarium and the comprehensive general and botanical libraries of the Museum proved invaluable to botanists outside the Museum, on whom responsibility for the major part of the work rested.

The year 1960 brought another enquiry instigated by the Treasury on the relations between Kew and the Department, aimed to prevent duplication of effort and wastage of resources, but regarded at the Natural History Museum as yet another attempt to enhance Kew at the expense of the Museum by placing it under Kew control. For many years relations between the two institutions had been harmonious, co-operative and non-competitive, with little or no duplication of effort, though spiced with some friendly academic rivalry, but they lacked bureaucratic formality. After resistance by the Museum's Director to Kew control of part of the Museum, it was proposed that the Director of Kew should be responsible for the gardens under the Ministry of Agriculture and the Trustees of the British Museum responsible for the taxonomic work in the Kew Herbarium and the Department of Botany. Since interest and knowledge of the garden staff and the scientific staff at Kew in each other's work and collections had been often rather remote, this was not an unreasonable suggestion: indeed, Lord Avebury had proposed in 1900 that Kew should be administered by the Trustees. In 1960 the Trustees had quite enough responsibility on their hands and the proposal was dropped. Instead there resulted in 1961 the formal Morton Agreement (taking its name from Sir Wilfred Morton, the chairman) for division of accession and research activities. This stated:

(a) The division of responsibility in respect of vascular plants (including Pteridophyta but excluding Gymnospermae) shall be on a geographical basis:—

British Museum	Kew
Europe	Asia

British Museum	Kew
North West Africa from the Atlantic Islands to Tunisia; S. Tomé and other W. African Islands, excluding Fernando Po; Angola North and Central America West Indies Arctic and Antarctic	Rest of Africa (including Madagascar and Mascarene Islands) South America Australasia (including Polynesia)

(b) The division of responsibility in respect of the remainder of the Plant Kingdom shall be by systematic groups as follows:—

British Museum	Kew
Algae (including Charophyta and Diatomae)	Fungi
Lichens	Gymnospermae
Bryophyta (Musci and Hepaticae)	

A further statement emphasizes that:

'By this means duplication in taxonomic research, in the curation of botanical collections and in the acquisition of specimens was avoided. Broadly it was agreed that the Royal Botanic Gardens, Kew, would be responsible for enquiries and investigations on the vascular plants of Asia, South America, Australia and the Islands of the Pacific, and most of Africa, and, with few exceptions, would incorporate specimens from those regions into its herbarium collections. The Museum would deal similarly with the vascular plants of Europe, North West Africa, North America, Costa Rica and the West Indies, and the Arctic and Antarctic regions. In addition, it was decided that the Museum should be responsible for taxonomic work and enquiries on Bryophyta, Algae, and Lichens, and the Royal Botanic Gardens, Kew should be responsible for Fungi, Gymnospermae, Orchidaceae and Gramineae.'

The Morton agreement resulted in the transfer by 1969 of the Kew specimens of Bryophyta, Algae and Lichens to the Department and of the Department's specimens of Fungi to Kew, such specimens being regarded for legal purposes as being on permanent loan. Although bound to accept this arrangement, neither institution has looked upon it as wholly satisfactory, but it has been interpreted flexibly so as to make the best use of the staff and facilities in both institutions as with the Department continuing research on the flora of Nepal and the Zambesi area. It has nevertheless provided a useful formal basis on which the building up of the national collections can continue without wasteful overlapping of facilities and effort, and against this background the correlation of activities and fraternal cooperation have developed very smoothly. The Department staff had always been allotted the charge of systematic groups whereas the Kew staff had always been allotted the charge of all systematic groups from certain main geographical areas in accordance with the concept of Kew as a British Empire botanical clearing house. The Kew staff changed in 1970 from a geographical to a systematic division of labour and the Morton Agreement then became less meaningful for Kew.

Dandy retired in 1966 and was succeeded as Keeper by Robert Ross (b. 1912) who, retiring in 1977, was succeeded by John F.M. Cannon (b. 1930). The years from 1960 onwards have been ones of steady progress in acquiring and incorporating collections and publishing systematic work based upon them. Publications associated with the Department, in addition to the *Flora Europaea* and *Conspectus Florae Angolensis* mentioned above, include the *Flora Zambesiaca* (1960 onwards) and *An Enumeration of the Flowering Plants of Nepal* (1978 onwards) while a number of monographic papers on *Allium, Epilobium, Buchenavia, Capartogramma, Elaphoglossom, Myrsinaceae, Columea, Oplonia, Hypericum, Argyranthemum, Chisocheton* and other groups have been published in the *Bulletin of the British Museum (Natural History)* Botany. A new departure in floristic work was a botanical survey of the island of Mull, Argyllshire, begun in 1966 and completed in 1970. This was in part a response to the specific responsibility for the British flora allocated to the Department through the Morton Agreement. Mull, off the west coast of Scotland, is a rugged island, the largest of the Inner Hebrides, with an area of 450 square miles (116,550 hectares) and great topographical and geological diversity affording widely divergent habitats for plants. The survey covered not only flowering plants and ferns but also mosses, lichens, fungi and marine and freshwater algae. It yielded much interesting scientific material, including many new records with among them unexpected extensions of range, and provided training in the field for junior members of the Department's staff. In all they found about 5,280 species and varieties in over 1,600 genera. The results were published in 1978 in a volume of 656 pages, *The Island of Mull: a Survey of the Environment and Vegetation*, edited by C. Jermy and J.A. Crabbe.

The Morton agreement in leaving within the Museum's orbit the majority of the cryptogams recognized the long tradition of scholarship the Museum had with these more primitive groups of plants. Indeed because the Museum lacked the imperial commitments of Kew with the vascular plants of colonial territories, the Department began in the second half of the nineteenth century to give much greater attention to cryptogams, at first by enlisting the services of amateur specialists, then by the appointment of staff members to deal with particular groups. Thus it has come to have an exceptionally large cryptogamic component. William Carruthers (1830-1922), who joined the Department as an assistant in 1859, contributed in 1864 an account of *Diatomaceae* to J.E. Gray's *Handbook of British Water-weeds*, a return for Gray, then Keeper of Zoology, to the cryptogamic studies of his youth. When Keeper, Carruthers employed a fellow Scot, the Rev. James Morrison Crombie (1830-1906), to prepare *A Monograph of the British Lichens, being a descriptive Catalogue of the Species in the Herbarium.* Crombie published Part 1 in 1894. Annie Lorrain Smith (1854-1937), also a Scot and an amateur, edited Crombie's manuscript Part 2 (1911) and then in 1918 and 1926 published a second edition of the two parts. She was an unofficial worker or 'Acting Assistant' in the Department from 1889 to 1933. Her book, *Lichens*, for the Cambridge Botanical Handbooks has become a classic. The first official lichenologist, Ivan Mackenzie Lamb (b. 1911) worked in the Department from 1935 to 1946, apart from absence during the 1939-1945 World War. Alan Henry Norkett (b. 1914), employed from 1933 to 1975 did much curatorial work on the lichen collection during this period. In 1955 Peter Wilfrid James (b. 1930) was appointed as lichenologist. The lichen herbarium was founded mainly on Crombie's collection and that of Churchill Babington. It was notably enriched by the purchase from the Linnean Society of London in 1963 of the collection of Erik Acharius (1757-1819), the founder of lichenology. In 1969 the Kew lichen herbarium was transferred to the Department on permanent loan. Thus the Department's lichen herbarium now contains nearly 300,000 species, probably the largest and richest in the world.

The study of Algae in the Museum likewise began in the nineteenth century. The Keeper of Manuscripts, Frederick Madden, coming to the Department in May 1847 with his children to look at specimens of seaweed was disgusted and angry to find the Department then had no collection. However, J.E. Gray's wife Emma, commemorated in the algal genus *Grayemma*, was deeply interested in seaweeds and by January 1886, when Antony Gepp (1862-1955), after graduating from Cambridge, was appointed as an assistant in charge of cryptogams, such a collection had been formed. George R.M. Murray, also a Scot, produced, with A.W. Bennett in 1889, a *Handbook of Cryptogamic Botany* followed in 1895 by an *Introduction to the Study of Seaweeds.* Gepp's main interest was in marine Algae as was that of Ethel Sarel Barton (1864-1922), an unoffical worker in the Department. After their marriage in about 1900, he and she produced significant publications on a wide range of Algae. Gepp continued to work in the Museum until within a short time of his death at the age of ninety-three, occasioned by a fall down Museum stairs. Geoffrey Tandy (b. 1900) joined the Department as a cryptogamist in January 1926 and worked principally on tropical and subtropical marine Algae. Sometimes confused, through close similarity of name, he and J.E. Dandy made known to the botanical world that they were different individuals by a joint paper 'On the identity of *Syringodium* Kütz' in the *Journal of Botany* 77: 114-116 (1939). Tandy achieved a dual reputation; he was known in the British Broadcasting Company as a great botanist and in the Department of Botany as a great broadcaster. He joined the Navy early in the 1939-1945 World War and never returned to botany afterwards. In 1953 the University of Birmingham presented the algal herbarium of E.M.M. Holmes and in 1969 the Kew collection came on permanent loan.

The diatom collection formed part of the Algae section until the appointment of Robert Ross in October 1936 to take charge of it, but material had been accumulating since 1856 when a British series had been purchased from William Smith (1808-1857), author of a *Synopsis of British Diatomaceae* (2 vols, 1853-1857). In 1868 the Museum bought the collection formed by the German algologist Friedrich Traugott Kützing (1807-1893). Thereafter collections from Gregory, Greville, Ralfs, Rylands, Roper, O'Meara, Deby, Comber, Wynne Baker, F.W. Payne, Adam, Barker, and Wise were acquired by purchase or bequest.

Bryophytes came under the general care of the cryptogamic staff such as Antony Gepp and Alan Henry Norkett, who finally devoted all his time to them. In 1957 Dunkery Hugh Dalby was appointed to take charge, an appointment which can be taken as establishing an independent section. The collection of bryophytes is probably the most comprehensive and important in the world and includes the herbaria of H.N. Dixon, W. Wilson and many other prominent workers.

Work in the Museum's mycological collection began with the cataloguing of specimens by Arthur Lister (1830-1908), a retired wine merchant, who took up the study of Myxomycetes, at the age of fifty-seven, in 1887 and produced in 1894 for the Museum *A Monograph of the Myxomycetes* with the help of his daughter Gulielma Lister (1860-1949). He was President of the British Mycological Society in 1906, she in 1912 and 1932. Gulielma produced a second edition of her father's work in 1911 and a third edition in 1926. Both were unofficial workers. The first staff member to work exclusively on the mycological collections was Vernon Herbert Blackman (1872-1967) employed from 1896 to 1906, when he resigned to become professor of botany at Leeds. John Ramsbottom (1885-1974) joined the Museum staff in 1910 and worked at mycology until his appointment as Keeper in 1930. Frances Lottie Stephens (later Mrs Balfour-Browne) was an unofficial worker on fungi from 1929 to 1936, when she joined the staff; she retired in 1967 and the mycological collections (apart from Myxomycetes) were transferred to Kew in 1969 and 1976.

The fern collections at the Museum received a remarkable increase through the purchase of the personal herbarium of John Smith (1798-1888), the Scottish gardener, who was from 1842 to 1864 Curator of the Royal Botanic Gardens, Kew and author of *Historia Filicum* (1875), and that of Carl Frederick Albert Christensen (1872-1942), the celebrated Danish pteridologist, compiler of the *Index Filicum* (1905-1906). In 1930 Arthur Hugh Garfit Alston (1902-1958) joined the staff to take charge of vascular cryptogams. After graduating at Oxford in 1924 he joined the Kew staff, then from 1925 to 1930 was keeper of the herbarium at the Botanic Gardens, Peradeniya, Sri Lanka (Ceylon), then from 1930 to his suicide in 1958 on the Department staff, serving from 1939 to 1945 in the Ministry of Home Security. Alston acquired a remarkably wide knowledge of tropical floras which made him a most valuable helper in allocating newly arrived and undetermined tropical specimens to their families and genera. He collected avidly in Sri Lanka during his service there, in northern South America, Indonesia and Europe, gathering in all nearly 20,000 specimens. His major interest was in the genus *Selaginella*, on which he published many papers, but his wider interest in ferns and fern-allies gave the Department an international reputation as a centre of pteridological research. He published five new genera and 187 new species. From 1937 to 1949 he edited the *British Fern Gazette.*

During the last two decades, a policy has gradually evolved which is aimed at ensuring the continued importance of the outstanding collections and library facilities, through a controlled introduction of new specialisations and techniques. Thus, the development of extensive research programmes using transmission and scanning electron microscopy has been especially significant. This has been particularly important for the study of diatoms, a group of minute Algae with very complex siliceous structures. Electron microscopy has also been of special significance for the Palynology Section which was formed to secure the Department's role in the developing study of pollen grains; this is shedding much new light on relationships between plant groups. Similarly, the Department has taken a lead in the use of computers for plant identification and the testing of some taxonometric programmes. When it became obvious that computers would play an increasing rôle in the handling of information, the appointment of a specialist to undertake research in computer identification soon followed. Techniques developed include the direct 'on-line' use of computers, together with their indirect use for the development and production of keys, both traditional and in the form of multi-access punched-card packs. The possiblity of automated plant description writing from data matrices containing standardised character codings is also being investigated. As the relative cost and size of electronic equipment is reduced, these opportunities will be of increasing importance for the biologist. The establishment of the Cytology Section is another instance of the introduction of more recent laboratory-based research in support of the traditional processes of taxonomy. Chromosomes often provide direct evidence of the course of evolution, which is invaluable, especially at the level of relationships between species. Finally, the study of fine-structure and histochemistry is shedding important light on the reproductive processes of plants, essential information for an eventual comprehensive understanding of plant relationships. In the days of Robert Brown, first Keeper of Botany, it was still possible for one man, admittedly in his case a botanical superman, to encompass the whole field of botany. Today, an increasingly high degree of specialization is necessary to ensure even a proper coverage of systematics and the immediately related fields.

To some it may seem that today's botanists are becoming increasingly remote from the plants they study. This however is quite untrue, and the Department places strong emphasis on the direct study of living plants through fieldwork and the culture of plants both at Chelsea Physic Garden and, for microscopic organisms, in the laboratories.

The earlier sections of this chapter have dwelt at length on the often acrimonious relationship between the Museum and the Royal Botanic Gardens, Kew. Today, when botanists are more conscious of the enormity of the task that still confronts them, close friendly cooperation is in everyone's best interests; with so much work waiting to be undertaken there is no place for petty jealousies. Nowadays the Keepers of the National herbaria meet annually, the Museum Keeper of Botany and the Keeper of the Herbarium at Kew being joined by the Director of the Royal Botanic Garden, Edinburgh, the third national institution which shares with the Museum and Kew a responsibility for systematic botany. At these meetings full information is exchanged about present and future programmes, collecting expeditions and other activities. This eliminates any possible conflict of interests, and opportunities for participation in projects based at each of the three institutions are explored. Much of the old rivalry may have been at a high level, while the ordinary botanists got on amicably with their studies. However, it is good to be able to conclude with this picture of positive and constructive collaboration at all levels.

Fig. 28. Indian Laburnum, Golden-shower Senna or Purging Cassia, *Cassia fistula,* a beautiful tree of India, Burma and Sri Lanka, with yellow flowers and long pods with laxative properties, as portrayed on the panelled ceiling of the Museum's main hall.

17

Department of
Library Services

T HE VITAL CONNECTION between books and specimens for research and information purposes in a natural history museum is not generally realized, and hence some explanation seems relevant. Both are needed for the identification and classification of organisms past and present, as also of minerals, which are major functions of the Natural History Museum.

Since the eighteenth century the number of known organisms has far exceeded the capacity of any one generation of available naturalists to describe and name them. Thus the first published description of an organism may long remain the only source of information about it. For systematic botany, zoology, palaeontology and mineralogy, the work of past generations as recorded in books, journals and pamphlets has a relevance and utility rare or unknown in other disciplines. For example, in chemistry a good textbook may make its predecessors obsolete and may itself be superseded by another within a few years. Standard monographs and revisions of complex groups of plants and animals slowly become out of date on account of discoveries made and new material accumulated since their preparation. Their replacement, however, may necessitate so much painstaking and time-consuming toil that many years may pass before a dedicated research worker tackles again the task of revision. Hence such works, especially if well illustrated, often have a long period of use. Moreover, to ascertain the correct use of a scientific name, reference must often be made to the first published description of an organism concerned. Lack of access to such descriptions, scattered as they are through a wide range of literature, is a severe handicap to taxonomic research in many countries without comprehensive libraries of long standing.

Taxonomists, particularly those concerned with the naming of European plants and animals, often need to consult scientific literature earlier than 1753 and 1758, the respective years of publication of Carl Linnaeus's *Species Plantarum* and *Systema Naturae* (10th edition) which are the internationally agreed starting points of modern botanical and zoological nomenclature. They also need to keep in touch with the latest literature in their own special fields, often spread through a wide range of journals. Linnaeus by the time of his death in 1778 had given names to roughly 4,000 species of animals and 7,100 species of flowering plants and vascular cryptogams. The latest general estimates put the number of known recent species in the animal kingdom at about 1,239,800 and in the vegetable kingdom at about 384,600, together with about 300,000 fossil species of plants and animals; new organisms, both living and fossil, are continually being described. Research workers must consult their descriptions in order not to give unnecessary new names to organisms already named and also not to use the same name for different organisms.

Lacking a good library, a natural history museum is like an arm without a hand. The Department of Library Services of the British Museum (Natural History) provides a coverage of relevant international literature unrivalled elsewhere, even though its far from complacent staff are ever conscious of deficiencies and seek to remedy them. The periodical list alone extends to about 17,600 serials, of which about 8,000 are in current publication. The complete catalogue of the Museum's holdings includes about 1,500,000 entries. It is in the interest of the whole international scientific community to maintain this superb reference collection; gifts of books, pamphlets and journals are as appreciated and useful now as they have been in the past, possibly more so, since the vast modern output of literature makes ignorance of relevant material all too easy. The present library holdings were not acquired without difficulty, their presence in the Natural History Museum is due to the zeal, persistence and diligence of a succession of librarians, well supported by the Trustees.

Whilst still in the British Museum at Bloomsbury, each scientific branch had its own library of working books in close proximity to the specimens and the scientific staff could also use the resources of the Main Library, including the Banksian Library transferred to the British Museum on the acquisition of Sir Joseph Banks's herbarium to which it was a necessary accompaniment. Charles Konig (Keeper of the Natural History Department) explained to the Select Committee of Enquiry in 1836 the increasing need to purchase books specifically for the Natural History Department. It was not, however, until 1845 that the Trustees first agreed to set aside regular grants for book purchase. The Mineralogy and Geology branch was granted £25 per annum, commencing in 1845, while Zoology and Botany received the same annual grant in 1847 and 1848 respectively. The large and comprehensive departmental libraries of today have grown from these humble beginnings.

The transfer to South Kensington in 1880 cut the scientific staff off from the general repository of books in the Main Library of the British Museum. The disadvantages of this had long been foreseen. The Trustees of the British Museum in 1880 called attention to the statement of the Select Committee of the House of Commons in their report of 10 August 1860 that 'should the Natural History collections be removed, the purchase of a special and comprehensive library for study and reference would become indispensable and that the formation of such a library would cost £30,000'. The estimate of cost naturally increased with time. Sixteen years later the departmental Keepers assessed the cost of the necessary natural history books for the Zoological Library at £40,000, for the Botanical Library at £15,000, the Mineralogical Library at £1,500 and the Geological Library at £2,000. Apparently they overlooked the need for a General Library.

The essential linkage of specimens and literature was by no means evident to high officials. In January 1877 and December 1878 the Lords Commissioners of the Treasury declined to make any provision for natural history libraries. However in January 1879, with most of the new building at South Kensington erected, their Lordships expressed the hope that the means of gradually forming such libraries at South Kensington might be forthcoming in future years; presumably they would have told a builder with a house half-built that bricks might gradually be forthcoming in future years. Albert Günther, the Keeper of Zoology, had stated that upwards of 10,000 volumes were constantly required in his very active department for reference in addition to those always kept in the departmental library. The Trustees in 1880 accordingly regretted that the formation of a library adequate for the requirements of the Natural History Museum was not begun earlier, Her Majesty's Government having failed to act upon their earlier representations. The Keeper of Printed Books at Bloomsbury, George Bullen (1816-1894) reported that the Main Library contained many duplicates of natural history books which could be transferred to South Kensington without injury to the general library. In practice this meant that if a natural history book existed, as many did, in both a coloured and an uncoloured state, the uncoloured one went to South Kensington and the coloured one, which would have been of greater use to naturalists, stayed at Bloomsbury. The Trustees then directed the

Principal Librarian, Sir Edward A. Bond (1815-1898), to apply to the Treasury for a grant of £5,000 to purchase books for the Natural History Museum during the ensuing financial year and to state that the same sum would be applied for yearly. In March 1880 Bond accordingly drafted for submission by the Trustees to their Lordships of the Treasury a memorandum which, in its cogent exposition of the need for adequate library facilities in a natural history museum, remains as true today as when written:

'My Lords,

1. The Trustees of the British Museum, being in daily expectation of receiving over the new building erected at South Kensington for the Natural History collections under their charge, have again taken into their most anxious consideration the conditions under which the removal of the collections from their present repository will be effected.

2. They feel themselves responsible not only for careful transference of the specimens but for their safe custody, arrangement, and future administration, in the building prepared for them.

3. Foremost among the difficulties that confront them in respect to administration is one which directly affects both the further formation and the practical use of the collections.

4. The final necessity for the work of classifying the specimens, and fixing the position of each in scientific order, is the command of books and treatises in which their exact character is determined.

5. Without free and ready access to such books the performance of the first and most essential duties of the staff must be utterly inefficient. Books are to them the tools by which they are enabled to select the novel or important objects from the host of specimens offered for purchase, to judge of their monetary or intrinsic value, to determine their names, to arrange them in systematic order, and to ascertain the extent and nature of desiderata, and the sources whence they can be obtained.

6. These are only the more immediate uses for which books are necessary, but unless the library be made efficient, scientific work within the establishment will be greatly impeded, if not brought to a standstill. The preparation of the descriptive catalogues, which are the means of making the contents of the Museum and the result of the labour done in it generally known, which form some of the principal elements in the development of the collections, and which have proved the greatest use in the colonies for the investigation of their natural products would have to be discontinued. And finally the large class of workers engaged in the

study of the various branches of the collections could no more be supplied with the books essential for their special line of enquiry except at such a distance from the specimens to be determined as would render it impossible to recognise the character described. This necessary supply of books has hitherto been found in the Museum General Library; but must now be sought elsewhere. The small collection of works which each department has for special use needs to be supplemented from a more general library comprising other technical works and also the Transactions of Academies and Learned Societies, scientific periodicals, books of travels, voyages, and illustrated works, often very costly.

7. The total number of works possessed by the Departments amounts to about 4,000 with a certain number of pamphlets and separate memoirs. And no great addition will be made by duplicates obtained from the general library since books cannot be withdrawn from the Royal, the Banksian, the Cracherode and Grenville collections.

8. The library difficulty was foreseen at the earliest time of a contemplated separation of the British Museum collections. In their Report of 1860 (Ordered to be printed, 10th August, 1860) the Select Committee of the House of Commons on the British Museum pointed out (p.xiii) the necessity of furnishing the Natural History departments with a sufficient library after their removal, and estimated (p. v) the cost at £30,000. More recently, the closer calculations of Keepers of Departments have shown that for the purpose of the collections not less than £58,000 ought to be provided for the purchase of books.

9. So long ago as December 1876 it was represented to Your Lordships (Mr Winter Jones to Treasury, 16 December, 1876) that if the Natural History collections were to be removed, provision to about this amount for a library would be necessary, and more than one application has been made for some instalment of it.

10. In a letter dated 27th January, 1879 (Treasury letter: 1063/79) the Trustees were informed by Mr William Law, that Your Lordships were unable at that time to make the required provision, but "hoped that the means of gradually forming libraries of reference at South Kensington might be forthcoming in future years".

11. Since then, the only contributions towards the whole amount required have been the two sums of £1,000 and about £2,500 out of savings on the general Museum votes for 1878-79, 1879-80, together with the value represented by a comparatively small

selection of duplicate works from the General Library. (Treasury
Letters: (1) 14 February 1879, Minerals-Botany: (2) 27 February
1880, 3726/80, Natural History generally).

12. At this moment, therefore, of expected commencement of the
removal of the collections, the Trustees find themselves
unprovided with the means of furnishing the Natural History
Museum with such a library as they consider indispensable, and
they are compelled to renew their request for the provision of
funds for this purpose.

13. The books required could not be suddenly procured, nor
would it be advisable to make purchases to a very large amount
within a short time.

14. The Trustees therefore propose that a sum of not less than
Five Thousand Pounds (£5,000) should be allowed annually for
the gradual formation of the library, commencing with the
financial year 1880-81; and not to cease until the library has been
brought to a state fully answering the required conditions.'

Unable to counter such considerations the Lords of the Treasury
authorized on 10 July 1880 expenditure of not more than £5,000 a year
for five years from 1881 onwards for the formation of a natural history
library; they also authorized expenditure on this of any savings out of
the 1880-81 voted allowance, since they would not provide any other
money during the current financial year. The Trustees accordingly
ordered that preference should be given to purchases of books needed
for the present work of departments and that they should be made
through joint agreement.

It was the desire of Sir Joseph Banks when he bequeathed his superb
natural history library to the British Museum in 1820 that it should
remain associated with his herbarium bequeathed at the same time, but
unfortunately the Law Officers of the Crown in 1882 opposed the
transfer of the Banksian Library from Bloomsbury to South
Kensington along with the Banksian herbarium and some of its
furniture. This legal difficulty could have been overcome then by Act of
Parliament but there was no one of Panizzi's forcefulness and status at
South Kensington to promote it. In consequence there remain virtually
unknown and rarely if ever consulted at Bloomsbury in the British
Library the only available copies in Britain of many important natural
history works; indeed of one work it has the only known surviving copy
in the world.

When the collections had been moved to South Kensington, there
was clearly a need for a General Library. This library was formed to
house works on subjects common to two or more of the departments,
such as journals, transactions and proceedings of many learned

societies, academies and universities, biographical, topographical and travel books, maps, etc, as well as material relevant to general science and biology. The departmental libraries at that time consisted of those for Mineralogy, Geology, Botany and Zoology. Until 1913 the Entomology books and journals formed part of the Zoology Library collection. After that date however they became a separate library gaining independence in 1936. In 1956 the Department of Geology became the Department of Palaeontology. The only other libraries to be formed in recent years are the library of the Sub-Department of Anthropology and the Library of the Sub-Department of Ornithology at Tring. The former was created in 1959 to serve the newly founded Sub-Department. Its collections were made up of material drawn from the Zoology, General and Palaeontology Libraries and from the outset until 1963 it was administered by the General Library, then the Palaeontology Library assumed responsibility. In 1971 the Museum's Bird Room collections, together with the Ornithological Library were transferred to a new purpose-built building adjoining the Zoological Museum at Tring, Hertfordshire. The Tring Library, supplemented by the large and valuable collection of ornithological books and journals held in the Rothschild Library there, is now probably the most comprehensive ornithological library in this country. The Department and Sub-Department libraries contain material relating exclusively to their special fields, plus useful general works such as atlases and dictionaries. They may be sub-divided for working convenience and in accordance with the objective of placing the literature as close to the working scientist as possible. The Departmental Libraries have always enjoyed a considerable degree of autonomy. Prior to 1946 they were responsible for arranging their own purchases and keeping their own accounts. They also undertook most of their own cataloguing. In 1946, however, the Trustees decided to centralize cataloguing, book purchases, accounts and book-binding programmes within the General Library.

A good library deserves a good librarian. In October 1881 the Trustees appointed Bernard Barham Woodward (1853-1930) as Assistant in Charge of the General Library, which was at first governed by a committee of the four Keepers of departments, William Carruthers (Botany), Alfred Günther (Zoology), Henry B. Woodward (Geology) and Lazarus Fletcher (Mineralogy). In 1884 the new Director of the Museum, William Henry Flower, took over its control. B. B. Woodward had worked in the Department of Printed Books at Bloomsbury since 1875 and he proved a very efficient librarian at South Kensington, keenly interested in the building up of the library and in bibliographical investigation. In this he was much helped by the antiquarian bookseller Frederick (Friedrich) Justen (1832-1906), proprietor of Messrs Dulau & Co., whose interest in the Museum libraries extended far beyond financial considerations and who was himself a generous donor. He was born in Bonn, Germany, but came to England at an early age, as did another enterprising and ambitious young German antiquarian bookseller, Bernard Quaritch, from whose firm the Natural History Museum also acquired important works. Justen's connexions in the second-hand book trade ranged all over Europe; he not only sought diligently for long runs of major journals and works but took much trouble in obtaining rare and obscure minor works, including pamphlets, which migh be useful to the Museum. Together with the Keeper of Botany, W. Carruthers, he became an executor of the botanist Friedrich M.F. Welwitsch (1806-1872) and was thereby involved in a long and worrying lawsuit with the King of Portugal on behalf of the Natural History Museum (p.293). For his services to botany William Philip Hiern named the genus *Justenia* of the family Rubiaceae in his honour.

Charles Davies Sherborn (1861-1942), the great natural history bibliographer, also did much to aid the growth of the Museum libraries. Sherborn, never officially a member of the Natural History Museum staff although long supported by the Trustees, spent much of his life in the libraries, especially when compiling his monumental *Index Animalium* (1902-1933). He began work on this in July 1890 by compiling a list of all the books and periodicals in every European language from 1758 to 1800 likely to contain descriptions of new genera or species of living or extinct animals, which was later printed in his *Index Animalium* sectio prima. That task, which occupied him for a year, gave him an unrivalled first-hand knowledge of zoological and geological literature as well as of the Museum's deficiencies, which Woodward, Justen and he sought zealously to remedy. About 2,000 volumes, according to J.R. Norman, obtained by his efforts passed on to the Museum Library shelves, 'not all of equal rarity but sufficiently so to evade the search of F. Justen'. Often he had to buy a rare book out of his own pocket for fear of its going elsewhere and then had to persuade the Museum to buy it. 'Many were the tussles he had with the successive Keepers of Zoology and Geology . . . His very persistence generally gained him his end, and if a Keeper proved adamant he would go away in high dudgeon, grumble for a day or two, and then present the book in his own name'. After what Sherborn described as 'the churlish action of the Royal Society' in refusing a grant towards the cost of printing his *Bibliography of the Foraminifera* (1888), because he had written 'a savage criticism of a foreigner', Justen informed Sherborn that he would publish it himself without seeing it and he did so. Little wonder that Sherborn wrote many years later: 'Justen was a great and true friend . . . He had the most extraordinary knowledge of natural history literature, and was a dear and amiable man'. To both Justen and Sherborn, users of the Museum libraries often owe much more than they can ever know.

By February 1888 the libraries within the Museum had grown so much as to be adequately representative of the whole of literature on natural history. Woodward accordingly began to prepare for publication a general catalogue arranged alphabetically by authors and places (for publications of corporate bodies) incorporating much bibliographic information. The first volume of the *Catalogue of Books, Manuscripts, Maps and Drawings in the British Museum (Natural History)* appeared in 1903, the second in 1904, the third in 1910, the fourth in 1913, the fifth in 1915 with a supplementary sixth volume in 1922, the seventh in 1933 and the eighth in 1940. As stated by F.C. Sawyer in *Bulletin of the British Museum (Natural History)* Historical Series, 4: 82 (1971), 'the proof sheets, besides being checked by the compiler, were sent to another member of the staff for examination. Whether by accident or thoughtful design the man selected by the Keepers was Professor F. Jeffery Bell, a zoologist known to be on unfriendly terms with the Librarian and who delighted in picking up any errors or omissions in the catalogue.' This source of tediously gained pleasure for Bell must have been galling for Woodward, whose standards of accuracy were certainly high, but paradoxically it heightened the value and repute of Woodward's work.

A by-product of the work of cataloguing was investigation into the dates of publication of major works issued in parts, and the information gained was incorporated in the catalogue. According to the international rules of nomenclature for botany and zoology, when two or more names have been given to the same organism the first published name to which there is no legitimate objection must be adopted as the correct name for the organism concerned. The precise dating of such names has thus a practical importance. Fortunately, while the catalogue was in preparation, Sherborn had cause to make numerous bibliographical enquiries for his *Index Animalium* and he generously gave Woodward much unpublished information. The two also collaborated in a number of papers in the *Annals and Magazine of Natural History, Journal of Botany, Proceedings of the Malacological Society* and *Proceedings of the Zoological Society*, giving the evidence for their conclusions. As a result the *Catalogue* became immediately a valuable bibliographical tool throughout the world for taxonomists, librarians and booksellers who could never visit the Museum itself.

B.B. Woodward served the Trustees until he retired in 1921. He should not be confused with his cousin Horace Bolingbroke Woodward (1848-1914), the celebrated geologist. According to Sherborn, H.B. Woodward was nicknamed the 'Humble Bee' in the Museum but B.B. Woodward was called ''Canary'' on account of his hair, but later in life was known as ''Bumble Bee'' because of his burly, bustling habit and his quarrelsome nature. . . These two names fitted each man exactly'.

Basil Harrington Soulsby (1864-1933) succeeded B.B. Woodward and had charge of the General Library until his retirement in 1930. He continued work on the supplementary volumes of the *Catalogue* but his most important contribution to the library was the formation of a remarkably comprehensive collection of works by or relating to the Swedish naturalist Carl Linnaeus (1707-1778). Every summer he visited Scandinavian and other continental libraries and bookshops and, being a man of private means, spent nearly £1,100 out of his own pocket towards the enrichment of the collection. His zeal culminated in the posthumous *Catalogue of the Works of Linnaeus*, second edition, published by the Trustees of the British Museum in 1933. It has been the policy of the Museum to increase this collection by continual additions and it now forms one of the finest collections of Linnaeana in the world.

Fig. 29. Basil Harrington Soulsby (1864-1933), Museum Librarian 1920-1930 (from *Svenska Dagbladet*, 2 September 1924).

Soulsby's successor as librarian was Alexander Cockburn Townsend (1905-1964), a genial urbane classical scholar with a wide knowledge of modern languages and, in particular, of French literature. He served from 1930 until his tragic death in a railway accident on the last day of 1964. During his tenure as Librarian the regular inflow of books and periodicals continued, interrupted only by the 1939-1945 World War and its aftermath.

Although the Trustees of the Museum agreed to centralise acquisitions, cataloguing, book-binding and library finance in 1946, Townsend's efforts to obtain administrative control of the departmental libraries and their staffs were unsuccessful.

The growing congestion in the General Library consequent on its makeshift accommodation, a state which had existed since 1880 because no part of the new building in South Kensington had been allotted for libraries, became a matter of concern to him. Urgent requests for adequate space were largely satisfied in 1958, when a new library was built in the North Block, with a spacious reading room and map room, a distinct contrast to the old corridor and basement book-stores which had served as the General Library since 1880. However, it was not until 1973, with the building of the North East Block library extension that all the book stock from outlying stores of the General Library could be brought together into their correct sequence with spacious, elegant and secure accommodation provided for the more valuable materials.

Townsend was succeeded in 1965 by Maldwyn Jones Rowlands (b. 1918), a professional librarian with a wealth of experience gained in three national scientific libraries, including periods as both Assistant and Deputy Librarian (1954-61) in the Natural History Museum.

The expansion in library services, acquisitions and staff has continued. In October 1975 a major change in library organisation occurred when the Trustees of the Museum, on the recommendation of a Library Survey Group which had been requested to examine the organization of the Museum libraries, decided to centralise the administration and control of all the libraries and to form the Department of Library Services. The Museum Librarian was henceforth officially designated Head of Library Services. The major objective, however, of keeping the relevant literature as close as possible to the working scientist was unaltered by these administrative changes. The close relationship between all the libraries in the Department and the Museum's scientific staff is of mutual benefit.

The continued expansion of the General Library accommodation has already been referred to; to this must be added the opening in 1973 of a new Zoology Library, while the Palaeontology Library moved to purpose-built premises in the new East Wing in 1977.

The making public of the library collections continued with the publication, for the first time, of a *List of Serial Publications held in the British Museum (Natural History) Libraries* in 1968; a 3rd edition was issued in 1980 (3 volumes). The *Bulletin of the British Museum (Natural History),* Historical Series, which has shown a substantial expansion in recent years, is edited within the Department of Library Services, which also provides editorial advice for Museum monographs in historical fields. As a consequence of the ever-growing collections of early and original material in the Museum's care, an archivist was appointed in 1973.

The original c.5,000 volumes brought to South Kensington from Bloomsbury now forms part of a library collection consisting of some 750,000 volumes of books, periodicals, pamphlets and reprints, 70,000 maps, and an extensive collection of original material.

Over the years the Museum libraries have been enriched not only by judicious purchases and exchanges of publications but also by numerous much appreciated gifts and bequests. In many instances they have served to create the fine collections of manuscripts and originals drawings. One of the earliest acquisitions of such material was in 1827 as part of the Banksian Collections (p.22). This included, among much else, the drawings and manuscripts of Georg Dionysius Ehret (1708-1770); the water colour drawings and pencil sketches of Sydney Parkinson (d. 1771) of plants made on James Cook's first voyage of circumnavigation as well as those by Johann Georg Adam Forster (1754-1794) and John Webber (1752-1793) from the second and third Cook voyages respectively. Also received in the Museum as part of the Banks collection were the zoological drawings of Parkinson, Forster and William W. Ellis (d. 1785) originating from the three Cook voyages. Franz Andreas Bauer (1758-1840), regarded by many as the finest botanical draughtsman of all time was employed by Banks in drawing plants at Kew Gardens. In 1841 Queen Victoria presented an extensive series of his drawings. Two years later the Lords Commissioners of the Admiralty presented the drawings by Franz's brother Ferdinand Lucas Bauer (1760-1826) made during the voyage of the *Investigator* (1801-1803). The Banksian library also provided a number of drawings of fossils including those of plants and fish from the Eocene rocks of Monte Balca (Italy).

In 1835 Thomas Hardwicke (1755-1835) bequeathed his drawings of Asiatic zoology whilst in 1859 the Museum purchased over 2,500 water colour drawings for *English Botany* by James Sowerby (1757-1822). The water colour drawings of Indian fossils by Hugh Falconer (1808-1865) were presented by his executor in 1867. In 1886 the Museum obtained

71. Professor Carl Frederick Abel Pantin (1899-1967), Chairman of Trustees 1963-1967.

72. East wing completed in 1975 and occupied by Department of Palaeontology in 1976-1977.

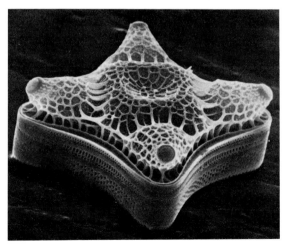

73. A marine diatom *(Triceratium pentacrinus)* photographed at × 520 magnification with the scanning electron microscope.

74. A thrips from sugar beet *(Hercinothrips femoralis)* female, photographed at × 115 magnification with the scanning electron microscope.

75. Aerial view of the Museums area of South Kensington, showing the Natural History Museum towers in line with the tower of the former Imperial Institute, the Albert Hall dome and the Albert Memorial. By courtesy of Aerofilms Ltd., 1976.

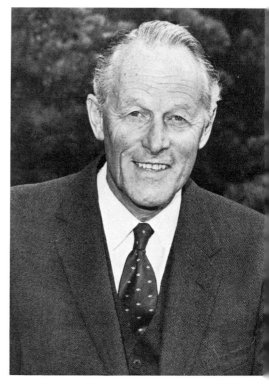

76. Sir Gavin Rylands de Beer
    (1899-1972), Director 1950-1960.

77. Sir Terence Charles Morrison-Scott
    (b.1908), Director 1960-1968.

78. Sir Gordon Frank Claringbull
    (b.1911), Director 1968-1976.

79. Dr. Ronald Henderson Hedley
    (b.1928), Director, appointed 1976.

by purchase the water-colours and pencil sketches made by Thomas Baines, (1825-1871) the explorer during an expedition to Mashonaland, Southern Africa.

A most important accession was the magnificent ornithological library formed by the ninth Marquess of Tweeddale (1824-1878) containing 698 works in 2,560 volumes, together with about 200 pamphlets, donated in 1887 by his nephew and heir R.G. Wardlaw Ramsay. At the same time Colonel Wardlaw Ramsay presented Lord Tweeddale's collection of Asiatic birds, comprising 20,186 specimens.

The libraries have been no less fortunate in their acquisitions in the twentieth century. In 1902 drawings by Thomas Watling (b. 1762) of natives, animals and plants from the neighbourhood of Port Jackson, Australia, were purchased. Sixty years later a presentation by Miss Eva Godman provided seventy-two water-colour drawings of scenery and natural history of New South Wales, Norfolk Island, etc made by George Raper (d. 1797) a Midshipman on H.M.S. *Sirius*.

The sixth Baron Walsingham (1843-1919) (p.212) made a gift of his superb collection of microlepidoptera and also his extensive entomological library which included the water-colour drawings of Jean Baptiste Godart (1775-1825) and M.P.A.J. Duponchel (1774-1846) for the *Histoire naturelle des Lépidoptères de France* (1820-1842) and 370 sheets of 2,709 water-colour drawings for *De Uitlandsche Kapellen* (1775, 1779-1782) by Pieter Cramer (d. 1779). In 1922 J.L. Murray presented the rich library of oceanographic and zoological works formed by his father Sir John Murray (1841-1914), editor of *Scientific Reports* resulting from the *Challenger* voyage of 1873-1876. Among the original material is a collection of sketches and outline drawings of invertebrate animals dated 1840-41 by Sir Joseph Dalton Hooker (1817-1911). In 1925 as part of the R.W. Lloyd Bequest the drawings, plates and manuscripts representing the work of Jacob Hübner (1761-1826) were received. In the same year Joan Gideon Loten's (1710-1789) collection of coloured drawings by P.C. de Bevere of birds, mammals, insects and plants of Sri Lanka and the Malay Archipelago was purchased.

In 1933 the executors of Sir Richard Owen presented an extensive series of his manuscripts and a large collection of original drawings on zoological subjects (see 'A catalogue of the Richard Owen collection of Palaeontological and Zoological drawings in the British Museum (Natural History)' by J.M. Ingles and F.C. Sawyer *Bulletin of the British Museum (Natural History)* Historical series 6: 109-197, 1979).

Surpassing in munificence all of the other donations was the bequest in 1937 by the second Baron Rothschild (1868-1937) of the Rothschild Zoological Museum at Tring, with its specimens, manuscripts, paintings, drawings (including 770 original water-colours which illustrated *British Entomology* (1824-1839) by John Curtis and associated library of some 30,000 volumes, many in fine bindings.

In 1964 the manuscripts and original water-colour drawings of *Specimens of British Minerals*, etc (1797) by Philip Rashleigh (1729-1811) were received as part of the collection bequeathed by Sir Arthur Russell.

Of the manuscript collections likely to be of special interest to historians of natural history as relatively unstudied sources are the correspondence of Albert Günther (1830-1914) with naturalists of many countries from 1850-1914, acquired from his grandson, A.E. Gunther in 1969 and subsequently; also correspondence of the Sowerby family of artists and botanists, geologists, mineralogists, entomologists, zoologists and antiquaries, comprising some 2,500 letters mostly dating before 1850, purchased also in 1969.

The General and Botany Libraries hold a large and growing collection of material relating to Sir Joseph Banks (1743-1820). It comprises original manuscripts and copies of material held in collections throughout the world. This important archive is a major source of reference for the historian of science and for those interested in the history of Australia.

More detailed information on the main collections may be found in Frederick C. Sawyer's 'A short history of the libraries and list of manuscripts and original drawings in the British Museum (Natural History)' in the *Bulletin of the British Museum (Natural History)* Historical series, 4: 79-204, 1971.

Not surprisingly the greatest use of the libraries is made by the scientific staff of the Museum, indeed the primary aim of the libraries is to act as 'the working libraries of the scientific staff'. However the libraries receive many visitors, some 15,000 a year, from all over the world. Research workers visiting the Museum's scientific departments also make extensive use of not only the collections of specimens but also of the resources of the Library Department. The libraries have also long been used by the various indexing and abstracting services, a particularly lengthy association existing with the *Zoological Record*. This is a most fitting liaison considering the wealth of the library collections and the importance of this indexing service to taxonomic research.

The Department of Library Services, through its fine and comprehensive collections, serves as both a national and an international reference centre for all of those undertaking taxonomic research.

Part V

An Era of Change and Independence 1950-1980

BY
A.P. COLEMAN
AND
H.W. BALL

18

Prelude to Change

DURING THE DECADE following the end of the 1939-1945 World War, the Museum was largely pre-occupied with picking up the pieces, both literally and metaphorically. Man-power, materials and money were all scarce. There was a serious shortage of accommodation through studies, storerooms and galleries being war-damaged and unusable, and these were only slowly repaired and refurbished. There was also a lack of storage cabinets; well into the 1950s parts of the collections had not been unpacked from their evacuation boxes. The staff complement, still at pre-war level, was further strained by the demands of national service. Nevertheless, the staff struggled to make the fullest use of the resources available to them in the preparation of exhibits for the rehabilitated galleries and to respond to the renewed use of the collections by scientific visitors.

A similar hiatus had occurred with the 1914-1918 World War. During the nineteenth century the British Museum built up an unrivalled collection and its staff, leaders in their various fields of study, enjoyed high international repute. This high tide in the Museum's reputation persisted into the first decade of the twentieth century, despite the proliferation of other museums, research institutes and universities that had begun in the later years of the Victorian era. However, after the 1914-1918 World War the heroic age of natural history, in which the Museum had played a significant part, was over. New sciences and disciplines began to appear; experimental studies became more fashionable, and there was a move from the museum into the laboratory and field. Not least, there was a hitherto unprecedented supply of well qualified and university-trained scientists who found these new fields for investigation much more exciting than traditional taxonomy. Moreover, although still a major institution, the Museum was now one among many competing, with varying degrees of success depending upon their resources, for natural history collections. It maintained its reputation for scholarliness, accuracy and objectivity, but through its traditional role as a centre for taxonomic research, it was not so responsive to changes in scientific fashions and attitudes as some younger and more overtly vigorous institutions.

The aftermath of the Second World War prompted more wide-reaching and profound changes than that of the First. Many young people, often after war service, attended universities and technical colleges, and there was a marked broadening in educational methods and outlook. From these factors emerged pressures which later impelled the Museum to undertake a more active educational role. The 'Festival of Britain' held in 1951 made the general public no less than the professional exhibitor aware of the impact and stimulus of the new and exciting display techniques introduced in it. Most far-reaching of all, television entered into more and more homes, and subtly combined education and entertainment, which had indeed long been an aim though not always an achievement of Museum policy; both archaeology and natural history became the subjects of a remarkable surge of general interest. In a different sphere, reduction of the working week provided more leisure time.

These factors combined to increase the number of visitors to museums and zoos. Moreover, the previously mentioned broadening of educational methods with their greater emphasis on stimulation of awareness resulted in an increased number of school parties visiting museums, and in the case of the Natural History Museum many travelling from schools far beyond the London area. Thus the times and circumstances had provided an expanding and more sophisticated public than hitherto, as well as a fresh and innovative impetus to display techniques. Unhappily, the Museum's resources were inadequate to enable it to meet fully this newly-emerged demand.

The importance of scientific research and technology was recognised not only in the successful prosecution of the 1939-1945 war, but in the subsequent redevelopment of the national economy. To devise means of attracting scientists of high calibre into the Civil Service, the Treasury set up in 1943 a Committee under Sir Alan Barlow (Second Secretary to the Treasury) as Chairman to make recommendations for reorganisation of the Scientific Civil Service. A Government White Paper *The Scientific Civil Service — Reorganisation and recruitment during the reconstruction period* (1945) adopted the Committee's proposals and an entirely new grading structure for scientific staff was introduced in 1947 throughout the Civil Service.

The war had inevitably seriously disrupted the work of the Museum, but it also provided time for reappraising the Museum's role and the balance of its diverse activities. In 1943 the Trustees, Director and Keepers were actively considering the future of the Museum after the war. In addition to considering priorities for building extensions and for reorganising the exhibits, they were greatly preoccupied with the staff structure in accordance with the Barlow Report, the implications of which for the Museum were still under discussion with the Treasury in 1946. Morale in the Museum at this time was low; salaries had fallen far below those available in comparable pre-war sectors, and negotiations with the Treasury proceeded only very slowly and with difficulty.

Part of the problem arose from the unity of the British Museum as a single institution and the objections of the Trustees and many of the staff to treating the component Museums differently. Thus, there was difficulty in reconciling proposals for scientific grading sought by the British Museum (Natural History) with those for the museum grades retained at the British Museum, Bloomsbury. Moreover, the Treasury was at first reluctant to accept the proposals, or even to consider the British Museum (Natural History) as a scientific research institution! However after long hard negotiation, the Museum was accepted as part of the Scientific Civil Service and the new grades were introduced from 1 January 1947.

Although the Museum had long been in substance a research institute, its inclusion in the Scientific Civil Service subtly reinforced a change of attitude that had begun to manifest itself in the war-time re-appraisal of the Museum's role. The Director and Keepers had anticipated that the conflicting demands on the time of a depleted staff during post-war reconstruction could only be resolved by some degree of reorganisation and changes in the balance of the staff and their duties, the very changes made feasible by the implementation of the Barlow Report. Its effect was to polarise the major commitments to research, curation and exhibition; the Scientific Officer class became freer to pursue their research, the Experimental Officer class (newly created in 1947) assumed increasing responsibility for the curation of the collections, while exhibition work fell increasingly into the hands of a specialist exhibiton staff.

Such changes could not take place overnight. However, there was a slowly increasing complement of specialist recruits to the scientific staff. Since the First World War, the scientific staff had largely been recruited from first-class honours graduates who, having succeeded in obtaining support for their candidature from a Principal Trustee and after passing a public examination (comprising papers on précis, simple mathematics and English — first-class honours not with-standing) were appointed to whichever vacancy was available; thus one who hoped to study birds was given charge of parasitic worms! In the 1950s appointments were made through the Civil Service Commission from candidates selected for their specialist knowledge and expertise. This, in turn, reflected a change that had occurred in the universities, now producing many more doctoral graduates compared with pre-war years. A further major change was the remarkable diversification in science combined with the blending of different disciplines. Paradoxically, the pursuit of many of these activities, e.g. comparative physiology, biochemistry, cytology and ecology, dependent as they were on a firm taxonomic foundation, served to underline the importance of the fundamental research commitment of the Museum. This was further emphasised by an increase in visitors to the scientific departments and increasing requests for assistance in a wide diversity of research projects being undertaken throughout the world.

For nearly two hundred years the story of the Museum had been one of apparent stability and at times even stagnation, but in a little more than a decade after the 1939-1945 World War, the Museum had changed from a somewhat removed and inward-looking institution into a more involved and outward-looking one.

19

Administering the Museum

GAVIN RYLANDS DE BEER, who became Director on 1 May 1950, was a scholar, a prolific writer, an accomplished linguist and a Fellow of both the Royal Society and the Society of Antiquaries. He was born on 1 November 1899, at Malden, Surrey, but spent the first thirteen years of his life in France. He attended the Ecole Pascal in Paris, Harrow School and Oxford University, where he read zoology. After years of teaching in Oxford, during which he wrote his *Vertebrate Zoology* (1928) *Embryology and Evolution* (1930) and *The Development of the Vertebrate Skull* (1937) he moved to University College, London, as Reader in Embryology in 1938. At the outbreak of the 1939-1945 World War he rejoined the Grenadier Guards (in which he had served as a Subaltern in 1918-1919) and worked as a Staff Officer at HQ 21 Army Group on psychological warfare, attaining the rank of Lieutenant Colonel. After the War he returned to University College where he was Professor of Embryology from 1945 to 1950.

His appointment as Director of the Natural History Museum gave him scope for furthering his own prestigious research and publications while at the same time seeking to provide the staff and resources for extending the Museum's scientific research which he regarded as its most important function. An insatiable curiosity combined with great erudition led him into a wide diversity of subjects far beyond his own scientific background. Indeed, de Beer reminded a Swiss scholar, who saw him working at his high desk, of an intellectual leader of the Renaissance. This analogy is perhaps heightened by de Beer's interest in turning back to and rethinking aspects of classical antiquity, as well as throwing new light on Darwin and the dawn of evolutionary theory. Between 1951 and 1961 he published a hundred articles, addresses and reviews, all scholarly, together with several books, i.e. *Speaking of Switzerland* (1952), *Sir Hans Sloane and the British Museum* (1953), *Archaeopteryx lithographica* (1954), *Alps and Elephants: Hannibal's March* (1955) and *The Sciences were never at war* (1960). He also gathered during this period some material used later in his *Reflections of a Darwinian* (1962), *Charles Darwin* (1963) and *Atlas of Evolution* (1964).

An event important to research and the Museum's relationship with other scientific institutions occurred with the passing of the British Museum Act, 1955, the introduction of which had been pushed aside year after year from lack of legislative time. It received the Royal Assent on May 6. This legalized the loan of Museum material for research as distinct from purely identification purposes, a practice which had in fact been carried on for years in ignorance or disregard of a 1753 Statute, and it permitted the destruction of objects which had become useless by reason of infestation or physical deterioration. When the Bill was before the House of Lords an amendment was introduced to prohibit the loan of type specimens in any circumstances and make it impossible for the Museum to reciprocate the cooperation of other institutions which lent their type specimens for study in the Museum. This was withdrawn after the Lord Chancellor and Lord Ilchester had informed the House of the Trustees' intent to draw up stringent regulations on the loan of type material.

In 1956 de Beer was appointed President of the Fifteenth International Zoological Congress to be held in London in 1958. This provided him, as a world authority on Darwin, with a fitting opportunity to celebrate the centenary of the joint communication of Charles Darwin and Alfred Russel Wallace 'On the tendency of species to form varieties; and on the perpetuation of varieties and species by natural means of selection' which had been presented to the Linnean Society at the Special Meeting of 1 July 1858, and published in the Society's *Journal of Proceedings Zoology* 3; no. 9: 45-62 (1858). This paper was a brief summary of Darwin's *The Origin of Species by Means of Natural Selection* (1859). De Beer set about organizing both the Congress and the Darwin-Wallace celebrations in the Museum with customary verve. He also prepared an exhibition in the main hall illustrating the fact of evolution and the forces determining it, which was opened by the Duke of Edinburgh on 11 June 1958. Associated with this was a Museum handbook entitled *Evolution*.

At the opening of the International Zoological Congress, de Beer demonstrated his abilities as a polyglot by making his Presidential Address in a succession of languages. Inevitably such a colourful character became the source of numerous stories, some apocryphal; but it is certainly true that, if he lacked inches, he did not lack self-assurance. Perched on a pile of cushions, he daily sallied forth from the Museum in his Rolls Royce into the tide of the traffic with an unassailable (and, in the event, justified) faith that it would part at his coming!

To some of the Museum's staff, their Director seemed rather remote. His interest in the broad issues of Museum policy did not extend to general matters of administration and management, which he left to the Secretary, Thomas Wooddisse (b. 1893), in the way that Directors before him had deepened on the redoubtable Charles Fagan (p.111). He freely expressed his awareness of 'the extraordinary favourable position which the Museum enjoys because of Wooddisse's tenure of the position of Secretary'.

Wooddisse first joined the Museum in 1919 after war service in the Black Watch and the King's African Rifles. He acquired an immense knowledge of the Museum and its needs in the course of several appointments in the Museum, including that of Accountant. From 1927 he worked closely with the Secretary to whom he was responsible for the executive work of the Museum and for the preparation of Trustees' papers. In 1935 he was appointed Secretary, in which capacity he served four Directors over a period of twenty-four years. After supervising the evacuation of Museum collections at the beginning of the Second World War, he was seconded to the Ministry of Home Security from 1941 until 1946, when he rejoined the Museum in time to organise their return. He also had to face up to the daunting tasks of effecting war damage repairs and of meeting urgent needs for new accommodation, equipment and staff. Despite the achievements of restoration during Kinnear's time, much remained to be done in 1950.

That much was accomplished in recruiting staff and providing new buildings in the 1950s despite severe post-war difficulties is largely attributable to Wooddisse's wisdom and judgement which was trusted by both the Treasury and the Museum staff. His quiet authority, patience and tact earned him the greatest respect from his colleagues; his clarity of expression is well documented in the Museum's archives. Wooddisse retired as Secretary in March 1959, having been made a Companion of the Imperial Service Order. He was re-employed on a part-time basis until 1962.

Gavin de Beer, who had been knighted in 1954, and on whom many other honours were bestowed, retired on 30 April 1960 after ten years of service as Director. From 1965 to 1972 he left England to settle at Bex in his beloved Switzerland. However, for reasons of health he decided to return to England and arrived at his home in Alfriston, Sussex, in May 1972. He died suddenly, after a heart attack, on 21 June 1972.

The significant advances made in the 1950s were but the prelude to twenty years of profound change in the 1960s and 1970s. Dr T.C.S. (later Sir Terence) Morrison-Scott, appointed Director in 1960 on the retirement of Sir Gavin de Beer, was eminently suited by experience and temperament to steer the Museum on its new course.

He was born in Paris on 24 October 1908. His scholarly interests, like those of his predecessor, spanned both arts and science. To a classical education at Eton and Oxford were added studies in zoology; he received a doctorate of science from the University of London. He joined the zoological staff of the Museum in 1936 and was assigned to the Mammal Room.

As an officer of the Royal Naval Volunteer Reserve, Morrison-Scott served with the Royal Navy from 1939 to 1945, being awarded the Distinguished Service Cross for gallantry during the invasion of Normandy. He took with him, amongst other things, an early acquired love of Horace's maxims and opinions, and an interest in the conservation of mammals. To those who knew him well, it should have been no surprise that Lieutenant-Commander Morrison-Scott while in command of the 12th flotilla of Tank Landing Craft, for the assault training of newly commissioned officers, had painted on his funnel the phrase from Horace Odes II, 3: *'Aequam memento rebus in arduis servare mentem...'* which, in very free translation, might be rendered 'Keep calm, amid difficulties,' or, more colloquially, 'Don't flap'.

Morrison-Scott returned to the Museum in 1945 to continue his work on mammals and take charge of the mammal section (p.189). Early in 1956, he became Director of the Science Museum, where he remained until his return to the Natural History Museum in 1960. In addition to his knowledge of the Museum and its taxonomic work, and the experience of higher administration he had acquired in the Science Museum, he brought with him well-tried qualities of leadership, an impressive presence, a keen sense of humour and a happy relationship with officials of the Treasury and other Government departments.

Morrison-Scott had played an active part in the Scientific Officers' Association, which had been formed in 1949 (p.353) to represent the interests of the scientific staff, particularly during the negotiations leading to the inclusion of the Museum within the Scientific Civil Service. Moreover, both in peace and war, he had seen the great importance of teamwork and he worked hard to foster a closer corporate spirit for the Museum as a whole. In the past, each Department had acted virtually as an institution within an institution, each Keeper jealously guarding his rights and privileges even to the extent of persuading the Director that he should obtain the permission of a Keeper to visit his Department. This territorial exclusiveness resulting from Bloomsbury tradition had become materially reduced with the passing of years, and Morrison-Scott aimed to eliminate any remaining vestiges of it by encouraging discussion and collaboration between the Keepers and with himself. But by a strange turn of fate, while endeavouring to cement the unity of his own Museum, he became a principal in the negotiations which led to its severance from its sister institution in Bloomsbury.

Thus, during much of 1962 and part of 1963, the Director was involved in discussions with Trustees, the Director of the British Museum (Sir Frank Francis), the Treasury and the Office of Parliamentary Counsel regarding the drafting of a British Museum Bill and its passage through Parliament. In this he was greatly assisted by the Secretary of the British Museum (Natural History), W.A. Ferguson (1902-1973), who had taken up his appointment on 1 April 1959, on the retirement of T.W. Wooddisse and had already served the Trustees for more than fifteen years in the British Museum at Bloomsbury. The Bill was 'to alter the composition of the Trustees of the British Museum (Natural History) to make new provision with respect to the regulation of the two Museums and their collections in place of that made by the British Museum Act, 1753...'

The desirability and validity of continuing the link between the two Museums under a joint governing body had long been disputed. In 1866 a petition urging the separation of the natural history collections from the art collections and library, each with its own administration, had been presented to the Chancellor of the Exchequer by a number of notable signatories, including the Presidents of the Royal, Linnean and Zoological Societies, Charles Darwin, T.H. Huxley, A.R. Wallace, Joseph Hooker, P.I. Sclater and other distinguished naturalists.

Eight years later, in 1874, a Royal Commission on science recommended that advantage should be taken of the contemplated migration to South Kensington to remove the Natural History Collections from the control of the British Museum Trustees. The result of both submissions was that the Trustees obtained powers in 1878 to move the collections without altering their control; though, in the event, the transfer of the Natural History Departments (as they had become in 1856-1857) to South Kensington in 1880 and the appointment of Director of the Natural History Department (*sic*) were important steps towards ultimate emancipation. Discontent rumbled on, and twenty years later, through the medium of a letter to *The Times* (dated 9 July 1898; p.77), Lord Kelvin, Sir George Stokes, Sir Michael Foster, Sir Arthur Rucker, Sir John Murray, Sir Francis Galton and others contended that the Director at South Kensington should not be under the control of the head official at Bloomsbury.

A more positive attempt to resolve the controversy was made in 1908 when in July a deputation to the Prime Minister, Mr H.H. Asquith, comprising Sir Frank Darwin and Professors Cossar Ewart, Adam Sedgwick, J. Graham Kerr, G.C. Bourne, S.J. Hickson and J.E. Marr, asked for a full official enquiry to be made and proposed that the Natural History Museum should have a separate Board of Trustees. While agreeing to convey the substance of the proposals to his fellow Trustees, and sympathising with the submission that the Director should have a free hand in managing his department, Asquith nevertheless pointed out that 'the Trustees are a statutory body with whom the Government is powerless to interfere'; and that 'Trustees, men of wide experience and great distinction, are equally cognisant of natural history and archaeology'. The deputation was manifestly not convinced, but received no satisfactory response from the Trustees and Government.

Undaunted, some of the protagonists resumed their assault late in the following year, 1909. The campaign, fought in the correspondence columns of *The Times*, opened with a letter from E. Ray Lankester attacking his old adversaries, the Trustees and the Museum's former Director and Principal Librarian, Sir E. Maunde Thompson, (p.78). Supporting fire came from Ewart, Sedgwick, Hickson and Bourne, who demanded a Royal Commission to enquire into the administration of the Natural History Museum and to prepare a more satisfactory scheme of reconstruction. The Trustees called to their defence the celebrated geologist Sir Archibald Geikie, who as President of the Royal Society was, *ex officio*, one of their number. He composed a reassuring letter in support of the *status quo*; and again the campaign was smothered in a blanket of masterly inactivity.

Twenty years elapsed before a gesture towards recognising the divergence of the component Museums was made in the British Museum Act passed in 1930, by which the Director of the Natural History Departments became responsible for their own funds and for the care and custody of the natural history collections. However, the Act made no move to meet the substance of the criticisms levelled at the institution over the previous sixty years, and the further representation made in 1946 through Sir John Graham Kerr on behalf of a number of eminent scientists again returned to the matter of the administration of the British Museum (Natural History), though in this instance it did not propose the removal of the Natural History Museum from the jurisdiction of the Trustees, or the separation of the Museums. The signatories, while praising the collections and the scientific contributions of the staff, commented that the Museum's 'administration and management is capable of great improvements and that, if such improvements were carried out, the services which the Museum renders to science and to the Nation would be greatly enhanced'. Their main concern was that the Trustees lacked the necessary expertise and specialist knowledge to evaluate the recommendations submitted by the Director affecting the work of the institution, or to ensure that it was efficiently conducted on progressive lines. In order to repair this omission, the signatories proposed that the Trustees should appoint 'an Advisory Committee containing eminent workers in the various branches of systematic and applied Natural History and leading teachers of general zoology, botany and geology both at the Universities and elsewhere', in other words themselves, and thus make the control of the Museum more closely analogous to that of other government research departments.

The response of the Trustees, signed on their behalf by the Archbishop of Canterbury, was to reject the proposal as 'both unnecessary and inexpedient', since they had confidence in the technical administration of the Director and his staff; and with regard to general policy, the Board of Trustees had 'specially elected representatives well qualified to safeguard the interests of science'.

When, nearly a century after the submission of the first representation by Darwin, Huxley, *et al*, the machinery of Government was at last set in train to separate the British Museum (Natural History) from the British Museum and to reconstitute the Board of Trustees, it was not the substance of the successive petitions which provided the motivation, but the need to prepare the way for building a National Library. Whilst undertaking the necessary legislation, the Government decided to take the opportunity of bringing the constitution of the British Museum and the British Museum (Natural History) up to date with a new legal structure appropriate to the modern status, importance and distinctiveness of the two Museums.

The Trustees were consulted regarding the framing of the Bill and set up a Sub-Committee to hold preliminary discussions with the Chief Secretary to the Treasury who represented the Prime Minister. They readily accepted that their existing General Board of fifty-one was unrealistic. Indeed their predecessors had recognised this in 1755 when they had placed responsibility for the day-to-day control of the British Museum departments in the hands of a Standing Committee (p.11) of eighteen Trustees, some of whom were specially selected for knowledge and experience of particular relevance to the subject areas covered by the Museum. The Trustees also agreed that *ex officio* and family appointments to the Board should be abolished and that tenure of office as a Trustee should no longer be for life. With some reservation over the number of appointments by the Prime Minister compared with co-options by the Board, the Trustees accepted for the British Museum a new Trustee body of twenty-five (a Trustee appointed by the Sovereign, fifteen appointed by the Prime Minister, four nominated by learned societies and five co-opted by the Trustees themselves).

However, the members of the Standing Committee of Trustees were as much opposed to the separation of the British Museum (Natural History) from the British Museum as had been their predecessors, and the matter was discussed at some length in both Houses of Parliament during the progress of the Bill. In Committee in the House of Commons the Rt Hon James Chuter Ede, CH, MP (himself a Trustee of the British Museum and member of the Trustees' Sub-Committee on the British Museum Bill) read the following extract from the minutes of the Standing Committee of the British Museum:

> '. . . there were renewed expressions of regret at the proposed separation of the British Museum (Natural History) from the British Museum (Bloomsbury), in view of the important links between the two institutions and the subject fields they represented. The Trustees expressed the hope that their views might be placed on record when the Bill was debated in Parliament, and that it should be stated that it was not the wish of the Trustees that the total separation of the two Museums should take place.'

The 'important links' lay chiefly in the fields of archaeology, anthropology and ethnology where the interests of the Museums overlapped; and to some extent also in the development and application of new methods of research. A deeper feeling stemmed from the preamble to the British Museum Act, 1753, which established the British Museum ('. . . all arts and sciences have connection with each other') and from the belief that it was philosophically wrong to separate the two cultures — the concept so admirably expounded in C.P. Snow's Rede Lecture at Cambridge in 1959. There was also a sentimental view that, as the Natural History Departments had shared not only in the origin of the British Museum but in its traditions and prestige over 210 years, something of psychological value would be lost by separating the Museum in South Kensington from that in Bloomsbury.

These views were not held by all the Trustees, at least one of whom considered it impossible for the two institutions to be managed properly unless each had its own distinctive and appropriate governing body. Certainly the Government regarded the separation of the two Museums as essential, pointing out that the Museum in South Kensington had long had its own Director and buildings and that it had in the course of time become important predominantly as a scientific institution; thus, the creation of a separate governing body was a logical step in the Museum's development. In the House of Lords the Earl of Cranbrook suggested that had the two Museums already been separate no-one would have thought of bringing them together. The British Museum (Natural History) was finally given its own Board of twelve Trustees, of whom eight were to be appointed by the Prime Minister, one by the Treasury on the nomination of the President of the Royal Society and three by the Trustees themselves. In response to the views of the British Museum Trustees about the separation of the two Museums, the Prime Minister expressed his willingness to try to find suitable people who would be prepared to serve simultaneously on the Boards of both Museums. The Government also took note of a suggestion that some consultative machinery of a permanent nature be established between the two Museums. Although this was not adopted it was decided, in order to preserve the historical link with the British Museum, that the name British Museum (Natural History) be retained. This accorded with the wishes of the Trustees and the Director.

An amendment to change the Museum's title to 'British Museum of Natural History' (which the Trustees had approved in 1936 on the recommendation of the Director, Tate Regan, but had soon afterwards rejected — p.132) was moved by Lord Cranbrook in Committee in the House of Lords on 6 May 1963. His reason was 'to make it abundantly clear that the British Museum (Natural History) is entirely separated from the British Museum at Bloomsbury'. He also pointed out that 'British Museum (Natural History)' was an awkward phrase to use and 'British Museum of Natural History' was 'more euphonious and more convenient', thus expressing the view of younger members of the Museum staff. In debate it was said, *inter alia,* that there had been a good deal of feeling against the separation of the South Kensington and Bloomsbury Museums and that a change in name would rub salt in the wounds. Moreover, scientists and naturalists abroad regarded the institution in South Kensington as the British Museum. The amendment was withdrawn.

However, the retention of the title 'British Museum (Natural History)' has its disadvantages. Despite persistent efforts to correct the misapprehension, there is still a tendency to regard the British Museum (Natural History) in South Kensington as a branch of the British Museum, Bloomsbury, as was the intent of the name when given.

In the early stages of drafting the Bill, the staff of the Museums was consulted on whether they wished to remain employees of a Board of Trustees, or become servants of the Crown. Of those in the British

Museum (Natural History) who voted, a very large proportion opted to serve a Board of Trustees. Under the Bill, as drafted, staff were to be appointed and employed by a Board of Trustees but given the same conditions of service as civil servants. This fully safeguarded their wishes and interests.

The British Museum Bill 1963 was duly enacted, receiving Royal Assent on 10 July 1963 and came into operation on 30 September 1963. The final separation from the British Museum was completed on 16 August 1965 with 'The British Museum (Transitional Provisions) Order 1965'. This vested in the Trustees of the British Museum (Natural History) the freehold of land and buildings at Tring and transferred to them, from the British Museum Trustees, interest in certain private funds and bequests, copyright of the natural history publications and the power of appointment to Trusts and other bodies. However, the 1963 Act made no provision for a share of the large General Purposes Fund vested in the British Museum Trustees to be made available to the British Museum (Natural History) as a result of which the latter is at an unfortunate disadvantage compared not only with the British Museum, but with its natural history equivalent in the Smithsonian Institution, Washington D.C., in lacking substantial private funds. The Trustees debated the possibility of raising from private sources a 'Natural History Collections Fund' of £100,000, but came to the conclusion that it would not be propitious to launch an appeal during the prevailing (and, sadly, all-too-familiar) period of financial stringency.

Nevertheless the Trustees received new powers under the Bill for the loan and disposal of specimens. For the first time they were empowered to lend objects for public exhibition abroad and to sell, exchange, give away or otherwise dispose of duplicate material.

On October 11 1963 the first meeting of the newly appointed Board of Trustees of the British Museum (Natural History) took place. Of the nine present, three had been members of the former Trustees' Standing Committee. Professor Carl Pantin F.R.S. was unanimously elected Chairman, thereby initiating the custom of the Chairman of Trustees being a scientist. Subsequently three more Trustees were co-opted, thus completing the complement of twelve members, eight of whom were professional scientists. A Building Committee of Trustees was formed in October 1967 and an Investment Committee in December 1968.

In the midst of deliberations on implementing the Act, the Director found the wording of section 8(1) of the Act irresistible: 'There shall be a ... common seal'. He obtained the Trustees' approval for a design for the official seal of the Board of Trustees which included *Phoca vitulina* (the common seal). Thus it is that the covers of the first two triennial reports submitted to Parliament in accordance with Section 7 of the Act bear the simple motif of a common seal with an unmistakable, though nor irreverent, smile (Fig. 30).

From the outset, the new Board of Trustees aimed to ensure that the authority of the Director matched his responsibilities, namely, that 'There shall be a Director... who shall be responsible to the Trustees for the care of all property in their possession and for the general administration of the Museum.' The all-important matter of the appointment and promotion of staff, which previously had required the prior approval of the three Principal Trustees and the Standing Committee of Trustees, became the responsibility of the Director, except for the appointments of Keepers and Deputy Keepers and the Secretary, which were made by the Trustees on the recommendations of the Director. The Secretary assisted the Director by dealing with many aspects of personnel management which hitherto had been brought to the Trustees for approval. These changes in organisation and control promoted a close and invaluable relationship between the Director and the Board of Trustees, and especially with the Chairman of Trustees who is consulted on important matters arising between Trustees' meetings. As a result, the management of the Musem has become both better coordinated and more cohesive, while the Director is seen much more clearly as the leader of a team of senior staff.

Only three months after the passing of the British Museum Act 1963 *The Report of the Committee of Enquiry into the Organisation of Civil Science*, (chaired by Sir Burke Trend) was published and accepted by the Government in 1964. At the Committee's request the Director had submitted a short factual statement on the Museum's research policy and expenditure and he gave oral evidence before them in January 1963. He urged that, especially in view of the international character of the Museum's work, the British Museum (Natural History) be allowed to continue as an independent body and that at least its capital needs for research should be considered with those of other institutions engaged in civil science, rather than with those of the national museums and galleries. This proved an important move in the Museum's transition from the world of the Arts to that of Civil Science. One outcome of the Trend Committee's recommendations was the setting up in January 1965 of a Council for Scientific Policy to advise the Secretary of State for Education and Science on relevant scientific matters and especially on the size of the scientific budget of the Department and its allocation to the Research Councils and other scientific bodies, including the British Museum (Natural History). On 1 April 1965 responsibility for the Museum's capital and current expenditure passed from the Treasury to the Department of Education and Science. Since the financial year 1966/67, its aims and requirements have been reviewed on a quinquennial basis by the Council for Scientific Policy and its successor in association with those of the Research Councils, instead of with the National Museums and Galleries.

By the time that Sir Terence Morrison-Scott retired from the directorship at the end of November 1968, as he had always intended, the Museum was on a new course. He left therefore with his mission accomplished, having obtained for the Museum the capital and other resources so long needed for the proper fulfilment of its scientific obligations.

With the approval of the Prime Minister, Dr G.F. (later Sir Frank) Claringbull was appointed Director by the Board of Trustees from 1 December 1968. In Claringbull the Trustees had chosen a scientist with a keen interest in education and exhibitions and a readiness to grasp the nettle of change. For the first time in the Museum's history, the appointment of a Director resulted from a publicly advertised competition organised by the Civil Service Commission.

Claringbull was educated at Finchley Grammar School and Queen Mary College, London, where his studies led to a doctorate of philosophy, and he was later elected a Fellow. He joined the Museum's Department of Mineralogy in 1935. After gaining experience in various sections of the Department he spent several months in 1938 at the University of Birmingham studying methods for the determination of crystal structure. In 1940 he was seconded to the Ministry of Supply at Birmingham to work on the crystallography of explosives and later for scientific duties to Special Operations Executive. His experience as a war-time 'boffin' developed in him a resourcefulness and attention to detail which were to stand the Museum in good stead. It also reinforced his innate receptiveness to new ideas.

On return to the Museum in 1945, he resumed work in X-ray crystallography before becoming acting Keeper of Mineralogy in 1952 and Keeper in 1953. During this time he published with Sir Lawrence Bragg a major work *Crystal Structures of Minerals*. Apart from his expertise in crystallography he was and still is an authority on gemstones and has held various offices including that of President both in the Mineralogical Society and the Gemmological Association.

The post-war period was one of significant developments in the fields of analytical and other techniques used in the determination of minerals and Claringbull ensured that the Museum's Department of Mineralogy became equipped with the instrumental means of analysis, including the electron microprobe. A man of great energy, he personally supervised the salvage of oceanographical specimens when in 1966 the 'Old War Room' (a massive underground structure used in the 1939-1945 World War as a Civil Defence control centre) became accidentally flooded through the failure of pumps. Without hesitation, he took off his shoes and socks and, rolling up his trousers, waded in to help his staff; thus damage to the collection was minimised. His seemingly boundless energy sometimes manifested itself to the consternation of fellow pedestrians in negotiating heavy traffic on Cromwell Road, just outside the Museum. This he was apt to cross with all the élan of an accomplished rugby half back.

A little over a year after Claringbull's appointment, on 11 December 1969, the Trustees held a special meeting to discuss matters of general policy. The implementation of their decisions, when linked with the advances in the scientific field, were to have far-reaching effects in the succeeding years. The meeting not only reviewed the proposed plans for the development of the South Kensington site (p.378) but also accepted two further suggestions by the Director. The first was to extend the scope of the exhibitions and (p.367) the second to increase substantially the space for exhibitions and education services. At the same meeting, the Trustees decided that the Museum's links with university departments should be further strengthened in an endeavour to stimulate interest in taxonomy. They also agreed that the Museum should investigate the application of a computer-based system for the indexing and retrieval of data about specimens, such as that being developed at the Sedgwick Museum, Cambridge.

This extension and diversification of the Museum's activities inevitably imposed greater demands on staff and resources and required that consideration be given to how the total programme was to be carried out. Although the Trustees agreed in general that the structure and organisation of the scientific departments were appropriate, they were acutely aware of the mounting administrative pressures and responsibilities imposed on the Director and on his Office. Consequently, the Trustees appointed Dr R.H. Hedley, the senior Deputy Keeper of the Department of Zoology to the newly created post of Deputy Director from 1 June 1971. In addition to taking a special interest in the coordination of scientific activities and in the development of policy for scientific research in the Museum, Hedley was to act for the Director when necessary and have special responsibility for the Library and all central service units including Biometrics, Electronic Data Processing and Electron Microscopy.

Further pressures on the Director's Office originated from activities generated by the Civil Service Department, created in 1969 as a result of the Fulton Committee Report. The Committee's remit was 'to examine the structure, recruitment and management, including training, of the Home Civil Service', and in its Report published in 1968 it made no less than 158 recommendations, many of which affected the Museum.

Two further important steps were taken to overcome the mounting administrative load. An Office Manager (a title later changed to Administration Officer) with a wider range of responsibilities than his predecessor had as Assistant Secretary was appointed. Secondly, an agreement was negotiated with the Department of Education and Science for a joint procedure on promotions and transfers covering the administrative staff of the Museum and the Department of Education and Science. The resulting intake of experienced, executive staff into the Museum for periods of several years, together with the provision of opportunities for promotion or further experience for Museum administrative staff, gave timely flexibility in staffing and freshness of approach to the Museum's growing administrative problems.

Unfortunately, at a time when the Museum was developing both its scientific and educational roles, it was, like other institutions, seriously affected by the financial measures introduced by the Government to combat inflation. Over the five-year period 1965 to 1969 the Museum's overall staff complement was allowed to increase by only two. In order to make some progress with exhibitions and education and to provide additional staff in essential central services, the Museum was obliged to make compensating reductions in the scientific departments. This seriously depleted supporting staff in several sections.

The Paymaster General first announced the Government's intention to introduce charges for admission to national museums and galleries in 1972. The Trustees, who had not been consulted and some of whom regretted the decision to end a long tradition of free access to the public galleries (charging for admission had been contemplated by the Government in 1923 but not introduced (p.122), were informed that this was a Government requirement. In the drafting of the necessary enabling legislation, the Trustees stood firm on several requirements: that admission to the Museum's scientific departments and libraries should continue to be free; that a single charge should be made for entry to the scientific complex of the Natural History Museum, the Science Museum, and the Geological Museum; that because of the lack of adequate restaurant facilities, a ticket should be usable any number of times on the day of issue; and that charges for admission to the Zoological Museum at Tring should be half those for South Kensington. All these points were accepted as were suggestions for the sale of season tickets and the free admission of schoolchildren under the age of sixteen, certain students, and old age pensioners. The Museum was obliged to recruit ten extra staff and the Department of the Environment had to erect specially designed kiosks near the main entrance in South Kensington, turnstiles inside the entrance were ruled out on grounds of safety as well as aesthetics. The Department of the Environment also had to supply ticket machines and other equipment and to provide a separate entrance for the staff. The introduction of the scheme was delayed not only in drafting the Bill and in its passage through Parliament, but in order not to breach phase 2 of the Government's counter-inflation programme. Charging for admission began on 2 January 1974 at 10p for adults and 4p for children in South Kensington. Charges of 5p and 2p respectively were introduced later in Tring where admission continued to be free while major adaptations and redisplay work were going on. The attendance at South Kensington fell to less than half that for the same period in 1973, but contrary to what might have been expected vandalism increased in the frequently empty galleries which were then that much more vulnerable. Although the Museum was allowed to retain receipts, less the cost of administration, this provided only a very small income. The scheme was abandoned on 29 March 1974 following a change of Government.

During the four years 1971 to 1974, ninety additional posts were added to the Museum's staff complement enabling the Director to overcome some of the worst deficiencies, which by now included the need for more staff in security and public safety and for the general management of two new buildings. However, this had to be done at the expense of funds available for scientific equipment, by further postponing the acquisition of necessary capital equipment, by restricting expenditure on bookbinding and by discontinuing vacation studentships for university undergraduates.

Just when major plans for the Museum's development were coming to fruition, the 'go-stop-go' economic pattern of the 1960s, to which the Museum had grown wearily accustomed, was overtaken by a world recession in 1972 and 1973, followed by a sharper decline in 1974 and 1975. Consequently, the Government introduced a number of firm budgetary controls, which imposed social as well as financial consequences on the Museum as on the nation as a whole.

Despite the discouraging economic prognosis, the Trustees and the Director were determined not to lose altogether the momentum generated in the past ten years. They decided to take careful stock of the Museum's organisation, work and finances and to pay even closer attention to staff matters. A number of major regroupings were put into effect. The Museum's education and exhibition activities were brought together from January 1975 to form a new Department of Public Services with Dr Roger Steele Miles (b.1937) as its Head, thereby facilitating the development and production of a new exhibition, and associating with it the Museum's educational services. From the same date, a Department of Central Services was established by the association of the Electron Microscopy, Radiography, Computing and Biometrics, and Publications Sections, the Photographic Unit and the various Workshops. Moreover, in October, the General Library and the Departmental Libraries were amalgamated to form a Department of Library Services (p.327). Further developments in 1976 were the creation of a Department of Administrative Services, with the Secretary at its head, and the formation of a separate and compact Directorate.

Sir Frank Claringbull retired on 31 May 1976, having been Director during an eventful period in which far-reaching plans had been developed for extending the public galleries and introducing an entirely new exhibition on modern biology (Chapter 21). His successor was Dr R.H. Hedley, who became Director from 1 June 1976. Hedley was educated at Durham Johnston School and King's College, University of Durham. Following post-graduate studies in zoology, for which he was awarded a doctorate of philosophy, he spent two years on national service in the Royal Regiment of Artillery. There his interest in sport — and perhaps a canny eye to gaining further experience in management — led him to qualify in his spare time as a Football Association referee. He joined the Museum's Department of Zoology in 1955 to work on protozoa and the value of his research and publications over the next thirteen years was recognised in the award of a doctorate of science by the University of Durham. From the start he maintained an interest in staff problems and was Chairman of the Museum's large staff association branch during the crucial period leading to the Museum's separation from the British Museum, Bloomsbury, in 1963. His appointments as Deputy Keeper of Zoology from 1964-1971 and Deputy Director since 1971 gave him valuable administrative experience in the Museum's largest scientific department; he gained additional experience by being Head of a Department responsible for the Electron Microscope and Electronic Data Processing Units; and by being responsible for the Museum's Library Services. As Deputy Director he had attended all meetings of the Trustees since 1971 and was therefore the first Director to assume his appointment already conversant, at first hand, with the Trustees' policy both for the scientific and educational activities of the Museum. Hedley was subsequently elected Honorary Secretary of the Zoological Society of London. However, in June 1980 he resigned this appointment, having found that his part-time duties as Honorary Secretary conflicted with his full-time responsibilities as Director of the Museum.

Consequent upon Hedley becoming Director, Mr A.P. Coleman (b.1922), who had been Secretary since July 1965, was appointed to be Deputy Director and Secretary to the Board of Trustees; and in October 1976, Mr R. Saunders (b.1933) was appointed to be Museum Secretary and Head of the Department of Administrative Services.

In facing the economic and social stresses of the 1970s, the Museum was fortunate that it possessed a sound base of good staff relations. Although staff associations existed in the British Museum and the British Museum (Natural History) before 1919, they had never been co-ordinated into a single, negotiating body. With the setting up of a Departmental Whitley Council in January 1920 these individual associations became officially represented in the discussion of local matters affecting staff. However, they were not represented on the National Whitley Council which considered central issues, such as salaries and conditions of service, until 1947 when the Museum adopted general Civil Service grading.

In the meantime, the British Museum (Natural History) had been authorised in 1931 to form its own Departmental Whitley Council of twenty members (eight 'Official Side' and twelve 'Staff Side'). Apart from the war years (there were no meetings from April 1939 to June 1947) it has operated ever since. Consultation on day-to-day business is conducted either at meetings of a small General Purposes Committee or more informally through discussion.

In 1949 a Scientific Officers' Association arose as a phoenix out of the ashes of the former Natural History Museum Staff Association. Thanks to the industry and imagination of its officers, it has been conspicuously successful in fulfilling its current object 'to bring the scientific staff of the British Museum (Natural History) into closer contact, so as to promote the exchange of ideas among them, and to encourage liaison with other scientists'. This it has done in a variety of ways, both academic and social, including lunch-time talks and film shows, field excursions, symposia and exhibitions. Far from conflicting with Whitley interests, it plays a most useful and important part in the promotion of good staff relations. Arising from the Fulton Committee's Report relating to the structure, recruitment and management of the Civil Service which was published in 1968, changes in the grading of staff have been introduced, including the integration of the former three classes of scientific staff into a single class.

Various measures intended to improve the lot of the Museum's staff, unfortunately burdened all levels of management in the Museum with the necessary, but time-consuming, attention to administrative innovation. Heads of Departments and Heads of Sections found their time increasingly taken up with meetings and with writing reports, and less and less with inspiring and coordinating the work of their staff. Not unnaturally, the senior scientific staff viewed this with mixed feelings. However, they recognised as important the needs for greater staff participation, for improving communications between management and staff, and for greater job satisfaction for the staff and accepted these needs as reflections of changing social attitudes in the population as a whole.

Other problems arose out of the prevailing economic pressures in that the Museum's overall resources (for education and science) remained level in real terms, and in order to meet non-scientific requirements, including the new exhibition scheme, reductions had to be made in the staff numbers and funds of the scientific departments in the period 1975 to 1978. This was bound to engender critical attitudes in some of the scientific staff towards the development of the exhibition programme.

In presenting the Museum's 'Forward Look' to the Advisory Board for the Research Councils in 1976 the Director said:

'For the first time in ninety-five years in South Kensington the two main functions of the BM(NH), one as a scientific institution and amenity and the other as a public amenity, are potentially vigorous. The objectives associated with both functions are now clearly defined and it is, I fear, a tragedy that our movement towards their achievement is being and may be further hampered. As a consequence of the redevelopment of the Exhibition coupled with 'zero growth' our scientific activity and productivity is losing financial and staff support. It is all the more unfortunate that this should happen at a time when the NERC Report on the Role of Taxonomy in Ecological Research and the interim report of the ABRC Taxonomy Review by Dr J.E. Smith both point [see also p.363] to the need for increasing activity in specified areas of both research and training.'

Unfortunately, because of the general economic situation, the Museum's funds were reduced in real terms from 1977 to 1980.

One area offered a new opportunity for supplementing the Museum's financial resources. While the number of visitors to the public galleries had increased from one million in 1966 to one and a half million in 1971, and to three million in 1977, their demand for natural history publications, souvenirs and gifts through the Museum's shops even exceeded this growth. Meeting this demand provided the opportunity to augment the Museum's finances.

The Museum's publications, scientific and popular, have played a prominent part in the dissemination of knowledge of natural history. Scientific papers and reports on the Museum collections are published in the *Bulletin of the British Museum (Natural History)* (p.151) as well as in monographs from time to time, handbooks, catalogues, indexes and publications on general subjects. Occasionally from its wealth of natural history drawings and illustrations, the Museum has published a prestigious work notable for superbly reproduced illustrations. More popular publications include a wide range of books, guides and leaflets, prints, wallcharts, postcards, models and other material related to natural history. To these has been added a new and outstandingly successful range of well illustrated gallery booklets prepared by the Museum's staff, each closely related to a specific phase of the new exhibition, and including its concepts and images, as well as references to enable the readers to explore the subject more widely. The first of the series *Human Biology, an Exhibition of Ourselves,* was given a specially created Children's Science Book Award by the New York Academy of Science.

By the mid 1970s the Museum's long-established policy of using the profits from the sale of its popular items to subsidize its scientific publications was proving inadequate to meet the unrelenting increases of publishing costs. In order to promote further cost effectiveness, a Publications Officer, Robert Cross (b.1925) with wide commercial experience was appointed in 1976, and within two years he and his staff had so successfully explored the production and marketing of publications and greatly increased the range of sales items that the Publications Section was not only self-financing, but was indirectly financing library exchanges with institutions throughout the world to a value of £15,000. This vigorous and outward-looking publications policy was one manifestation of the response of the Museum to the realities of life in a rapidly changing world.

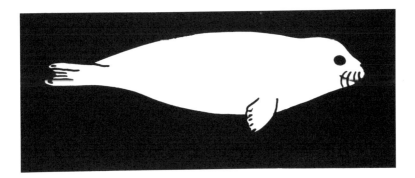

Fig. 30   Seal design on cover of Museum reports.

20

In the Interests
of Science

I N 1963 THE new Board of Trustees lost no time in reviewing the
work of the Museum and assessing its requirements in the light of a
number of reports with recommendations by the Director, Sir Terence
Morrison-Scott. They adopted as the basis of their policy a paper on
'The Function of the British Museum (Natural History)' which the
Director had submitted to the Trend Committee in January 1963
(p.347). This defined the activities and aims of the Museum thus: 'The
original function of the natural history departments of the British
Museum was that of its other departments — enlightenment of the
philosophically curious. With the growth of the collections and the
development of science the function of the Museum began, however, to
evolve differently from that of the arts museums. Today the original
educational and cultural function, greatly expanded and modernised
though it is, represents only some 12 per cent of the Museum's effort.
The major part, behind the scenes, is concerned with investigations
centred on the rich and ever growing research collections, serviced by
numerous laboratories and libraries; the whole forming what is
probably the most comprehensive research institution of its kind in the
world. The research carried out has, broadly speaking, two aims; a
general philosophical aim and a specialist aim.

'The general aim of the five departments (Zoology, Entomology,
Palaeontology, Mineralogy and Botany) is to discover as much as
possible about the natural history of the groups concerned, together
with their inter-relationships and interactions. One of the
justifications, if any indeed are required, of this general philosophical
aim is well expressed in the preamble to the British Museum Act 1753:

356

" . . . all Arts and Sciences have a Connexion with each other, and Discoveries in natural Philosophy and other Branches of speculative Knowledge, for the Advancement and Improvement whereof the said Museum or Collection was intended, so and may, in many instances give Help and Success to the most useful Experiments and Inventions."

'The more specialised research is in the field of taxonomy, or systematics: that is to say the identification and classification of living organisms, fossils and minerals. These studies, contributing as they do to the elucidation of the mechanisms and course of evolution, are of considerable philosophical importance, but their material importance lies in the many applied fields where an exact knowledge of the identity of organisms and minerals is essential to success. The work of the Museum is in fact basic to much research and practice in, for example, medicine, veterinary science, anthropology, agriculture, forestry, fisheries, the storage of perishable products, and the mining and oil industries.

'Another of the Museum's functions is related to its role as an international institution: to provide facilities for visiting scientists from all over the world. This is a two-way service since the Museum benefits from the interchange of views and materials.

'A function which is increasing in importance with the growth of the universities is liaison with their scientific departments, who send vacation students to study material not available anywhere else in this country. Members of the Museum's staff also act as extramural supervisors to graduates proceeding to a higher degree. Here again there is mutual benefit in the exchange of information about new techniques and methods.

'Finally, though scientific research is now the major activity, the Museum retains its original educational role, which it discharges by means of its exhibition galleries, lectures, films, children's centre, and popular publications.'

The Trustees turned their attention first to the scientific work of the Museum on which approximately seven-eighths of the Museum's funds were spent. In December 1963 the Chairman of Trustees wrote to the Second Secretary to the Treasury.

'As I think you will realise, the new body of Trustees is taking a much closer interest in the development of the Natural History Museum than the previous body was in a position to do: as indeed it seems to have been the clear intention of Parliament that they should do. We have been greatly impressed with the volume, quality and importance of the work which is going on in the research departments; by the enthusiasm of the staff and by the happy atmosphere which seems to prevail. But we have been astonished at the relatively small shoestrings on which they are working.'

The Chairman of Trustees pressed strongly for new posts and for a start to be made on the new buildings 'which have been repeatedly asked for' and singled out for attention several other items of special importance, especially the inadequacy of the Purchase Grant, an annual sum which then covered the purchase of scientific books and periodicals as well as the acquisition of specimens, the mounting of expeditions and provision of field training. The provisions of new buildings was needed not only for the housing of collections but also for the rapidly increasing number of scientists and students using the Museum. The total accommodation requirements were highlighted as an urgent need in the Report published in 1963 of a Committee appointed by the Council of the Royal Society 'To consider the whole question of the need for taxonomists and provision of taxonomic training', which further drew attention to the need for additional staff in some fields of the Museum's work, and for adequate provision for expeditions overseas. All these recommendations confirmed and strongly supported the Trustees' own conclusions. The Report also recommended that 'closer links between the universities and the national institutions should be encouraged, particularly with respect to post- graduate training'. Further to this end, in the following year the Council of the Royal Society met with the Vice-Chancellors of twenty-six universities in the United Kingdom to discuss what revisions of university regulations were necessary to enable post-graduate research students to work for a large proportion of their time at the Museum, where this was appropriate to their research.

A further development occurred in 1965 when the Council for Scientific Policy set up a Working Party under the chairmanship of Sir Gordon Sutherland, F.R.S., to undertake a study aimed at improving liaison between universities and Government research establishments over the whole field of science. In giving evidence to the Working Party and to a University of London Academic Council Sub-Committee on Relationships with Research Institutes, the Director drew attention to the facilities which the Museum had to offer to undergraduates, and to University research workers, whether at the post-graduate or post-doctoral level. Grants available for work in the Museum included Vacation Studentships, Vacation Consultancies and Research Fellowships.

It has already been shown (p.335) that a significant change occurred in the recruitment of scientific staff during the 1950s. The unprecedented accession of specialist staff included former university teachers, most of whom retained close links with the universities. They found at the Museum a wealth of biological and geological material sufficient to provide the source for many life-times' research, and so welcomed the opportunity of making suitable parts of it available to research students whom they jointly, if informally, supervised in collaboration with former university colleagues. The new official blessing did more than confer respectability on a covert relationship, it made jointly supervised projects easier to effect and, not least, it provided a greater sense of satisfaction for the Museum staff.

New staff, new subjects, new techniques brought in their train demands for new and much more sophisticated equipment. An Electron Microscope Unit, which the Trustees agreed was essential to the Museum's scientific work, was established in 1964 equipped with two transmission electron microscopes, ancillary equipment and preparation rooms. A scanning electron microscope, a new development in the field of electron microscopy first put on the market in 1965, was obtained in 1966. The Trustees also approved the acquisition in 1965 of an electron probe micro-analyser which had been developed at Cambridge in collaboration with a member of the Museum staff. The equipment facilitated the rapid and non-destructive analysis of minerals, and in particular the investigation of meteorites, of which the Museum has the most representative collection in the world. A laboratory for X-ray fluorescence analysis was set up in 1967 in the Department of Mineralogy, so providing a rapid means of elemental analysis of geological specimens, especially rocks.

On a less spectacular, though no less important level, by 1967 a programme was well advanced for providing the scientific departments with the modern optical microscopes essential for much of their work, although requirements for other equipment had for the time being to remain unfulfilled through lack of funds.

These changes, profound as they were, represented a phase (appropriately for an institution concerned with the history of life) of accelerated evolution. They were by no means unique to the Museum, for the whole diversity of the nation's research organisation and universities were responding similarly to the changes in structuring, organisation and funding that were taking place in civil science. For the greater part of its history, the Museum had been largely self-contained and concerned with its own interests and priorities. Now it had to be responsible to national needs and, no less important for its continued advancement, it had to be seen to be effective. In common with the Research Councils, its activities fell within the aegis of the Council for Scientific Policy whose Preparatory Group visited the Museum in July 1972 to see something of its scientific work and to discuss requirements for the next financial year. Two months later the Council for Scientific Policy was replaced by a new Advisory Board for the Research Councils (A.B.R.C.) under the chairmanship of Sir Frederick Dainton. The terms of reference of the A.B.R.C. were:

  a. to advise the Secretary of State [The Rt Hon. Shirley Williams M.P.] on her responsibilities for Civil Science with particular reference to the Research Council system, its articulation with the universities and Departments, the support of postgraduate students and the proper balance between international and national scientific activities;

  b. to advise the Secretary of State on the allocation of the science budget among the Research Councils and other bodies (including the Museum), taking into account funds paid to them by customer Departments and the purposes to which such funds are devoted;

  c. to promote close liaison between the Councils and the users of their research.

In December 1972 the Chairman of Trustees, Director, Deputy Director and Secretary attended an informal meeting with Sir Frederick, one of his A.B.R.C. colleagues and the Secretary of the A.B.R.C. to discuss a paper 'Background Aims and Priorities of Scientific Research in the British Museum (Natural History)' which had been circulated by the Director. As a consequence of this meeting a Working Group on Natural History Research was appointed by the A.B.R.C. under the Chairmanship of Professor Sir Alan Hodgkin, P.R.S. 'to discuss with the staff of the Natural History Museum their plans for scientific research activities over the next ten years and to report to the Advisory Board'. The Working Group visited the Museum in March 1973, toured various departments and had discussions with Professor Williams (representing the Trustees), the Director, Deputy Director and Secretary. In a subsequent report, the Working Group stated 'our general impression of the Museum's research effort and technical competence is very favourable'. They made a number of recommendations, all of which were endorsed by the Advisory Board and accepted by the Board of Trustees, the most far-reaching of which was to introduce a system of Visiting Groups to the five scientific departments in sequence which commenced in 1974.

In general, the terms of reference of the Visiting Groups were 'to examine and comment on the scientific work of the Department with reference to:

  a. *Curation and advisory work.* The state of the collections and the services to the scientific community by way of identifications and advice, and

80. Sir Arthur Landsborough Thomson (1890-1977), Chairman of Trustees 1967-1969.

81. Sir James Eric Smith (b.1909), Chairman of Trustees 1969-1974.

82. Professor Alwyn Williams (b.1921), Chairman of Trustees 1975-1979.

83. Professor Thomas Richard Edmund Southwood (b.1931), Chairman of Trustees from 1980.

84. Meteorite pavilion, showing part of the Mundrabilla iron meteorite found in 1966 in Australia.

85. 'Man's Place in Evolution' exhibition opened in 1980.

86. 'Introducing Ecology' exhibition opened in 1978.

87. 'Human Biology, an Exhibition of Ourselves' opened in 1977.

88. Children's Centre in the north hall, initiated by Jacqueline Grizel Palmer (1918-1961) in 1948 to provide guidance and information for children and foster their interest in natural history.

b. *Research.* The scope of and priorities for research in relation to present and likely future trends in taxonomy; the initiation of new lines of inquiry and/or the termination of work which, for the time being at least, may have come to the end of its usefulness.'

Visiting Groups submitted their reports with recommendations direct to the Board of Trustees, leaving the Trustees to decide whether the recommendations should be accepted.

A further outcome of the Hodgkin Working Group is that short accounts of current scientific work have been sent annually to appropriate university departments and scientific institutions in the United Kingdom. Reviews have also been made from time to time to ensure that there is no unnecessary duplication of scientific work between the Museum and the Royal Botanic Gardens, Kew, the Royal Botanic Gardens, Edinburgh (p.309) or the Institute of Geological Sciences (p.251).

As the result of another recommendation by the Working Group, the A.B.R.C. appointed a Taxonomy Review Group in 1974 chaired by Dr J.E. (later Sir Eric) Smith, C.B.E., F.R.S. (until 31 December 1974, Chairman of the Museum's Board of Trustees) 'to review current and future needs for taxonomy and the facilities required in the United Kingdom to meet them; and to report to the Advisory Board for the Research Councils with recommendations'.

The Museum had since the 1950s been establishing and strengthening its links with universities and allied research institutions but after the separation from the British Museum the pace quickened. Considerable progress had been made in establishing close associations at working level between the Museum's staff and members of university departments and other institutions in Britain and overseas. University researchers in the field of taxonomy almost always need to refer to the Museum's study collections, and post-graduate students often spend time working in the Museum's scientific departments. Museum staff collaborate in projects, including expeditions and field and laboratory studies, with scientists from universities and other bodies. All meet fellow workers at scientific gatherings and many, by long tradition, through serving as officers and members of Councils and Committees of scientific societies. Museum staff also served as members of University Boards of Studies, as Visiting or Associate Lecturers, and examiners of postgraduate theses, and there has been a long tradition of their acting as informal supervisors of research students. This contribution now became formalized.

An important innovation was the authorization by the Department of Education and Science in 1972 for the Museum to award up to a maximum of six post-graduate studentships related to the Museum's fields of expertise and tenable for three years. In the same year, the first of what was to become a number of Natural Environment Research Council (N.E.R.C.) Institute studentships was awarded to the Museum. These were subsequently augmented by studentships funded by the Department of Education of Northern Ireland and the Potato Marketing Board. Other sources of studentships are the Natural Environment Research Council, C.A.S.E. (Co-operative Awards in Sciences of the Environment) and the Science Research Council C.A.S.E. (Co-operative Awards in Science and Engineering) schemes. In addition, Museum staff continue to act as supervisors under individual agreements with university and polytechnic departments; and the Museum offers each year a limited number of Sandwich Course Studentships and Vacation Studentships. The Museum also provides demonstration facilities for classes from universities, colleges and teaching hospitals and helps the Open University.

If the impetus for such collaboration arose from a sense of obligation and the desire of the Trustees and staff to further and extend the scientific activities of the Museum, the benefits accruing have by no means been one-sided. The Museum supervisors derive a refreshing stimulus from contact with students; and the latter have in many instances made welcome contributions to the collections. The many distinguished scientists from all over the world who yearly study the Museum's collections and libraries provide yet another stimulus. The very considerable amount of collaboration between the Museum and other research institutions and the diversity of the scientific contribution is now widely appreciated on an international scale.

However it must be acknowledged that, not infrequently such visitors have been a source of embarrassment in having exposed the inadequacies of much of the accommodation and equipment available. The lack of adequate facilities for the visitors had been a constant source of concern since their numbers began to swell immediately after the war, and this deficiency combined with the commitment to providing space for 'in-house' research students placed an even greater pressure on the Museum's accommodation resources.

The period 1975-1979 was particularly significant for far-ranging reviews of the work of the Museum's scientific departments, and for re-assessment of priorities for taxonomic research, both in the United Kingdom and overseas. Reports from the Visiting Groups to Palaeontology (1974), Entomology (1975), Mineralogy (1976), Zoology (1977) and Botany (1978) were received and considered by the Board of Trustees in consultation with the Director and the Head of Department concerned. The Trustees approved various recommendations made by the Visiting Groups and put them into effect. Others await implementation when resources or opportunities allow.

Two important surveys which incorporated reviews of the Museum's work resulted in recommendations important for confirming the validity of its research strategy. *The Role of Taxonomy in Ecological Research* (1976), a report by the Natural Environment Research Council, and *Taxonomy in Britain: The Report of the Advisory Board for the Research Councils Review Group in Taxonomy* (1979) helped to determine and evaluate the needs and priorities for taxonomic research and where additional funds might be used to best effect. Both Reports confirmed the importance of adequate curation of the collections and the relevance of taxonomy as the basis for applied studies in the agricultural, environmental, geological and medical sciences.

The Reports, combined with those of the Visiting Groups to the Museum's scientific departments, emphasized that urgent attention should be given to appropriate new fields of research and also to the training of taxonomists. Unfortunately, not only was the Museum unable to respond to these needs, but it was obliged to reduce by fourteen posts, the curatorial staffing of the scientific departments and to restrict severely funds necessary for technical equipment and travel in order to meet some of the Museum's essential non-scientific requirements. This was a particularly painful decision for the Board of Trustees, who fully accepted these recommendations in the Advisory Board for the Research Councils' Taxonomy Report which affected the Museum and in particular recommendation 5 which reflected what had long been their policy:— 'We recommend that the British Museum (Natural History), the Royal Botanic Gardens and other institutions which maintain the national collections of non-living reference specimens make the curation of these collections and their development for education and research the central purpose of their programmes.' A long-standing dialogue with the Royal Botanic Gardens, Kew, had achieved a general agreement regarding respective areas of botanical responsibility and a similar understanding relating to geology had been established with the Institute of Geological Sciences, South Kensington (p.251).

In addition to his long-standing and close associations with these institutions, the Director continued to strengthen the liaison between the Museum and the Universities, Research Councils and the Royal Society. His success was evidenced by the growing number of research students who subsequently undertook their training either wholly or in part at the Museum, many of them supported by Research Council grants.

In addition Museum staff supervised a large number of university-based students who spent widely varying lengths of time at the Museum. Despite its restricted scientific staffing the Museum was nevertheless able to recruit several of the students who had shown the special abilities and potential which it required.

Although unable to increase its scientific staffing overall, the Museum continued to benefit from the help freely given by a number of taxonomists, both professional and amateur, who by invitation worked on the collections, thereby supplementing the work of the Museum's staff. A number who had given outstanding and continuing benefactions and services to the Museum were awarded Honorary Associateships by the Board of Trustees which accorded them the special privilege of using the Museum's facilities as if they were members of the Museum staff.

Despite this valued support, the staffing situation now differed greatly from that of the inter-war years, when the Museum could rely upon the services of outside specialists working for minimal payment, to augment its much smaller, permanent staff. Now, there were not even minimal funds and few under-employed specialists! Thus, gaps remain in the Museum's coverage, and in its ability adequately to fund the full range of its activities.

However, in the balance of progress this limitation, made inevitable by the state of the national economy, was heavily outweighed by the remarkable improvement in the Museum's image and status in the scientific world during the 1960s and 1970s. From appearing to many as a somewhat isolated, introspective and old-fashioned part of the British Museum it emerged as a separate modern well-equipped and outward-looking scientific institution. Not only had it become much more closely integrated into the network of biological and geological activities but it actively sought to collaborate with universities and with other scientific institutions at home and abroad. At a time when the fundamental importance of taxonomy was gaining renewed recognition the Museum accepted the challenge of its responsibility in a rapidly changing world. Conscious of its heritage and of its dependence on the free flow of material and information it determined to seize every opportunity to forge new friendship and to enhance its unrivalled study collections for the benefit of science.

21

The Public Face
of the Museum

AFTER THE Second World War the lack of staff, furniture and
fittings made exhibition work disappointingly slow.
Unfortunately, funds did not allow the installation of exhibits planned
for display during the Festival of Britain in 1951.

Some advance was however made in the late 1950s with the
redevelopment of the Botany Gallery (p.307) and the evolution
exhibition in the main hall.

Morrison-Scott informed the Trustees in December 1963 of his
dissatisfaction at the lack of resources for exhibition work and stressed
the need eventually to increase the exhibition staff and to reorganise its
programme. The Trustees, having decided that their first duty was to
concentrate on scientific needs, were obliged to postpone a review of the
Museum's educational functions. They recognised that it was not
reasonable to expect large additional resources for its educational
activities as well as for its scientific work. Nevertheless, during
1963-1968 a number of major exhibits were introduced in the public
galleries; the most important was the new Insect Gallery opened in
October 1968.

By 1968, with the Museum's scientific function firmly established,
the Trustees began to turn their attention to the public side of the
Museum's activities. They could hardly have chosen a more
appropriate time. An International Seminar held that year in Poland
on 'The Museum and the New Public' stressed the importance of
museums responding to rising levels of public education and to the
burgeoning quest for knowledge. A conference of the Committee for
Education and Cultural activities of the International Council of
Museums held in Russia in 1968 on the theme of 'Education in

Museums', drew attention to the need to regard education as a primary function of museums. Delegates addressed themselves to problems of perception and of providing direct contact between visitors and exhibits, in short to answering the question: 'How can we help the visitor to look with greater understanding?' They agreed that museum educationalists should become informed of new trends and techniques in teaching.

In Britain an editorial in the March 1969 issue of the *Museums Journal* seemed to catch the new spirit by noting that 'the enterprise, the imagination, the stimulus the new public wants are not be found in conformity to fashion, but in the offer of what they cannot otherwise see; in revelation.'

Other events suggested that the time had come for museums and perhaps the British Museum (Natural History) especially to change the whole approach to the visiting public. The advance of science and the marvels of modern technology were dramatically brought home to the public in July 1969 by live television pictures of man first setting foot on the moon. At about this time a growing public interest in nature was further stimulated by a world-wide awakening to the menace of pollution. A United Nations Report on 'Problems of Human Environment' published in 1969 prepared the way for European Conservation Year 1970.

In 1969 Britain led the world in making a university level of education available to the ordinary man or woman, by founding, under Royal Charter, the Open University. To overcome its special problems of communicating knowledge to its students at a distance and in part through the media of radio and television, the Open University further developed educational technology. This was of particular relevance to the Museum with its difficult task of conveying complex biological and geological concepts to a wide variety of visitors.

The social importance of museums was not to be overlooked. In a restive age museums faced a challenging opportunity to entertain as well as interest. The Chairman of the Standing Commission on Museums and Galleries, the Earl of Rosse, may well have had this in mind when in his address to the 1968 Conference of the Museums Association in London, he said that museums had a vital part to play in helping to fulfil 'the quests for inner contentment and for realisation of man's highest capabilities'. For all these reasons, it was time for the Museum to make a bold and imaginative move by redeveloping its presentation of natural history and its services to the public.

From the beginning, Claringbull took personal control of exhibitions and education work; early in 1969 he began to improve facilities for the public, including the provision of a new Children's Centre, a comfortable waiting area near the main entrance and a new bookshop.

When members of the Standing Commission on Museums and Galleries visited the Museum on 17 June 1969 the Director took the opportunity to discuss with them the need for more staff and funds for exhibitions and educational services. In order to ascertain the requirements of schools, the interest of visitors in natural history displays and the use made of the public galleries and facilities, a series of surveys was carried out in 1970 and 1971. In consequence, the bookshop was enlarged, the Museum Guide improved, a number of automated audio and visual aids were introduced and new facilities for schools were provided. Completion of major outstanding projects in the current exhibition programme received high priority. The Meteorite Pavilion was completed in June 1970 and about a third of the Fossil Mammal Gallery was opened to the public in the following month. Plans were developed and put into effect for refurbishing the showcases improving the lighting and labelling of specimens in the Zoological Museum, Tring, while retaining its essential Victorian character. The last of the major items was accomplished with the opening of the entire Fossil Mammal Gallery on 14 February 1972.

At their meeting on 11 December 1969 the Trustees had adopted two suggestions made by the Director. The first was to extend the scope of the exhibitions to embrace the experimental as well as the older structural approach to biology and thus deal with ecology, physiology and molecular biology, as well as the diversity of life. The second was to increase the space for exhibitions and education services in order to overcome severe overcrowding, allow for new exhibitions and provide proper facilities for the public.

Hitherto, each Department had been responsible for its own exhibition programme and for preparing the exhibits, although latterly they had been able to enlist the aid of a small exhibition section. Since the preparation of exhibits was only one of the many calls on the time of the scientific staff, the quality of the end-product varied according to the degree of commitment of each individual to this particular duty.

Despite the innovatory aim of the Museum's first Director, Sir William Flower, that exhibits should provide education and entertainment (p.75), between 1881 (when the Museum was opened in South Kensington) and 1925, displays consisted largely of systematic series of specimens sometimes with little or no accompanying information or supporting illustration. If the very young and the academically privileged found stimulation from this passive approach the vast majority of visitors, whose interests and intellectual abilities fell between these extremes, did not, They had nothing to help them organise or extend their knowledge. From 1925 a more didactic approach began to be introduced, but as late as 1943, when plans were being prepared for the reopening of the exhibition galleries after the war, a memorandum from the Director (Sir Clive Forster Cooper) to the Trustees cites criticism that the exhibits were 'too scientific and dull' that there was 'not enough natural history'. He then went on to comment that 'generally speaking the arrangment in the Museum seems to have been rather haphazard and without underlying plan', and that much of it could be best described as 'exhibited storage' and overcrowded storage at that. He further commented that there was often too great a diversity of aim owing to the lack of consultation and consideration, as well as inconsistency in the end product arising from varying abilities and even lack of interest.

At that time the Director's control of exhibits still did not extend beyond the main hall, a demarcation established more than fifty years earlier by Sir William Flower (p. 69). However, Forster Cooper proposed that an exhibition section should be set up under his control which should be responsible for undertaking all exhibition work, although Keepers would still decide what was to be exhibited in their galleries, as well as provide staff to collaborate in the preparation of the exhibits. As guidelines for the content of the exhibits, he recommended that consideration should be given to the special needs of (1) the adult visitor with no particular bent, but whose interest can be stimulated; (2) the visitor with special interest in a particular study, i.e. the scientific 'amateur'; (3) children, who could be best approached through the agency of guide lecturers; (4) the professional student. The need for a centralised exhibition section was largely agreed by the Keepers and Deputy Keepers. While approving the proposal, the Trustees foresaw problems in persuading the Treasury of the necessity for the very modest staff increases envisaged. Events proved them right, and even ten years later only a bare nucleus had been formed.

By this time, the early 1950s, attitudes to, and expectations of exhibition display had begun to change drastically, as has been described elsewhere (p. 366). Attempts were made to meet these new demands, but the resources then available were wholly inadequate. However, as the financial situation eased, a more ambitious exhibition programme was initiated, and the Botany, Entomology and Fossil Mammal Galleries were the outcome of this new and more enterprising approach. But, these self-same galleries served to emphasise the inadequacy of the rest of the exhibits, and to point to the necessity of a major reconsideration of the Museum's exhibition policy.

Such then was the vast scale of the Director's problem in devising an entirely new exhibition scheme that he had no precedent from which to work. A preliminary move made by his predecessor towards an eventual reorganisation of exhibition work had been to arrange two exploratory visits to the U.S.A. and Canada by the Secretary and the Keeper of Palaeontology in 1967 and 1969, to study and report on the development of exhibitions and the planning of new buildings. In addition to making recommendations on planning the East (Palaeontology) Wing they stressed in their report the need for a master plan to be drawn up for a comprehensive new exhibition and referred to evidence at an American museum of the successful use of a scientist-designer partnership in the design of a new exhibition though the exhibition was never produced owing to lack of funds.

Subsequently the Director visited a number of museums in the U.S.A. with the Exhibition Officer to study exhibition work at first hand. He had long recognised the need to demonstrate new biological ideas and developments and to make a bold new approach to the task of mounting exhibitions along scientific lines. Such ideas had been discussed by a number of eminent workers at an international symposium on 'Natural History Museums and the Community', held at the Swedish Museum of Natural History in 1969. This symposium, at which the Director was a contributor, helped to set the scene for work on a new exhibition scheme for the Museum.

Claringbull set up a panel of thirteen of the Museum's scientific staff, of which he was chairman, to consider the whole concept and presentation of natural history in the Museum and in February 1973 he presented to the Trustees a paper entitled 'A proposal for a new approach to the visiting public'. This concluded that the existing exhibition failed because it was primarily concerned with the diversity of nature, and omitted some three-quarters of its rightful subject matter. It was piecemeal and conceptually static, neglectful of natural processes and interactions, and reflected to its loss the division of the Museum into five separate departments. The paper noted that, since the eighteenth-century the inception of the British Museum, natural history had changed from the collecting and cataloguing of curiosities for the cabinets of leisured men, to a discipline affecting us all, the study of the world in which we live. The Director recommended that a new exhibition should be planned to present to the interested layman an integrated view of modern biology. The aim was to attract an audience representative of the population as a whole and in order to ensure that the exhibits were readily comprehensible to the broadest spectrum of visitors, the exhibits were to be designed for a fifteen year old 'target audience', i.e. such that anyone aged fifteen (or more) with average mental development, general knowledge and vocabulary would be able to grasp easily any argument presented. They should also show how living things interact with each other and with their physical environment; describe the chemical and physical processes that keep them alive; introduce the concepts of heredity and evolution, of ecosystems and energy cycles; and examine man's role in the living world. The suggested contents of the proposed new exhibition were grouped into four main themes — the subject matter of which would overlap widely: Man; Ecology; Life processes and behaviour; Evolution and diversity. The Trustees received these proposals with enthusiasm and asked the Director to proceed with his plans and to report progress after a year. The Chairman of the Standing Commission on Museums and Galleries, who with other members of the Commission visited the Museum on 18 May 1972 expressed strong support for the new exhibition proposals to the Paymaster General (Lord Eccles) who was then ministerially responsible for museums and galleries.

Detailed proposals for the first three of the themes, prepared by independent working parties of scientific staff, were completed by the end of 1972. The fourth theme, which covered the field of the Museum's existing exhibition, was to be developed later. It was intended that the new exhibition should be flexible enough to allow rapid modification and updating and that the fulfilment of the scheme depended on a major extension to the public exhibition space. In order to assess public reaction, it was proposed that the first phase of the new exhibition should replace the existing Fish and Reptile Galleries, fishes and reptiles being displayed in another part of the Museum.

During 1973 proposals for the Evolution and Diversity theme were prepared, and Dr R.S. Miles (who had chaired the panel concerned with Life Processes and Behaviour) was seconded from the Department of Palaeontology to assist the Director by co-ordinating the efforts of three new committees of staff, each of which was given the task of developing one of the four main themes to the pre-design stage. Altogether about forty scientific staff were directly involved, but interest was generated among many more. In the meantime, the Department of the Environment had agreed to participate in the new exhibition scheme, not only by providing the necessary adaptations and engineering services, but by producing contract drawings, arranging contracts and by supervising the production and installation of the exhibition stands, funishings and fittings. The Museum was to design the exhibits and to prepare or let contracts for the necessary artwork and models.

Once the broad approach to the new exhibition had been established and the respective roles of the Museum and the Department of the Environment agreed, it became possible to augment and reorganise the Exhibition Section to undertake its new work. This entailed, among other things, recruiting designers and graduate biologists who, with selected volunteers loaned temporarily from the Museum's scientific departments, formed designer-scientist partnerships to research and design specific parts of the exhibition. This innovation was to prove a striking success.

By the end of 1974 a pilot exhibition on Human Biology had been developed by Miles and a small team of scientific staff with advice from a number of educational research and educational technology consultants. A management consultant with wide experience as a systems analyst and in planning courses for the Open University, was employed part-time to produce a detailed programme for the pilot scheme and to assess requirements of resources. Human Biology was deliberately chosen as the subject for the pilot exhibition chiefly to show that, for the first time, Man was to be treated fully as an important part of natural history. It was, however, to discover the public response to natural history exhibits which departed from the familiar objects and settings of the past. It was also chosen to demonstrate the Museum's intention to present exhibits covering the modern biological sciences and to show that they were germane to everyday life.

In January 1975 the Museum's education and exhibition activities were brought together to form the Department of Public Services with Miles as its head. Such a change was necessary for the successful continuance of the new exhibition scheme.

In its Second Report published in March 1976, the A.B.R.C. recorded its support of the Museum's plan to develop its exhibits, and recommended that £1m should be set aside in 1979/80 and the following financial years towards the first phase of a major new exhibition building. The Secretary of State for Education and Science, to whom the Report was submitted, approved this recommendation.

In 1977 the first phase of the new exhibition scheme, *Human Biology,* was opened to the public. In 1978 the second entitled *Introducing Ecology,* providing a simple introduction to ecology, showing how plants and animals interact with each other and their own living surroundings, to form an energy-sharing ecosystem, was opened. These two phases together with *Dinosaurs and their Living Relatives,* which was completed in the main hall in 1979, clearly showed how the new philosophy for exhibitions was being applied.

Perhaps the most important innovation of the new exhibition scheme — and one which is unique in the United Kingdom — is a facility not only for updating the exhibits in the light of scientific development, but for continually assessing their effectiveness. Much is learned from large-scale sample surveys of visitors, and from studying the behaviour of visitors in the galleries in response to exhibits. Still more important, what is learned can be applied in a constant process of improvement. The evaluation programme has confirmed the broad acceptability of the exhibition scheme and the new displays have made a very favourable impression on the public. Visitor surveys in 1977, 1978 and 1979 showed that the Hall of Human Biology had become the Museum's most popular gallery and, of more importance, that the Museum was achieving its objective of communicating concepts of modern biology to its visitors. Surveys conducted in 1979 showed that, as had been hoped, the new exhibition had a strong appeal to secondary schools, and that casual visitors shared this preference.

It was particularly encouraging to the Museum as a national institution to know that of the increasing number of secondary school parties who contacted the Museum in advance of their visits in 1979, 72% came from outside London, and 25% from more than 100 miles away.

The first three phases of the new exhibition engendered a lively discussion in the Museum world. Inevitably such a radical change in the Museum's approach to the visiting public raised apprehensions and misapprehensions. Mistaken fears that the dinosaurs were to be hidden away in the basement were allayed by their appearance in a new exhibition, in the main hall, and contrary to another unfounded rumour the full-size model of a blue whale remains on display in the Whale Hall. The loss of displays in the Fish and Reptile Galleries to make room for the Hall of Human Biology was an understandable point of criticism, even though specimens of fish and reptiles were put on display elsewhere in the Museum. Some members of academic circles, and of the Museum staff, were dismayed at the change from the old-style of systematic display, using natural objects, to what to them seemed a modernistic 'gimmicky' presentation of an alien subject, using only photographs and cleverly designed models. Several found the change itself too stark; others felt that the academic world should have been more closely involved in planning the new exhibition as a whole, unaware that such advice had been sought and obtained.

With the appearance of further phases of the exhibition and evidence that the Museum was applying lessons it had learned from the first phase, adverse criticism diminished. Indeed, the early opposition which had manifested itself especially in correspondence in *Nature*, the *Biologist* and the *Museums Journal* became outweighed by support for the Museum's exhibition policy: while school teachers and educationalists at home and museums and scientific institutions abroad were from the outset unwaveringly in favour of the Museum's objectives and enterprise. At the height of the controversy the Trustees' views were made perfectly clear. In his speech on the occasion of the opening of

Introducing Ecology in October 1978 the Chairmen of Trustees, Dr Alwyn Williams F.R.S. said:

> '. . . the Board of Trustees stand unanimously behind the staff in the way they handle exhibitions . . . Indeed we go so far as to congratulate publicly all employees of the Museum for what they have done in the past, what they are doing at present and what they plan to do in the future in entertaining and educating the public and also in advancing the cause of science.'

The Trustees' faith in the high standard of the Museum's exhibition work was further demonstrated when they gave unanimous support to the Museum's entry in November 1979 for the National Heritage Museum of the Year Award for 1980. These awards sponsored annually by *The Illustrated London News* in conjunction with the National Heritage Memorial Fund, 'are intended to commend and encourage praiseworthy innovations for the benefit and enjoyment of the museum visiting public and in particular imaginative use of museum resources for this purpose.' The Museum was judged to be the 'Museum of the Year' for 1980 and, in addition to a prize of £2,000, received *The Illustrated London News* trophy, a porcelain sculpture by Henry Moore, for display for one year. The Trustees decided to devote the prize money towards setting up an annual bursary to enable young curators and exhibition staff from other United Kingdom museums to spend a short period gaining experience in the Public Services Department of the Museum.

With the development of the new exhibition and the increase in the number of visitors, it became necessary to consult external educationalists on how the Museum's education service might be made more appropriate and effective. As a result plans were made for a Visitor Resource Centre to deal with enquiries, and for a Teachers' Room equipped with a self-service display of leaflets and other teaching-aids. The Museum's own teaching staff, who previously had spent their time on guide-lecture tours and lectures to student parties, were asked instead to train and help school teachers to use their time in the Museum profitably. To assist school children and others in full-time education, a wide and improved range of books, brochures and leaflets was provided. Packs of printed material were designed for use by family parties and related to particular exhibits and topics and to certain activities in which parents and children could share. Other resources, such as conducted tours for junior school parties by teaching auxiliaries, the Children's Centre and clubs and the public lecture programme have continued successfully and further facilities are planned so that all types of visitors are provided with an appropriate service. Unfortunately owing to the shortage of funds not all the

Museum's educational aims, especially the production of special travelling exhibits for circulation to provincial museums, can be attained in the foreseeable future.

22

Space,
The Eternal Problem

ACCOMMODATION HAS BEEN a constantly recurring theme throughout this account of the Museum's history. Resolving the competing requirements and priorities of the study collections, staff, scientific visitors, exhibitions and facilities for the public has required from successive Directors the special abilities of a Grand Master of Chess.

After the 1939-1945 World War, the endeavours of Kinnear to renovate and extend the Museum met with success in 1950 when war-damaged roofs were made good and work on the Entomology block, which had been suspended during the war, recommenced. Discussions with the Ministry of Works about a new North Block which Kinnear began in 1948 were continued by de Beer in the early 1950s at the request of the Trustees. Plans were, so far as possible, related to estimated requirements of accommodation for the next fifty years which de Beer had obtained from the Keepers in 1952. Planning in the South Kensington area was complicated by the need to allow expansion space for the Imperial College of Science and Technology and for the westward extension of the Science Museum (p.102). The interrelated problems of the three institutions were resolved by 1954 when, as a result of the Government's policy for developing technical education as a means of increasing industrial productivity, the Treasury gave approval for part of the Museum's proposed North Block to proceed. This comprised a ten-storey north-west tower linked to a three-storey central building to the north of the Museum's main halls. The tower was to rehouse the mammal collection from temporary storage on the Science Museum site in order that the Science Museum might be extended westwards. The central building was to provide a Lecture

Hall, a General Library, accommodation for the education staff and a few studies for the Department of Zoology. All this was accomplished by 1959, including a bridge to the Science Museum.

In the meantime the opportunity was taken to renovate serious war damage sustained in the eastern upper gallery of the Waterhouse building, to construct a mezzanine floor, thereby providing more space for exhibition purposes and for the storage of botanical collections. Work commenced in 1955 and was completed in 1958. In November 1959, when a proposed extension to the Geological Museum threatened a further encroachment on the Natural History Museum's land, the Trustees made an important and definite statement of policy:

> 'Their trust is not limited in time, and they cannot doubt that the progress of the sciences represented in the British Museum (Natural History) will in the future require additional buildings both for research and for educational display, and these, which must be contiguous to the existing building, would occupy the land as planned in the Interim Report of the Royal Commission on National Museums and Galleries of September 1928. There is no chance of obtaining alternative land contiguous to this museum. The density of building already in existence in the South Kensington area forces the Trustees firmly to resolve that any further building erected on the land allotted to them must be for the Museum of which they are Trustees.'

Welcome though it was, the new building programme completed in de Beer's time left unresolved major problems of space for four of the five scientific departments. The immediate needs of the Department of Botany alone were met by a reallocation of accommodation within the Museum which gave them the whole upper floor of the main building.

When Morrison-Scott became Director in 1960, by far the highest priority among the Museum's requirements was for new buildings to accommodate the vast and increasing collections and to provide studies and laboratories for the scientific staff and facilities for increasing numbers of visiting scientific workers. The Director had been pressing the Treasury for new research buildings since his appointment and a deputation of the Trustees to the Minister of Science in July 1962 presented a memorandum urging early action on completing the North Block and on building a West Wing. These proposals were far from new. The eventual provision of West and East Wings and a North Block had been shown on a site plan appended to the Interim Report of the Royal Commission on National Museums and Galleries dated 1 September 1928. But in the intervening years, although these intentions had been successively resuscitated in the mid 1930s and 1940s, they had been overtaken by changed priorities and circumstances, including the bequest by Lord Rothschild of the Tring Museum in 1937.

A major stumbling block to progress had been that the Museum had to compete with other national museums and galleries for inclusion in a long-term programme of new building for which the annual allocation of funds was wholly inadequate. The Standing Commission on Museums and Galleries, to whom the Treasury had given the unenviable task of deciding priorities between institutions, acknowledged that they were not competent to judge the research requirements of the Museum. However, in October 1964 the Treasury wrote to the Museum that it seemed to them wrong in principle to try to deal with the National History Museum's requirements of scientific buildings out of the context of other expenditure in the scientific field, but added that detailed arrangements to implement the Trend Report (p.347) had yet to be worked out. In the meantime, the Treasury agreed to consider a case for the completion of the North Block and, in their Seventh Report, published in 1965, the Standing Commission on Museums and Galleries gave their support for new building schemes to relieve overcrowding in the scientific departments.

In July 1966 the Director and the Secretary met the Preparatory Group of the Council for Scientific Policy and outlined the Museum's building needs. The Director presented a case for a building at Tring, for the completion of the North Block principally for the Department of Palaeontology, and for building a West Wing for the Departments of Zoology and Entomology in South Kensington. As so large a programme would be unacceptable to the Council for Scientific Policy, the Director reluctantly agreed to the West Wing scheme being temporarily set aside. The Chairman of the Council for Scientific Policy (Sir Harrie Massey, F.R.S.) visited the Museum to see something of its work and of its need for new accommodation, and subsequently the Council for Scientific Policy recommended approval of the Museum's building programme (the West Wing excluded) to the Secretary of State for Education and Science.

Sketch plans for completing the North Block had already been prepared in collaboration with the Ministry of Public Building and Works, but further development of these made it apparent that the volume of building required would exceed the planning density for the area, and for this reason and other architectural considerations it was decided to build an East Wing for the Department of Palaeontology and a North-East Tower for staff of other departments.

The decision to press for a new building at the Museum's outstation at Tring was the outcome of a Trustees' Meeting there in September 1965 in order to consider the exchange of accommodation between the

'Bird Room', which occupied the equivalent of two whole floors of the Entomology Building in South Kensington, and the Lepidoptera collections in Tring. This necessitated the erection of a new building at Tring, which eventually solved two serious problems simultaneously: the preservation of the very valuable collections of bird skins which had been kept in deplorable conditions in accommodation 'temporarily' loaned to them some thirty years earlier; and the needed reorganization of the entomological collections at South Kensington, including those at Tring, for which much extra space was required. The Ministry of Public Building and Works' scheme for demolishing the single-storey 'Insect Room' at Tring in order to erect a new building, received planning approval, but met with some local opposition. However, the Minister of Public Building and Works, the Rt Hon Robert Mellish, MP, visited Tring in March 1969 and after meeting the Member of Parliament for Hemel Hempstead, local Councillors and officials, and others, decided that the project should proceed.

In addition to new accommodation, the scientific departments badly needed new storage cabinets for their collections. In many sections the provision of cabinets had lagged so far behind the acquisition of new material that a great many specimens were housed in temporary storage boxes and were not only inaccessible, but at constant risk of damage from overcrowding. Fortunately, this serious deficiency had been largely resolved by 1968.

At the special meeting of Trustees held on 11 December 1969, the Chief Architect of the Ministry of Public Building and Works informed the Trustees that there were only two potential schemes for increasing the area of accommodation on the site in South Kensington — one was to build a West Wing; the other to demolish the single-storey galleries to the east and west of the main hall and to erect buildings of several storeys on the same sites. In view of this they decided that, in anticipation of the eventual saturation of the South Kensington site, the long-term possibility of acquiring land at Tring for the scientific departments should be explored. However, they agreed that the pressing needs of the Departments of Zoology and Entomology for more accommodation should be met in a West Wing scheme in South Kensington.

The Museum's staff had long become adept at achieving that oft-quoted impossibility of fitting a quart into a pint pot; but even they had problems when the quart swelled to a gallon. However, 1970 ended with work on three new buildings progressing simultaneously, action symbolic of the Museum's vigour and evidence of the recognition by the Council for Scientific Policy of the value of the Museum's work. The foundation stone of the new building at Tring had been laid by Sir

Landsborough Thomson in May of that year, and work on the North East Tower and on the sub-structure of the East Wing had been started in June and December respectively.

In 1971 the new building at Tring was completed, the move of the ornithological collections to Tring effected and the enormous task begun of incorporating into specially designed cabinets the reference collection of some one and a quarter million bird skins as well as of organising the collections of skeletons, eggs, and bird material pre-served in ethyl alcohol. This move not only safeguarded the bird collections, but enabled the extensive and important collections of Lepidoptera, bequeathed by the late Lord Rothschild, to be brought from Tring to the Entomology Building in London as had always been intended. The incorporation of the bird skin collection was well advanced by July 1972 when H.R.H. The Duke of Edinburgh honoured the Museum by declaring open the new building at Tring.

In South Kensington, work started on the main construction of the East Wing which was to accommodate the Department of Palaeon-tology in May 1972 (part of the foundation having been laid in 1970); and the new North East Tower building was ready in February 1973 for occupation by members of the administrative, exhibition, computer and biometrics staff, as well as providing greatly improved studio facili-ties for the photographic unit and much-needed expansion space for the General and Zoology libraries.

Gratifying though it was to have these buildings either completed or in the course of construction, they by no means met the Museum's total needs. Thus the Advisory Board to the Research Councils (A.B.R.C.) Working Group which had visited the Museum in 1973 (p.360) recommended that the Trustees 'should consider whether, once the current building project has been completed, any further steps are needed to improve the cramped conditions under which some of the research is at present carried out and to provide accommodation for visiting research workers'. Estimates for a Northwest Tower building (as part of a new West Wing development) had already been included in the Museum's Forward Look to provide urgently needed accom-modation for the Department of Zoology, and the matter was pressed again in presenting the Museum's requirements in 1973.

By no means the least important of the recommendations made by the Hodgkin Working Group in 1973 was that the Department of Education and Science should re-examine the arrangements for fund-ing capital developments at the Museum to ensure that it did not suffer any disadvantage compared with other national museums in the provision of adequate exhibition areas, educational services, and fac-ilities for the public. This was both reassuring and opportune for a

Government White Paper published in May 1971 on 'Future Policy for Museums and Galleries' had shown that, whereas schemes had been approved for extending the public areas at other national museums, none had been included for the British Museum (Natural History). In August 1972 the Department of Education and Science reaffirmed that expenditure related to exhibitions was to be chargeable to the Arts and Libraries budget. This meant that for the limited funds available the Museum's scheme had to compete with major schemes which the Arts and Libraries Branch had already approved for the other national museums and galleries. The Museum had no real hope of success. However, following the acceptance of the Hodgkin Working Group recommendation, the A.B.R.C. decided to consider all the Museum's requirements, whether for science or education, as charges on the science budget of the Department of Education and Science. Indeed, they regarded the new exhibition scheme as an important means of attracting young students to scientific careers. In 1974 the Department of Education and Science agreed that, if the East Infill scheme (below) were approved by the Secretary of State for Education and Science, its cost would be borne by their science budget.

The question of a West Wing development had been considered in the 1972 when the Building Committee of Trustees received from the Department of the Environment feasibility studies of the whole of the Museum's site in South Kensington which led to two building proposals. One was for the erection of East and West five-storey Infill Blocks; the other for the construction of a West Wing facing Cromwell Road and Queen's Gate, plus a tower block to the west of the Whale Hall. On the recommendation of their Building Committee, the Trustees decided to give priority to the first of these proposals in view of the growth in the number of visitors from 1 million in 1966 to 1½ million in 1971, the serious lack of facilities for the public and the need for more space for new exhibitions. They noted that an East Infill building could most conveniently be erected after the Department of Palaeontology and its collections had moved into the East Wing, and left empty large parts of the former Palaeontology Galleries. Members of the Standing Commission on Museums and Galleries, when they visited the Museum in May 1972, expressed approval of the Trustees' proposals for extending the public areas by means of Infill Blocks. Based on the advice given by the Department of the Environment, the Museum submitted a case to the Department of Education and Science in July 1972 for approval in principle for an East Infill block and, eventually, a West Infill block.

This self-evident demand for space to satisfy the increasing needs of the public had to be balanced against the equally pressing needs for the accommodation necessary to enable the Museum to meet its commitments as a progressive international research organization. Fortunately, in the second half of the 1970s some headway was made by the completion of the East Wing in November 1975, which was occupied by the Department of Palaeontology in 1976 and formally opened on 24 May 1977 by the Secretary of State for Education and Science, the Rt Hon. Shirley Williams M.P. The move of the Palaeontology staff and their collections freed space which was suitably adapted for use by the Department of Mineralogy and occupied by them in July 1979. It also provided some small easement for the Department of Zoology and Botany.

Further welcome relief accrued in 1976 when an outstation of the Museum was established in a group of three adjacent buildings at the former United States Air Force base at South Ruislip which enabled unsatisfactory accommodation at Acton and elsewhere to be given up and space to be provided for the design, construction and storage of exhibits, and for those parts of the collections which could not be housed at South Kensington.

Even so, such was the need for space that when the Whale Research Unit of the Institute of Oceanographic Sciences moved with its collections to Cambridge in 1977, the Museum re-occupied after more than fifty years a wooden building which, although far below standard in accommodation, afforded some minor relief for the Department of Zoology. Notwithstanding these modest gains by the Department of Zoology its real needs remained largely unsatisfied, as did the longer term requirements of the Department of Entomology. Together these two — by far the largest of the scientific departments — presented a very serious problem which, as had long been recognised, could only be resolved by a very large new building.

In establishing their overall strategy for the Museum, the Trustees placed great importance on the maintenance of the highest scientific standards of the institution through the scientific departments being in close association and the exhibition design staff being in close proximity to their scientific colleagues. They also regarded it as essential that the Museum's unrivalled libraries and other essential support services, including costly equipment, should be managed centrally and be readily available to the scientific staff and scientific visitors. It was further considered as no less important that the public should continue to be able to bring enquiries and specimens for identification direct to the scientific staff. All these considerations and the Museum's close links with the University of London, learned scientific societies such as the Royal Society, the Linnean Society, the Zoological Society of London, the Geological Society of London, the Mineralogical Society of Great Britain and Ireland, the Royal Entomological Society of London, and other institutions such as the Royal Botanic Gardens, Kew, convinced the Trustees that the Museum's operations must be maintained on the site in South Kensington. They believed it to be an integral part of the complex of Museums and scholarly institutions which had evolved in South Kensington over the past century in accordance with Prince Albert's far-sighted hope.

This framework of basic policy and the advice of the Department of the Environment on making the fullest use of the South Kensington site led to the logical conclusion that provision should be made for the public in the centre of the site and for the departments on the periphery: the geological departments (Palaeontology and Mineralogy) to the east linked with the Institute of Geological Sciences; and the Zoology and Entomology departments to the west and north. The plans for geology (which were accomplished by 1979) had been accorded top priority in the 1960s before plans had been developed for the new exhibition. In the 1970s the Trustees decided that the needs of the public must take precedence over those for biological science.

Reference has already been made (p.378) to the advice given by the Department of the Environment that the single-storey galleries to the east and west of the Central and North Halls should be demolished and infill blocks several storeys high erected instead. The Trustees accepted this advice only after very serious consideration of its implications on the main Waterhouse building. The cleaning of the beautiful terracotta façade had been undertaken as part of the celebration of European Architectural Heritage year, 1974, as well as the cleaning and special lighting of the walls and ceiling panels of the main hall. However, the single-storey galleries were both architecturally and aesthetically much inferior to the main galleries and, while regretting the necessity of demolishing them, the Trustees were convinced, bearing in mind financial as well as functional considerations, that their obligation to the public could not satisfactorily be met in any other way.

The Directorate of Ancient Monuments and Historic Buildings of the Department of the Environment, who advised the Trustees, were equally aware of their own responsibility for the care and integrity of the Waterhouse building, which was listed as a Grade I building. They therefore took great care when first presenting their plans for the East Infill Scheme to the Royal Borough of Kensington and Chelsea in March 1976, to ensure full and frank discussion with the Royal Fine Art Commission and with the Historic Buildings Board of the Greater London Council.

Members of the Historic Buildings Board visited the Museum in September 1976 to inspect the site of the proposed East Infill and to consider the Department of the Environment proposals, and subsequently commented that they 'considered that the proposals made a fundamental change in the plan form of Waterhouse's design — a plan which had admirably served the needs of the 'showcase' museum of the later nineteenth century but one which could not be made to serve the forms of museum layout essential to this important institution today. Some regret was expressed at the extent of change envisaged but it was also agreed that the galleries to be demolished are not a part of the main architectural display in Waterhouse's building, which remains well preserved today and which — with one proviso, that light should appear through the clerestory windows on the eastern side of the Central Hall — would remain unaffected. The consensus of opinion on the major issue was that the needs of the Museum should take precedence over the preservation of the existing plan form.'

It was subsequently necessary to modify the design of the East Infill in order to conform with new building regulations and safety requirements. This entailed the inclusion of an extra floor to make up for the loss of mezzanine floors, and the siting of the cafeteria on the roof. However, the broad concept of the scheme was not changed otherwise and the effect on the existing building in terms of demolition work was not changed at all.

The modified design was submitted in 1978 to the Local Authority and the Royal Fine Art Commission. Objections to the design were considered at Department of the Environment meetings which were held in the Museum in July and October, 1978. These were chaired at the request of the Department, by Sir Arthur Drew (Chairman of the Trustees' Building Committee) and were attended by representatives of the Royal Fine Art Commission, the Historic Buildings Council, the Greater London Council, the Royal Borough of Kensington and Chelsea, the Victorian Society, the Department of Education and Science and the Museum. The principal objections were to the increase in the height of the building since the original design was approved in 1976 and to the demolition of the single-storey galleries. To overcome the first of these objections the Department of the Environment recommended, and the Trustees agreed, to remove one floor from the modified design thereby ensuring that the roof would not be seen from street level.

Understandably the Victorian Society took the unequivocal view that the Museum should be maintained in content as well as fabric as a splendid example of Victorian culture. Other objectors to demolition of the single-storey galleries suggested that additional galleries could be provided instead in the basement, elsewhere on the South Kensington site or on another site. The Museum pointed out that using the basement would provide only a fraction of additional space required and there would be no alternative accommodation for most of the collections, staff, and equipment which would be displaced. The other suggestions were equally impracticable since the Department of the Environment advised that there was no other location within the South Kensington site on which the substantial spatial requirements for the public could be provided. In addition the principal undeveloped areas to the west and north-west of the site could not be used without conflicting with the need to arrange research and other activities on the periphery. Several alternative designs for building on the East Infill site, retaining part or all of the existing Waterhouse structure, were considered at the October 1978 meeting, but all gave rise to objections, and most of the objectors pressed for a public inquiry.

After giving full consideration to the outcome of the two Department of the Environment meetings, the Trustees decided that they should adhere to their policies and plans for new East and West Infill buildings for the public, and for the planned new buildings on the west and north-west of the site to be reserved for scientific purposes. In response to a written question submitted in the House of Lords by Lord Winterbottom on 6 December, 'Whether a decision has yet been taken to hold a public inquiry into the proposed East Infill Block at the Natural History Museum, Kensington', the Baroness Birk as Parliamentary Under-Secretary of State of the Department of the Environment replied that 'In view of the public interest and concern that has been expressed, the Government have decided that it could be appropriate to hold a non-statutory public inquiry into the proposal and this will be arranged as soon as possible.' Shortly afterwards Mr J.B.S. Dahl, R.I.B.A., F.R.I.P.S. of the Department of the Environment was appointed as Inspector for the public inquiry.

The inquiry took place in the Conversazione Room of the Museum between 5 and 14 June, addresses being given by the Museum and the opposing Greater London Council and the Royal Borough of Kensington and Chelsea. Representatives of the Victorian Society, The Kensington Society and the South Kensington and Queensgate Residents Association also gave evidence. Although the inquiry was open to members of the public, no report of it appeared in the national press. Other than those directly involved or in supporting roles there were present from time to time during the public inquiry a total of less than a dozen members of the public and about a dozen members of the Museum staff.

The height of the proposed East Infill Building was no longer a problem. The real objection was to the demolition of the single-storey galleries. It became clear that, through an oversight by the local authority, the Victorian Society and the local residents' associations had not been consulted in 1976 when the original plans for the East Infill had been submitted.

The Museum pointed out that, since 1972 when a case had first been made for an East Infill block, the numbers of visiting public had increased to three million in 1977. In consequence circulation space round the existing exhibition was now totally inadequate and the whole educational purpose of the Museum was being thwarted.

Much time was devoted to tentative outline plans introduced during the course of the public inquiry. Proposals attempting to solve the Museum's problems without having first ascertained the Museum's precise needs were rebutted by the Museum's Counsel and witnesses as failing to meet these requirements.

After the closing addresses, the Inspector spent the afternoon of 14 June touring the Museum site and buildings. Thereafter, he reported his findings and recommendations to the Secretary of State for the Environment.

On 8 August 1980 the Secretary of State, the Rt. Hon. Michael Heseltine M.P., ended two years of uncertainty by making known his decision on the enquiry in response to a written question in the House of Commons. He said that he accepted the Inspector's recommendation that the Museum's plans should be allowed to proceed, subject to minor alterations to the design of structures on the roof of the new building to lower its profile.

And so the Museum, whose organisation, work and plans had been so thoroughly examined by independent assessors since gaining its independence in 1963, ended its first hundred years in South Kensington, clear in its obligations and objectives, proud of the high regard in which it was held in the worlds of science and education and more determined than ever to serve as fully as possible the needs of science and the public in the fields of natural history.

Appendices

Appendix A

Principal Librarians and Senior Natural History Officials of The British Museum, Bloomsbury, with their periods of office.

Principal Librarians	Periods of office
Gowin Knight (1713-1772)	1756-1772
Matthew Maty (1718-1776)	1772-1776
Charles Morton (1716-1799)	1776-1799
Joseph Planta (1744-1827)	1799-1827
Henry Ellis (1777-1860)	1827-1856
Anthony (Antonio) Panizzi (1797-1879)	1856-1866
John Winter Jones (1805-1881)	1866-1878
Edward Augustus Bond (1815-1898)	1878-1888
Edward Maunde Thompson (1840-1929)	1888-1909
Frederic George Kenyon (1863-1952)	1909-1930

Keepers (Under-Librarians) of Natural History Department (originally Department of Natural and Artificial Productions)

James Empson (d. 1765)	1756-1765
Matthew Maty (1718-1776)	1765-1772
Daniel Carlsson Solander (1733-1782)	1773-1782
Paul Henry Maty (1745-1787)	1782-1787
Edward Whitaker Gray (1748-1806)	1787-1806
George Shaw (1751-1813)	1806-1813
Charles (Carl) Dietrich Eberhard König (1774-1851)	1813-1838

Keepers of Botanical Branch (after 1856, Department of Botany)

Robert Brown (1773-1858)	1836-1858 (from 1827 to 1835 Keeper of the Banksian Botanical Collection)
John Joseph Bennett (1801-1876)	1859-1870
William Carruthers (1830-1922)	1871-1895

Keepers of Mineralogical and Geological Branch (in 1857 split into Departments of Geology and Mineralogy)

Charles (Carl) Dietrich Eberhard König (1774-1851)	1838-1851
George Robert Waterhouse (1810-1888)	1851-1857

Keepers of Geology

George Robert Waterhouse (1810-1888)	1857-1880
Henry Woodward (1832-1921)	1880-1901

Keepers of Mineralogy

Mervyn Herbert Nevil Story-Maskelyne (1823-1911)	1857-1880
Lazarus Fletcher (1854-1921)	1880-1909

Keepers of Zoological Branch after 1856, Department of Zoology)

John George Children (1777-1852)	1837-1840
John Edward Gray (1800-1875)	1840-1875
Albert Charles (Carl) Lewis (Ludwig) Gotthilf Günther (1830-1914)	1875-1895

Superintendent of Natural History Departments

Richard Owen (1804-1892)	1856-1884

Appendix B

Directors and Senior Officials of The British Museum (Natural History), South Kensington, with their periods of office.

Superintendent

Richard Owen (1804-1892)	1881-1884

Directors

William Henry Flower (1831-1899)	1884-1898
Edwin Ray Lankester (1847-1929)	1898-1907
Lazarus Fletcher (1854-1921)	1909-1919
Sidney Frederic Harmer (1862-1950)	1919-1927
Charles Tate Regan (1878-1943)	1927-1938
Clive Forster Cooper (1880-1947)	1938-1947
Norman Boyd Kinnear (1882-1957)	1947-1950
Gavin Rylands de Beer (1899-1972)	1950-1960
Terence Charles Stuart Morrison-Scott (b.1908)	1960-1968
Gordon Frank Claringbull (b. 1911)	1968-1976
Ronald Henderson Hedley (b. 1928)	1976-

Deputy Directors

Ronald Henderson Hedley (b. 1928)	1971-1976
Arthur Percy Coleman (b. 1922)	1976-

Museum Secretaries

Charles Edward Fagan (1855-1921)	1889-1919 (Assistant Secretary) 1919-1921 (Secretary)
George Frederick Herbert Smith (1872-1953)	1921-1930 (Assistant Secretary) 1930-1935 (Secretary)
Thomas Wooddisse (b. 1893)	1935-1959 (Secretary)
William Alexander Ferguson (1902-1973)	1959-1965 (Secretary)
Arthur Percy Coleman (b. 1922)	1965-1976 (Secretary)
Raymond Saunders (b. 1933)	1976 - (Secretary)

Keepers of Zoology

Albert Charles (Carl) Lewis (Ludwig) Gotthilf Günther (1830-1914)	1875-1895
William Henry Flower (1831-1899)	1895-1898
Edwin Ray Lankester (1847-1929)	1898-1907
Sidney Frederic Harmer (1862-1950)	1909-1921
Charles Tate Regan (1878-1943)	1921-1927
William Thomas Calman (1871-1962)	1927-1936
Martin Alister Campbell Hinton (1883-1961)	1936-1945
Norman Boyd Kinnear (1882-1957)	1945-1947
Hampton Wildman Parker (1897-1968)	1947-1957
Francis Charles Fraser (1903-1978)	1957-1964
John Philip Harding (b. 1911)	1964-1971
John Gordon Sheals (b. 1923)	1971-

Keepers of Entomology

Charles Joseph Gahan (1862-1939)	1913-1927
Ernest Edward Austen (1867-1938)	1927-1932
Norman Denbigh Riley (1890-1979)	1932-1955
William Edward China (b. 1895-1979)	1955-1960
John Priestman Doncaster (b. 1907)	1960-1968
Paul Freeman (b. 1916)	1968-

Keepers of Geology (after 1956, Palaeontology)

Henry Woodward (1832-1921)	1880-1901
Arthur Smith Woodward (1864-1944)	1901-1924
Francis Arthur Bather (1863-1934)	1924-1928

William Dickson Lang (1878-1966)   1928-1938
Wilfred Norman Edwards (1890-1956)   1938-1955
Errol Ivor White (b. 1901)   1955-1956)
                                                           1956-1966
Harold William Ball (b. 1926)   1966-

Keepers of Mineralogy

Lazarus Fletcher (1854-1921)   1880-1909
George Thurland Prior (1862-1936)   1909-1927
Leonard James Spencer (1870-1959)   1927-1935
George Frederick Herbert Smith (1872-1953) 1935-1937
Walter Campbell Smith (b. 1887)   1937-1952
Frederick Allan Bannister (1901-1970)   1952-1953
Gordon Frank Claringbull (b. 1911)   1953-1968
Alfred Allinson Moss (b. 1912)   1968-1974
Arthur Clive Bishop (b. 1930)   1974-

Keepers of Botany

William Carruthers (1830-1922)   1871-1895
George Robert Milne Murray (1858-1911)   1895-1905
Alfred Barton Rendle (1865-1938)   1906-1930
John Ramsbottom (1885-1974)   1930-1950
George Taylor (b. 1904)   1950-1956
James Edgar Dandy (1903-1976)   1956-1966
Robert Ross (b. 1912)   1966-1977
John Francis Michael Cannon (b. 1930)   1977-

Museum Librarians

Bernard Barham Woodward (1853-1930)   1881-1920
Basil Harrington Soulsby (1864-1933)   1920-1930
Alexander Cockburn Townsend (1905-1964)   1930-1964
Maldwyn Jones Rowlands (b. 1918)   1965-

Appendix C

Trustees of the British Museum (Natural History) appointed between
1963 and 1980.

Boyd of Merton, The Viscount, P.C., C.H.   September 1963-December 1975
Bulman, Professor O.M.B., F.R.S.   October 1963-December 1970
Buxton, Aubrey L.O., M.C.   November 1969-September 1973
Callan, Professor H.G., F.R.S.   October 1963-July 1966

Casson, Sir Hugh, K.C.V.O., P.R.A.	January 1976 to date
Clapham, Professor A.R., C.B.E., F.R.S.	October 1965-September 1975
Cranbrook, The Earl of, C.B.E.	September 1963-September 1973
Dainton, Professor Sir Frederick, F.R.S.	December 1973 to date
Deer, Professor W.A., F.R.S.	February 1967-December 1975
Dodd, Professor J.M., F.R.S.	January 1975 to date
Drew, Sir Arthur, K.C.B.	December 1972 to date
Dunham, Professor K.C., F.R.S.	September 1963-October 1966
Elliott, Sir Hugh, Bt, O.B.E.	October 1971 to date
Fogg, Professor G.E., F.R.S.	December 1975 to date
Goodman, Sir Victor, K.C.B., O.B.E., M.C.	September 1963-October 1966
Harris, Professor T.M., F.R.S.	September 1963-September 1973
Harrison, Professor, R.J., F.R.S.	January 1978 to date
Hill, Professor A.V., C.H., O.B.E., F.R.S.	September 1963-September 1965
§ Pantin, Professor C.F.A., F.R.S.	September 1963-January 1967
Perrin, Sir Michael, C.B.E.	February 1974 to date
Radcliffe, The Viscount, G.B.E.	September 1963-September 1969
Rothschild, The Hon Miriam	January 1967-December 1974
§ Smith, Dr J.E., C.B.E., F.R.S.	September 1963-December 1974
§ Southwood, Professor T.R.E., F.R.S.	November 1973 to date
Sutton, Professor J., F.R.S.	November 1975 to date
§ Thomson, Sir Landsborough, C.B., O.B.E.	October 1963-September 1971
Valentine, Professor D.H.	January 1975 to date
Whittington, Professor H.B., F.R.S.	January 1980 to date
§ Williams, Dr A., F.R.S.	January 1971-December 1979
Winnifrith, Sir John, K.C.B.	October 1967-October 1972
Zuckerman, The Lord, O.M., K.C.B., F.R.S.	January 1967-December 1977

§ Chairman of Trustees, from 1963 onwards. Prior to 1963 His Grace the Archbishop of Canterbury, as senior Principal Trustee, when present at meetings of the Trustees, took the chair. Last to hold this office was the Most Rev. and Right Honourable Arthur Michael Ramsey D.D.

Professor C.F.A. Pantin	October 1963-January 1967
Sir Landsborough Thomson	May 1967-September 1969
Dr J.E. Smith	October 1969-December 1974
Dr A. Williams	January 1975-December 1979
Professor T.R.E. Southwood	January 1980-

Appendix D

Number of Visitors to the Museum from the date of opening

Date	Number	Date	Number
1881	231,284	1885	421,350
1882	278,027	1886	382,742
1883	277,331	1887	358,178
1884	375,231	1888	372,802

Date	Number	Date	Number
1889	361,046	1935	666,147
1890	355,682	1936	638,141
1891	375,906	1937	520,463
1892	351,917	1938	528,183
1893	408,208	1939	358,034
1894	413,572	1940	Closed
1895	446,737	1941	Closed
1896	453,956	1942	59,767
1897	422,607	1943	137,195
1898	419,004	1944	51,017
1899	422,290	1945	Closed
1900	485,288	1946	56,266
1901	417,691	1947	298,271
1902	433,619	1948	414,180
1903	486,733	1949	502,092
1904	470,557	1950	503,294
1905	566,313	1951	425,908
1906	472,557	1952	407,821
1907	497,437	1953	400,935
1908	517,043	1954	602,202
1909	535,116	1955	612,667
1910	515,562	1956	692,593
1911	435,684	1957	762,626
1912	455,613	1958	813,210
1913	486,320	1959	764,959
1914	420,914	1960	804,201
1915	433,581	1961	897,989
1916	402,673	1962	819,736
1917	423,128	1963	928,422
1918	422,805	1964	780,634
1919	455,736	1965	956,231
1920	527,701	1966	1,059,149
1921	479,476	1967	1,108,107
1922	498,841	1968	1,331,547
1923	492,500	1969	1,368,061
1924	521,901	1970	1,489,142
1925	507,225	1971	1,509,949
1926	511,313	1972	1,517,373
1927	569,318	1973	1,876,078
1928	567,273	1974	1,701,003
1929	541,198	1975	2,503,303
1930	506,407	1976	2,959,000
1931	537,170	1977	3,075,088
1932	602,918	1978	2,788,824
1933	606,712	1979	2,754,294
1934	631,782	1980	2,285,153

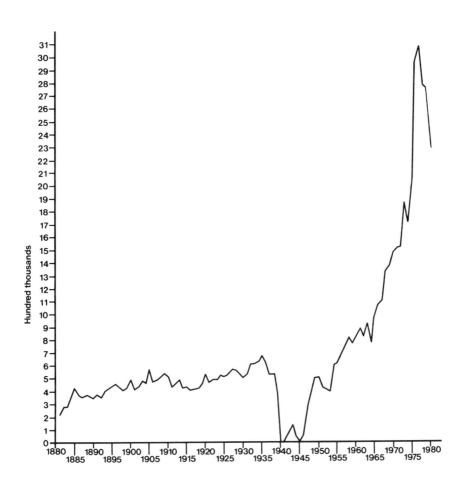

Fig. 31.   Number of Visitors to the Museum 1880-1980.

Index